UN CONVENTION ON THE LAW OF THE SEA AND THE SOUTH CHINA SEA

Contemporary Issues in the South China Sea

Series Editors: Shicun Wu, National Institute for South China Sea Studies, China; Keyuan Zou, University of Central Lancashire, UK

The South China Sea involves a wide array of complex issues covering sovereignty over islands and reefs, maritime delimitation, maritime security, cooperation against piracy and terrorism, resource development and environmental protection, all of which require extensive research. The area's importance largely results from one-third of the world's shipping transiting through its waters and that it is believed to hold huge oil and gas reserves beneath its seabed. Several countries have made competing territorial claims over the South China Sea with such disputes being regarded as Asia's most potentially dangerous source of conflict. This series seeks to provide thoughtful consideration of these issues from a variety of interdisciplinary perspectives. It provides an opportunity for early career researchers as well as established scholars to publish theoretically informed monographs and edited volumes that engage with key issues in this region.

Also in the series

Non-Traditional Security Issues and the South China Sea
Shaping a New Framework for Cooperation
Edited by Shicun Wu and Keyuan Zou

Major Law and Policy Issues in the South China Sea
European and American Perspectives
Edited by Yann-huei Song and Keyuan Zou

UN Convention on the Law of the Sea and the South China Sea

Edited by

SHICUN WU, MARK VALENCIA AND NONG HONG
National Institute for South China Sea Studies (NISCSS)

Routledge
Taylor & Francis Group
LONDON AND NEW YORK

First published 2015 by Ashgate Publishing

2 Park Square, Milton Park, Abingdon, Oxfordshire OX14 4RN
52 Vanderbilt Avenue, New York, NY 10017

Routledge is an imprint of the Taylor & Francis Group, an informa business

First issued in paperback 2020

British Library Cataloguing in Publication Data
A catalogue record for this book is available from the British Library

The Library of Congress has cataloged the printed edition as follows:
UN Convention on the Law of the Sea and the South China Sea / edited by Shicun Wu, Mark Valencia and Nong Hong.
pages cm. -- (Contemporary issues in the South China Sea)
Other title: United Nations Convention on the Law of the Sea and the South China Sea
Includes bibliographical references and index.
ISBN 978-1-4724-5295-5 (hardback)
1. United Nations Convention on the Law of the Sea (1982 December 10)
2. Law of the sea--South China Sea Region. 3. Territorial waters--South China Sea Region. I. Wu, Shicun, editor. II. Valencia, Mark J., editor. III. Hong, Nong, editor. IV. Title: United Nations Convention on the Law of the Sea and the South China Sea.
KZA1120.3.U5 2015
341.4'50916472--dc23
2015008094

ISBN 978-1-4724-5295-5 (hbk)
ISBN 978-0-367-66869-3 (pbk)

Contents

PART III: PRACTICES OF UNCLOS AND THE SOUTH CHINA SEA

List of Figures and Tables

Figures

Tables

Notes on Contributors

Shicun Wu, PhD in history, is President and Senior Research Fellow of the National Institute for South China Sea Studies, and Deputy Director of the Collaborative Innovation Center of South China Sea Studies, Nanjing University. Dr Wu's research interests cover the history and geography of the South China Sea, maritime delimitation, maritime economy, international relations and regional security strategy. His main single-authored books include *Solving Disputes for Regional Cooperation and Development in the South China Sea: A Chinese Perspective* (Woodhead Publishing, 2013), *A Study on the South China Sea Disputes* (Hainan Publishing House, 2005) and *The Origin and Development of the Nansha Disputes* (Ocean Press, 1999). His main edited books include: *Recent Developments in the South China Sea Dispute: The Prospect of a Joint Development Regime* (Ashgate, 2014), *Securing the Safety of Navigation in East Asia: Legal and Political Dimensions* (Woodhead Publishing, 2013), *Maritime Security in the South China Sea* (Ashgate, 2009), *Selective Studies on World Famous Island Economic Bodies* (World Knowledge, 2006) and *Collection of Documents Relating to South China Sea Issues* (Hainan Publishing House, 2001). Dr Wu has published widely in academic journals and been the subject of frequent media interviews as a senior commentator on South China Sea issues.

Mark J. Valencia is an internationally known maritime policy analyst, political commentator and consultant focused on Asia. He has been a speaker at the World Knowledge Forum in Seoul and numerous other important international meetings. He was a senior fellow with the East-West Center for 26 years where he originated, developed and managed international, interdisciplinary projects on maritime policy and international relations in Asia. Most recently he was a visiting senior scholar at China's National Institute for South China Sea Studies. Before joining the East-West Center, Dr Valencia was a lecturer at the University Sains Malaysia and a technical expert with the UNDP Regional Project on Offshore Prospecting based in Bangkok. He earned a PhD in Oceanography and a Diploma in the Asian Overseas Career Program from the University of Hawaii, and a MA in Marine Affairs from the University of Rhode Island. Dr Valencia has also been an associate of the National Asia Research Program co-sponsored by the National Bureau of Asia Research and the Woodrow Wilson Center, a visiting senior fellow at the Maritime Institute of Malaysia and a visiting senior scholar at Japan's Ocean Policy Research Foundation. He was a Fulbright fellow to Australia (2007) and to Malaysia (1985), an Abe fellow, a DAAD (German Government) fellow, an International Institute for Asian Studies (Leiden University) visiting fellow, and a

US State Department-sponsored international speaker. He has also been a consultant to international organizations (e.g. IMO, UNDP, UNU, PEMSEA); government institutions and agencies (e.g. Canada, Japan, Malaysia, the Republic of Korea, Singapore, Taiwan, Vietnam and the United States); and numerous private entities (e.g. Shell, CONOCO, and legal firms dealing with maritime issues). Dr Valencia has published some 15 books and about 100 articles in peer-reviewed journals and has been a frequent contributor to prominent public media such as the *Far Eastern Economic Review*, *International Herald Tribune*, *Asia Wall Street Journal*, *Japan Times*, *South China Morning Post* and *Straits Times*. Selected major policy relevant works include *The Proliferation Security Initiative: Making Waves in Asia* (Adelphi Paper 376, International Institute for Strategic Studies, October 2005), *Military and Intelligence Gathering Activities in the Exclusive Economic Zone: Consensus and Disagreement* (co-editor, Marine Policy Special Issues, March 2005 and January 2004); *Maritime Regime Building: Lessons Learned and Their Relevance for Northeast Asia* (Martinus Nijhoff, 2002); *Sharing the Resources of the South China Sea* (with Jon Van Dyke and Noel Ludwig, Martinus Nijhoff, 1997); *A Maritime Regime for Northeast Asia* (Oxford University Press, 1996); *China and the South China Sea Disputes* (Adelphi Paper 298, Institute for International and Strategic Studies, 1995); *Atlas for Marine Policy in East Asian Seas* (with Joseph Morgan, University of California Press, Berkeley, 1992); and *Pacific Ocean Boundary Problems: Status and Solutions* (with Douglas Johnston, Martinus Nijhoff, 1991).

Nong Hong is Director of Research Center for Oceans Law and Policy at the National Institute for South China Sea Studies (NISCSS). Dr Hong received her PhD in the interdisciplinary study of international law and international relations from the University of Alberta, Canada and held a postdoctoral fellowship in the university's China Institute. She was ITLOS-Nippon Fellow for International Dispute Settlement (2008–2009), and Visiting Fellow at the Center of Oceans Law and Policy, University of Virginia (2009) and at the Max Planck Institute for Comparative Public Law and International Law (2007). She is also a research fellow with China Institute, University of Alberta. Her research takes an interdisciplinary approach to examining international relations and international law, with focus on international relations and comparative politics in general; ocean governance in East Asia; law of the sea; international security, particularly non-traditional security; and international dispute settlement and conflict resolution. Her most recent publications include *UNCLOS and Ocean Dispute Settlement: Law and Politics in the South China Sea* (Routledge, 2012); *Recent Developments in the South China Sea Dispute* (co-edited with Shicun Wu, Routledge, 2014); *Maritime Security Issues in the South China Sea and the Arctic: Sharpened Competition or Collaboration?* (co-edited with Gordon Houlden, China Democracy and Legal System Publishing House, 2012); 'Beyond Oil and Gas: Alternative Fields and Models of Joint Management', in Shicun Wu and Nong Hong (eds), *Recent Developments in the South China Sea Dispute: The Prospect of a Joint*

Development Regime (Ashgate, 2014), pp. 241–56, 'China's Newly Formed Coast Guard and its Implication for Regional Maritime Disputes', *Ocean Yearbook*, 28 (2013) pp. 611–30; 'The Energy Factor in the Arctic Dispute: A Pathway to Conflict or Cooperation?', *Journal of World Energy Law & Business* (2012).

Judge José Luis Jesus is the former president (2008–2011) and a current member (since 1999) of the International Tribunal for the Law of the Sea. He earned his law degree at the School of Law at the Classical University of Lisbon in 1978 and an international law certificate and master's degree in government and politics from Saint John's University, New York, in 1985. He has since served as Chairman of the Group of 77 for the Law of the Sea (1986); Ambassador and Deputy Permanent Representative of Cape Verde (1987–1991); Ambassador and Permanent Representative of Cape Verde to the United Nations in New York (1991–1994); President of the United Nations Security Council (July 1992 and November 1993); Ambassador of Cape Verde to Portugal, Spain and Israel (1994–1996); Secretary of State for Foreign Affairs and Cooperation (1996–1998); Minister of Foreign Affairs and Communities (1998–1999); Chairman of the National Commission on the Delimitation of Maritime Boundaries, Cape Verde; and legal consultant for technical assistance in the drafting of fisheries legislation, FAO, amongst many other accomplishments. He has been a lecturer at several seminars on the law of the sea, humanitarian law and international relations. In addition, he has authored publications in the fields of the law of the sea and humanitarian law, extradition and procedures at ITLOS.

Helmut Tuerk has been a judge of the International Tribunal for the Law of the Sea since 2005 and was its Vice-President from 2008 to 2011. He had served as the legal advisor of the Austrian Federal Ministry for Foreign Affairs and later as Ambassador to the United States and the Holy See as well as Director-General of the Office of the Austrian Federal President. For many years he was a member of the Austrian Delegation to the Third United Nations Conference on the Law of the Sea and in 1997–1998 served as President of the Meeting of States Parties to the United Nations Convention on the Law of the Sea. Judge Tuerk is the author of numerous publications in the field of international law, in particular the law of the sea.

Hasjim Djalal is former Ambassador-at-Large for the Law of the Sea and Maritime Affairs, Indonesia. He was Director of Treaty and Legal Affairs of the Indonesian Department of Foreign Affairs (1976–1979) and Director General for Policy Planning (1985–1990). He has served at the Indonesian embassies in Belgrade, Guinea (Africa), Singapore, Washington, DC and as Ambassador/Deputy Permanent Representative of Indonesia to the UN in New York (1981–1983), Ambassador to Canada (1983–1985), Germany (1990–1993) and Ambassador-at-Large for the Law of the Sea and Maritime Affairs (1994–2000). He participated fully in the Third UN Law of the Sea Conference (1973–1982) and in its implementation thereafter, as well as in other maritime activities, nationally, regionally and internationally until now. He was President of the International Seabed Authority (ISA) in Jamaica (1995, 1996), and currently serves as Chairman of the Finance Committee of the ISBA. Since 1989 he has been the initiator and convener of the Workshop Process on Managing Potential Conflicts in the South China Sea, and has been involved in development of maritime cooperation in the Indian and Pacific Oceans. Currently, he is a member of Indonesian Maritime Council, senior advisor to the Indonesian Minister for Maritime Affairs and Fisheries, and to Indonesian Naval Chief of Staff, and lectures at universities and other high learning institutions in Indonesia. He has written extensively on the law of the sea and regional issues. His books include *Indonesian Struggle for the Law of the Sea* (1979), *Indonesia and the Law of the Sea* (1995), *Indonesian Foreign Policy in the 1990s* (1997), *Preventive Diplomacy in South East Asia: Lessons Learned* (2003), *Seeking Lasting Peace in Aceh* (2006), and numerous articles in Indonesia and abroad.

Vesselin Popovski, Senior Academic Programme Officer, United Nations University, undertakes research and post-graduate teaching and supervision in the field of international relations, peace and security, international law, human rights, international criminal justice, and governance. He has published numerous books and articles in peer-reviewed journals. He took part in two major international initiatives and co-authored their reports: (1) International Commission on Intervention and State Sovereignty (ICISS) and its 2001 report 'Responsibility to Protect' that led the way to the adoption by the UN General Assembly of the 'Responsibility to Protect' norm in 2005; and (2) Princeton Project on Universal Jurisdiction that developed and published 'Princeton Principles of Universal Jurisdiction' (2001). He is currently a member of the International Working Group on 'Principles and Guidelines for the Elimination of Discrimination Against Persons Affected by Leprosy', created to develop a Plan of Action following General Assembly resolution A/RES/65/215 (2010). Another major project that Popovski initiated, developed and materialized is *Legality and Legitimacy in Global Affairs* (Oxford University Press, 2012), co-edited with Richard Falk and with chapters from some of the world's top scholars. Popovski also championed the project *Towards the Dignity of Difference* with Andy Knight and Mojtaba Mahdavi (Ashgate, 2012). His research and collaborations on trends and innovations in governance materialized in a UNU Press series of books, co-edited with Shabbir Cheema: *Building Trust in Government* (2010), *Engaging Civil Society* (2010) and *Cross-Border Governance in Asia* (2011). He also wrote chapters for, and co-edited, many books.

Stuart Kaye is Professor of Law within the Australian National Centre for Ocean Resources and Security at the University of Wollongong, and academic leader of the Sustaining Coastal and Marine Zones theme area within the university's flagship Global Challenges Programme. He was formerly the Dean of Law at the

University of Western Australia having been appointed Winthrop Professor of Law in July 2010. He held a chair in law at the University of Melbourne from 2006 to 2010 and was Dean and Professor of Law at the University of Wollongong between 2002 and 2006. He holds degrees in arts and law from the University of Sydney, winning the Law Graduates' Association Medal, and a doctorate in law from Dalhousie University. He is admitted as a barrister of the supreme courts of New South Wales, Tasmania and Queensland. He was elected a fellow of the Royal Geographical Society in 2007 and a fellow of the Australian Academy of Law in 2011.

André Tahindro is a former official of the Division for Ocean Affairs and the Law of the Sea (DOALOS), in the UN Office of Legal Affairs, New York, from 1986 to 2011. During his service with DOALOS, Tahindro had general responsibilities on matters relating to the law of the sea, in particular issues regarding the conservation, management and sustainable use of marine fishery resources. He had been responsible for the preparation of the reports of the UN Secretary-General to the General Assembly on sustainable fisheries. He has been secretary of the Informal Consultations of States Parties to the UN Fish Stocks Agreement (2002–2010); secretary of the Review Conferences on the UN Fish Stocks Agreement (2006 and 2010); secretary of the ad hoc Working Group of the Whole for the Regular Process for global reporting and assessment of the state of the marine environment, including socio-economic aspects (2009–2010); and secretary of the UN informal consultations on the annual resolution of the UN General Assembly on sustainable fisheries (1996–2010). He has prepared for DOALOS several studies on: EEZ, protection of the marine environment and marine biodiversity, and State practices. He has been the DOALOS focal point on cooperation and coordination with FAO, RFMO/As, NGOs, UNEP and WTO for the conservation and management of marine fishery resources (1993–2011). Before joining the UN, Tahindro had served with the Ministry of Foreign Affairs of Madagascar, in Algiers, Geneva and New York (1974–1986). He was a member of the delegation of Madagascar to the Third United Nations Conference on the Law of the Sea and the Preparatory Commission for the International Seabed Authority and the International Tribunal for the Law of the Sea (1977–1986).

Clive Schofield is Professor and Director of Research at the Australian Centre for Ocean Resource and Security (ANCORS), University of Wollongong, Australia. ANCORS is Australia's sole academic centre devoted to multidisciplinary research on national and international ocean law, policy, management, and maritime security. He currently holds an Australian Research Council Future Fellowship. He previously served as Director of Research at the International Boundaries Research Unit (IBRU), University of Durham, United Kingdom. Dr Schofield is a political geographer and international legal scholar whose research interests relate to international boundaries and particularly maritime boundary delimitation. He holds a PhD (geography) from the University of Durham, UK and an LLM from the University of British Columbia, Canada. He has researched and published primarily on issues related to the delimitation of maritime boundaries, geo-technical issues in the law of the sea, maritime security and regarding maritime boundary disputes and their resolution. He has published over 100 book chapters and scholarly articles and is co-author (with Professor Victor Prescott, Emeritus Professor of Geography, University of Melbourne) of the book *The Maritime Political Boundaries of the World* (Martinus Nijhoff, 2005). He has also been involved in the peaceful settlement of boundary and territory disputes, for example through the provision of technical advice and research support to governments engaged in boundary negotiations and in dispute settlement cases before the International Court of Justice.

Donald R. Rothwell is Professor of International Law, and Head of School at the ANU College of Law, Australian National University (ANU) where he has taught since July 2006. His research has a specific focus on law of the sea, law of the polar region, and implementation of international law within Australia as reflected in over 160 articles, book chapters and notes in international and Australian publications. Rothwell has authored, co-authored or edited 17 books including most recently his co-edited work with Alex Oude Elferink and Erik Molenaar, *The Law of the Sea and Polar Regions: Interactions between Global and Regional Regimes* (Brill, 2013), and *Law of the Sea* (Edward Elgar, 2013). Major career works include *The International Law of the Sea* (Hart, 2010) with Tim Stephens, and *The Polar Regions and the Development of International Law* (Cambridge University Press, 1996). Rothwell is also coordinating editor of the *Oxford Handbook on the Law of the Sea* (2015) and co-editor of the *Australian Year Book of International Law*. In 2012 he was appointed as rapporteur of the International Law Association (ILA) Committee on 'Baselines under the International Law of the Sea'. He has acted as a consultant or been a member of expert groups for UNEP, UNDP, IUCN and the Australian government, and acted as advisor to the International Fund for Animal Welfare (IFAW). In 2012 Rothwell was also appointed an inaugural ANU Public Policy Fellow by the ANU Vice-Chancellor, Professor Ian Young.

Clive R. Symmons has taught international law, with a specialization in the law of the sea, over many years, both in the UK and Ireland. He is currently visiting research fellow at the School of Law, Trinity College, Dublin and has also recently acted as adjunct professor, Marine Law and Ocean Policy Centre, National University of Ireland, Galway. His many publications, and presentations at conferences, particularly in more recent years, reflect his law of the sea research interests; and his books include *The Maritime Zones of Islands in International Law* (1979), *Ireland and the Law of the Sea* (1st and 2nd editions, 1993/2000), *Historic Waters in the Law of the Sea: A Modern Re-Appraisal* (2008), and most recently his editorship of *Selected Contemporary Issues in the Law of the Sea* (2011). He has been a member of several maritime law study groups, including the ILA Committee on Legal Issues of the Outer Continental Shelf; and has acted as an adviser on law of the sea issues to the Irish Government, as well as an expert witness for the US Federal Government in two rounds of Supreme Court litigation between the United States and the State of Alaska on maritime issues, including more recently, the question of possible historic waters within the Alexander Archipelago (in early 2000) as claimed by the State of Alaska in the case of *Alaska v. US*. He is currently acting as one of the commentators in the forthcoming *United Nations Convention on the Law of the Sea: Commentary* (ed. A. Proelss) to be published by C.H. Beck.

Keyuan Zou is Harris Professor of International Law at the Lancashire Law School of the University of Central Lancashire (UCLan), United Kingdom. He specializes in international law, in particular law of the sea and international environmental law. Before joining UCLan, he worked in Dalhousie University (Canada), Peking University (China), University of Hannover (Germany) and National University of Singapore. He has published over 60 refereed English papers in 30 international journals. His recent books include *China-ASEAN Relations and International Law* (2009), *Maritime Security in the South China Sea* (co-edited, 2009), *International Law in East Asia* (co-edited, 2011) and *Conflict Management and Dispute Settlement in East Asia* (co-edited, 2011). He is a member of the editorial boards of the *International Journal of Marine and Coastal Law*, *Ocean Development and International Law*, *Journal of International Wildlife Law and Policy*, *The Polar Journal*, and the *Chinese Journal of International Law*, as well as a member of the advisory board of the China *Oceans Law Review*.

Robert Beckman heads the ocean law and policy programme as well as being Director of the Centre for International Law, a university-wide research centre at the National University of Singapore (NUS) which was established in 2009. Professor Beckman is also an associate professor at the NUS Faculty of Law, where he has taught for more than 35 years. He currently teaches Ocean Law & Policy in Asia and International Regulation of Shipping. Professor Beckman lectures in the summer programme at the Rhodes Academy of Oceans Law & Policy in Rhodes, Greece. He is an expert on the issues of law of the sea in Southeast Asia, including piracy, maritime security, the South China Sea and the Straits of Malacca and Singapore. His latest publications include 'The UN Convention on the Law of the Sea and the Maritime Disputes in the South China Sea', *American Journal of International Law*, 107 (2013), pp. 142–63; Robert C. Beckman and Clive H. Schofield, 'Defining EEZ Claims from Islands: A Potential South China Sea Change', *The International Journal of Marine and Coastal Law*, 29 (2014), pp. 193–243.

Michael Sheng-ti Gau is Professor at the Institute of Law of the Sea, Taiwan Ocean University. He holds the degrees of LLB (Taiwan University), LLM (Cambridge), LLM (London) and PhD (Leiden), all specializing in public international law. Professor Gau has been legal advisor for and commissioned by the Ministry of the Interior, Fishery Agency of Council of Agriculture, Ministry of Economics, Ministry of Health and Ministry of Foreign Affairs on numerous research projects on law of the sea legal issues, negotiations in Regional Fisheries Management Organizations like ICCAT, SPRFMO and WCPFC, as well as WTO fishery subsidies negotiations, and Taiwan's participation in IGOs like ICAO, OIE, WHO, etc. For the past six years, Professor Gau has been focusing on outer continental shelf, CLCS and the South China Sea legal issues, with articles in publications including *Ocean Development and International Law*, *Chinese Journal of International Law*, *Journal of East Asia* and *International Law*. Professor Gau has been Administrator for the Taiwan Regional Round of the Philip C. Jessup International Law Moot Court Competition since 2000. Born in 1963, Dr Gau is married and lives by the mouth of the Tam-sui River in Taipei.

Introduction

The South China Sea: UNCLOS and State Practice

Shicun Wu, Mark J. Valencia, and Nong Hong

The United Nations Convention on the Law of the Sea (UNCLOS) was agreed in 1982—some 30 years ago—and has been in effect for nearly 20 years, since 1994. Although some 163 countries have ratified the Convention, the interpretation and implementation of and compliance with many of its provisions are uneven and inconsistent. Indeed some of the Convention's key provisions are ambiguous and controversial. Moreover customary law evolves with state practice and technological innovation.

These legal "grey" areas have particular relevance in this complex geographic region where many key terms and regimes remain undefined—and controversial—like legitimate baselines, rocks and islands, marine scientific research, due regard, peaceful uses and threat of use of force. More important, the practice of South China Sea littoral states and users often arguably differs from that proscribed by UNCLOS. Indeed there are clearly differences in interpretations between some littoral countries as well as between them and the maritime powers. As a result littoral countries and users of the South China Sea have had many disputes involving the content of jurisdictional and navigational regimes and there have been several serious international incidents. Such incidents are likely to increase in frequency and intensity as interpretations and practice diverge from more traditional and restrictive views of the law. The United States in particular may find it increasingly difficult to maintain its expansive interpretation of navigational freedoms and its rather narrow view of coastal state jurisdiction. The South China Sea countries may thus be critical in shaping interpretations of UNCLOS elsewhere. To prevent conflict, it is imperative that a consensus be built on critical aspects of the Convention that are presently unclear and subject to different interpretation.

This book reviews the implementation of the 1982 UNCLOS in the South China Sea. Special focus will be on the differences between UNCLOS and state practice and the evolution of the meaning of terms that are key to states peacefully exercising their maritime rights and fulfilling their duties in the South China Sea.

Part I address the dispute settlement mechanism of UNCLOS. In Chapter 1, Jesus addresses the contribution of the compulsory jurisdiction mechanism to the effective application of the dispute settlement system of UNCLOS. He concludes that the judicial work of the International Tribunal for the Law of the Sea (ITLOS) has been heavily dependent on the compulsory jurisdiction mechanism built into UNCLOS's innovative dispute settlement system. He argues that this compulsory jurisdiction plays a pivotal role in keeping the settlement dispute system alive and has contributed to maintaining the delicate balance of interests in UNCLOS.

Tuerk in Chapter 2 affirmed the role of ITLOS as an essential feature of the dispute settlement system and one of four means under UNCLOS for the settlement of disputes entailing binding decisions. The author highlights that ITLOS has earned a reputation for the expeditious and efficient management of cases and has made substantial contributions to the interpretation of UNCLOS and to the further development of international law.

Part II includes four chapters on some concepts in UNCLOS which are relevant to the South China Sea. In Chapter 3, "Military Activities in Foreign EEZs," Mark J. Valencia points out that the South China Sea in particular has become a cockpit of frequent but largely sub-rosa confrontations between Chinese vessels and aircraft and US surveillance platforms such as U2s, EP-3s, the US Navy ocean surveillance vessel *Impeccable* and the oceanographic survey ship *Bowditch.* He summarizes the larger geopolitical context as well as the US/China strategic military convergence, describes a worst-case scenario, raises questions regarding the "legality" of certain practices, and then suggests preventive arrangements and ways forward.

Hasjim Djalal, in Chapter 4, argues that the "due regard" provisions seek to balance the rights and interests of the coastal states and the rights and interests of other states. Some accidents with regard to these issues have taken place in the past in the South China Sea, causing political tensions between the states and injuring peace and stability in the South China Sea area. States parties of UNCLOS therefore should fulfill their obligations under UNCLOS "in good faith" and exercise their rights, jurisdictions, and freedoms in a manner that would not constitute "abuse of right."

In Chapter 5, Popovski reaffirms that the texts in UNCLOS are somewhat insufficient in settling a clear regime for the peaceful use of oceans and should be enriched in order to elaborate on the positive facets of the idea of "peaceful use." States should view the notion from a wide perspective. There is no doubt that they should not conduct military activities or test nuclear bombs in the oceans, should also bear more obligations and should also keep in mind the sustainability of the environment and development.

Chapter 6, authored by Stuart Kaye, considers the differences in approach and interpretation by states in respect of "military survey," "hydrographic survey," and "marine scientific research." UNCLOS established for the first time in international law, a regime for the regulation of marine scientific research, which provided a range of rights and obligations for coastal and flag states. This chapter considers the arguments for and against the distinguishing of "military survey" and "hydrographic survey" from "marine scientific research" under Part XIII, and also considers related state practice.

In Chapter 7 André Tahindro suggests that introducing the concept of regional common heritage in the South China Sea, in addition to previously adopted confidence-building measures, may provide a step forward in that direction. Regional common heritage would not purport to solve territorial sovereignty and maritime jurisdictional disputes in the South China Sea. It may however instill a better sense of regional identity and induce a possible joint stewardship in the conduct of marine activities in the South China Sea, pending a solution to current maritime disputes.

Part III comprises seven chapters that address the practice of UNCLOS in the South China Sea. In Chapter 8, Clive Schofield reviews state practice concerning baselines and insular features in the South China Sea. He outlines the various distinct types of baseline provided for under UNCLOS, highlighting key issues and uncertainties. The latter part of the chapter then offers a systematic and critical analysis of the baselines practice of the South China Sea littoral states. The chapter concludes by addressing some of the technical, legal, and political issues arising from the baselines practice of the South China Sea states.

Donald Rothwell, in Chapter 9, addresses and assesses the freedom of the seas and navigational rights and freedoms under UNCLOS. Consideration is given to how these rights are recognized in the territorial sea, within international straits, within archipelagic waters, the exclusive economic zone, and the high seas.

Clive Symmons, in Chapter 10, critically examines the supposed Chinese claim to historic waters in the South China Sea, including the inter-relationship of such a claim with the doctrine of historic rights. The problems relating to definition of historic waters and the supposed rules and sub-rules relating to the doctrine are specifically applied to the situation in the South China Sea. Conclusions are drawn accordingly on such a claim, including what impact the pending request of the Philippines for arbitration under UNCLOS provisions may have on this issue.

Chapter 11 contributed by Keyuan Zou attempts to discuss a couple of legal issues surrounding the U-shaped line and its implications for the future resolution of the islands disputes as well as maritime boundary delimitation in the South China Sea. He concludes that the U-shaped line had existed for more than half a century before the adoption of UNCLOS and even before the adoption of the 1958 Geneva Conventions on the Law of the Sea. The historic rights deriving from this line cannot be disregarded.

Robert Beckman's chapter analyzes the dispute settlement system in UNCLOS by reviewing the system of compulsory binding dispute settlement set out in Part XV of UNCLOS. It then examine the limitations and optional exceptions to the system of compulsory binding dispute settlement. The author also examines the advisory jurisdiction of ITLOS.

Nong Hong, in Chapter 13, addresses both the legal and political impact of state practice. The attitude toward international law, participation in UNCLOS negotiation, maritime legislation and dispute settlement practice of relevant states is considered in turn to elaborate the practice of littoral states of the SCS.

Michael Sheng-ti Gau, in Chapter 14, discusses the hidden legal obstacles in the Notification and Statement of Claim produced by the Philippines to initiate the Sino-Philippine Arbitration on January 22, 2013. Article 9 of Annex VII to UNCLOS and other relevant rules are applied to demonstrate that the Tribunal has no jurisdiction over the disputes brought by the Philippines against China, while the Philippines' claims may not be deemed to be well founded in fact and in law.

PART I:
Dispute Settlement Mechanism under UNCLOS

Chapter 1
The Contribution of the Compulsory Jurisdiction Mechanism to the Effective Application of Dispute Settlement System of the 1982 United Nations Convention on the Law of the Sea: The Case of ITLOS

José Luis Jesus

This chapter attempts to assess the contribution of the procedure of compulsory jurisdiction to the effective application of the UNCLOS[1] dispute settlement system, by reference, especially, to the work of ITLOS. I will start by making a few observations related, namely, to the important role of the Convention's dispute settlement system in ensuring the workability, as well as the integrity, of the Convention's legal regime. Then, I will attempt to highlight the pivotal role so far played in this regard by the compulsory jurisdiction provisions of that settlement system.

The negotiators of the Convention were fully aware that the great mission they were embarking upon during the Third UN Conference,[2] of addressing "all issues relating to the law of the sea,"[3] meant that a giant step was being taken, as they were negotiating a thorough regulation for the world's oceans, setting up new frontiers, laying down the main rules for the partition of vast ocean space amongst countries and distributing entitlements to vast resources.

Those negotiators were certainly very much aware that the scope, the structure, and the content of their end-product—that is the Convention—would have enormous implications on States' relations concerning ocean affairs and, to a great extent, would change, in a fundamental way, the very perception of the sovereignty of the coastal State over vast maritime space or its ownership and control over substantial marine resources.

---

1 See Part XV of the 1982 UN Convention on the Law of the Sea. See also Section 5 of Part XI, Annex VI and Annex VII to the same Convention.

2 The negotiations in the Third United Nations Conference on the Law of the Sea started in 1973 and came to an end in 1982, with the adoption of the Law of the Sea Convention

3 See 1982 Law of the Sea Convention, Preamble, para. 1.

The mission of the framers of the Convention was, thus, one of enormous responsibility. Responsibility in securing the achievement of a negotiated set of rules that would command the consensual support of States, but also, and most importantly, responsibility in ensuring the creation of conditions that would promote the integrity and the effective application of the Convention.

As the Convention is the fruit of a complex interplay of give-and-take that took place in the Conference, it reflects a delicate balance, translated into a network of different national interests interwoven therein.

Pivotal in maintaining this delicate balance was the design of a carefully crafted dispute settlement system, as the only mechanism put in place that could possibly guarantee the peaceful implementation of such an important international regulation for the seas in its multiple aspects. In a way, the integrity of the balance of interests achieved in the Convention's legal regime would ultimately be ensured by the activation of this built-in dispute settlement system.

This settlement dispute system, though drawing heavily on past experiences, includes a set of innovative features, never before seen in international adjudication. It did so, I suspect, because otherwise, the workability of this settlement system would probably encounter tremendous hurdles, which, if they were to happen, could eventually compromise the effective and peaceful implementation of the whole legal regime established in the Convention, a situation that would benefit no one, as the Convention is "an important contribution to the maintenance of peace, justice and progress for all peoples of the world."[4]

I chose to address here today, as my main observation, one of the most salient points of those innovative features of the Convention's dispute settlement system, from the point of view of its contribution toward making that settlement system both workable and effective: I am referring to the procedure of compulsory jurisdiction.

By compulsory jurisdiction in this context, I mean the possibility that one of the parties to a dispute has to activate one of the means of settlement of dispute referred to in Article 287 of the Convention, by instituting proceedings against the other party.

To be more to the point, I will center my observations on the actual use by States parties of the compulsory procedure in the framework of the law of the sea disputes and the contribution of such procedure not only to ensure the integrity of the Convention's legal regime, but also to the judicial work of the International Tribunal for the Law of the Sea (the Tribunal).

The Convention's settlement system marks a departure from past experience, in that it subjects disputes arising out of the application or interpretation of the Convention to the general rule of compulsory jurisdiction, within the meaning stated before.

Of course, the Convention makes some exceptions to this general rule, namely:

4 Ibid.

a. in cases where parties agree at any time to settle a dispute between them concerning the interpretation or application of this Convention by any peaceful means of their own choice;[5]
b. in cases where there are limitations on applicability of Section 2 of Part XV;[6]
c. in cases where States may opt out, regarding certain categories of disputes.[7]

I shall not deal with these limitations and exceptions in this chapter, as this would divert me from my chosen theme.

Even when one takes into account these limitations and exceptions to the applicability of the compulsory procedure set forth in Section 2 of Part XV, there remains a great number of potential disputes that inexorably fall within that compulsory jurisdiction, if States have not chosen the same means of dispute settlement referred to in Article 287;[8] in the cases involving seabed activities related disputes; and in the special cases of urgent proceedings.[9] This is what, in my view, maintains the vitality of the Convention's dispute settlement system and, by implication, the integrity of the delicate balance of States' rights and interests translated into the Convention's provisions.

This compulsory procedure mechanism made it possible for the filing of all cases that so far have been submitted to the Annex VII arbitration. It is also the reason why the Tribunal has so far received 22 cases in a relatively short period of time since its entry into operation. Indeed, the majority of these cases submitted to the Tribunal were based, directly or indirectly, on the compulsory procedure provisions of the Convention.

Although Annex VII arbitration is the default procedure, and therefore it is the means of settlement of disputes chosen by Article 287 of the Convention to receive the disputes submitted under the compulsory jurisdiction procedure, exception being made, of course, for seabed activities related disputes, the Tribunal shares with the Annex VII arbitration the default status, albeit in a more limited way, and to this extent the Tribunal's judicial work is and has been the beneficiary of the compulsory jurisdiction mechanism established in the Convention.

Indeed, some provisions of the Convention grant to the Tribunal a special treatment in, at least, four circumstances. These four circumstances are:

a. the exclusive jurisdiction of the Tribunal's Seabed Disputes Chamber regarding disputes and requests for advisory opinions related to activities in the Area;[10]

5 Ibid., Art. 280.
6 See ibid., Art. 297.
7 Ibid., Art. 298.
8 Ibid., Art. 287, paras 3 and 5, Annex VII to the Convention.
9 Ibid., Arts 292 and 290, para. 5.
10 Ibid., Arts 187, 191.

b. the residual jurisdiction of the Tribunal in prompt release cases;[11]
c. the special and unique jurisdiction, conferred on the Tribunal by the Convention, to entertain requests for provisional measures pending the constitution of an arbitral tribunal under Annex VII of the Convention;[12]
d. the authority, expressly granted to the President of the Tribunal by Annex VII, to appoint arbitrators to an arbitral tribunal at the request of a party and in consultation with both parties.[13]

On the Exclusive Jurisdiction of the Tribunal's Seabed Disputes Chamber

The Convention recognizes the exclusive jurisdiction of the Tribunal's Seabed Disputes Chamber to entertain both disputes arising out of interpretation or application of the provisions of the Convention concerning activities in the Area, and requests for advisory opinions made by the Assembly or the Council of the Authority "on legal questions arising within the scope of their activities."[14] Thus, the framers of the Convention granted an important preferential treatment to the Tribunal, via its Seabed Disputes Chamber. Indeed, none of the other "means of dispute settlement" referred to in Article 287 of the Convention has jurisdiction to deal with such disputes or requests.[15, 16]

Thus, a whole set of potential disputes or requests for advisory opinions concerning an important Part of the Convention[17] dealing with the Seabed activities is reserved for the Tribunal Seabed Disputes Chamber. Recently, this special treatment given to the Seabed Chamber by the Convention made it possible for the advisory case, Case N. 17, to be filed with that Chamber.

---

11 Ibid., Art. 292, para. 1.

12 Ibid., Art. 290, para. 5.

13 Ibid., Annex VII, Art. 3.

14 See ibid., Art. 191.

15 See Carl-August Fleischhauer, "The Relationship Between the International Court of Justice and the Newly International Tribunal for the Law of the Sea in Hamburg," *Max Planck Yearbook of United Nations Law* (1997), 1:332. See also Dame Rosalyn Higgins' statement at the tenth anniversary of the International Tribunal for the Law of the Sea.

16 There are, however, two narrow exceptions to this rule: First, the parties to a dispute between States concerning the interpretation or application of Part XI of the Convention and related annexes may choose a chamber of the Tribunal or refer the dispute to a three-member ad hoc chamber of the Seabed Disputes Chamber itself (see Art. 188, para. 1 (a)); second, a party to a dispute concerning a contract or a plan of work may request that it be submitted to binding commercial arbitration.

17 Part XI and related Annexes and the NY Agreement.

Prompt Release of Vessels and Crews

The Convention confers on the Tribunal a residual jurisdiction to entertain cases of prompt release of vessels from detention, either for alleged non-compliance with laws and regulations concerning living resources in the exclusive economic zone that are adopted by the coastal State in conformity with the Convention or for pollution of the marine environment. Other courts and tribunals referred to in Article 287 may exercise jurisdiction in cases of prompt release of vessels and crews if the parties so agree. If, however, as is usually the case, no such agreement is reached within 10 days from the date of the detention of the vessel,[18] the flag State may institute a prompt release case on a compulsory basis only before the Tribunal.

This residual jurisdiction gives the Tribunal an edge over other courts or tribunals referred to in Article 287, by conferring upon it, after the 10-day period, an exclusive compulsory jurisdiction to entertain vessels prompt release cases under Article 292 of the Convention.

The flag State has thus the option of bringing a prompt release case before the Tribunal 10 days after the detention of the vessel, irrespective of whether the detaining State agrees or not with the flag State's choice of the Tribunal as the forum to entertain the prompt release case.

As a result of this residual jurisdiction, the Tribunal has received nine cases of prompt release of vessels and crews from detention for alleged violation of fisheries regulations in the exclusive economic zone. All these cases were introduced by the flag State or on its behalf. No such cases have been instituted before any other court and tribunal referred to in Article 287 of the Convention.

Provisional Measures Pending the Constitution of an Annex VII Arbitral Tribunal

Provisional measures pending the constitution of an Annex VII arbitral tribunal is another example of preferential treatment accorded to the Tribunal by the Convention, entailing an exclusive compulsory jurisdiction.[19]

This procedure is an innovation in international adjudication; it allows a party to a dispute that has been submitted to an arbitral tribunal under Annex VII of the Convention to file for interim measures before the Tribunal, pending the constitution of that arbitral tribunal.

The request for provisional measures may also be made to any court or tribunal referred to in Article 287 if both parties to the dispute so agree. If, as has always been the case, no such agreement is reached within two weeks from the notification of the institution of Annex VII arbitration, either party to the dispute

18 See Art. 292, para. 1, of the Convention.

19 Ibid., Art. 295, para. 5.

may introduce the request for provisional measures to the Law of the Sea Tribunal and only to this tribunal.

This special treatment explains why the Tribunal, and no other court or tribunal of those listed in Article 287, has received six such cases. The *Bluefin Tuna Cases* (joined), the *MOX Plant Case*, the *Land Reclamation Case*, the *Ara Libertad Case*, and, most recently, the *Arctic Sunrise Case*, were all instituted before the Tribunal under provisions entailing compulsory jurisdiction.

Annex VII Special Authority

Another special situation, although of a different nature, that may facilitate the institution of a case before the Tribunal has to do with the role granted to its president by Annex VII to the Convention.

Under Annex VII arbitral tribunal, the parties to a dispute are to agree on the appointment of three of the five arbitrators that compose the arbitral tribunal. If, within 60 days from the notification of institution of arbitral proceedings, the parties cannot agree on these appointments or on an entity to make them, either party may request the president of the tribunal to do so in consultation with both parties.

The recourse to the president of the tribunal brings the parties to Annex VII arbitration closer to the Law of the Sea Tribunal. In some instances, as a result of the consultations held by the president of the tribunal with the parties in the context of the appointment of the arbitrators, the parties may end up transferring the case from arbitration to the Law of the Sea Tribunal. Financial considerations may play a major role in this regard, as the costs of arbitration are not negligible and these costs can be substantially reduced if the case is transferred to the Law of the Sea Tribunal.

Moreover, States parties to a dispute, after years of consultations and negotiations, are sometimes left with no alternative other than to institute Annex VII arbitral proceedings (for which the instituting party does not require the agreement of the other disputant party). At times, the recourse to Annex VII arbitration is a first step toward possible referral of the dispute to another third party procedure, such as the Law of the Sea Tribunal. Once Annex VII arbitration has been instituted, considerations of costs reduction and time effectiveness in the management of the case may lead the parties to agree to refer the case to the Tribunal.

On five occasions, cases that were initially brought up as an Annex VII arbitration were later transferred to the Tribunal by agreement of the parties: This happened in the "Saiga" 2 case, in the Swordfish Stocks case, in the case concerning the delimitation of the maritime boundary in the Bay of Bengal, in the Louisa case and in the Virginia G case.

From this brief note, one draws two important conclusions: First, the judicial work of the Tribunal has been heavily dependent on the compulsory procedure mechanism built into the Convention's innovative dispute settlement system, either directly, as in the cases of prompt release and requests for provisional measures pending the constitution of the Annex VII arbitral tribunal, or indirectly, as in the cases on the merits brought before the Tribunal, as a result of transfer to it of cases previously submitted under compulsory jurisdiction to Annex VII arbitration; second, the Convention's compulsory procedure plays, and has been playing, a pivotal role in keeping the settlement dispute system alive, not only as a useful, but also at times as the only outlet available to States to solve their law of the sea disputes with other States, disputes which otherwise may have been unmanageable for lack of agreement between the parties as to the choice of forum for their settlement. In so doing, the compulsory jurisdiction has contributed to maintaining the integrity and the delicate balance of States' interests as reflected in the Convention.

References

Fleischhauer, Carl-August, "The Relationship Between the International Court of Justice and the Newly International Tribunal for the Law of the Sea in Hamburg," *Max Planck Yearbook of United Nations Law* (1997), 1:332.

Higgins, Dame Rosalyn, Statement at the tenth anniversary of the International Tribunal for the Law of the Sea.

NY Agreement, Part XI and related Annexes.

United Nations Convention on the Law of the Sea.

Chapter 2
UNCLOS and the Contributions of ITLOS

Helmut Tuerk

As another chapter addresses the dispute settlement system of the United Nations Convention on the Law of the Sea (UNCLOS), I will now concentrate on the position of the International Tribunal for the Law of the Sea (ITLOS) within that system and highlight the contributions this Tribunal has already made to the interpretation of the Convention and to the law of the sea in general.[1] Let me, nevertheless, recall that the negotiators at the Third United Nations Conference on the Law of the Sea, to which I had the privilege of belonging, strongly believed that compulsory third-party dispute settlement should be an essential feature of the new Convention.[2] This was obviously motivated by the wish to safeguard the many delicate compromises and to secure, as far as possible, a uniform interpretation and application of this instrument.[3] The newly created International Tribunal for the Law of the Sea constitutes an essential feature of the dispute settlement system, although, as you are aware, it is only one of four means under UNCLOS for the settlement of disputes entailing binding decisions. The term 'Tribunal', which may lead to some confusion in particular with respect to *ad hoc* tribunals, was used in order to distinguish this new institution from the International Court of Justice (ICJ). In choosing the method to resolve a dispute States parties are accorded a great deal of flexibility as otherwise consensus on enshrining compulsory dispute settlement in the Convention could not have been achieved.[4]

I wish to point out that the question of establishing a special tribunal within the framework of UNCLOS was originally dealt with in the context of the

---

1 This presentation is mostly based on Chapter 7 of H. Tuerk, *Reflections on the Contemporary Law of the Sea* (Leiden and Boston: Martinus Nijhoff, 2012), 121–57.

2 J.E. Noyes, 'Judicial and Arbitral Proceedings and the Outer Limit of the Continental Shelf', *Vanderbilt Journal of Transnational Law*, 42 (2009): 3; see also J.E. Noyes, 'Compulsory Third-Party Adjudication and the 1982 United Nations Convention on the Law of the Sea', *Connecticut Journal of International Law*, 4 (1988–9): 677–9; see further J.E. Noyes, 'The International Tribunal for the Law of the Sea', *Cornell International Law Journal*, 32 (1999): 115–16.

3 R.R. Churchill, 'Some Reflections on the Operation of the Dispute Settlement System of the UN Convention on the Law of the Sea During its First Decade', in D. Freestone, R. Barnes and D.M. Ong (eds), The Law of the Sea: Progress and Prospects (Oxford/New York; Oxford University Press, 2006).

4 N. Klein, *Dispute Settlement in the UN Convention on the Law of the Sea* (Cambridge: Cambridge University Press, 2005), 54.

creation of the International Seabed Authority. This new tribunal was to be one of the principal organs of the Authority, following the example of the ICJ – the 'principal judicial organ of the United Nations'.[5] In the course of the negotiations this approach was, however, abandoned in favour of establishing a full-fledged Tribunal for the settlement of all law of the sea disputes as an autonomous international organization, not part of any other organ set up by UNCLOS, with a special Seabed Disputes Chamber.[6] As regards the composition of ITLOS added weight has been given to developing countries in comparison to the ICJ.[7]

ITLOS is open to States parties to the Convention, other States, as well as other entities, such as international organizations and natural or legal persons in any case expressly provided for in Part XI of the Convention.[8] Although its jurisdiction is not as broad *ratione materiae* as that of the ICJ, being confined to matters provided for in the Convention and related instruments, it is thus more comprehensive *ratione personae*. One could say that access is probably the most significant difference between ITLOS and the ICJ.[9]

Before dealing with the jurisprudence of the Tribunal, let me briefly outline its jurisdiction: in principle, it includes any dispute relating to the law of the sea. It is, however, subject to limitations spelled out in Article 297 UNCLOS and optional exceptions to the compulsory procedures according to Article 298. In two instances ITLOS has compulsory jurisdiction: that is Article 290(5) regarding provisional measures, pending the constitution of an arbitral tribunal, and Article 292 concerning the prompt release of vessels and/or crews. The Tribunal may also exercise jurisdiction over disputes relating to the interpretation or application of treaties which are already in force, and concern the subject-matter covered by the Convention, provided that all the parties to that treaty so agree.[10]

---

5 Article 1, Statute of the ICJ.

6 A.O. Adede, 'The System for Settlement of Disputes under the United Nations Convention on the Law of the Sea: A Drafting History and a Commentary', *Publications on Ocean Development*, 10 (1987): 173–4; see also A.K. Escher, 'Release of Vessels and Crews before the International Tribunal for the Law of the Sea', in E. Valencia-Ospina (ed.), *The Law and Practice of International Courts and Tribunals: A Practitioner's Journal* (Leiden; Martinus Nijhoff, 2004), 237–8.

7 A.E. Boyle, 'The International Tribunal for the Law of the Sea and the Settlement of Disputes', in J.J. Norton et al. (eds), *The Changing World of International Law in the Twenty-First Century* (The Hague/London/Boston; Kluwer Law International, 1998), 118.

8 See Article 20, Statute of the Tribunal, Annex VI to UNCLOS.

9 A.E. Boyle, 'Dispute Settlement and the Law of the Sea Convention: Problems of Fragmentation and Jurisdiction', *International & Comparative Law Quarterly*, 46/1 (1997): 51; see also R. Wolfrum, 'Verfahren zur Freigabe von Schiffen vor dem Internationalen Seegerichtshof', in R. Lagoni and M. Paschke (eds), *Seehandelsrecht und Seerecht: Festschrift für Rolf Herber zum 70. Geburtstag* (Hamburg; Lit Verlag, 1999), 568.

10 Article 22, Statute of the Tribunal.

In addition, the jurisdiction of ITLOS may derive from relevant clauses included in international agreements related to the purposes of UNCLOS.[11] At present, there are 11 such multilateral and five such bilateral agreements containing provisions making specific reference to the dispute settlement procedures of Part XV of the Convention.[12] It is important to note that with respect to these agreements, the procedures of Part XV apply, whether a party to the agreement is a State party to the Convention or not.

UNCLOS does not contain any provision conferring advisory jurisdiction on the Tribunal in its full composition, which, however, on the basis of Article 138 of its Rules 'may give an advisory opinion on a legal question if an international agreement related to the purposes of the Convention specifically provides for the submission to the Tribunal of a request for such an opinion'.[13] In adopting that rule ITLOS prepared itself for possible requests for advisory opinions in case such competence were to be entrusted to it by future agreements. On 28 March 2013, the full Tribunal, for the first time, received a request for an Advisory Opinion from the Sub-Regional Fisheries Commission, located in Dakar, Senegal, comprising seven Member States – Cape Verde, the Gambia, Guinea, Guinea-Bissau, Mauritania, Senegal and Sierra Leone, which are all parties to UNCLOS. The questions put to ITLOS, *inter alia*, relate to the obligations of the flag State in cases of illegal, unreported and unregulated (IUU) fishing activities within the exclusive economic zone of third-party States and to the extent of liability of the flag State for such fishing activities conducted by vessels sailing under its flag.[14]

Although advisory opinions are non-binding they provide a flexible mechanism for clarifying the interpretation of the law. As States and other users of UNCLOS seem to differ on the interpretation and application of certain of its provisions, I am convinced that requests to ITLOS for advisory opinions will prove to be a useful tool to assist parties in narrowing their differences on a given legal point

---

11 See Guide to Proceedings before the Tribunal (2009/1), at 6, available at: www.itlos.org.

12 See ibid., Annex 1, at 39, listing these agreements; see also Statement by Mr Doo-young Kim, Deputy Registrar of ITLOS, reproduced as Appendix G to the Report of the First Meeting of Regional Fishery Body Secretariats Network, at 4, FAO doc. FIEL/R837 (12–13 March 2007).

13 The respective Article 138 of the Rules of the Tribunal is based on Article 21 of its Statute, which states that the jurisdiction of the Tribunal comprises 'all disputes and all applications submitted to in in accordance with this Convention and all matters specifically provided for in any other agreement which confers jurisdiction on the Tribunal'. See generally H. Tuerk, 'Advisory Opinions and the Law of the Sea', in M. Pogacnik et al. (eds), *The Challenges of Contemporary International Law and International Relations – Liber Amicorum Dr. Ernest Petric* (Nova Gorica; European Law Faculty of Nova Gorica, 2011), 365–83; see also H. Caminos, 'The International Tribunal for the Law of the Sea: An Overview of its Jurisdictional Procedure', in A. Del Vecchio (ed.), *New International Tribunals and New International Proceedings* (Milano; Giuffrè Editore, 2006), 22.

14 ITLOS Press Release No. 190, 28 March 2013, available at: www.itlos.org.

and to facilitate the settlement of disputes through negotiations. Such opinions may even prevent maritime disputes from arising at all.

The Seabed Disputes Chamber, to which I have already referred, is composed of 11 judges and constitutes a 'tribunal within a tribunal'. It has been granted exclusive and compulsory jurisdiction over disputes arising out of the exploration and exploitation of the international seabed 'Area'.[15] It is important to note that the decisions of the Chamber are enforceable in the territories of the State parties in the same manner as judgments or orders of the highest court of the State party in whose territory the enforcement is sought.[16] In that respect the functions of the Seabed Disputes Chamber might well be compared to that of a constitutional court.[17] The Chamber may further be requested by the Assembly or the Council of the International Seabed Authority to give an advisory opinion 'on legal questions arising within the scope of their activities'.[18] The Council of the Authority has already submitted one such request for advisory opinion with which I will deal later.

Since ITLOS became operational in 1996, 22 cases have been submitted to it, concerning questions such as the lawfulness of enforcement measures taken against foreign vessels in the exclusive economic zone, the use of force at sea, the prompt release of detained vessels and crews, the protection of fishery resources and of the marine environment as well as the delimitation of maritime areas. Of these cases 16 were settled by way of litigation, two were discontinued further to agreement between the parties, one was the Advisory Opinion given by the Seabed Disputes Chamber, and three are in progress. There are three kinds of contentious cases which have been or are being dealt with by ITLOS: provisional measures, prompt release of vessels and/or crews, and cases relating to the merits.

ITLOS may be requested to prescribe provisional measures in two situations, first according to Article 290 (1) where a dispute on the merits has been submitted to it, and second on the basis of Article 290 (5) when such a dispute has been submitted to an arbitral tribunal, pending its constitution.[19] In order to prescribe provisional measures, the Tribunal must consider that the measures are required

---

15 See also Presentation by Judge H. Tuerk, Vice-President of ITLOS, at the Seminar on Exploration ad Exploitation of Deep Seabed Mineral Resources in the Area: Challenges for Africa, and Opportunities for Collaborative Research in the South Atlantic Ocean, Abuja, Nigeria, 24 March 2009, at 9–10, available at: www.itlos.org.

16 Article 39, Statute of the Tribunal.

17 R. Wolfrum, 'Advisory Opinions: Are They a Suitable Alternative for the Settlement of International Disputes?', presentation, in R. Wolfrum and I. Gätschmann (eds), *International Dispute Settlement: Room for Innovations?* (Heidelberg: Springer, 2012), 53.

18 Article 191 UNCLOS.

19 Judge R. Wolfrum, President of ITLOS, Statement to the Sixth Committee of UNGA, 20 October 2006, at 5, available at: www.itlos.org. According to Judge Wolfrum it is also of interest to note that under the Straddling Fish Stocks Agreement of 1995 the Tribunal is empowered to prescribe provisional measures to protect the rights of the parties as well as to prevent damage to the fish stocks in question.

by the urgency of the situation and that, *prima facie*, the arbitral tribunal to be constituted would have jurisdiction.

Provisional measures are binding upon the parties to the dispute and they may not only be prescribed by the Tribunal to preserve the respective rights of the parties, but also to 'prevent serious harm to the marine environment', which reflects the importance UNCLOS attaches to environmental protection. ITLOS may also follow up the measures it has prescribed by requesting the parties to submit reports on compliance.[20] Let me also point out that no cases requesting provisional measures under Article 290 have so far been submitted to any other court or tribunal having jurisdiction under the Convention.

The Tribunal has to date been seized with requests for provisional measures in seven cases: the *M/V Louisa Case*, Saint Vincent and the Grenadines v. Spain, in connection with an application on the merits, the other six pending the constitution of an arbitral tribunal – the *Southern Bluefin Tuna Cases*, Australia and New Zealand v. Japan, the *MOX Plant Case*, Ireland v. United Kingdom, the *Case concerning Land Reclamation by Singapore in and around the Straits of Johor*, Malaysia v. Singapore, the *ARA Libertad Case*, Argentina v. Ghana, and recently the *Arctic Sunrise Case*, Netherlands v. Russian Federation.

In the *M/V Louisa Case*,[21] Saint Vincent and the Grenadines requested the Tribunal, in particular, to order the release of that vessel and its tender held by Spain for alleged violation of Spain's historical patrimony. In its Order of 23 December 2010, the Tribunal found that it was no 'real and imminent risk' that irreparable prejudice may be caused to the rights of the parties or to the marine environment on account of degradation of the vessel, considering the assurances given in this respect by Spain. In the circumstance of the case, the Tribunal saw no requirement to prescribe provisional measures.

The *Southern Bluefin Tuna Cases*,[22] the *MOX Plant Case*[23] and the *Land Reclamation Case*[24] also related to the protection of the marine environment. These cases have enabled the Tribunal to contribute to the development of international

20 Judge R. Wolfrum, President of ITLOS, Statement to the Informal Meeting of Legal Advisers of Ministries of Foreign Affairs, 24 October 2005, at 5, available at: www.itlos.org.

21 *M/V Louisa* (Saint Vincent and the Grenadines v. Spain), Provisional Measures, Order of 23 December 2010, ITLOS Press Releases No. 154, 24 November 2010, 8 December 2010, 157, 20 December 2010, available at: www.itlos.org.

22 ITLOS, *Southern Bluefin Tuna* (New Zealand v. Japan; Australia v. Japan), Provisional Measures, Order of 27 August 1999, 2 ITLOS Reports (1999), at 280–336, reprinted in 38 ILM 1624 (1999); ITLOS Press Releases No. 27, 26 August 1999, and No. 28, 27 August 1999, available at: www.itlos.org.

23 ITLOS, *MOX* (Ireland v United Kingdom), Provisional Measures, Order of 3 December 2001, 5 ITLOS Reports (2001), at 89-112, reprinted in 41 ILM 405 (2002); ITLOS Press Releases No. 61, 29 November 2001, and No. 62, 3 December 2001.

24 *Case concerning Land Reclamation by Singapore in and around the Straits of Johor* (Malaysia v. Singapore), Provisional Measures, Order of 8 October 2003, 7 ITLOS

environmental law, in particular by emphasizing the duty of cooperation,[25] the notion of prudence and caution, and the importance of procedural rights, as essential components of environmental obligations. In its orders for provisional measures, the Tribunal followed the line of adopting a pragmatic approach and prescribing measures which, in its view, would assist the parties to find a solution.[26] The record of the Tribunal on environmental disputes can certainly be considered as a positive one.

The *ARA Libertad Case*[27] related to the detention of that Argentine warship in the Port of Tema, near Accra, where the ship had arrived on a courtesy visit on 1 October 2012. As the vessel's departure from this port was prevented by the authorities of Ghana pursuant to a decision of the High Court of Accra taken in connection with a commercial lawsuit, Argentina instituted arbitration proceedings under Annex VII to UNCLOS and thereupon requested ITLOS, to prescribe provisional measures against Ghana with respect to the detention of the vessel. On 15 December 2012, the Tribunal unanimously delivered its Order,[28] considering that 'in accordance with general international law, a warship enjoys immunity' and that 'any act which prevents by force a warship from discharging its mission and duties is a source of conflict that may endanger friendly relations among States'.

ITLOS, therefore, prescribed that Ghana shall forthwith and unconditionally release the frigate *ARA Libertad*, ensure that the frigate, its commander and crew are able to leave the port of Tema and the maritime areas under the jurisdiction of Ghana, and ensure that the *ARA Libertad* is resupplied to that end.[29] The ship was released as prescribed by the Tribunal and, on 19 December 2012, left the maritime areas under the jurisdiction of Ghana. Argentina and Ghana recently settled their dispute on the merits of this case. The echo to that Order of ITLOS was overwhelmingly positive as a clear decision was taken on a matter of principle – the immunity of warships.

The largest number of cases the Tribunal has so far dealt with concerned the prompt release of vessels and crews. According to Article 73 (2) of UNCLOS, arrested fishing vessels and their crews must, however, be promptly released upon the posting of a bond or other security. Whenever it is alleged that the detaining

---

Reports (2003), at 10–64, available at: www.itlos.org; ITLOS Press Release No. 83, 6 October 2003 and No. 84, 8 October 2003, available at: www.itlos.org.

25 See also P. Weckel, 'Les premieres applications de l'article 290 de la Convention sur le droit de la mer relatif a la prescription de mesures conservatoires', *Revue Générale de Droit International Public*, 109/4 (2005): 838.

26 R. Wolfrum, 'The Tenth Anniversary of the International Tribunal for the Law of the Sea', *Romanian Journal of International Law*, 2/3 (2006): 76.

27 *ARA Libertad* (Argentina v. Ghana), Provisional Measures, Order of 15 December 2012, available at: www.itlos.org; ITLOS Press Release No. 182, 14 November 2012; No. 183, 22 November 2012; No. 184, 28 November 2012; No. 185, 28 November 2012; No. 186, 13 December 2012 and No. 188, 15 December 2012, available at: www.itlos.org.

28 See Order of 15 December 2012, paras 95 and 97.

29 Ibid., para. 108 (1).

State has not complied with that duty, the flag State of the vessel is entitled under Article 292 to request the release of the vessel before any court or tribunal agreed upon by the parties or, failing such agreement within 10 days from the time of the detention, before a court or tribunal accepted by the detaining State under Article 287 UNCLOS or before ITLOS, unless the parties otherwise agree.[30]

ITLOS has so far ordered the release of the vessel and/or its crew upon the posting of a reasonable bond in altogether six cases: *M/V Saiga I*,[31] Saint Vincent and the Grenadines v. Guinea; *Camouco*,[32] Panama v. France; *Monte Confurco*,[33] Seychelles v. France; *Volga*,[34] Russia v. Australia; *Juno Trader*,[35] Saint Vincent and the Grenadines v. Guinea-Bissau; and *Hoshinmaru*,[36] Japan v. Russia. The *M/V Saiga I Case* concerned the prompt release of an oil tanker and its crew, the other cases involved fisheries disputes.

Let me emphasize that ITLOS has developed a coherent jurisprudence in respect of prompt release cases, making it clear that it may be seized not only where no bond has been set but also where it considers that the bond set by the detaining State is unreasonable, and that it has the ultimate competence to decide on the amount. In this connection it has established a number of relevant factors for determining the reasonableness of bonds or other financial security.[37] The Tribunal has also observed that Article 292 provides for a quick, independent remedy during which local remedies could not normally be exhausted.[38] In those

30 Article 292 (1) UNCLOS.

31 *M/V Saiga I* (Saint Vincent and the Grenadines v. Guinea), Prompt Release, Judgment of 4 December 1997, 1 ITLOS Reports (1997), at 16–38, reprinted in 37 ILM 360 (1999); ITLOS Press Release No. 9, 21 November 1997, available at: www.itlos.org.

32 *Camouco* (Panama v. France), Prompt Release, Judgment of 7 February 2000, 4 ITLOS Reports (2000), at 10–37, available at: www.itlos.org; ITLOS Press Release No. 35, 7 February 2000, available at: www.itlos.org.

33 *Monte Confurco* (Seychelles v. France), Prompt Release, Judgment of 18 December 2000, 4 ITLOS Reports (2000), at 86–117, available at: www.itlos.org; ITLOS Press Releases No. 41, 15 December 2000, and No. 42, 18 December 2000, available at: www.itlos.org.

34 *Volga* (Russia v. Australia), Prompt Release, Judgment of 23 December 2002, 6 ITLOS Reports (2002), at 10–41, available at: www.itlos.org; ITLOS Press Releases No. 74, 20 December 2002, and No. 75, 23 December 2002, available at: www.itlos.org.

35 *Juno Trader* (Saint Vincent and the Grenadines v. Guinea-Bissau), Prompt Release, Judgment of 18 December 2004, 8 ITLOS Reports (2004), at 17–92; ITLOS Press Releases No. 92 Corr. 1, 1 December 2004, and No. 95, 18 December 2004, available at: www.itlos.org.

36 ITLOS Press Releases No. 110, 6 July 2007, No. 111, 2 August 2007, and No. 112, 6 August 2007, available at: www.itlos.org.

37 See 4 ITLOS Reports (2000), at 31, para. 67, 6 ITLOS Reports (2002), at 32, para. 65, and 8 ITLOS Reports (2004), at 41, para. 85; see also T.A. Mensah, 'Provisional Measures in the International Tribunal on the Law of the Sea', *Zeitschrift für ausländisches öffentliches Recht und Völkerrecht*, 62(1/2) (2002): 46.

38 See Panama v. France concerning the fishing vessel *Camouco* (note 32).

cases where members of the crew were still being detained it was determined that they should be free to leave the respective country without any conditions.

It is important to note that in prompt release proceedings, ITLOS may deal only with the question of the release of the vessel without prejudice to the merits of any case before the appropriate domestic forum in respect of the vessel, its owner or its crew. In its jurisprudence, it has strictly applied this requirement of the Convention. The prompt release procedure is also characterized by its swiftness, as the Tribunal, according to its Rules, must give priority to such applications over all other proceedings.[39] In its practice, ITLOS has acted in prompt release proceedings with remarkable efficiency and speed, having delivered its decisions within the timeframe of approximately one month. The urgency of these proceedings is justified in view of the financial burden resulting from the detention of a vessel as well as humanitarian considerations regarding detained crews.[40]

No decision was taken by ITLOS with respect to the other three applications for prompt release submitted to it. In the case of the *Grand Prince*,[41] Belize v. France, the Tribunal found that it had no jurisdiction under Article 292 UNCLOS as the applicant failed to establish that Belize was the flag State of the vessel when the application was made. The *Chaisiri Reefer 2 Case*,[42] Panama v. Yemen, was removed from the Tribunal's list of cases following an agreement between the parties. In the *Tomimaru Case*,[43] Japan v. Russia, the competent Russian courts had decided to confiscate the vessel for the alleged infringement of national fisheries legislation in the Russian exclusive economic zone. In its Judgment of 6 August 2007 ITLOS expressed the view that a final domestic decision to confiscate eliminates the provisional character of the detention of the vessel rendering the procedure for its prompt release without object and that it was therefore not called upon to give a decision thereon. I, however, also wish to point out that the Tribunal noted that confiscation decided in 'unjustified haste' would jeopardize the implementation of Article 292. Such a decision should thus not be taken in such a way as to prevent the ship-owner from having recourse to available

39 Article 112 of the Rules of the Tribunal, available at: www.itlos.org.

40 Judge R. Wolfrum, President of ITLOS, Statement to the Informal Meeting of Legal Advisers of Ministries of Foreign Affairs, 24 October 2005, at 5, available at: www.itlos.org; Wolfrum, 'The Tenth Anniversary of the International Tribunal for the Law of the Sea' (note 26), at 76.

41 *Grand Prince* (Belize v. France), Prompt Release, Judgment of 20 April 2001, 5 ITLOS Reports (2001), at 17–46, available at: www.itlos.org; ITLOS Press Releases No. 47, 19 April 2001, and No. 48, 20 April 2001, available at: www.itlos.org.

42 *Chaisiri Reefer 2 Case* (Panama v. Yemen), Prompt Release, Judgment of 13 July 2001, 5 ITLOS Reports (2001), at 82–4, available at: www.itlos.org; ITLOS Press Releases No. 51, 5 July 2001, and No. 52, 16 July 2001, available at: www.itlos.org.

43 *The Tomimaru Case* (Japan v. Russian Federation), Prompt Release, Judgment of 6 August 2007, available at: www.itlos.org; ITLOS Press Releases No. 110, No. 111, and No. 112, 6 August 2007, available at: www.itlos.org.

domestic judicial remedies, or as to prevent the flag State from resorting to the prompt release procedure set forth in the Convention.

Let me now briefly refer to the four cases relating to the merits the Tribunal has so far been seized with:

In the *M/V Saiga (No. 2) Case*,[44] Guinea alleged that providing fishing vessels with gasoil – bunkering – off its coast was an offence under its customs laws, while Saint Vincent and the Grenadines claimed that the bunkering of vessels is within the freedom of navigation in the exclusive economic zone. In its Judgment of 1 July 1999 ITLOS declared that Guinea had violated the rights of Saint Vincent and the Grenadines in arresting the *Saiga*, and awarded the applicant monetary compensation. The Tribunal also made several important pronouncements concerning issues such as freedom of navigation, enforcement of customs laws, nationality of claims, reparation, use of force in law enforcement activities, hot pursuit and the question of the genuine link between the vessel and its flag State, thereby making an important contribution to the development of international law regarding these aspects. Let me just point out that ITLOS declared that under UNCLOS a ship is to be considered as a unit, everything on it and every person involved or interested in its operations – irrespective of their nationality – are treated as an entity linked to the flag State.

The *Case concerning the Conservation and Sustainable Exploitation of Swordfish Stocks in the South-Eastern Pacific Ocean*, Chile v. European Community[45] – now the European Union – dealt with by a Special Chamber of the Tribunal, has so far been the only case where one of the parties was an international organization. The Order of the Chamber of 16 December 2009 placed on record the discontinuance of the proceedings by agreement of the parties which, *inter alia*, provides for a definitive commitment to cooperate in the long-term conservation and management of the swordfish stocks in the South-Eastern Pacific. A dispute that had divided Chile and the European Union for about 20 years could thus be brought to a satisfactory conclusion.[46]

---

44 *M/V Saiga II* (Saint Vincent and the Grenadines v. Guinea), Merits, Judgment of 1 July 1999, 3 ITLOS Reports (1999), at para. 155; ITLOS Press Release No. 23 and Supplement No. 1, 1 July 1999, available at: www.itlos.org.

45 *Swordfish Stocks in the South-Eastern Pacific Ocean* (Chile v. European Community), Order of 20 December 2000, Order of 29 December 2005, 9 ITLOS Reports (2005), Order of 16 December 2009, ITLOS Press Releases No. 43, 21 December 2000; No. 45, 21 March 2001; No. 87, 7 January 2004; No. 102, 29 December 2005; No. 117, 30 November 2007; No. 129, 11 December 2008 and No. 141, 17 December 2009, available at: www.itlos.org.

46 See Remark by the President of the Special Chamber, Justice Chandrashekhara Rao; ITLOS Press Release 141, 17 December 2009, at 2, available at: www.itlos.org.

The *Dispute concerning delimitation of the Maritime Boundary between Bangladesh and Myanmar in the Bay of Bengal*, Bangladesh v. Myanmar,[47] was the first maritime delimitation case submitted to ITLOS. Bangladesh requested the Tribunal to delimit the maritime boundary with Myanmar in the Bay of Bengal with respect to the territorial sea, the exclusive economic zone and the continental shelf, including the part of the continental shelf beyond 200 nautical miles from the baselines.[48]

In its Judgment of 14 March 2012, the Tribunal, having found that there was no agreement within the meaning of Article 15 UNCLOS between the Parties, decided to delimit the territorial sea by drawing an equidistance line. In this connection, it gave full effect to St. Martin's Island, which is under the sovereignty of Bangladesh but lies opposite Myanmar's mainland coast.[49] In respect of the exclusive economic zone and continental shelf within 200 nautical miles, the Tribunal applied the equidistance/relevant circumstances method, following the three-stage approach developed in the most recent international jurisprudence on the subject. ITLOS thus began by constructing its own provisional equidistance line, it then determined that the cut-off effect produced by the concavity of Bangladesh's coast constituted a relevant circumstance and decided to adjust the provisional equidistance line for this reason.[50]

As regards the continental shelf beyond 200 nautical miles ITLOS was faced with the problem that neither Party had established the outer limits of the continental shelf pursuant to Article 76, paragraph 8, UNCLOS, and that the Commission on the Limits of the Continental Shelf had not yet made any recommendations to the parties in this regard. Nevertheless, the Tribunal found that it had jurisdiction to delimit the continental shelf in its entirety and that it should not refrain from exercising it. In the view of the Tribunal, it would have been contrary to the object and purpose of the Convention not to resolve the existing impasse between the Parties. Inaction by the Commission and the Tribunal, two organs created by the Convention to ensure the effective implementation of its provisions, would leave the Parties in a position where they might be unable to benefit fully from their rights over the continental shelf.[51] Under the specific circumstances of the case, ITLOS concluded that the Parties had overlapping entitlements to the continental shelf beyond 200 nautical miles and proceeded to delimit that area by applying the equidistance/relevant circumstances method. In this connection, it decided that

---

47 *Dispute concerning Delimitation of the Maritime Boundary between Bangladesh and Myanmar in the Bay of Bengal* (Bangladesh v. Myanmar), Judgment of 14 March 2012, ITLOS Press Releases No. 140, 16 December 2009; No. 142, 29 January 2010; No. 169, 26 August 2011; No. 174, 8 March 2012, and No. 175, 14 March 2012, available at: www.itlos.org.

48 Memorial of Bangladesh, Vol. I, 1 July 2011, at 49, 50, available at: www.itlos.org.

49 Judgment of 14 March 2012, paras 166–9, available at: www.itlos.org.

50 Ibid., paras 297 and 323–40, available at: www.itlos.org.

51 Ibid., paras 392–4, available at: www.itlos.org.

the adjusted equidistance line delimiting the continental shelf within 200 nautical miles would continue in the same direction beyond the 200-nautical-mile limit of Bangladesh until it reached the area where the rights of third States might be affected.[52]

In interpreting provisions of UNCLOS, the Tribunal took into consideration the existing jurisprudence of courts and tribunals, in particular that of the ICJ, which it reaffirmed in a number of respects. It went beyond these confines only as required to decide issues that had so far not been addressed in international adjudication, especially regarding the delimitation of the continental shelf beyond 200 nautical miles. In this respect that judgment may also provide guidance for the future resolution of disputes of a similar nature.

It is worth noting that ITLOS decided this highly complex maritime boundary case, which was actually three cases in one, within a rather short time of 27 months. The judgment has rightly been called a 'landmark decision', even a 'historic and major milestone in international law', particularly with respect to UNCLOS. It can certainly be considered as a fair solution to the dispute that had existed for over 36 years and was also regarded as such by Bangladesh and Myanmar, which both expressed their satisfaction at the judgement. Let me in this connection point out that Bangladesh succeeded in gaining access to a continental shelf beyond 200 nautical miles, while the area south of St. Martin's Island where Myanmar had started exploitation activities remained on its side of the delimitation line. A highly important aspect of the judgment is furthermore that it potentially unlocked a situation where both Myanmar and Bangladesh were prevented from exploiting the natural resources of the continental shelf beyond 200 nautical miles.

The *M/V Louisa Case*,[53] Saint Vincent and the Grenadines v. Spain, concerned that vessel which had been boarded, searched and detained by Spanish authorities on 1 February 2006 while lying in a Spanish port. The flag State, Saint Vincent and the Grenadines, maintained that the *M/V Louisa* was engaged in conducting surveys of the sea floor with a view to locating oil and gas deposits. According to the Spanish authorities, the vessel was seized in connection with criminal proceedings instituted in respect of the alleged commission of 'the crime of possession and depositing weapons of war', together with the 'continued crime of damaging Spanish historical patrimony'. Several persons were arrested and detained in Spain for different periods in connection with these criminal proceedings. Saint Vincent and the Grenadines requested ITLOS, *inter alia*, to declare that Spain had violated a number of provisions of UNCLOS, including Article 87 relating to the freedom of navigation, and to declare that the detention of the individuals was unlawful and abused their human rights in violation of the Convention.

In its Judgment of 28 May 2013, ITLOS came to the conclusion that none of the provisions invoked by the Saint Vincent and Grenadines could serve as a basis

52 Ibid., paras 461–2, available at: www.itlos.org.

53 *M/V Louisa* (Saint Vincent and the Grenadines v. Spain), Judgment dated 28 May 2013, available at: www.itlos.org.

for the claims it had submitted. As regards the treatment of persons connected with the M/V 'Louisa', Saint Vincent and the Grenadines also contended a violation of Article 300 UNCLOS relating to 'good faith and abuse of rights', a claim that was, however, only submitted after the closure of the written proceedings. ITLOS considered that reliance on that article generated a new claim in comparison to the claims presented in the Application and held that it could not allow a dispute brought before it by an application to be transformed in the course of proceedings into another dispute which is different in character. Therefore, Article 300 UNCLOS could not serve as a basis for the claims submitted. ITLOS thus concluded that no dispute concerning the interpretation or application of the Convention existed between the Parties at the time of the filing of the Application and that it had no jurisdiction *ratione materiae* to entertain the case before it.

On 1 February 2011, the first advisory opinion was rendered by ITLOS, to be precise by its Seabed Disputes Chamber, following a request by the Council of the International Seabed Authority pursuant to Article 191 UNCLOS[54] which related, in particular, to the legal responsibilities and obligations of States parties to the Convention with respect to the sponsorship of activities in the international seabed 'Area'. The Chamber unanimously rendered its Opinion, stating that there is an obligation of 'due diligence' of sponsoring States under the Convention and related instruments and that these States are bound to make 'best possible efforts' to secure compliance by the sponsored contractors. These obligations apply equally to developed and developing States, unless specifically provided otherwise in the applicable provisions. The Chamber, *inter alia*, also held that the Convention requires the sponsoring State to adopt, within its legal system, laws and regulations and to take administrative measures to ensure compliance by the contractor with its obligations and to exempt the sponsoring State from liability.[55]

This advisory opinion was received very favourably by the International Seabed Authority and the international community at large. It turned out to be instrumental for the Authority in the discharge of its tasks under UNCLOS and also constitutes an important guideline for States parties to the Convention intending to engage in deep seabed mining. As the exploitation phase with respect to the international seabed 'Area' is drawing closer, further requests for advisory opinions may well be addressed to the Seabed Disputes Chamber.

---

54 See Decision by the Council of the ISA, ISA doc. ISBA/16/C/13, 6 May 2010, available at: www.isa.org.jm/files/documents/EN/Press/Press10/SB-16-19.pdf; see also Seabed Disputes Chamber of the International Tribunal for the Law of the Sea, Responsibilities and Obligations of States Sponsoring Persons and Entities with Respect to Activities in the Area, Advisory Opinion, 1 February 2011, at para. 1; ITLOS Press Releases No. 147, 14 May 2007; No. 148, 19 May 2007; No. 150, 29 July 2010; No. 151, 20 August 2010; No. 152, 6 September 2010; No. 160, 19 January 2011; No. 161, 1 February 2011, available at: www.itlos.org.

55 Ibid., at para. 242.

The three cases currently on the docket of ITLOS are the *M/V Virginia G Case*,[56] Panama v. Guinea-Bissau, the already mentioned Request by the Sub-Regional Fisheries Commission for an Advisory Opinion and the *Arctic Sunrise Case*.[57] The *M/V Virginia G Case* concerns a Panamanian-flag vessel, which was arrested in the exclusive economic zone of Guinea-Bissau under the allegation of providing fuel to fishing vessels without the necessary authorization. Oral proceedings in this case were held in September 2013 and a judgment is expected in April 2014, while the Request for an Advisory Opinion will be dealt later in that year. The *Arctic Sunrise Case* relates to the detention of that icebreaker and its crew in the Russian port of Murmansk. The ship had been used by Greenpeace International to stage a protest directed against a Russian off-shore fixed platform in the Barents Sea.

In conclusion, let me sum up that ITLOS in its almost 16 years of existence has established a reputation for the expeditious and efficient management of cases,[58] and has made substantial contributions to the interpretation of UNCLOS and to the further development of international law.[59] The Tribunal has the competence and means under the Convention to deal with a wide range of disputes and has, when appropriate, also adopted a pragmatic approach in order to assist the parties to find a satisfactory solution to their dispute. The continued and significant contribution of ITLOS to the settlement of disputes by peaceful means in accordance with Part XV of UNCLOS is also regularly being noted with satisfaction by the UN General Assembly.[60]

I further wish to highlight that while UNCLOS does not grant the Tribunal the privilege of being the default procedure, which is as you know is arbitration, some of its provisions nevertheless accord it a more favourable treatment. These relate to the exclusive jurisdiction of the Seabed Disputes Chamber regarding the international seabed 'Area', the residual jurisdiction of ITLOS in prompt release cases, the special and unique jurisdiction conferred upon it to entertain requests for

---

56 *The M/V Virginia G Case* (Panama v. Guinea-Bissau), Judgment of 14 April 2014, ITLOS Press Releases No. 168, 5 July 2011; No. 179, 31 October 2012; No. 180, 6 November 2012; No. 199, 19 August 2013; No. 210, 8 April 2014 and No. 211, 14 April 2014, available at: www.itlos.org.

57 *The Arctic Sunrise Case* (Kingdom of Netherlands v. Russian Federation), Order of 22 November 2013, ITLOS Press Releases No. 201, 21 October 2013; No. 202, 25 October 2013; No. 203, 30 October 2013; No. 204, 19 November 2013 and No. 205, 22 November 2013, available at: www.itlos.org.

58 Judge R. Wolfrum, President of ITLOS, Statement to the Report of the Tribunal to the Sixteenth Meeting of States parties to UNCLOS, 19 June 2006, at 5, available at: www.itlos.org.

59 See also M. Kamto, 'Regard sur la jurisprudence du tribunal international du droit de la mer depuis son entrée en fonctionnement (1997–2004)', *Revue générale de droit international public*, 109/4 (2005): 828; see further Wolfrum, 'The Tenth Anniversary of ITLOS' (note 26), at 76.

60 See for instance UN General Assembly Resolution 65/37 of 7 December 2010, Oceans and the Law of the Sea, at op. para. 37.

provisional measures pending the constitution of an arbitral tribunal under Annex VII to UNCLOS, and the authority, granted to the President of the Tribunal by Annex VII, to appoint members of an arbitral tribunal at the request of one of the parties and in consultation with both of them[61] – an authority of which has already been made use of on several occasions.

The creation of ITLOS has from the very beginning been subject to a certain degree of criticism as being unnecessary and risking a fragmentation of international law.[62] The evidence so far, however, suggests that the danger of conflicting jurisdiction has been widely overestimated. Fragmentation of the law of the sea has thus far not occurred and in my view is not likely to occur in the future. The Tribunal is regularly referring to the judgments of the ICJ and the Court is closely following the work of ITLOS, and especially its already well-developed jurisprudence on provisional measures[63] as well as its pronouncements with respect to maritime delimitation. It has rightly been pointed out that it is important to see the range of courts and tribunals acting under the Part XV of UNCLOS as contributing to a coherent body of law.[64] As the international community will in the future be facing ever new challenges in ocean activities, most certainly also in this region with the world's largest ocean, the work of ITLOS may be gaining ever more in importance in the years to come.

References

Adede, A.O. 'The System for Settlement of Disputes under the United Nations Convention on the Law of the Sea: A Drafting History and a Commentary', *Publications on Ocean Development*, 10 (1987): 173–4.

Boyle, A.E. 'Dispute Settlement and the Law of the Sea Convention: Problems of Fragmentation and Jurisdiction', *International & Comparative Law Quarterly*, 46/1 (1997): 51.

61 Judge J.L. Jesus, President of ITLOS, Keynote Speech on 'The Role of ITLOS in the Settlement of Law of the Sea Disputes', Globalization and the Law of the Sea, Washington, DC, 2 December 2010, at 6, available at: www.itlos.org. This authority has already been made use of on several occasions.

62 See also Boyle, 'ITLOS and the Settlement of Disputes' (note 7), at 120; Boyle, 'Dispute Settlement and UNCLOS' (note 9), at 37; see further Klein, *Dispute Settlement in the UN Convention on the Law of the Sea* (note 4), at 55; see also R. Rayfuse, 'The Future of Compulsory Dispute Settlement under the Law of the Sea Convention', *Victoria University Wellington Law Review*, 36 (2005): 698; see further Churchill 'Some Reflections on the Dispute Settlement System of UNCLOS During its First Decade' (note 3), at 416.

63 Dame R. Higgins, President of the ICJ, Speech at the 10th Anniversary of ITLOS, Hamburg, 29 September 2006, available at: www.icj-cij.org.

64 M. Wood, 'The International Tribunal for the Law of the Sea and General International Law', *The International Journal of Marine and Coastal Law*, 22/3 (2007): 353.

Boyle, A.E. 'The International Tribunal for the Law of the Sea and the Settlement of Disputes', in J.J. Norton et al. (eds), *The Changing World of International Law in the Twenty-First Century* (The Hague/London/Boston; Kluwer Law International, 1998), 118.

Caminos, H. 'The International Tribunal for the Law of the Sea: An Overview of its Jurisdictional Procedure', in A. Del Vecchio (ed.), *New International Tribunals and New International Proceedings* (Milano; Giuffrè Editore, 2006), 22.

Churchill, R.R. 'Some Reflections on the Operation of the Dispute Settlement System of the UN Convention on the Law of the Sea During its First Decade', in D. Freestone, R. Barnes and D.M. Ong (eds), *The Law of the Sea: Progress and Prospects* (Oxford/New York; Oxford University Press, 2006).

Escher, A.K. 'Release of Vessels and Crews before the International Tribunal for the Law of the Sea', in E. Valencia-Ospina (ed.), *The Law and Practice of International Courts and Tribunals: A Practitioner's Journal* (Leiden; Martinus Nijhoff, 2004), 237–8.

Kamto, M. 'Regard sur la jurisprudence du tribunal international du droit de la merdepuis son entrée en fonctionnement (1997–2004)', *Revue générale de droit international public*, 109/4 (2005): 828.

Klein, N. *Dispute Settlement in the UN Convention on the Law of the Sea* (Cambridge: Cambridge University Press, 2005).

Mensah, T.A. 'Provisional Measures in the International Tribunal on the Law of the Sea', 1/2 *Zeitschrift für ausländisches öffentliches Recht und Völkerrecht*, 62 (2002): 46.

Noyes, J.E. 'Compulsory Third-Party Adjudication and the 1982 United Nations Convention on the Law of the Sea', *Connecticut Journal of International Law*, 4 (1988–9): 677–9.

Noyes, J.E. 'The International Tribunal for the Law of the Sea', *Cornell International Law Journal*, 32 (1999): 115–16.

Noyes, J.E. 'Judicial and Arbitral Proceedings and the Outer Limit of the Continental Shelf', *Vanderbilt Journal of Transnational Law*, 42 (2009): 3.

Rayfuse, R. 'The Future of Compulsory Dispute Settlement under the Law of the Sea Convention', *Victoria University Wellington Law Review*, 36 (2005): 698.

Tuerk, H. 'Advisory Opinions and the Law of the Sea', in M. Pogacnik et al. (eds), *The Challenges of Contemporary International Law and International Relations – Liber Amicorum Dr. Ernest Petric (Nova Gorica; European Law Faculty of Nova Gorica,* 2011), 365–83.

Tuerk, H. *Reflections on the Contemporary Law of the Sea* (Leiden and Boston: Martinus Nijhoff, 2012).

Weckel, P. 'Les premieres applications de l'article 290 de la Convention sur le droit de la mer relatif a la prescription de mesures conservatoires', *Revue Générale de Droit International Public*, 109/4 (2005): 838.

Wolfrum, R. 'Advisory Opinions: Are They a Suitable Alternative for the Settlement of International Disputes?', in R. Wolfrum and I. Gätschmann (eds), *International Dispute Settlement: Room for Innovations?* (Heidelberg: Springer, 2012).

Wolfrum, R. 'The Tenth Anniversary of the International Tribunal for the Law of the Sea', *Romanian Journal of International Law*, 2/3 (2006), 66–78.

Wolfrum, R. 'Verfahren zur Freigabe von Schiffen vor dem Internationalen Seegerichtshof', in R. Lagoni and M. Paschke (eds), *Seehandelsrecht und Seerecht: Festschrift für Rolf Herber zum 70. Geburtstag* (Hamburg; Lit Verlag, 1999).

Wood, M. 'The International Tribunal for the Law of the Sea and General International Law', *The International Journal of Marine and Coastal Law*, 22/3 (2007): 353.

PART II: Concepts of UNCLOS Relevant to the SCS

Chapter 3
Military Activities in Foreign EEZs: An Update[1]

Mark J. Valencia

Introduction and Background[2]

Rapid advances in technology – in space, in the air and on and under the sea – are changing both the art of intelligence gathering and its manifestations. This in turn is creating confusion, uncertainty and disputes regarding 'appropriate' behaviour in others' maritime jurisdictional zones. Already there are calls – which eventually may become shouts – for a review and revision of the 'rules of engagement' and relevant laws, including the Law of Sea.

The United States has been undertaking drone attacks for years under its broad interpretation of the 'right to self-defence'.[3] But such attacks actually undermine the rule of law and make US allies uneasy as the rationale could one day be used to justify attacks against them or the United States itself. Already two of the world's leading law faculties have concluded that targeted drone killings violate international law.[4] In many cases these drones overfly other countries and their maritime jurisdictional regimes. Indeed Pakistan's very public but futile angst over what it says are violations of its sovereignty by US aerial drones[5] may be only a forerunner of coastal countries' similar protests regarding violations of their ocean security and marine scientific research (MSR) regimes.

The South China Sea in particular has become a cockpit of frequent but largely sub-rosa confrontations between China and US surveillance platforms such as

---

1 This chapter is a significantly revised and updated version of Mark J. Valencia, 'Foreign military activities in Asian EEZs: conflict ahead?', National Bureau of Asian Research, Special Report #27, May 2011, and other previous work. If in particular situations little or nothing has changed, the analysis and language are the same.

2 An earlier version of this section without references was published by *Nautilus*, 30 August 2011.

3 Roger Cohen, 'Doctrine of silence', *New York Times*, 28 November 2011.

4 Ramesh Thakur, 'Is America now becoming an international outlaw?', *New York Times*, 3 September 2013.

5 Cohen, *supra* n. 3.

Global Hawks,[6] U2s, EP-3s,[7] the US Navy ocean surveillance vessels *Impeccable*[8] and *Victorious*[9] and the oceanographic survey ship *Bowditch*.[10] But these incidents are only the tip of an iceberg of 'wicked' possibilities and a harbinger of more to come. This chapter summarizes the larger political context including US/China military rivalry, describes a stark worst-case scenario, examines the advances in drone technology and its role in the rivalry, and then suggests preventive arrangements and ways forward.

Converging Strategic Trajectories

The convergence of the United States' and China's strategic trajectories is likely to increase the frequency and perhaps the intensity of maritime incidents. US Admiral Mike Mullen, then Chairman of the Joint Chiefs of Staff says that the US military perceives China as undergoing a 'strategic shift, where they are moving from a focus on their ground forces to a focus on their navy, and their maritime forces and their air force'.[11] Being more specific, then US Secretary of Defence Robert Gates said China's investment in anti-ship weapons and ballistic missiles could threaten America's primary way to project power and help allies in the Pacific.[12] Making the US response perfectly clear, Gates said simply that 'the U.S. will increase its military presence in Asia',[13] while Michelle Flournoy, then Undersecretary of Defence for Policy, elaborated that 'the United States is strengthening alliances with the Philippines, Singapore and Thailand and must do more with Indonesia and Vietnam'.[14] The United States is also deepening its military relationship with Australia and Malaysia. Meanwhile, some analysts say

---

6 http://www.af.mil/AboutUs/FactSheets/Display/tabid/224/Article/104516/rq-4-global-hawk.aspx. The RQ-4 Global Hawk is a high-altitude, long-endurance, remotely piloted aircraft with an integrated sensor suite

7 en.wikipedia.org/wiki/Lockheed_EP-3.

8 en.wikipedia.org/wiki/USNS_Impeccable_(T-AGOS-23).

9 en.wikipedia.org/wiki/USNS_Victorious_(T-AGOS-19). Chinese ships followed and harassed the USNS *Impeccable* in the South China Sea on 9 March 2009.

10 According to *Wikileaks*, in 2008, the US government complained that 'China's activities regarding USNS Victorious constitute serious harassment and escalate the risk of miscalculation'.

11 Robert Burns, 'Gates sees wider U.S. military presence in Asia', Staradvertiser.com, 4 June 2011.

12 'U.S. sends destroyer to region amid Spratlys tension', *Manila Standard Today*, 5 June 2011.

13 'United States/Australia/Asia: U.S. military to expand presence in Asia', *Channel News Asia*, 7 November 2010.

14 Lisa Daniel Flournoy, 'Asia will be heart of U.S. security policy', *American Forces Press Service*, 29 April 2011.

that China's perceived bullying of ASEAN South China Sea claimants has pushed them towards the United States.[15]

This change in US strategy or at least in emphasis was originally being undertaken under the guise of stepping up pressure on Pyongyang[16] – but there is little doubt in Beijing that the United States has it in mind as well. Indeed, the recently released US National Military Strategy states that it is 'concerned about the extent and strategic intent of China's military modernization and its assertiveness in space, cyberspace, in the Yellow Sea, East China Sea, and South China Sea'. 'To safeguard U.S. and partner nation interests, the United States will be prepared to demonstrate the will and commit the resources needed to oppose any nation's actions that jeopardize access to and use of the global commons and cyberspace, or that threaten the security of our allies.'[17]

To back up its 'rebalancing', the United States is developing the US Air Sea Battle Concept in response to what it sees as China's 'anti-access area denial strategies' (A2/AD).[18] The concept 'centers on networked, integrated attack-in-depth to disrupt, destroy and defeat A2/AD'. In the first stage, 'air and naval forces attack-in-depth to disrupt the adversary's intelligence collection and command and control used to employ A2/AD weapons systems'.[19] The EP3, *Bowditch* and *Impeccable* military intelligence gathering, including target mapping and submarine tracking, can be seen in this context. So too can the US transition to increased use of UAVs (drones), USVs, USSVs and stealth littoral combat vessels in the region. But their frequent intrusions into Chinese air and sea space are considered by China's leaders to be like 'flies at a picnic', and some Chinese think tank analysts have said China is intent on developing counter measures.

> What is China's intent?
>
> A combination of economic and geo-strategic factors related to security merge to form the strategic motivation for a historically unique Chinese defence perimeter that extends hundreds of miles out to sea. The strategic drivers for Beijing are: the 'core' issue of Taiwan itself; the fact that the vast majority of China's unresolved security issues are maritime in nature (and U.S. arms sales

15 Michel Moran, 'China's naval rise is not as threatening as U.S. would like', *DOOH Insights*, 26 June 2011.

16 'U.S. considers boosting force in Asia: Pentagon', *Joong Ang Daily*, 28 January 2011.

17 Chairman of the Joint Chiefs of Staff, National Military Strategy of the United States of America 201, 8 February 2011.

18 Sam Bateman, 'U.S. Air Sea battle: countering China's anti-access strategies', *RSIS Commentaries*, No. 82, 19 May 2011; David Axe, 'U.S. drones vs. China', *The Diplomat*, 23 May 2011.

19 Headquarters, Marine Corps, The Air-Sea Battle Concept, summary, DVIDS, 10 November 2011; William Kazer, Larry M. Wortzel, Interview, *China Real Time*, 2013.

> to it); the reality that its economic development depends upon imports of raw materials and exports of finished goods that travel mainly by sea; and, perhaps most importantly, the fact that China's economic centre of gravity is located along its eastern seaboard, exposed to attack from the sea.[20]

Given this strategic perspective, China was shocked by the US rapid aggressive response to the 1996 crisis of the Taiwan Strait and is determined not to let that happen again.

However, Beijing argues that China is on a path of peaceful development and is not a threat to its neighbours. China's leaders want this to be true. But as any strategist will tell you, intentions can change in an instant. What really matters are the military capabilities that China will possess when its counter-intervention force is completed. Will China be able to defeat US forward-deployed forces and prevent additional US forces from reaching East Asia in the event of a conflict? The Obama 'rebalancing' strategy is designed to reassure friends and allies in East Asia of the overall American staying power in Asia in the face of a rising China.

Regarding the South China Sea, China maintains that it is committed to peace and stability there[21] and is simply defending its security and sovereignty and preventing what it perceives as isolation and 'containment'. It also denies that it is or will inhibit freedom of navigation. But some say that it is China's intent to regain its historic hegemony over a large part of the South China Sea and thereby Southeast Asia.[22] And its still vague claim to the waters and/or certain rights within its nine-dashed line claim raises the possibility of a historic waters claim, in which traditionally there is no freedom of navigation.

To China it is the United States (and the Philippines and Vietnam in exploring for petroleum in Chinese-claimed areas) that has become more assertive. It believes that the Obama Administration is trying in general to boost the confidence of Southeast Asian nations to stand up to China.[23] Senator McCain's public call for the United States to help ASEAN in the South China Sea matter did nothing to diminish this impression.[24] Neither did US Senator Jim Webb's political backing of Vietnam through a resolution in the US Senate condemning Chinese 'use of

---

20 Globalasia.org, 21 December 2012.

21 Tanya Fang, 'Territorial dispute main concern at dialogue', *Today*, 6 June 2011; Guanglie Liang, 'A better future through security co-operation', Speech, Shangri-la Dialogue, 5 June 2011.

22 Steven Mosher, 'Does the PRC have a grand strategy of hegemony', Testimony presented to the Subcommittee on Oversight and Investigations, The Hon. Dana Rohrabacker, Chairman, International Relations Committee, U.S. House of Representatives.

23 Lachlan Carmichael, 'Obama reviving U.S. clout in Asia as China stumbles', *AFP*, 30 July 2010.

24 Shaun Tandon, 'Build unified ASEAN in South China Sea: McCain', *AFP*, 20 June 2011.

force'.[25] The United States and allies Japan and South Korea just completed 'routine' joint exercises in the East China Sea.[26] Moreover the US Navy holds annual Southeast Asia Co-operation and Training (SEACAT) exercises with the Philippines, Brunei, Indonesia, Malaysia, Singapore and Thailand.[27] Diplomatic vitriol peaked when Chinese Vice Foreign Minister Cui Tiankai warned the United States to restrain other countries from 'provoking' Beijing regarding the South China Sea disputes lest Washington itself be drawn into it.[28]

Some leaders in China – particularly in the military – seem convinced that the 'die is cast' and that the United States is trying to draw ASEAN or some of its members (e.g., its allies the Philippines and Thailand) and Australia,[29] together with Japan and South Korea, into an alliance to constrain if not contain China. Indeed it appears to China and analysts alike that the United States is enlisting several of its allies in its ASB strategy particularly in maritime ISR (Intelligence, Surveillance and Reconnaissance).[30] If this perception is confirmed, China will struggle to break out politically and militarily, setting the stage for rivalry and tension in the years ahead.

Indeed, according to Western analysts, China's navy appears increasingly intent on challenging US naval supremacy in the Western Pacific.[31] China's launch of its first aircraft carrier certainly drew the attention of the US military establishment.[32] More ominous are indications that China's military is influencing its foreign policy and that China has launched a strategy of politics and actions 'to remake global norms and institutions, transforming the world as it transforms itself'.[33] Worse, 'the reins of civilian control over the PLA [are] quite loose. The PLA's warnings are not necessarily intended as aggressive threats but rather as stern declarations of deterrence in order to underscore what China believes to be an asymmetry of resolve'.

Clearly factions in the United States and China are on a strategic collision course, with perhaps one bellwether being the military activities of US assets in Chinese waters, particularly its EEZ. China has warned against 'any military

25 Jason Folkmanis, 'U.S. says S. China Sea events "troubling" after Vietnam meeting', *Bloomberg*, 13 June 2011.

26 ROK, 'U.S. and Japan conduct naval exercise', *Yonhap*.

27 'U.S. Navy in South China Sea exercise with ASEAN', *UPI*, 17 June 2011.

28 'China warns U.S. over Spratlys ahead of Hawaii meeting', *Associated Press*, 22 June 2011.

29 Greg Sheridan, 'Trade and defense: our China line', *The Australian*, 25 June 2011.

30 Carlyle Thayer, 'American grand strategy: Power and purpose in the 21st Century', 64th Strategy Forum, U.S. Naval War College, 18–19 June 2013.

31 'China's naval ambitions', *New York Times*, 1 January 2011; 'China blasts PH anew on Spratlys claim', *Philippine Daily Inquirer*, 9 June 2011.

32 Brahma Chellaney, 'Deception by the boatload', *China World*, 19 June 2011.

33 Andrew Scobell, 'Is there a civil military gap in China's peaceful rise?' *Parameters*, Summer 2009.

acts in our exclusive economic zone without permission'.[34] This warning was of course rejected by the United States diplomatically and in its actions. 'The risk of miscalculation between the U.S. and China may be higher than many assume and once a crisis or confrontation develops, the potential for unintended escalation is significant.'[35] In such situations, it may be wiser to forego exercising a perceived right in order to preserve the peace. This is the political context of US–China military maritime relations.

US–China Maritime Relations

The United States and China have a 1998 Military Maritime Co-operation Agreement (MMCA) which provides a forum to discuss such issues. But over the past 11 years the mechanism has failed to play an effective role.[36] Even the US principal negotiator involved has said that it is 'of limited effectiveness because it is held hostage by China over U.S. actions in carrying out our stated obligations under the Taiwan Relations Act'.[37] Moreover there is little evidence that military to military and strategic dialogue have reduced mistrust or raised transparency.[38] China's well-known three obstacles to bilateral defence co-operation with the United States remain in place: US arms sales to Taiwan; US intelligence gathering in China's EEZ; and the FY2000 National Defence Authorization Act restrictions on military interaction with the PLA.

In fact on the military front, the trend in relations is negative. China has always been sensitive to US use of force in international relations and believes it is an attempt to spread American hegemony.[39] China's vehement opposition to the 2010 US–South Korean naval exercises in the Yellow Sea should be viewed in this context. It is disconcerting to China to say the least that the United States is expanding missile 'defence' co-operation with Japan and South Korea and may do so with the Philippines.[40] China is also concerned that the United States is deploying another X-Band radar system in Japan, this one in the middle of the

34 Ian Johnson and Martin Fackler, 'China addresses rising Korean tensions', *New York Times*, 26 November 2010.

35 Sheridan, *supra* n. 29.

36 2009 U.S.-China Defense Consultative Talks (DCT) Small Group Session, U.S. Embassy, Beijing, 1 July 2009.

37 Bruce Lembum, 'U.S.–Taiwan relations are threat to China', *Defense News*, 8 November 2012.

38 Kenneth Lieberthal and Wang Jisi, 'Addressing U.S.-China strategic distrust', John L. Thorton China Center, Brookings, March 2012, pp. 7–33.

39 Bonnie S. Glaser and Deep Pal, 'How will China react to a military strike on Syria?', CSIS,Strategic Insights and Bipartisan Policy Solutions,5 September 2013.

40 http://www.globalresearch.ca/threat-to-china-pressure-on-south-korea-to-join-u-s-anti-ballistic-missile-defense-system/5389304.

archipelago.[41] Fan Changlong, one of China's three most senior military officers, has called on the PLA to 'speed up various preparations for sea battles' and 'improve maritime deterrence and combat capabilities'.[42] In the South China Sea, potential 'collusion' between the United States, the Philippines and Vietnam to work together on regional security co-operation is viewed by China as 'potentially presenting a military coalition designed to offset China's growing military presence in the South China Sea'.

However, according to a recent report by the US National Defence University, 'nothing would be more destructive of Sino-American relations and Asia's security dynamics than a decision by China to threaten a military confrontation in order to change a U.S. course of action Beijing perceived as threatening its interests in the South China Sea'.[43] US Secretary of Defence Chuck Hagel has recently warned that 'a growing number of maritime incidents and tensions in disputed Asian waters increase the risk of a dangerous international confrontation'.[44] And CINCPAC Admiral Samuel Locklear recently cautioned that 'What we need in the South China Sea is a mechanism that prevents us turning our diplomacy over to young majors and young [naval] commanders ... to make decisions at sea that cause a problem [that escalates] into a military conflict that we might not be able to control'.[45]

China is currently no match militarily for the United States in a full military conflict. However, there may come a day when it is – and the United States is taking no chances. It is particularly concerned with China's fleet of submarines – and now with its drone development programme. In the last decade China has acquired 12 Russian Kilo-class subs and built by itself two types of nuclear powered subs – the Jin-class which carries ballistic missiles, and the Shan-class attack subs. China plans to build at least five Jin-class SSBN so that, like the United States, it can have a near-continuous presence at sea of this third-leg of the nuclear deterrent triad. China has recently built a submarine base at Yulin, Hainan with 11 submerged tunnel openings to accommodate its new subs. Thus, the US concern with, and focus on, Yulin.

Beijing has long sought to prevent other countries from carrying out surveillance or surveying operations within its EEZ. In 2002, China enacted a law against the undertaking of such activities in its EEZ without its permission. It has subsequently recorded at least 200 incidents of US vessels collecting intelligence in its EEZ, but generally has avoided confrontation. However, it has tried to

41 *The Japan Times*, 28 January 2013.

42 'Stay out of sea disputes China warns U.S.', *France Press*, 14 September 2013.

43 Wendell Minmick, quoting Paul Godwin and Alva Miller, 'Chinese signaling for conflict: A predictive pattern', newdefensenews.com, 28 April 2013.

44 'Hagel issues warning over Asian maritime dispute', *The Gulf Today*, 29 August 2013.

45 Michael Marina, 'China, Japan engage in new invective over disputed isles', *Reuters*, 8 February 2013.

enforce its interpretation of the law several times against the *Bowditch*, a US hydrographic survey vessel, and against the *Impeccable*, a US ocean surveillance vessel, resulting 'in international incidents'.

The real issue here is China's expanding blue-water navy capabilities and its new submarine base at Yulin. Obviously it wants to protect its 'secrets' in the area including the activities and capabilities of its submarines and the morphology of the sea bottom. And, just as intently, the United States wants to know as much as it can about China's submarine capabilities and the area it may one day have to do battle in. Thus such incidents are likely to be repeated and become ever more dangerous.

Instead of just surveying the ocean bottom and hydrographic variables like the *Bowditch*, to aid in the future navigation of its own subs and detection of underwater threats, the *Impeccable* was probably tracking Chinese submarines – which is one part of its mission. Indeed it may have been trying to determine at what distance it could detect the subs exiting China's Yulin base. It was also likely mapping the navigational channels from Yulin to facilitate targeting in case it one day becomes necessary to bottle them up. Because China does not have a similar capability to monitor the US fleet and ocean bottom off its ports, the *Impeccable* 'intrusion' was humiliating to the Chinese navy, potentially emasculating its submarine nuclear weapon capability and greatly frustrating its military leadership. For China, this was – and is – a very 'unfriendly' act and is well-known as such to the United States. This explains the strong Chinese reaction.

However, China and the United States may have quietly reached some sort of interim understanding regarding US military activities in its EEZ. Otherwise, we would be reading about more such incidents. Admiral Willard has told the US Senate that the Chinese navy had not exhibited the same level of assertiveness in 2011 that it did in 2010.[46] Willard attributed this change in China's behaviour to the strong American response regarding such actions and the resumption of US–China military talks. Perhaps so, although in late June 2011, Chinese jets chased away a US surveillance jet [rumoured to be a drone – a Global Hawk] over the Taiwan Strait.[47] Despite China's protests that such flights 'severely harmed mutual trust and were a major obstacle to better military ties', US Admiral Mullen 'vowed to press ahead with such surveillance flights'.[48]

A high-level meeting of Chinese and US defence officials was held in Washington, DC on 10 December 2010, and dealt with such maritime security issues. Also US Defence Secretary Gates visited China between 10 and 14 January 2011. And Gates met China's Defence Minister Guanglie Liang at the Shangri-la Dialogue in Singapore in June 2011. The MMCA met in June 2013

46 'Chinese navy less assertive in 2011: U.S. Admiral', *AFP*, 12 April 2011; 'U.S. Admiral: Chinese Navy less hostile in disputed waters', *Top Market News*, 13 April 2011.

47 Bill Gertz, 'Chinese jets chase U.S. surveillance jet over Taiwan Strait', *The Washington Times*, 25 July 2011.

48 'China protests U.S. spy flights near its coast', *Reuters*, 27 July 2011.

in Honolulu – but without any noticeable breakthrough. The two countries have agreed to have their militaries conduct a joint humanitarian assistance and disaster relief exercise and to make use of a special telephone link.[49] Moreover, to prevent 'brush-ups' from triggering 'tactical miscalculations', collision protocols have been established so 'unintended maritime incidents do not escalate'.[50] The legal positions of the protagonists regarding military activities in EEZs are dealt with in detail elsewhere, but suffice it to say here that the two continue to fundamentally and vehemently disagree in principle and actions.[51]

Worst Scenario: Could a Maritime Conflict Really Trigger a US–China War?[52]

On 26 August 2013 a rather frightening op-ed appeared in the *Los Angeles Times*. It was lead-authored by David Gompert – until recently the second-highest-ranking US intelligence official in the Obama Administration. What was scary was his sober assessment of the possibility that a conflict in the maritime arena could trigger a China–US Armageddon – at least for Asia. This is not a new thought but heretofore had been the realm of fiction writers, warmongers, wolf-criers and video-game makers.

There is now little doubt that China and the West are going to clash. They are already competing in both military and civilian areas and more fundamentally in values and the pursuit of political power. The as yet unanswered questions are will the conflicts become 'physical' and, if so, how and why?

China – according to Gompert – is particularly worried about a long war in which the technically superior US forces would prevail. So the Chinese military is developing plans and tactics for early and swift strikes to take out US carriers, air bases, and command and control networks, including satellites.[53] 'Chinese surveillance sensors and communication links are the 'common technological threads that sew together A2/AD' and for that matter ASB. The US military has

49 Jens Kastner, *Asia Times Online*, 25 May 2011.

50 Rowan Callick, 'Top gun warns of military rivalry', *The Australian*, 3 June 2011.

51 Raul (Pete) Pedrozo, 'Coastal state jurisdiction over marine data collection in the Exclusive Economic Zone', in Peter Dutton (ed.), *Military Activities in the EEZ*, China Maritime Studies Institute, No. 7, pp. 23–36, December 2010; Mark J. Valencia, 'Not an Impeccable argument', The Nautilus Institute, www.nautilus.org/publications/essays/napset/.../09026Valenica.html, 23 June 2010; Mark J. Valencia, 'Tempting the Dragon', The Nautilus Institute, www.nautilus.org/publications/essays/napset/.../09020Valencia.html, 23 June 2010; Mark J. Valencia, 'The Impeccable incident: Truth and consequences', www.chinasecurity.us/pdfs/Valencia.pdf.

52 Mark J. Valencia, 'Could a maritime conflict start a Sino-American war?', *The Japan Times*, 2 September 2013.

53 Daniel Blumenthal, 'A Sino-American proxy war?' *Foreign Policy*, 18 September 2013.

countered with its 'air-sea battle' plan 'designed to cripple China's C4 ISR,[54] i.e., missile launchers, air and submarine bases and command and control centres before they can be unleashed'.[55] And it has supposedly asked South Korea to join the US-led missile defence systems. The United States is therefore trying to detect and determine the most vulnerable link in China's C4 IRS chain for targeting if and when necessary.[56] This is where the 'ISR' could make the difference.

Gompert argues that, as a result, '*crisis instability*' involving the two is increasing rapidly. Crisis instability occurs when 'the price of failing to attack before the opponent does means *defeat*. Each side knows the other is thinking the same way and so has all the more incentive to act pre-emptively if war seems imminent. Or probable. Or maybe just possible. Given the penalty for attacking second, such spiralling logic can turn confrontation into conflagration'.[57]

This is where maritime issues come in. The US 'rebalance' towards Asia and China's inexorable rise puts their naval and air forces in close proximity – especially at sea. Gompert identifies several flash points that could trigger war including the China/Japan territorial and jurisdictional disputes in the East China Sea. Here a first 'strike' would be a tactical necessity as the occupier of the features would have a decided advantage.[58] Moreover, from a perch in and around the islands, China could exert more pressure on Taiwan and enhance its legitimacy in claiming other islands in the Ryukyu chain. On the other hand Obama's indecisiveness on Syria has led Japan to wonder if and how the United States would respond to an occupation of the disputed islands by China.[59] The allies reiterated their concern with China's behaviour at their October 2013 Two Plus Two Ministerial Meeting. The ministers affirmed that the Alliance should remain well positioned to deal with a range of persistent and emerging threats to peace and security, as well as challenges to international norms. Among these are: *coercive and destabilizing behaviours in the maritime domain.*[60]

Also dangerous is the conflict between US views and backup actions regarding 'freedom of navigation' of its surveillance ships and aircraft in China's 200 nm EEZ and China's views on the limits of this principle. The United States considers 'freedom of navigation' in the South China Sea a 'national security interest'.

---

54 Command, control, communications, computers, intelligence, surveillance and reconnaissance.

55 http://www.japantimes.co.jp/opinion/2013/09/02/commentary/world-commentary/could-a-maritime-conflict-start-a-sino-american-war/.

56 Anton Wishik and Matthew Durnin, *Space, China's Tactical Frontier*, Interview with NBR, 23 May 2012; Kazer, *supra* n. 19.

57 http://www.latimes.com/opinion/op-ed/la-oe-gompert-kelly-war-china-u-s--20130826-story.html.

58 Ibid.

59 http://thediplomat.com/2014/05/chinas-oil-rig-gambit-south-china-sea-game-changer/.

60 Joint Statement Kerry/Hagel-Kishida/Onodera Meetings, *The Nelson Report*, 2 October 2013.

On 17 July, the *Washington Times* reported that in June 2013 Chinese vessels 'harassed' the US Navy ocean surveillance vessel *Impeccable* in what the US Navy claims were 'international waters' about 100 nm from Hainan.[61] The mission of the *Impeccable* is to use both passive and active low frequency sonar arrays to enable detection and tracking of undersea threats – enemy submarines, mines and torpedoes.

In the June 2013 *Impeccable* incident, the Chinese vessel warned the US Navy vessel that 'it was operating illegally and that China had not granted permission for it to be there'.[62] This reflects the differing positions that underlie these incidents. As Admiral Locklear said, 'the U.S. position is that those activities are less constrained than what the Chinese believe', and 'the U.S. and China disagree on UN definitions of controlled waters'.

China is among some 165 nations that have ratified the 1982 UN Convention on the Law of the Sea (UNCLOS). The United States is among a small minority that has not, although it maintains that most of it is binding customary law. However, customary law is constantly evolving based on state practice, as are the meanings of specific terms used in the Convention.

For example, there is no such thing as 'international waters'. According to the Convention, there are internal waters, territorial waters, the exclusive economic zone and the high seas, each with their own regime regarding freedom of navigation. 'International waters' is a term used by the US Navy to indicate areas where it thinks it has unconstrained navigational freedom. The term is imprecise and confusing and its use should be discontinued.

The last time such an incident occurred was in March 2009. In that incident the United States sent a guided missile destroyer to escort the sub-hunting *Impeccable*. China could have responded in kind. At the time a Pentagon spokesperson explained that 'Chinese ships and aircraft routinely steam or fly near U.S. navy ships in this area. However these actions [regarding the *Impeccable*] were considerably more aggressive and unprofessional than we have seen, and greatly increased the risk of collision or miscalculation'.

This set the stage for a worst-case scenario of confrontation between warships and the incalculable consequences. US officials including presidential spokesperson Robert Gibbs said publicly that 'the US Navy will continue to operate in the South China Sea' and 'we expect the Chinese to observe international law around that'. However, cooler heads prevailed – beginning with President Obama. He 'stressed the importance of raising the level and frequency of the U.S.-China military-to-military dialogue in order to avoid future incidents'. And then US Secretary of Defence Robert Gates said he did not think China was trying to prevent the US Navy from operating in the South China Sea and that he hoped armed escorts would not be needed in the future.

61 Ships and submarines participating in RIMPAC exercises, 27 July 2012.

62 William Cole, 'Chinese help plan for huge war game near isles', *Honolulu Star Advertiser*, 25 July 2013.

There is some confusion regarding the latest incident. If it occurred as described some say it would represent a more aggressive Chinese stance against American close-in surveillance. But US PACCOM Commander Admiral Samuel J. Locklear, who was interviewed shortly before the incident surfaced publicly, played down any possible provocative Chinese behaviour. He said that 'in areas that are close to the Chinese homeland – that we have been able to conduct operations around each other in a very professional and increasingly professional manner'.

China's Defence Minister General Chang met US Defence Secretary Chuck Hagel in Washington on 19 August 2013 and they announced that their countries would take steps to improve military to military relations. He did not mention the incident. However, Youfei Guan, foreign affairs spokesperson for China's Defence Ministry, complained about stepped-up, close-in surveillance by the United States, explaining that 'Any country would feel uneasy and threatened under such high-frequency reconnaissance'.[63] And he added that 'American vessels and planes are coming closer to Chinese planes and ships in China's exclusive economic zone'. General Chang warned that 'no one should underestimate our will and determination in defending our territory, sovereignty and *maritime rights*' [emphasis added].

The critical questions are: if in a crisis, China's military leaders advised its political leaders that US forces were preparing for war and China's only chance to avoid defeat was to strike first – would Beijing say 'no'? And if senior US military leaders advised the president that China was preparing for a pre-emptive strike would he or she risk the loss of key assets by waiting?

Technological Advances and International Legal Questions

The rapidly increasing use of spy planes including UAVs (unmanned aerial vehicles) such as the ever improving Global Hawk, and spy ships including unmanned surface vessels (USVs) and now unmanned underwater vessels (UUVs), and their missions are rapidly outstripping relevant laws and regulations.[64]

63 'China accuses U.S. of increasing surveillance', UPI.com, 22 April 2013.

64 On remote sensing and surveying, see William Sargent, 'Under seas maps under wraps', *The Christian Science Monitor*, 31 March 1987; Peter J. Brown, 'U.S. satellites shadow China's submarines', *Asia Times*, 13 May 2010; and 'U.S. doesn't comment, but has acknowledged monitoring North's military', MNSBC.com, 29 April 2006. On submarines, see Loren B. Thompson, 'Outside view: Shrinking U.S. sub fleet', *United Press International*, 3 January 2007. Most submarine missions in the Central Command area are devoted to intelligence collection, such as eavesdropping onshore communication. Submarines are one of the few reconnaissance tools that can act on the information they obtain. On spy planes, see Christopher Drew, 'U-2 spy plane evades the day of retirement', *New York Times*, 21 March 2010; and Andrew Chester, 'USAF planes to help U.K. fill SIGINT', *Defense News*, 22 March 2010. On drone programmes and unmanned capabilities, see Northrop Grumman team, individual contributions to Global Hawk Program recognized

Many platforms seem designed and destined to operate in foreign air and sea space without authorization,[65] i.e. in, over and under EEZs, archipelagic waters and even territorial seas.

Examples abound. Remote sensing from satellites and high-flying surveillance aircraft have for decades undertaken MSR and surveys in other EEZs without the permission – or even the knowledge – required by the 1982 UNCLOS. The US Air Force is developing Conventional Strike Missile technology that supposedly could hit targets at supersonic speeds anywhere in the world with just 60 minutes' notice.[66] Of course these missiles require targets, and targeting is presumably enabled or enhanced by satellites and drones. Meanwhile, the US Navy is refining the Fire Scout – a vertical take-off and landing tactical unmanned aerial vehicle to provide situational awareness, ISR and targeting data. It also carries its own array of weapons.[67] The United States' new X-47 B drone can land and take-off from an aircraft carrier, giving the United States a huge edge in power projection.[68]

Indeed, the race is now on among the world's navies to develop fleets of crewless vessels capable of missions on and under the water. The United States and Israel are among the industry leaders. China, India, Singapore, Israel, the UK and France are in the mix.[69] Others are buying off the shelf. For example Australia is purchasing a fleet of maritime super drones called Tritons to survey the Indian Ocean – and probably Chinese ships and submarines as well.[70]

High-tech unmanned submersibles are currently being assigned to mine countermeasure (MCM) operations, naval ISR roles, and anti-submarine warfare (ASW) missions.[71] There are generally two kinds of UUVs used in military operations: autonomous undersea vehicles (AUVs) and those that are remotely operated. They are changing the very way in which maritime security operations

by U.S. air forces, *Primezone*, 11 April 2005; Christina Mackenzie, 'Governments spend millions on sophisticated drones', *International Herald Tribune*, 13 June 2005; 'Remote controlled vessels unveiled', *Today*, 18 May 2005; and Eric Talmadge, 'Japan gets U.S. pitch to buy spy drones', *Associated Press*, 8 April 2010. Meanwhile China and other Asian states are upgrading their own; 'U.S. Navy drones: coming to a carrier near China?', *Associated Press*, 16 May 2011.

65 Michael Richardson, 'U.S. turns to drones to counter China', *The Japan Times*, 5 January 2012.

66 *Global Security News*, 24 June 2011. www.dtic.mil/cgi-bin/GetTRDoc?AD=AD A601181.

67 Steve Duda, 'Navy tests mean green killing machine', *Earth Techling*, 18 October 2011.

68 http://www.examiner.com/article/northrop-grumman-s-x-47b-is-tested-on-the-u-s-s-harry-s-truman.

69 Seth Robson, Maritime drones make waves among navies worldwide, *Stars and Stripes*, 3 August 2011.

70 http://globalaviationreport.com/tag/australia-to-buy-triton-uav/.

71 W.J. Hennigan, 'Submarine drones need to be autonomous', naval experts say, *Los Angeles Times*, 10 February 2013.

are conducted. Moreover many of these UUVs can be weaponized and some can launch aerial drones through torpedo tubes.

Also in development is the sea glider – a small, energy efficient, winged AUV. This vessel uses a unique form of propulsion in which a small pump fills and empties a chamber, changing the vehicle's buoyancy and allowing it to ascend and descend as a means of moving forward. While most gliders can only move at speeds of up to half a knot, these vessels have extremely low energy demands which allows them to stay at sea for months at a time. Although gliders currently lack the situational awareness needed to avoid obstacles and detection by adversaries, their endurance and ability to operate stealthily due to a lack of noise-producing engines makes them ideal candidates for IRS missions. Gliders can also be deployed by submarines to detect and locate a passing ship without the vessel realizing it is being tracked.

The United States in particular is placing heavy emphasis on developing maritime drones for missions that will include IRS.[72] Indeed the result is a huge asymmetry in favour of the United States in control and use of space, air and seas. Moreover, due to the drawdown in Afghanistan and the US 'pivot', the navy is releasing ISR assets for use in Asia.[73] US Chief of Naval Operations Admiral Gary Roughead believes that 'unmanned underwater systems will become extensions to the submarines, can become extensions to aviation, manned or unmanned, as far as sensing the battle space'.[74]

> But its [the pursuit of unmanned systems] also going to be important politically, because I believe the future will be one where the sensitivities of sovereignty, a nation's claim to control its own land, to be able to focus on that which is there, that the idea of large footprints ashore, improved facilities ashore, may not always be guaranteed as we have become used to over these past years.

His successor Admiral Greenert says simply that the undersea drones will enable the United States to retain 'our edge' in that environment.[75]

On the horizon are modular floating 'bases' (Afloat Forward Staging Bases) that can be carried on commercial container ships and assembled in foreign EEZs. Already the US Navy has deployed a prototype floating base, the Ponce, in the Persian Gulf.[76] As if is this is not enough to concern military and foreign affairs

---

72 David Axe, 'The U.S. Navy's belated robot revolution', worldpoliticsreview.com, 16 December 2011.

73 William Cole, 'Navy vessels due in Asia-Pacific area', *Honolulu Star Advertiser*, 10 April 2013.

74 Admiral Gary Roughead delivers remarks at 2011 AVVSI Unmanned System Symposium and Exhibition, 19 August 2011.

75 'Navy Chief: Robotic subs might span oceans', www.wired.com, March 2012.

76 'U.S. Navy's new floating base gets a workout in Gulf', kitsapsun.com, 22 September 2012.

planners and legal officers, the new US naval emphasis is on the littoral.[77] Indeed, two new US littoral combat ships with deployable USVs have been deployed to Singapore. This new focus on the littoral seems destined to violate the prior notification/authorization regime for military vessels that some countries like China, India, Indonesia and Vietnam have for their 12 nm territorial seas, let alone the innocent passage regimes.

No other country can match the United States' array of robotic aircraft and sea craft, particularly its range and advanced weapons and sensors, coupled with the necessary satellite and telecommunications support systems.[78] But drones are now generally considered relatively cheap weapons and highly effective reconnaissance tools. Others like Russia and China are engaging in crash programmes to catch up. China reportedly has more than two dozen UAV models. But little is known of their actual capabilities. Drone acquisition has now become a worldwide phenomenon. Indeed, more than 50 countries have purchased aerial surveillance drones, and many have started in-country development programmes to weaponize them.

The situation is clearly beyond international regulation and control. Thus continued intrusive probes are likely to generate frustration and resentment that may translate into the forcible halting of such 'intrusions' when and if detected. In addition to objecting to the *Impeccable* and *Bowditch*, China has complained bitterly that Japan's reconnaissance activities are undermining China's security.[79] But China itself also undertakes *passive* intelligence gathering of Japanese assets. The United States has deployed Global Hawks over the DMZ of the Korean Peninsula where they can 'keep watch' over all of North Korea and an adjacent part of China as well.[80] Perhaps more alarming is that Taiwan regularly gathers aerial intelligence over the East and South China Seas.[81] Guam-based Global Hawks now fly surveillance missions over the disputed islands in the East China Sea and those to be 'placed' in the Philippines will surveil disputed areas in the South China Sea.[82] Further, the United States would like to establish drone bases in Darwin and maybe the Cocos Islands,[83] a proposal which has already drawn objections from Indonesia whose maritime space and land lies between Australia and the South China Sea.[84]

77 Burns, *supra* n. 11.

78 http://www.washingtonpost.com/world/national-security/global-race-on-to-match-us-drone-capabilities/2011/06/30/gHQACWdmxH_story.html.

79 'Japan's reconnaissance missions undermine China's security interests: Defense ministry', *Xinhua*, 26 October 2010.

80 'Global Hawk set to watch over North Korea', *Unmanned Aerial Vehicle News*, 15 September 2011.

81 http://chinadailymail.com/2014/07/14/taiwan-using-drones-to-spy-on-china/.

82 'U.S. to provide PHL satellite surveillance assistance over maritime territory', *GMA News*, 4 May 2012; 'U.S. Navy eyes stationary ships in Singapore', *Reuters*, 16 December 2011.

83 'Australia backs security pact with U.S.', India: report, *Reuters*, 30 November 2011.

84 www.internationalaffairs.org.au/wp-content/uploads/2014/…/Past-Issues.pdf.

The scale and scope of maritime and airborne intelligence collection activities are expanding rapidly in many countries, involving levels and sorts of activities quite unprecedented in peacetime. They are not only becoming more intensive; they are generally more intrusive. Indeed, stepped up drone missions may even be considered a prelude to impending warfare. They will generate tensions and more frequent crises. They will produce defensive reactions and escalatory dynamics, and they will lead to less stability in the most affected regions, especially in Asia. These activities may even create a 'Grotian Moment' in which rapid and radical changes in technology and means of warfare greatly accelerate the formation of customary international law.[85] Indeed, China may already be building a case for customary law limiting such activities.[86]

Cyber War Games

The US president now has the authority to order pre-emptive cyber-strikes if he has credible evidence that the United States is about to experience a major cyber-attack.[87] Cyber-attacks could emanate from vessels and aircraft in EEZs. Harold Koh believes that 'if the physical consequences of a cyber-attack [would cause] the kind of physical damage that dropping a bomb or firing a missile would, that cyber-attack should be considered a use of force'.[88] The head of the US military's newly created Cyber Command revealed that he is establishing 13 teams to carry out offensive cyber-attacks in response to a major cyber-attack against the United States.[89] What is not said but is obvious, is that when the US computer warriors probe for vulnerabilities to collect intelligence, they are also identifying potential cyber targets. China maintains that it has been repeatedly cyber-probed by the United States, testing the PLA's capabilities.[90] In 2012, hackers crashed tens of thousands of computers in South Korea, and tried to steal South Korean and US military secrets.[91] The US tactical concern is that China could use cyber-attacks

85 Michael Scharf, *Recognizing Grotian Moments*, Cambridge University Press, 2013.

86 Jia Yong Ming, 'On dissection of disputes between China and the United States over military activities in Exclusive Economic Zone by the Law of the Sea docs', Shanghai Academy of Social Sciences.

87 'U.S. OKs pre-emptive cyber-strike', *The Japan Times*, 5 February 2013.

88 http://www.state.gov/s/l/releases/remarks/197924.htm.

89 Mark Mazetti and David Sanger, 'Security leader says U.S. would retaliate against cyber-attacks', *New York Times*, 12 March 2013.

90 'Creating a new model for U.S.-China relation at the Obama – summit', *World*, 5 June 2013.

91 The U.S. has recently added cyber-attacks as a possible *casus belli*. Dan de Luce and Shaun Tandon, 'U.S. Australia vow joint response in cyber war', *Google*, 5 September 2011. 'In the event of a cyber-attack that threatens the territorial integrity, political independence or security of either of our nations, Australia and the United States would consult together and determine appropriate options to address the threat,' a joint statement said.

to delay or degrade a US military response in the region because of 'the vagaries of international law and policy surrounding nation-state responses to apparent network attacks'.[92]

The United States acknowledges that a cyber-attack could threaten US territorial integrity and security.[93] Indeed it has agreed to a new clause in the ANZUS treaty that gives 'cyber-attacks the same weight' as missile or bomb attacks or physical invasions.[94] Cyber-probing of foreign networks can be conducted from aircraft or vessels as part of ISR. At the tip of the ISR build up in the Pacific is the RQ-4 Global Hawks based in Guam and Block 40 aircraft with electronically scanned array radar (AESA). China's military is well-aware of these new US assets and is developing counter strategies to deal with them.[95] But advanced US intelligence capabilities using, unmanned surveillance and reconnaissance gathering platforms will soon be able to penetrate sophisticated detection systems to collect detailed information.[96]

A crucial question is whether some of the electronic warfare activities conducted in or above the EEZ can be considered to be inconsistent with the UN Charter and thus the peaceful purposes clauses of the Convention. Particularly relevant are *active* SIGINT activities conducted from aircraft and ships, some of which are deliberately provocative, intending to generate programmed responses. Other SIGINT activities intercept naval radar and emitters, enabling them to locate, identify and track (and thus plan electronic or missile attacks against) surface ships and submarines. Still others may interfere with communication and computer systems. These activities appear to involve far greater interference with the communication and defence systems of the targeted coastal state then any traditionally passive intelligence-gathering activities conducted from outside national territory. Is this a threat of use of force and a violation of sovereignty as some contend?

Stretching and Testing the Legal Limits

The rapid expansion of the aerial, surface and submarine drone fleets – and the drive to weaponize them – and aggressive active probing and 'tickling' raise potential game-changing questions regarding agreed rules, 'customary' international law and expected behaviour. The Law of the Sea does not adequately deal with these

92 Jim Wolf, 'China cyber capability endangers U.S. forces', report, *Reuters*, 28 January 2012.

93 Greg Sheridan, 'New Australia-U.S. push deals India into Pacific', *The Australian*, 17 September 2011.

94 'No reason to get even close to Uncle Sam', *Smh.com*, 14 November 2011.

95 'U.S. gears up to meet China threat', *Eurasia Review*, 2 September 2011.

96 David Fulghum, 'Recon needs grow for South China Sea region', *Aviation Week*, 17 October 2011.

alleged aspects of freedom of navigation. But it does contain relevant key terms that are left undefined – and are now the subject of disagreement.

Critical questions include the following.[97]

Is a country legally correct to assert 'freedom of navigation and overflight of the high seas' to justify the operations of its military aircraft and vessels in foreign EEZs?

The answer depends in part on what exactly the aircraft and vessels were/are doing – which is usually classified. However in the case of the US EP-3 incident it has been speculated that the SIGINT plane was not just passively 'listening', but was actively 'tickling' China's onshore defence communications in order to elicit and observe a response, and perhaps even interfering with shore-to-submarine communications. China has recently engaged in passive intelligence gathering in the EEZs of Guam and Hawaii[98] and US military supporters and analysts are quick to point this out as evidence of China's hypocrisy. But this argument may be disingenuous. It is likely that Chinese capabilities and activities are so substantively inferior to and different from those of the United States as to be in a separate, much lower category (e.g., passive listening versus active probing or electronic interference).[99]

The US position is that such activities are allowed under Article 58 of UNCLOS, which provides that in the EEZ 'all states enjoy subject to the relevant provisions of this Convention, the freedoms ... of navigation and overflight ... and other internationally lawful uses of the sea related to these freedoms, such as those associated with the operation of ships, aircraft'. In other words, the United States is arguing that such intelligence-gathering activities are 'other internationally lawful uses of the sea ... associated with the operation of ships and aircraft', and compatible with the other provisions of the Convention. But are they – particularly the new active and autonomous intelligence-gathering methods? More to the point, does the United States as a non-party to the Convention have the legitimacy to cite and interpret its provisions in its favour? And if the US position is to rely on the 1958 Treaty on the Freedom of Navigation on the High Seas, which it *has* ratified, then is it implying it does not recognize the UNCLOS sanctioned EEZ and the Convention's provisions thereon?

The United States argues that it participated in the drafting of these UNCLOS provisions and that their negotiating history supports its position. Moreover, it says,

---

97 EEZ Group 21, Guidelines for Navigation and Overflight in the Exclusive Economic Zone, A Commentary, Ocean Policy Research Foundation, Tokyo, Japan 2006; Mark J. Valencia, 'Foreign military activities in Asian EEZs: conflict ahead?', National Bureau of Asian Research, Special Report #27, May 2011.

98 Daniel Ten Kate, 'China spurns arbitration as U.S. joins Japan on sea stance', *Bloomberg*, 2 June 2013.

99 The overall level of China's unmanned aircraft technologies still lags '15 to 20 years' behind Western countries; Yunli Zhang and Jiao Wu, 'China rebukes drone reports', *China Daily USA*, 25 September 2013.

the Convention's provisions are now customary international law. Others however argue that the Convention is a series of package deals and that non-ratifiers are not entitled to the 'benefits' of particular trade-offs while eschewing their part of the bargain. Further, the EEZ and its regime were created by the Convention, not customary law, and the EEZ is *sui generis*, not high seas or 'international waters'. Moreover, regulations and interpretation of the EEZ regime and key terms in the Convention are evolving rapidly through state practice and non-ratifiers like the United States have no legitimacy to interpret them to their advantage. For example, Australia recently banned Japanese whaling vessels from its EEZ. 'The government strongly objects to whaling vessels passing through Australia territorial seas or our exclusive economic zone', said Environment Minister Tony Burke.[100] Russia has promulgated legislation regulating shipping on the Northern Sea Route, including in its EEZ.[101] Others have proposed abolishing 'sovereign immunity' or allowing application of environmental protection to warships.[102]

China argues that the activities of the EP-3 and the *Impeccable* are an 'abuse of rights' prohibited by UNCLOS Article 300, i.e., the unnecessary or arbitrary exercise of rights, or interference with the exercise of rights by another state. It also alleges violation of the UNCLOS peaceful purposes provision in Articles 88, 141 and 301, and of their resource rights and environmental obligations in the EEZ.[103] This in turn goes back to exactly what these platforms were/are doing and to the issue of 'due regard to the rights and duties' of *each other*. Although such due regard in the EEZ is required by the Convention, it is undefined.

China also alleges that these activities constitute a non-peaceful threat of use of force, that the United States was 'preparing the battle field', and that the activity thus endangered China's security, a violation of the UN Charter[104] as well as the

100 Australia blasts Japan after whaling ships EEZ incursion, *The Japan Times*, 2 February 2013.

101 Caitlyn L. Antrim, *The Ocean Law Daily*, 1 August 2012.

102 Hiroke Sasaki, Military activities in the oceans and the 'sovereign immunity' provision. https://www.sof.or.jp/en/report/pdf/201203.pdf

103 Peter Pedrozo, 'The U.S.-China incidents at sea agreement: A recipe for disaster', *Journal of National Security Law and Policy*, 6; 207, July 2012.

104 Relevant excerpts from the UN Charter:

Article 2

The Organization and its Members, in pursuit of the Purposes stated in Article, shall act in accordance with the following Principles.

All Members shall refrain in their international relations from the threat or use of force against the territorial integrity or political independence of any state, or in any other manner inconsistent with the Purposes of the United Nations.
The Purposes of the United Nations are (among others):

Law of the Sea. Finally China points out that the Convention does not explicitly distinguish between MSR, hydrographic surveys and military surveys as activities in the EEZ requiring coastal state consent.[105]

But what constitutes a threat of use of force inconsistent with the UN Charter and UNCLOS? It is generally understood that the Charter prohibition includes the demonstrated intent to use or indirect use of armed force. For example, Japan has declared that Chinese warships, by locking in their fire-control radar on Japan's vessels, may have violated the Charter.[106] Moreover the Charter and subsequent legal developments in the UN system have not taken into account highly advanced technologies, in particular the latest intensive and intrusive electronic warfare capabilities.

Is the United States legally correct that the *Bowditch* is undertaking hydrographic surveys and is therefore not subject to the EEZ consent regime for marine scientific research (MSR)?

Again the answer is neither simple nor straightforward and again we need know what type of data was/is being collected in China's EEZ. The United States argues that hydrographic and military surveys – although undefined – are military activities, differentiated from in the language of the Convention and exempt from arbitration.[107] But China disagrees. If such a case were ever brought to the

---

To maintain international peace and security, and to that end: to take effective collective measures for the prevention and removal of threats to the peace, and for the suppression of acts of aggression or other breaches of the peace, and to bring about by peaceful means, and in conformity with the principles of justice and international law, adjustment or settlement of international disputes or situations which might lead to a breach of peace;

'China views the legal obligation of the "peaceful purpose" provision in a broad way. It believes it includes the obligations to refrain from any action which would infringe upon the national security interest of coastal countries, the obligation to respect and observe laws and rules formulated by coastal countries for maintaining their national security interest, and the obligation to submit to executive measures taken by coastal countries to maintain peace, tranquility and good order in their maritime space.'

'Some countries carry out "military hydrographic survey" activities in the EEZs of coastal states without their permission. China believes that in a military sense, this is a type of battlefield preparation and thus a threat of force against those countries, thus violating the principle of peaceful use of the sea.'

(Summary of paper presented by Xizhong Cheng, Research Fellow, China Institute for International Strategic Studies, Beijing, China); *The Regime of the Exclusive Economic Zone: Issues and Responses*, p. 30 (A Report of the Tokyo Meeting, 2003).

105 Haiwen Zhang, 'Is it safeguarding the freedom of navigation or maritime hegemony of the United States?', http://chinesejil.oxfordjournals.org/content/9/1/31.short.

106 'China provocation slammed', *The Japan Times*, 8 February 2013.

107 'Survey' activities seem to be distinguished in the 1982 UNCLOS from (marine scientific) research activities *on UNCLOS provisions relating to innocent passage*. Convention

UNCLOS dispute resolution mechanism, the arbitration panel – not the United States – would determine whether they are MSR or not.

But some argue that for intent and purpose they cannot be neatly differentiated and are essentially the same. They say the very reason that the Convention's consent regime was established for MSR is that information collected thereby may have economic value or may be used to undermine the security of the state. Some of the scientific information and data obtained by military surveys may be of great value for commercial exploitation as well as to achieve military objectives. For example, detailed US naval side-scan sonar charts of its west coast EEZ, when released, proved invaluable to geologists searching for volcanically active rift zones potentially rich in metallic sulphides. If such information regarding the seabed of a foreign coastal state's EEZ should be released to the private sector, its collection could have been a violation of Article 300 requiring good faith and non-abuse of rights. By then, of course, it would probably be too late, although compensation might be in order. Thus in terms of use there seems to be an overlap with data collected in MSR; coastal states who perceive the issue this way may try to prevent such data collection.

Similarly, trends in technology and the need for broader 'hydrographic' data have conflated hydrographic surveying with MSR. Indeed, hydrographic data now have much wider application than safety of navigation and some of its uses are associated with the rights and duties of a coastal state in its EEZ. It is becoming increasingly difficult to argue that hydrographic data collected today will not have some economic or security value in future. Thus similar considerations would now seem to apply to the conduct of hydrographic surveying in the EEZ as apply to

---

Article 19(2) refers to 'research or survey activities'; and Articles 21(1) and 40 mention 'marine scientific research and hydrographic surveys (survey ships)'. Convention Part XIII is devoted solely to marine scientific research, with no reference to surveys. To some this indicates that hydrographic and survey activities do not fall under the regime of Part XIII. 'Hydrographic surveys', which are generally 'to obtain information for the making of navigational charts and safety of navigation, and includes determination of one or more of several classes of data in coastal or relatively shallow areas – depth of water, configuration and nature of the natural bottom, directions and force of currents, heights and times of tides and water stages, and hazards of navigation – for the production of nautical charts and similar products to support safety of navigation'. 'Military surveys', 'refer to activities undertaken in the ocean and coastal waters involving marine data collection (whether or not classified) for military purposes, and can include oceanographic, marine geological, geophysical, chemical, biological and acoustic data. Equipment used can include fathometers, swath bottom mappers, side scan sonars, bottom grab and coring systems, current meters and profilers'. 'While the means of data collection used in military surveys may sometimes be the same as that used in MSR, information from such activities, regardless of security classification, is intended not for use by the general scientific community, but by the military', EEZ Group 21, Guidelines for Navigation and Overflight in the Exclusive Economic Zone, A Commentary, Ocean Policy Research Foundation, Tokyo, Japan 2006.

the conduct of MSR there. In sum, the distinction between different categories of surveying and MSR hinges on more than intent and the initial purpose of collecting the data. Indeed, it seems that the potential economic and security value and utility of the data to the coastal state should also be considered.

However, a plain reading of UNCLOS Article 258 should put the US arguments to rest. It provides that '*the deployment and use of any type of scientific research* installation or *equipment* in any area of the marine environment shall be subject to the same conditions as are prescribed in this Convention for the conduct of marine scientific research in any such area'. It seems difficult to avoid the conclusion that this applies to the *Bowditch* – and the *Impeccable* – and that their deployment of such equipment in a foreign EEZ requires the consent of the coastal state.

Are Military Exercises Allowed in the EEZ?

Traditionally the freedom of the high seas included the use of the high seas for military manoeuvres or exercises, including the use of weapons. This freedom has been incorporated in the 1982 UNCLOS, and it has been generally asserted, particularly by maritime states, that it applies also to the EEZ. However, upon signing, ratifying or acceding to the Convention, several states, including Bangladesh, Brazil, Cape Verde, Pakistan, Malaysia, Myanmar, Uruguay and, most recently, Thailand declared that such military activities are not permitted in their EEZ without the consent of the coastal state. The United States has taken the position that 'military activities, such as ... launching and landing of aircraft ... exercises, operations ... [in the EEZ] are recognized historic high seas uses that are preserved by Article 58'. The United States continues to assert this position and it backs it up with its 'Freedom of Navigation' programme, sailing naval vessels in and through areas other nations have declared 'off-limits' to such practices without their consent.

Some analysts have concluded that state practice and authoritative commentators are divided on whether military manoeuvres, and particularly those involving the use of weapons, in the EEZ of a foreign state without its consent are internationally lawful uses of the sea. They argue that simple naval transit and manoeuvres are part of the freedom of navigation. But they find it more difficult to agree that an extended test of weapons, such as laying of depth charges, launching torpedoes, firing artillery or the covert laying of arms within an EEZ, are included among the 'normal' uses associated with the operation of ships and aircraft and pay 'due regard' to the rights and duties of the coastal state, especially their duty to protect the environment including its fish and mammals. Moreover, the legality of military manoeuvres and ballistic exercises that temporarily prevents other states from using an area of their EEZ remains unresolved.

Military activities in the EEZ were a controversial issue during the negotiation of the text of the 1982 UNCLOS and continue to be so in state practice. Some coastal states contended that other states cannot carry out military exercises or manoeuvres in or over their EEZ without their consent. Their concern is that such uninvited military activities – like 'gun boat diplomacy' – could threaten their national security or undermine their resource sovereignty. Other states specifically argue the opposite. Indeed, maritime powers such as the United States insist on the freedom of military activities in the EEZ out of concern that their naval and air access and mobility could be severely restricted by a global EEZ enclosure movement. The debate continues and one aspect of it is the dispute over freedom of intrusive intelligence gathering.

The Convention provides that in cases where it does not specifically attribute rights or jurisdiction to the coastal or other states within the EEZ, any dispute between the states parties should be resolved on the basis of equity and in the light of all the relevant circumstances, taking into account the respective importance of the interests involved to the parties as well as to the international community as a whole (Article 59). So which is more equitable or more valuable to the international community – the right to spy to 'prepare the battle field' and to select targets, or the right to ban such activities in one's EEZ? Another relevant question is 'whether such intelligence activities can be deemed inherently hostile to the security interest of the coastal state so as to make it impossible or difficult for the state conducting the intelligence activities to respect either the "peaceful purposes" limitation or the "due regard" limitation'.[108] The UNCLOS negotiators apparently thought it necessary to retain this provision – even in the face of a Singapore proposal to delete it 'because it was unnecessary if the Convention clearly gives *only* resources jurisdiction [in the EEZ] to the coastal state'[109]

Such disputes imply that certain UNCLOS provisions formulated in a very different political and technological era must be interpreted in the light of these new circumstances – or renegotiated. But any such negotiations – with a weakened United States, a non-existent Soviet Union and a rising China – may have very different results than before, when the United States and the Soviet Union joined diplomatic forces to strongly influence the freedom of navigation provisions in favour of maritime powers.

Needed now is an agreement on a set of voluntary guidelines for military and intelligence-gathering activities in foreign EEZs and on definitions of permitted and prohibited conduct there. Such guidelines would provide indicators of friendly (and unfriendly) behaviour and help parties avoid unnecessary incidents without banning any activities outright. Specific guidelines have been proposed by a group of international experts sponsored by Japan's Ocean Policy Research Foundation.[110] The most relevant of these voluntary guidelines would be the increasingly meaningful obligation to only use the ocean for peaceful purposes and to refrain from the threat or use of force. These might be elaborated by examples. The

108 Sienho Yee, 'Sketching the debate on military activities in the EEZ: An editorial comment', *Chinese Journal of International Law*, 9(1) 2010, pp. 1–7.

109 Quoted in Satya Nandan and Shabatai Rosenne (eds), 2 UN Convention on the Law of the Sea 1982: A commentary, 2002, 568, para. 59.3.

110 See EEZ Group 21, *supra* n. 97.

guidelines would also discourage provocative acts such as collecting information to support the use of force against the coastal state, or more relevant now – interfering with naval electronic systems. However, the United States has rejected any and all such guidelines – voluntary or not – as unacceptable.

Nevertheless, at the 'Sunnylands Summit', President Xi reportedly offered an initiative on rules of behaviour in air and maritime domains.[111] Also, US CINCPAC Locklear has recently been quoted as saying that 'a "code of conduct" would allow the military to understand the boundaries of what they can do in the best interest for a peaceful solution'.[112] Maybe this is an idea whose time has come. If the United States really means it when it says its 'rebalancing' is not aimed at China, it should exercises some restraint regarding such sensitive actions. Indeed, the United States could reduce its surveillance activities in China's EEZ.[113] Proponents for this option argue that there are alternative ways to collect the information and that the information collected is not worth the risk of incidents that could lead to a crisis. However, opponents say that alternative methods are less effective and incapable of collecting certain types of information, that reducing these activities would decrease US military preparedness, and that such a reduction could be seen as a Chinese victory in resisting these operations, thus serving as a precedent and undermining the US security commitment to the region. And the beat goes on.

Ways Forward

Despite the bravado, bluster and propaganda from both sides, the answers to these questions are not a legal 'slam dunk' for any 'side'. Unless the issues are addressed and resolved, more incidents and possible conflict lie ahead. It is therefore particularly important that mechanisms be instituted to address these particular 'hot button' issues dotting the broad new geopolitical canvas.

There are several possible ways forward, each with its own complexities.

China/United States Bilateral Agreement

China and the United States could upgrade the MMCA discussions from the operational level to the policy level.[114] So far the United States simply repeats

111 http://www.japantimes.co.jp/opinion/2014/10/16/commentary/world-commentary/u-s-china-skirmishes-beg-for-guidelines-on-spying/.

112 Asian Security Forum addresses cyber-attacks, South China Sea, *Hindustan News*, 5 June 2013.

113 'Maritime territorial and EEZ disputes involving China', *Congressional Research Service*, p. 32.

114 Agreement Between the Department of Defense of the United States of America and the Ministry of National Defense of the People's Republic of China to Establish a Consultation Mechanism to Strengthen Military Maritime Safety, http://www.fas.org/

its navigational freedom arguments and China proposes that the US refrain from intelligence gathering in China's EEZ. It was hoped that such discussions might eventually lead to an INCSEA agreement similar to that between the United States and the Soviet Union at the height of the Cold War. But even that would only be a basic agreement on appropriate and inappropriate behaviour when platforms of both parties encounter each other at sea. It would not address the source of the problem nor resolve the issues for the broader Asian community.

Perhaps China can tolerate passive ELINT data collection but active 'tickling' and interference with communications is the real problem. If so, perhaps the two sides could agree that each should refrain from: (1) provocative acts, such as stimulating, exciting, or probing the defensive systems of the coastal state; and (2) collecting information to support the use of force against the coastal state. Perhaps they could work towards a formal Dangerous Military Activities[115] agreement on the following points:

1. The activities of another state in the EEZ of coastal state should not interfere with the communications, computer and electronic systems of the coastal state or make broadcasts that adversely affect the defence or security of the coastal state.
2. The coastal state should not interfere with the communications, computer and electronic systems of the user state's vessels and aircraft in and over the coastal state's EEZ.
3. In order to make the first two points effective, states should conclude agreements guaranteeing mutual non-interference with communications, computers and electronic systems.

Using the International Tribunal for the Law of the Sea to Sort Out Differences

In the best of worlds, the United States would ratify the Convention and agree to have the Tribunal decide these issues. Ratifying the 1982 UNCLOS would enhance US legitimacy in arguing the issues, bolster its position in favour of rules-based behaviour, give it a seat at the table in discussions of EEZ rights and generally advance its strategic image and position.

But this is probably a non-starter. The difficult US domestic political environment precludes ratification any time soon and, even if it did ratify, the United States would probably exercise its right to decline application of compulsory dispute settlement procedures to those disputes concerning military activities. However,

---

nuke/control/sea/text/us-china98htm; 'China urges U.S. to reduce surveillance operations', http://U.S.Chinesembassay.org/eng/zt/t581108.htm.

115 These elements were included in the US/Soviet INCSEA and DMA agreement.

defining 'military activities' would be up to the judges of the Tribunal, a possible problem for the US position.[116]

Nevertheless, the train has left the station. If the United States prefers clarity it needs to stop stonewalling and spouting the same stale rhetoric, and focus, engage, acknowledge and adjust. Otherwise such incidents are likely to continue, hardening hearts and minds in China and beyond.

A Regional Approach

Several prominent Southeast Asian thinkers suggest that it is time for Asia to take the lead in regional security matters.[117] Indeed, ASEAN is struggling to maintain its 'centrality' in security matters in the region. Perhaps it is time for a bold regional initiative to forge an understanding among all Asian countries regarding what are considered hostile and non-hostile acts in EEZs. Perhaps this could be undertaken by the Asean Defense Ministers Meeting. The approach would be for ASEAN to negotiate a declaration on conduct similar to the *Declaration on the Conduct of Parties in the South China Sea* but focused on military activities, especially intelligence gathering in EEZs. The language would hopefully be more specific than the rather vague admonition in the 2002 ASEAN–China Declaration on the Conduct of Parties in the South China Sea to exercise self-restraint in the conduct of activities that would complicate or escalate disputes and affect peace and stability'.[118]

The next step would be to invite China and others to join the agreement, perhaps through the ADMM-Plus which has already agreed to 'establish practical measures to reduce vulnerability to miscalculation and avoid misunderstanding and undesirable incidents at sea'.[119] However, this may be difficult for China because such an agreement would require that China deny itself the technological advantage it enjoys vis-à-vis all ASEAN countries except perhaps Singapore. But such a sacrifice would be proof of China's benign intent towards the region, leaving it up to the United States and Japan to either join or decline to do so – at some political cost. These agreements could also be bilateral between any relevant Southeast Asian countries or those involved in the region like the DOCs between

---

116 http://nautilus.org/napsnet/napsnet-policy-forum/intelligence-gathering-the-south-china-sea-and-the-law-of-the-sea/.

117 Kishore Mahbubani and Simon Chesterman, 'Pragmatic Asia can bolster global stability', *Japan Times*, 3 March 2010; Yoichi Funabashi, 'A 21st century vision for alliance', *Pacific Forum CSIS, PacNet*, no. 7, 18 February 2010.

118 Governments of the Member States of ASEAN and the Government of the People's Republic of China, *Declaration on the Conduct of Parties in the South China Sea* (Phnom Penh, 4 November 2002), http://www.aseansec.org/13163.htm.

119 U.S. Department of Defense, Post-ASEAN Defense Ministers Meeting – Plus Press Conference in Bandar Seri Begawan, Brunei, 29 August 2013.

China and the Philippines, and Vietnam and the Philippines.[120] The end result would be the same – a norm against provocative military activities in foreign EEZs. Indeed, needed urgently is a fundamental agreement as to what is and is not considered 'unfriendly' military behaviour in EEZs.

References

Antrim, Caitlyn L., *The Ocean Law Daily*, 1 August 2012.

'Asian Security Forum addresses cyber-attacks, South China Sea', *Hindustan News*, 5 June 2013.

'Australia backs security pact with U.S., India: Report', *Reuters*, 30 November 2011.

'Australia blasts Japan after whaling ships EEZ incursion', *The Japan Times*, 2 February 2013.

Axe, David, 'U.S. drones vs. China', *The Diplomat*, 23 May 2011.

Axe, David, 'The U.S. Navy's belated robot revolution', worldpoliticsreview.com, 16 December 2011.

Bateman, Sam, 'U.S. Air Sea battle: Countering China's anti-access strategies', *RSIS Commentaries*, No. 82, 19 May 2011.

Blumenthal, Daniel, 'A Sino-American proxy war?' *Foreign Policy*, 18 September 2013.

Brown, Peter J., 'U.S. doesn't comment, but has acknowledged monitoring North's military', MNSBC.com, 29 April 2006.

Brown, Peter J., 'U.S. satellites shadow China's submarines', *Asia Times*, 13 May 2010.

Burns, Robert, 'Gates sees wider U.S. military presence in Asia', Staradvertiser.com, 4 June 2011.

Callick, Rowan, 'Top gun warns of military rivalry', *The Australian*, 3 June 2011.

Carmichael, Lachlan, 'Obama reviving U.S. clout in Asia as China stumbles', *AFP*, 30 July 2010.

Chairman of the Joint Chiefs of Staff, National Military Strategy of the United States of America 201, 8 February 2011.

Chellaney, Brahma, 'Deception by the boatload', *China World*, 19 June 2011.

Chester, Andrew, 'USAF planes to help U.K. fill SIGINT', *Defense News*, 22 March 2010.

'China accuses U.S. of increasing surveillance', UPI.com, 22 April 2013.

'China blasts PH anew on Spratlys claim', *Philippine Daily Inquirer*, 9 June 2011.

'China's naval ambitions', *New York Times*, 1 January 2011.

'China protests U.S. spy flights near its coast', *Reuters*, 27 July 2011.

'China provocation slammed', *The Japan Times*, 8 February 2013.

120 Hasjim Djalal, Remarks on the Concept of 'Freedom of Navigation', in Myron H. Nordquist, Tommy T.B. Koh and John Norton Moore, *Freedom of Seas, Passage Rights and the 1982 Law of the Sea Convention*, Brill, 2009.

‘China warns U.S. over Spratlys ahead of Hawaii meeting’, *Associated Press*, 22 June 2011.
‘Chinese navy less assertive in 2011: U.S. Admiral’, *AFP*, 12 April 2011.
Cohen, Roger, ‘Doctrine of silence’, *New York Times*, 28 November 2011.
Cole, William, ‘Chinese help plan for huge war game near isles’, *Honolulu Star Advertiser*, 25 July 2013.
Cole, William, ‘Navy vessels due in Asia-Pacific area’, *Honolulu Star Advertiser*, 10 April 2013.
‘Creating a new model for U.S.-China relation at the Obama – summit’, *World*, 5 June 2013.
Djalal, Hasjim, ‘Remarks on the Concept of “Freedom of Navigation”’, in Myron H. Nordquist, Tommy T.B. Koh and John Norton Moore (eds), *Freedom of Seas, Passage Rights and the 1982 Law of the Sea Convention*, Brill, 2009.
Drew, Christopher, ‘U-2 spy plane evades the day of retirement’, *New York Times*, 21 March 2010.
Duda, Steve, ‘Navy tests mean green killing machine’, 18 October, 2011.
Fang, Tanya, ‘Territorial dispute main concern at dialogue’, *Today*, 6 June 2011.
Flournoy, Lisa Daniel, ‘Asia will be heart of U.S. security policy’, *American Forces Press Service*, 29 April 2011.
Folkmanis, Jason, ‘U.S. says S. China Sea events “troubling” after Vietnam meeting’, *Bloomberg*, 13 June 2011.
Fulghum, David, ‘Recon needs grow for South China Sea region’, *Aviation Week*.
Funabashi, Yoichi, ‘A 21st Century vision for alliance’, *Pacific Forum CSIS, PacNet*, no. 7, 18 February 2010.
Gertz, Bill, ‘Chinese jets chase U.S. surveillance jet over Taiwan Strait’, *The Washington Times*, 25 July 2011.
Glaser, Bonnie S. and Pal, Deep, ‘How will China react to a military strike on Syria?’, CSIS, Strategic Insights and Bipartisan Policy Solutions, 5 September 2013.
‘Global Hawk set to watch over North Korea’, *Unmanned Aerial Vehicle News*, 15 September 2011.
Guanglie, Liang, ‘A better future through security co-operation’, Speech, Shangri-la Dialogue, 5 June 2011.
‘Hagel issues warning over Asian maritime dispute’, *The Gulf Today*, 29 August 2013.
Hennigan, W.J., ‘Submarine drones need to be autonomous, naval experts say’, *Los Angeles Times*, 10 February 2013.
‘Japan’s reconnaissance missions undermine China’s security interests: Defense ministry’, *Xinhua*, 26 October 2010.
Jia, Yongming, ‘On dissection of disputes between China and the United States over military activities in Exclusive Economic Zone by the Law of the Sea docs’, Shanghai Academy of Social Sciences.
Johnson, Ian and Fackler, Martin, ‘China addresses rising Korean tensions’, *New York Times*, 26 November 2010.

Kate, Daniel Ten, 'China spurns arbitration as U.S. joins Japan on sea stance', *Bloomberg*, 2 June 2013.
Lembum, Bruce, 'U.S.-Taiwan relations are threat to China', *Defense News*, 8 November 2012.
Lieberthal, Kenneth and Wang, Jisi, 'Addressing U.S.-China strategic distrust', John L. Thorton China Center, Brookings, March 2012, pp. 7–33.
Mackenzie, Christina, 'Governments spend millions on sophisticated drones', *International Herald Tribune*, 13 June 2005.
Mahbubani, Kishore and Chesterman, Simon, 'Pragmatic Asia can bolster global stability', *Japan Times*, 3 March 2010.
Marina, Michael, 'China, Japan engage in new invective over disputed isles', *Reuters*, 8 February 2013.
Mazetti, Mark and Sanger, David, 'Security leader says U.S. would retaliate against cyber-attacks', *New York Times*, 12 March 2013.
Minmick, Wendell, 'Chinese signaling for conflict: A predictive pattern', quoting Paul Godwin and Alva Miller, newdefensenews.com, 28 April 2013.
Moran, Michel, 'China's naval rise is not as threatening as U.S. would like', *DOOH Insights*, 26 June 2011.
Mosher, Steven, 'Does the PRC have a grand strategy of hegemony', Testimony presented to the Subcommittee on Oversight and Investigations, The Hon. Dana Rohrabacker, Chairman, International Relations Committee, U.S. House of Representatives.
'Navy Chief: Robotic subs might span oceans', www.wired.com, March 2012.
'No reason to get even close to Uncle Sam', *Smh.com*, 14 November 2011.
Pedrozo, Peter, 'The U.S.-China incidents at sea agreement: A recipe for disaster', *Journal of National Security Law and Policy*, 6; 207, July 2012.
'Remote controlled vessels unveiled', *Today*, 18 May 2005.
Richardson, Michael, 'U.S. turns to drones to counter China', *The Japan Times*, 5 January 2012.
Robson, Seth, 'Maritime drones make waves among navies worldwide', *Stars and Stripes*, 3 August 2011.
'ROK, U.S. and Japan conduct naval exercise', *Yonhap*, 16 July 2014.
Roughead, Gary, remarks delivered at 2011 AVVSI Unmanned System Symposium and Exhibition, 19 August 2011.
Sargent, William, 'Under seas maps under wraps', *The Christian Science Monitor*, 31 March 1987.
Sasaki, Hiroke, 'Military activities in the oceans and the "sovereign immunity" provision'; https://www.sof.or.jp/en/report/pdf/201203.pdf.
Scharf, Michael, *Recognizing Grotian Moments*, Cambridge University Press, 2013.
Scobell, Andrew, 'Is there a civil military gap in China's peaceful rise?', *Parameters*, Summer 2009.
Sheridan, Greg, 'New Australia-U.S. push deals India into Pacific', *The Australian*, 17 September 2011.

Sheridan, Greg, 'Trade and defense: Our China line', *The Australian*, 25 June 2011.
'Stay out of sea disputes China warns U.S.', *France Press*, 14 September 2013.
Talmadge, Eric, 'Japan gets U.S. pitch to buy spy drones', *Associated Press*, 8 April 2010.
Tandon, Shaun, 'Build unified ASEAN in South China Sea: McCain', *AFP*, 20 June 2011.
Tandon, Shaun and de Luce, Dan, 'U.S. Australia vow joint response in cyber war', *Google*, 5 September 2011.
Thakur, Ramesh, 'Is America now becoming an international outlaw?', *New York Times*, 3 September 2013.
Thayer, Carlyle, 'American grand strategy: power and purpose in the 21st Century', 64th Strategy Forum, U.S. Naval War College, 18–19 June 2013.
Thompson, Loren B., 'Outside view: Shrinking U.S. sub fleet', *United Press International*, 3 January 2007.
United States/Australia/Asia: U.S. military to expand presence in Asia, *Channel News Asia*, 7 November 2010.
'U.S. Admiral: Chinese Navy less hostile in disputed waters', *Top Market News*, 13 April 2011.
'U.S. considers boosting force in Asia: Pentagon', *Joong Ang Daily*, 28 January 2011.
U.S. Embassy, Beijing, '2009 U.S.-China Defense Consultative Talks (DCT) Small Group Session', 1 July 2009.
'U.S. gears up to meet China threat', *Eurasia Review*, 2 September 2011.
'U.S. Navy eyes stationary ships in Singapore', *Reuters*, 16 December 2011.
'U.S. Navy in South China Sea exercise with ASEAN', *UPI*, 17 June 2011.
'U.S. Navy's new floating base gets a workout in Gulf', kitsapsun.com, 22 September 2012.
'U.S. OKs pre-emptive cyber-strike', *Japan Times*, 5 February 2013.
'U.S. to provide PHL satellite surveillance assistance over maritime territory', *GMA News*, 4 May 2012.
'U.S. sends destroyer to region amid Spratlys tension', *Manila Standard Today*, 5 June 2011.
Valencia, Mark J., 'Could a maritime conflict start a Sino-American war?', *The Japan Times*, 2 September 2013.
Valencia, Mark J., 'Foreign military activities in Asian EEZs: Conflict ahead?', National Bureau of Asian Research, Special Report #27, May 2011.
Wishik, Anton and Durnin, Matthew, 'Space, China's tactical frontier', Interview with NBR, 23 May 2012.
Wolf, Jim, 'China cyber capability endangers U.S. forces', report, *Reuters*, 28 January 2012.
Yee, Sienho, 'Sketching the debate on military activities in the EEZ: An editorial comment', *Chinese Journal of International Law*, 9(1) 2010, pp. 1–7.

Zhang, Haiwen, 'Is it safeguarding the freedom of navigation or maritime hegemony of the United States?', http://chinesejil.oxfordjournals.org/content/9/1/31.short.

Zhang, Yunli and Jiao, Wu, 'China rebukes drone reports', *China Daily USA*, 25 September 2013.

Chapter 4
'Due Regards' and 'Abuse of Rights' in UNCLOS

Hasjim Djalal

Due Regards

A state has no obligation to cooperate with other states. But if an act of a state or government result in causing damage to other states, the act of the state is likely to result in compensating the other states. Thus, even in a civil war or in domestic violence, a country has to act and exercise its sovereign rights with 'due regards' or 'due diligence', thus avoiding damage to other states or to their interests.

Article 56 (2) of UNCLOS clearly states that: 'In exercising its rights and performing its duties under this Convention in the EEZ, the coastal States shall have due regard to the rights and duties of other states and shall act in a manner compatible with the provisions of the Convention.'[1] At the same time, the other states exercising their rights and performing their duties in the EEZ of other coastal states, shall also 'have due regard to the rights and the duties of the coastal State and shall comply with the laws and regulations adopted by the coastal State in accordance with the provisions of this Convention and other rules of international law' (Article 58 (3) of UNCLOS).

Thus, the 'due regard' provisions seek to balance the rights and interests of the coastal states and the rights and interests of other states.

In practice, it may not be easy to seek this balance, such as in the conduct of military exercises and intelligence-gathering activities in the EEZ of other countries. Some accidents with regard to these issues have taken place in the past in the South China Sea, causing political tensions between the states, and injuring peace and stability in the South China Sea area. For this reason, a number of law of the sea personalities had undertaken consultations in various places in the past, such as in Bali (June 2002), Tokyo (February 2003), Honolulu (December 2003), Shanghai (October 2004) and Tokyo (2005), trying to formulate 'guidelines' for the freedom of navigation and over-flight in the EEZ, particularly regarding the military exercises and intelligence-gathering activities in the EEZ so that foreign military interests will not collide with the need of the coastal state to protect its sovereignty and security. Unfortunately the efforts have not been conclusive.

---

1 Unless otherwise noted, all further references are to the United Nations Convention on the Law of the Sea 1982 (UNCLOS).

UNCLOS 1982 has a lot of provisions with regard to 'due regards' situation, such as:

The rights of all states to *lay sub-marine cables and pipelines* in the continental shelf (Article 79 (1) of UNCLOS). But in doing so, they should do it with 'due regard' to the cables or pipelines already in place or in position (Article 79 (5) of UNCLOS). They should take into account the possibilities of repairing existing cables or pipelines which shall not be prejudiced or prevented by the laying of new cables or pipelines (Article 79, paragraph 5).

The coastal states have the rights to establish conditions for cables or pipelines in their territory or territorial sea, or over cables and pipelines constructed or used in connection with the exploration of its continental shelf or of exploitation of its resources, or the operation of artificial islands, installations and structures under its jurisdiction (Article 79 (4) of UNCLOS).

Administratively, the Council of the ISBA (International Seabed Authority) can also establish its subsidiary organs, but in doing so, it has to do it with 'due regard' to the economy and efficiency and to the principle of equitable geographical distribution and of special interests. For this reason, during the election for the membership of the Council and the governing board of the Enterprise, 'due regard should also be paid to the desirability of rotation of membership' (Article 161 (4) of UNCLOS), the equitable geographical distribution and of special interests and the need for members qualified and competent in the relevant technical questions (Article 160, paragraph 2d and Article 163, paragraph 4), and the necessity to secure the highest standard of efficiency, cooperation and integrity in recruiting the staff of the Authority (Article 167, paragraph 2).

When removing an abandoned or disused installation at sea in order to ensure safety of navigation, such activities of removal must also have 'due regard' to fishing, the protection of the marine environment, and the rights and duties of other states (Article 60 (3)). Appropriate publicity shall be given to the depth, position and dimension of the installations or structures not entirely removed.

When fishing for 'anadromous' stocks beyond the outer limits of the EEZ, states shall maintain consultation with a view to achieving agreement on terms and conditions of fishing for such anadromous stocks and such fishing should give 'due regard' to 'the conservation requirements and the needs of the State of origin' of the stocks (Article 66, paragraph 3 (a)).

The high seas are open to all states (Article 87 (1)). But in exercising their rights on the high seas, state should exercise them with 'due regard' to the interests of other states in their exercise of the freedom of the high seas and the rights under the Convention with regard to activities in the international seabed area (Article 87, paragraph 2).

Conversely, the activities in the ISA (International Seabed Area) on mineral deposits shall also be conducted with 'due regard' to the rights and legitimate interests of any coastal states across whose jurisdiction such deposits lie (Article 142, paragraph 1 of UNCLOS) and to the special interests and needs of developing states, in particular the landlocked and geographically disadvantaged state (LLGDS) (Article 148 of UNCLOS).

With regard to the *archaeological and historical objects* found in the ISA, particular regard should also be paid to the preferential rights of the state or country of origin, or the state of cultural origin, or the state of historical and archaeological origin of the objects (Article 149).

In promoting development and transfer of marine technology, 'due regard' shall also be given to the legitimate interests and the rights and duties of the countries of holders, suppliers and recipients of the marine technology (Article 267).

With regard to *navigation*, a coastal state in certain cases has the rights to exercise jurisdiction on board foreign ships passing through its territorial sea, to arrest any person or to conduct any investigation in connection with any crime committed on board the ship during its passage, but in doing so, the local authorities 'shall have due regard to the interests of navigation' (Article 27 (4)), in the sense that it should not cause hindrance to navigation.

On the other hand, with regard to *over-flights of state aircraft* in transit passage over 'straits used for international navigation', they also should operate at all times with 'due regard' to the safety of navigation (Article 39 (3)a) so that they would not cause harm to themselves as well as to the countries concerned.

Even the rights of the coastal state (for instance, Canada) to adopt and enforce its laws and regulations with regard to navigation in the 'ice-covered area' in its EEZ in the Arctic Ocean, will have to do it with due regard to the rights of others and should base it on the best available scientific evidence (Article 234).

Therefore it could be concluded that the 'due regard provisions' attempt to secure a good balance between the various interests of all parties involved, in the sense that neither sovereignty or sovereign rights of the coastal states, nor the freedoms of navigation and over-flight of other states, could be exercised with 'absoluteness', but should always be exercised with responsibility and by taking into account the interests of others. Otherwise, it may result in some kind of state responsibility and liability.

In some cases, the notion of 'due regards' may not be specifically mentioned in UNCLOS, but I understand that in exercising their rights under UNCLOS, the states should also pay attention to the rights of others; thus they also include the provision of 'due regards'. These may be implied in various cases, such as in exercising sovereignty over archipelagic waters and territorial sea, the coastal shall respect 'innocent passage' of foreign vessels, 'transit passage' in straits used for international navigations, and the 'archipelagic sea lane passage' through archipelagic waters. In fact, in establishing the sea lanes through the archipelagic waters in accordance with UNCLOS, Indonesia has already negotiated 19 rules with the relevant maritime powers (see below, and has enacted those rules into its legislation on navigation and over-flight on and over the archipelagic sea lanes (Government Regulation No. 37/2002). Similarly, Indonesia had also enacted into Government Regulation No. 36/2002 the rules and regulations with regard to 'innocent passage' in the archipelagic waters in accordance with the provisions of

UNCLOS. Equally, in determining baselines, either for territorial sea or straight archipelagic baselines, they should also observe various rules and regulations that take into account the interest of other states, either for navigation purposes and in some cases, based on argument, even for traditional rights of neighbouring states that may be affected (Article 47 (6)).

Abuse of Rights

Although a state may have sovereignty, sovereign rights or jurisdictions in maritime space, it should also not 'abuse' those rights that may bring damage to other states. Under traditional international law a breach of international obligation may entail 'compulsory jurisdiction' of the international court and may result in reparation or compensation to be made for that breach of an international obligation.[2]

The court, including the ITLOS, dealing with any claim shall determine the existence of the abuse of legal process and therefore can drop the case '*prima facie*' (Article 294 of UNCLOS) if the legal process is abused. States parties of UNCLOS therefore should fulfil their obligations under UNCLOS 'in good faith' and exercise their rights, jurisdictions and freedoms in a manner that would not constitute 'abuse of right' (Article 300).

'Abuse of rights' engaged by virtue of international law by sovereign states can result in state responsibility of that state. A state therefore should not and could not act in an arbitrary manner, in such a way as to inflict upon another state injury which cannot be justified.[3] For example, the duty of a state not to interfere with the flow of a river to the detriment of other riparian states.[4] (In fact, some of the Mekong River countries were worried several years ago that the building up of a number of dams in the mountains and the diversion of waters of the Lancang-Mekong River may affect the interests of other riparian states of the lower Mekong River.)

Even in the exercise of sovereignty, sovereign rights, and other jurisdictions of a state in maritime affairs, a state should not 'abuse' those rights that would be detrimental to other states or even to the 'marine environment' and the 'sustainability' of the marine resources.

Therefore, the state parties to UNCLOS have obligations to fulfil in good faith their responsibilities and to exercise their rights, jurisdictions and freedoms recognized in the Convention in such a way that would not constitute 'an abuse of rights' (Article 300). They shall refrain from any threat or use of force against the territorial integrity or political independence of any state and shall act in a manner that would respect the principles of international law, particularly the UN Charter,

2 International Court of Justice Statute, Art. 98

3 L. Oppenheim, *International Law: A Treatise, Longmans, Green and Co., Ltd.*, 8th edn (London, 1966), p. 345.

4 Ibid., p. 346.

UNCLOS, and other international and regional arrangements. In fact, most of those rights of states recognized in UNCLOS should be exercised and implemented by the states concerned in accordance with the mechanism and procedures provided in the Convention, such as in determining 'baselines', the limits of 'continental margin', settlement of maritime boundaries, and so forth.

Nineteen Sea Lane Rules[5]

1. Ships and aircrafts in sea lanes will not disturb or threaten the sovereignty, territorial integrity or independence and national unity of Indonesia. They will not carry out any action that would contravene principles of international law as embodied in the United Nations Charter.
2. Except for situations involving force majeure or distress, aircrafts in archipelagic sea lanes passage shall not land in Indonesian territory, including territory in the sea lanes. Ships and aircrafts in archipelagic sea lanes passage shall not deviate more than 25 nautical miles to either side of axis lines during passage, provided that such ships and aircrafts shall not navigate closer to the coasts than 10 per cent of the distance between the nearest points on islands bordering the sea lanes.
3. Foreign civil aircrafts passing through sea lanes must comply with international rules of civil aviation as established by ICAO.
4. While exercising sea lanes passages, foreign warships and foreign military aircrafts are not allowed to conduct war exercises or use live ammunition nor to conduct a war game. They are to proceed without delay through or over the sea lanes in the normal mode solely for the purpose of continuous, expeditious and unobstructed transit.
5. Foreign warships and military aircrafts, as well as ships using nuclear energy, passing through sea lanes, are recommended to inform the Indonesian Government (namely, the Commander of the Indonesian Armed Forces) in advance for the purpose of safety of navigation and to take the necessary preparatory actions should something untoward happen.
6. Ships carrying nuclear materials, except warships and other government ships operated for non-commercial purposes, are required to notify the Commander of the Indonesian Armed Forces in advance in accordance with the Convention on the Physical Protection of Nuclear Materials; are requested to comply with the Code for the Safe Carriage of irradiated nuclear fuel, plutonium and high level radioactive waste in flasks on board ships (INF Code); and are required to comply with other international conventions dealing with transportation or carriage of dangerous goods, hazardous materials and noxious substances.

5 Hasjim Djalal, Indonesia's Archipelagic Sealanes, in Robert Cribb and Michele Ford, "Indonesia Beyond the Water's Edge", ISEAS, Singapore, 2009, pp. 64–65.

7. Foreign military aircrafts flying above the sea lanes must observe the safety of civil aviation and monitor emergency frequencies, and are requested to maintain contact with the authorized air traffic controllers.
8. Transiting foreign ships and/or aircrafts should move carefully in sea lanes which are full of economic activities (either fisheries or mining), should exercise caution in limited navigational areas, and are prohibited from entering within 500 meters of safety zones around oil and gas installations, and should always observe and be careful with respect to the underwater cables and pipelines.
9. Foreign fishing vessels must keep their fishing gear stowed during transit, and are prohibited from carrying out fishing activities while in transit.
10. Transiting ships through sea lanes have to follow generally accepted international navigational rules for the safety of navigation and to be careful, and show due regard for local shipping as well as activities of local fishermen.
11. Ships in sea lanes passage shall comply with all generally accepted international standards regulating pollution of the marine environment from vessels and ships using sea lanes shall not dump wastes or other matter or discharge poisonous or dangerous materials while in Indonesian water.
12. All ships are prohibited from cleaning their tanks or polluting Indonesian waters while in transit.
13. All passing ships are not allowed to stop or anchor or to move back and forth while passing without any legitimate reason, except in case of force majeure or in distress. Transiting ships shall navigate in the normal mode solely for the purpose of continuous, expeditious and unobstructed transit.
14. Transiting ships are not allowed to disembark persons or goods and transfer them to other ships in contravention of customs, financial, immigration or health rules of Indonesia, or to carry out other activities in contravention of those rules.
15. Ships and transiting aircraft are not allowed to carry out survey works or marine scientific research, including taking water samples for the purpose of investigation during passage. They shall not interfere with survey or marine scientific research activities carried out by Indonesia in the sea lanes or there above.
16. Transiting ships and aircrafts are prohibited from carrying out unauthorized broadcasting or to emit electromagnetic signals that are aimed at interfering with national telecommunications systems and are prohibited from establishing direct communications with unauthorized persons or certain groups in the territory of Indonesia.
17. Transiting ships shall always meet the generally accepted international requirements for the safety of navigation.
18. To the maximum extent established by applicable international agreements, shippers, cargo owners and ship owners are strictly liable individually or collectively for the damage caused by them including to pay compensation

to Indonesia, either by way of applicable international agreements or otherwise. They shall be insured as required accordingly. Such liability and insurance shall also include compensation for the damage, including direct, consequential or environmental, to Indonesia. The Flag State of a ship entitled to sovereign immunity shall bear international responsibility for damages caused to Indonesia by the non-compliance of the ship with international law.

19. For purposes of the safety of navigation and the safety of Indonesia, foreign tankers, vessels using nuclear energy, foreign vessels carrying nuclear substances and other dangerous goods, foreign fishing vessels, as well as foreign warships passing through Indonesian waters from one part of the Exclusive Economic Zone or the High Seas to another part of the Exclusive Economic Zone or High Seas are recommended to pass through the sea lanes.

References

Cribb, R. and Michele Ford, "Indonesia Beyond the Water's Edge", ISEAS, Singapore, 2009.

International Court of Justice Statute.

Oppenheim, L. *International Law: A Treatise, Longmans, Green and Co., Ltd.*, 8th edn (London, 1966).

Chapter 5
UNCLOS and the Peaceful Use of the Sea

Vesselin Popovski

The 1982 United Nations Convention on the Law of the Sea (UNCLOS) is the culmination of years of evolution in maritime regulations. It can be regarded as the 'constitution' for the peaceful use of the seas and oceans, aimed to reduce conflict and to maintain peace at sea. UNCLOS enjoys almost universal acceptance and is one of modern public international law's greatest achievements. In terms of its significance, the declaration and the guarantees for the peaceful use of the sea in UNCLOS are as important as the abolishment of war as an instrument of policy and the pronouncement of the maintenance of peace as the main purpose in Article 1 of the UN Charter. Composed of a total of 320 articles and nine annexes, covering every matter related to the marine sphere, UNCLOS declares in its preamble that the State Parties recognize the Convention 'as an important contribution to the maintenance of peace, justice and progress for all peoples of the world'.[1] UNCLOS therefore has become a comprehensive global legal order for the maritime sphere, promoting the peaceful use of the seas and oceans among other things, balancing the maritime rights and obligations of states, and creating legally binding arrangements according to international law.

UNCLOS was born from a vision of the peaceful use of the sea, developed long before its adoption. The *Pacem in Maribus* (PIM) Conferences began in 1970 upon the initiative of Elisabeth Mann Borgese (1918–2002) who later founded the International Ocean Institute (IOI)[2] to become the initial secretariat for the Conference on the law of the sea. The PIM Conferences provided a forum where the interconnected challenges of the maritime space could be considered in their entirety and have played a crucial role in the formulation and promotion of principles and rules later to substantiate UNCLOS. The 23rd Conference held in 1995 in Costa Rica in particular was a significant achievement linking peace at sea with the UN 'Agenda for Peace'. Table 5.1 lists the themes of all the PIM Conferences.

1 UNCLOS, Preamble, http://www.un.org/depts/los/convention_agreements/texts/unclos/closindx.htm.

2 The IOI (http://www.ioinst.org/) is international non-governmental organization with headquarters in Malta, established officially in 1972. Paul Hoffman, then the Administrator of the UNDP, became Honorary President. Informally, the IOI activities go back to 1968 when preparations began for the first PIM Conference.

Table 5.1 Themes of all PIM conferences

1	Malta, 1970	Quiet Enjoyment: Arms Control and Police Forces for the Oceans
2	Malta, 1971	A Constitution for the Oceans
3	Malta, 1972	Economic Potential of the Oceans
4	Malta, 1973	Regional Cooperation in the Caribbean
5	Malta, 1974	The Common Heritage of Mankind
6	Okinawa, 1975	The Sea We Would Like to See
7	Mexico, 1976	Law of the Sea and Latin America
8	Algeria, 1977	Law of the Sea and the New International and Economic Order
9	Yaounde, 1978	Africa and the Law of the Sea
10	Vienna, 1980	Monitoring of Ocean Processes, the Surveillance of Uses, and the Enforcement of Agreed Rules of Management and Conservation
11	Mexico, 1981	National Legislation and the New Law of the Sea
12	Colombo, 1982	Marine Sciences and the New Law of the Sea
13	Norrtalje, 1984	The Denuclearization of the Oceans
14	USSR, 1985	Technical, Legal, Environmental and Economic Aspects of Shipping
15	Valletta, 1987	Commemoration of 20th Anniversary of Maltese Initiative UNCLOS III
16	Halifax, 1988	Ocean Technology, Development Training and Transfer
17	Moscow, 1989	Peace in the Oceans: The New Era
18	Rotterdam, 1990	Ports as Nodal Points in a Global Transport System
19	Lisbon, 1991	Ocean Governance: National, Regional, Global Institutional Mechanisms of Sustainable Development in the Oceans
20	Valletta, 1992	Ocean Governance: Model for Global Governance in the 21st Century
21	Takaoka, 1993	Ocean Governance: A Model for Regional Seas in the 21st Century
22	Madras, 1994	Sustainable Development and Regional Cooperation
23	San Jose, 1995	Potential Contributions of Ocean Governance and Law of the Sea to the Implementation of Secretary General's 'Agenda for Peace'
24	Beijing, 1996	Oceans in the 21st Century
25	Malta, 1997	Common Heritage and the 21st Century
26	Canada, 1998	Crisis of Knowledge: Directions for Learning/Informed Decision-Making for Oceans
27	Fiji, 1999	Oceans in New Millennium: Challenges and Opportunities for Islands
28	Hamburg, 2000	The European Challenge
29	Cape Town, 2002	The Ocean in the New Economy
30	Kiev, 2003	Ocean Governance and Sustainable Development: Ocean and Coasts: Glimpse in the Future
31	Townsville, 2005	Building Bridges to Integrated Oceans Governance: Linking Ocean Science, Engineering, Science and Policy
32	Malta, 2007	Waves of Change: Women, Youth and the Sea
33	Beijing, 2010	International Conference on Oceans, Climate Change and Sustainable Development: Challenges to Oceans and Coastal Cities
34	Bangkok, 2013	International Forum on Sustainable Governance of the Ocean

Pacem in Maribus as a Driver for UNCLOS

The idea of peace at sea (*Pacem in Maribus*) and the first Conferences became the main driver for the adoption of UNCLOS. In December 1968, the UN General Assembly (UNGA) expanded its Seabed Committee to 42 members, making it a standing committee under the name 'Committee on the Peaceful Uses of the Seabed and the Ocean Floor beyond the Limits of National Jurisdiction'.[3] Three months later the UN Secretary-General U. Thant wrote to Robert H. Hutchins, President of the Center for the Study of Democratic Institutions at the University of California Santa Barbara (UCSB) proposing the first *Pacem in Maribus* (PIM) meeting in Malta. The meeting was chaired by H.S. (Shirley) Amerasinghe of Sri Lanka, who took an active role chairing many early PIMs and who would be later elected President of the UNCLOS III in 1973. Amerasinghe was the most prominent individual at the first PIM, being one of more than 260 participants from industry, science, government and academia. Forging strong personal relationships was the key for negotiating success and the influence of those who participated in the first or subsequent PIM meetings was significant. Many of those individuals who contributed to PIM advocated for the adoption of UNCLOS III itself.

Elisabeth Mann Borgese, who worked at Hutchins' centre, led the organizational work for the February, May and June 1968 planning meetings, leading up to PIM I in 1970. In May 1969 she travelled to Washington and New York, meeting with Senator Claiborne Pell, Professor Louis Henkin, the Indian and Yugoslav Ambassadors to the UN and to Washington and others.[4] Senator Pell confirmed to Borgese that the American government was encouraging the scientific cooperation during the international ocean decade in order to get away from the remaining legal and political questions before the adoption of the regime. As the Soviet Union was gradually taking refuge in the disarmament issues, Pell suggested that there might be a possibility for the developing and non-aligned nations to fill this vacuum and to give cohesion and meaning to the Russian and the American efforts, which, if left isolated, would go nowhere. After talking to Pell and his staff, Borgese discussed the problems and the opportunities with the Indian and Yugoslav Ambassadors to the UN and to Washington and both of them made clear that Yugoslavia and India would be willing to become more pro-active in negotiating and adopting the UNCLOS, and Borgese suggested that a few key people from the Third World be brought together for the Preparatory Conference.[5] Besides India and Yugoslavia, these might include Ceylon (Mr Amerasinghe), Tanzania or Ghana, Jamaica

3 See R.-J. Dupuy and D. Vignes, *A Handbook on the New Law of the Sea* (Dordrecht: Nijhoff, 1991), 169–70.

4 Elisabeth Mann Borgese, *Pacem in Maribus* (New York: Dood and Mead, 1973).

5 Ibid. See also her book *The Drama of the Oceans* (New York: Harry N. Abrams, 1975); her lecture 'Complexities of a Sea Change' (1976); for a comprehensive historical account see also Aldo Chircop, Scott Coffen-Smout and Moira McConnel (eds), *Ocean Yearbook* 26 (The Hague: Martinus Nijhoff, 2012).

(Mr Richardson) and Sweden. The Preparatory Conference on the continental shelf and on the legal framework consisted of a total of about 20 participants, who were invited by Senator Pell to meet at the Institute for the Law of the Seas of the University of Rhode Island in February 1968. Senator Pell, chairing the Senate Foreign Relations Committee, invited Borgese to testify in July 1969 on the draft Ocean Space Treaty that he had introduced in the 90th Congress in March 1968,[6] and her testimony revealed a strong interest in moving towards functional jurisdiction and away from the distinct regime of terrestrial property law to one of non-territorial ocean areas beyond national jurisdiction.[7] She argued that the real obstacle was the legal tradition and the mentality of the oil and mining industries that are very land-oriented and based on the law of the land. The law of the land is rooted in concepts of inalienable ownership – as Borgese reported to the Senate Foreign Relations Committee – whether this be private or state ownership, but 'there is a function non-territorial area beyond the limits of national jurisdiction in the strict sense, in which area laws are made which are neither strictly national nor strictly international'.[8] Contrasting the law of the land with the law of the seas was a theme repeated in many of Borgese's lectures.[9] She also further developed the theme of functional as opposed to geographic sovereignty and regulation, writing that the 'structure of the constitution is defined by the function of regulating pollution, conservation, planning, not by the geographic area to which it is applied. The function is generalizable. The definition of the area is not'.[10]

Supplementing the three planning sessions in Rhode Island and Santa Barbara, five separate Preparatory Conferences were held in 1970: on Arms Control and Disarmament; on the Legal Framework for an Ocean Regime and the Continental Shelf and Limits of National Jurisdiction; on Planning and Development; on the Role of Enterprises in an Ocean Regime; and on Ecology and the Role of Science and Scientists in an Ocean Regime. The third conference on Planning and Development was carried out jointly by Borgese's Centre and the United Nations Institute for Training and Research (UNITAR) and considered to be a success particularly with respect to the involvement of the UN in the process, and as a source of new ideas and approaches.[11] The participants were a mix of

6 Senator Pell, Senate Res. 263, U.S. 90th Congress, 2d Sess., 114 Cong. Rec. 5181. Borgese testified before the same committee again in 1976 at Pell's invitation, Cong. Rec., Senate S 18140 October 26.

7 Statement of E.M. Borgese Before the Senate Committee on Foreign Relations, July 1969, Relating to S. Res. 33, a Resolution to Define and promote an International Regime for the Peaceful Uses of Ocean Space beyond the Limits of National Jurisdiction, EMB fonds, MS-2-744, Folder 177.6.

8 Ibid.

9 'The Ocean Regime', a lecture to the Association of International Law and International Relations, Bucharest [1969], EMB fonds MSS-2-744, Folder 147.7, 3ff.

10 Borgese, 'The World Communities', *The Center Magazine*, 1971, 12.

11 Wolfgang G. Vitzthum, Memorandum to Senior Fellows, 6 March 1970, EMB fonds MSS-2.744, Folder 183.12, 1, identifies participants from the UN Michael Hardy,

scientists, diplomats and UN officials: Aaron Danzig; Paul Fye, oceanographer and President of Woods Hole; Frank LaQue, metallurgist and retired Vice President of International Nickel Company Inc.; Arvid Pardo; Duke Pollard, Permanent Mission of Guyana to the UN; C.V. Ranganathan, Permanent Mission of India to the UN; Ambassador E.R. Richardson, Embassy of Jamaica to the United States; Louis Sohn; Warren Wooster, Scripps Institution of Oceanography, La Jolla; Vladimir Pavicevic, Yugoslav Foreign Affairs Ministry.

Borgese generated significant support for the ocean projects, also lecturing to outside audiences and promoting her ideas abroad. She continued to lecture and arrange relevant meetings at her Center.[12] These included a February 1971 meeting to consider new and revised draft treaty proposals beyond those discussed at the 1968 planning meeting.[13] Her lecture, 'The Ocean Regime', in January 1969 emphasized that whatever organization ended up embodying the ocean regime,[14] it could not be the United Nations, which is not suited for tasks like those assigned to the Regime, rather it should be an organization independent from the United Nations—like the World Bank or the IAEA—yet it must be in some way connected with it: it must emanate from it; it must be legitimatized by it. The regime would not become a 'super state ... More likely it is going to be a flexible system of cooperative world communities'.[15] This vision for a full-fledged international organization for the oceans, akin to the World Bank or the IAEA, never got off the ground. Borgese therefore presented a modified version of the model at the first PIM meeting using 'The Ocean Regime' as a discussion document, but by organizing certain PIM breakout sessions on the model. Her idea of creating a new oceans organization gained no traction in the UNCLOS III process itself and was not a model adopted by the 1982 UN Convention on the Law of the Sea.[16]

Wolfgang Graf Vitzthum, writing about his spring 1970 meetings on behalf of the Center to promote PIM in New York, Princeton and Washington, reported:

Jean Pierre Levy, Oscar Schachter (UNITAR Deputy Executive Director), Reginald Smith and Ralph Townley.

12 See Center Memos, EMB fonds, MS-2-744, Folder 37.18: (1) EMB Memo – Center Dialogue 26 January 1970, attached: two unpublished pieces by EMB, 'The Ocean Franchise' and 'Arms and the Ocean Bed'; (2) EMB Memo – Center Dialogue 13 October 1971, Yugoslav Constitutional Law as a Model for World Law and The Law of the Seas; (3) Center Dialogue 15 October 1971, Draft Ocean space Treaty for discussion with EMB and AP [Arvid Pardo], attached is Malta's draft submitted to the General Assembly, UN Doc. A/AC.138/53, 23 August 1971.

13 EMB, Memo to participants in the Dialogue, 4 February 1971, 'Proposed Agenda Monday Feb 8–Wed 10, 1971', EMB fonds, MS-2-744, Folder 122.22

14 'Speeches and Articles by Elisabeth Mann Borgese, 1970–1973', *CAMC Collection*, 43, https://gustavus.edu/library/archives/college/manuscripts/CAMC0043.php. Borgese was invited to deliver *The Ocean Regime* to the House of Lords.

15 Ibid., 19.

16 R.B. Levering and M.L. Levering, *Citizen Action for Global Change: The Neptune Group and Law of the Sea* (Syracuse: Syracuse University Press, 1999).

> the Centre seems to be one of the few institutions remaining active in oceans. Thus, many people were looking at us and the *Pacem in Maribus* project as the arena for the development of new ideas, or, at least, for an effort to think things through. One of the advantages of our work … seems to be, at least from the view of people on Capitol Hill, that we have so many non-Americans involved in the project.[17]

Shigeru Oda observed that PIM I 'did not produce any particularly remarkable conclusion', yet allowed for 'extensive discussions' of President Nixon's May 1970 statement regarding support for a treaty establishing a regime for seabed resources.[18]

Two years after PIM I, in 1972, the PIM board established the International Ocean Institute (IOI) in cooperation with the United Nations Development Programme (UNDP) and the government and the University of Malta. This initiative enjoyed the support of the Mediterranean members of the Seabed Committee, meeting in Malta separately from any PIM convocation. The statute of the international organization states that IOI's purpose is 'to promote research on the peaceful uses of ocean space and its resources, including the regulation of such uses'. In its formative years, the IOI focused on a four-pronged programme of research, the *Pacem in Maribus* convocations, publication of the *Ocean Yearbook*, and training, all of which have continued to this day. Once established, IOI convened all future PIM meetings and pursued other research projects, some strategically chosen for relevance to the ongoing negotiations at UNCLOS III. The IOI in its first years concentrated mainly on further development of various Mediterranean projects and its Planning Council became responsible for four projects a year, which are elaborated in three regional conferences a year in different parts of the world, plus one *Pacem in Maribus* convocation in Malta. This kept up the levels of interest for several years, paving the way for UNCLOS, maximizing the possibilities of direct input and influence with regard to various governments.

By September 1972, IOI had consultative status both with the Food and Agriculture Organization (FAO) and the United Nations Environment Programme (UNEP), and later would acquire such with UNCLOS too. Its function was twofold: to supply documentation and information and to be useful to the smaller nations, especially those of Africa and Asia who do not have the staff and the documentation they need in the development of their maritime policy. In 1972, IOI participated in the landmark UN Conference on the Human Environment, represented among others by Sidney Holt, who would later become IOI Director. In 1974, IOI obtained observer status for the first substantive session of UNCLOS III in Caracas. IOI Board Members who participated actively in UNCLOS III included Amerasinghe, who served as Chair of the Board, and Jens Evensen, who

17 Vitzthum, Memorandum to Senior Fellows, Folder 183.12, 2.

18 Shigeru Oda, *Fifty Years of Law of the Sea* (The Hague: Martinus Nijhoff, 2003), 372.

was an original IOI Board Member, but later resigned in 1975, feeling that his position as Norwegian Cabinet Minister was incompatible with his role at the IOI.

Defining Peace at Sea

'Peace' has been traditionally defined in military and security terms. The word 'peace', or the expressions 'peaceful purpose' or 'peaceful use', are mentioned many times in UNCLOS, and not only in Article 301, prohibiting the threat or use of force. For example Article 88 of UNCLOS states that the high seas are reserved for peaceful purposes, Articles 138 and 141 demand that the use of the Area is exclusively for peaceful purposes, Article 19 determines that passage in the territorial sea which is prejudicial to the peace is inconsistent with the Convention and coastal states may respond accordingly, and Article 240 *urges* that marine scientific research is to be carried out exclusively for peaceful purposes.

Article 301 is of a paramount importance and it reads very similar to Article 2/4 of the UN Charter, urging States exercising their rights and performing their duties under the Convention, to refrain from any threat or use of force against the territorial integrity or political independence of any State, or in any other manner inconsistent with the principles of the Charter of the United Nations.

Peaceful use of the sea under the UNCLOS regime is also specifically listed in Article 279 dealing with safe passage, marine research and the obligation to settle disputes peacefully. Finally, Part XV of UNCLOS is one of the most elaborate mechanisms on dispute settlement ever codified in any international treaty.

UN Initiatives Promoting a Peaceful and Sustainable Use of the Oceans

The initiatives taken by the United Nations regarding the use of the oceans do not all relate specifically to the peaceful use of the sea, but may nevertheless be of interest to this book. First, the UN declared the year 1998 to be the International Year of the Oceans. This designation provided individual organizations and governments with an important opportunity to raise public awareness and understanding of the ocean and related issues. Many activities also took place at the individual state level.

Second, in 1999, the UN put in place an online Atlas of the Oceans,[19] an inter-agency initiative led by the FAO, which presents itself as 'an Internet portal providing information relevant to the sustainable development of the oceans. It is designed for policy-makers who need to become familiar with ocean issues and for scientists, students and resource managers who need access to databases and approaches to sustainability'.

19 Atlas of the Oceans, http://www.oceansatlas.org.

Third, in 2006, the UNGA adopted the Resolution A/RES/60/30 on the oceans and the law of the sea,[20] reaffirming its support for UNCLOS, encouraging UN Member States to make every effort to implement it better, and enjoining them to do more to protect the oceans. This is but one of several UNGA resolutions regarding the maritime sphere. Fourth, as a result of a UNGA resolution passed in December 2008, the UN officially recognized the 8th of June as 'World Oceans Day', which was celebrated from 2009 onwards. The concept of a World Oceans Day was first proposed in 1992 by the government of Canada at the Earth Summit in Rio de Janeiro, Brazil, and it had been unofficially celebrated every year thereafter. Since 2002, the Ocean Project and the World Ocean Network have helped promote and coordinate World Oceans Day celebrations worldwide by supporting events organized by aquariums, zoos, museums, conservation organizations, universities, schools and businesses. Every year, an increasing number of countries and organizations have been using World Oceans Day as an opportunity to celebrate the world's oceans and our personal connection to the sea. Secretary-General Ban Ki-moon marked the first official World Oceans Day of 2009 with the following words: 'The first observance of World Oceans Day allows us to highlight the many ways in which oceans contribute to society. It is also an opportunity to recognize the considerable challenges we face in maintaining their capacity to regulate the global climate, supply essential ecosystem services and provide sustainable livelihoods and safe recreation.'[21]

Fifth, the Rio+20 summit of 2012 was held under the theme 'The Future We Want: Summit on Sustainable Development' and included many recommendations relating to the oceans and seas, especially with regard to their sustainable use. Finally, within two months of the Rio+20 summit, Ban Ki-moon launched a major initiative, his comprehensive Ocean Compact,[22] first announced on 12 August 2012 at the Yeosu International Conference (South Korea) that commemorated the 30th anniversary of UNCLOS. According to Ban Ki-moon, 'the Ocean impact sets out a strategic vision for the UN System to deliver more coherently and effectively on its oceans-related mandates, consistent with the Rio+20 outcome. It provides a platform for all stakeholders to collaborate towards achieving "Healthy Oceans for Prosperity"'.[23] Its aim is thus to strengthen the UN system-wide coherence in delivering on its oceans-related mandates, and it is expected to build upon the range of existing and ongoing activities of UN organizations to assist Member States to implement UNCLOS and other relevant global and regional conventions.

---

20 See Resolution A/RES/60/30, http://oceansbeyondpiracy.org/sites/default/files/un_general_assembly_resolution_60-30.pdf.

21 Ban Ki-moon, 'Message on World Oceans Day', 2008, http://www.un.org/News/Press/docs/2009/sgsm12289.doc.htm.

22 United Nations, Ocean Compact, http://www.un.org/depts/los/ocean_compact/oceans_compact.htm.

23 Ibid.

UN Organs Involved in Work on the Maritime Sphere

As mentioned earlier, there are several UN agencies whose work touches the maritime domain. The following two organs, however, are entirely focused on it. The first is UN Oceans,[24] which can best be described as an inter-agency coordination mechanism on ocean and coastal issues within the UN system. Its mission is to enhance cooperation and coordination among secretariats of the international organizations and bodies concerned with ocean-related activities. The United Nations University has been listed as a potential future member. UN Oceans holds regular meetings, whose minutes are published online at www.unoceans.org/Documents.htm.

The second oceans-focused organ of the UN is the Division for Ocean Affairs and Law of the Sea (UN-DOALOS) of the Office of Legal Affairs. It has been consistently recognized for its important contribution to the wider acceptance of UNCLOS, and for its work towards a rational and consistent application of the Convention. Its mandate, as spelled out by the UNGA and in the UN Secretary-General's Bulletin, is to carry out the responsibilities of the Convention and fulfil the functions associated with its entry into force.

Threats to the Peaceful Use of the Seas

In his first World Oceans Day statement, the UN Secretary-General Ban Ki-moon identified three criminal activities that pose a threat to peace and security on the oceans.[25] These are piracy and armed robbery (notably in terms of their effect on UN international law); smuggling of illegal drugs; and trafficking of persons. Other threats include nuclear tests and incidents connected to inter-state territorial disputes. Of those threats, the UN has in recent years placed a particular focus on piracy. The UNGA has addressed the issue in many resolutions in the last decade, and also more recently piracy has been addressed by the Security Council in several thematic discussions, leading to resolutions.[26]

Conclusion

The idea of the peaceful use of the sea, *Pacem in Maribus* (PIM), has laid a solid foundation for the development of the law of the sea, leading to UNCLOS. In fact one may argue that UNCLOS would have been impossible without the excellent work that the PIM Conferences have done since 1970. Committed, energetic

24 See UN Oceans, http://www.unoceans.org.

25 Ban Ki-moon, 'Message on World Oceans Day'.

26 See Peter Lehr, 'Security Council Resolutions on Somali Piracy', in V. Popovski and T. Fraser, eds, *The Security Council as Global Legislator* (London: Routledge, 2014).

individuals, such as US Senator Pell, Robert H. Hutchins, Elisabeth Mann Borgese, H.S. (Shirley) Amerasinghe of Sri Lanka and others contributed their tireless efforts to persuade governments and international organizations to support the work leading to the adoption of the Convention. The International Ocean Institute has become the initial secretariat for the Conference on the law of the sea whereas the PIM Conferences provided the platform for continuous dialogue where challenges of the law of the sea could be debated in detail. All this work played a crucial role in the formulation and promotion of principles and rules codified in UNCLOS.

The peaceful use of the sea is represented throughout the UNCLOS regime and specifically listed in many of the articles of the Convention – such as non-use of force, safe passage, marine research, obligation to settle disputes peacefully. Many UN initiatives were adopted to promote the peaceful and sustainable use of the oceans, such as declaring the year 1998 as the International Year of the Oceans to raise public awareness and understanding of the ocean and related issues. The Atlas of the Oceans is another strong inter-agency initiative led by the FAO – a rich portal providing latest updated information on the sustainable development of the oceans, designed for both policy-makers, for scientists and resource managers who need access to databases and approaches to sustainability.

The chapter also addresses the UN organs that have been created, such as UN Oceans – an inter-agency coordination mechanism on ocean and coastal issues to enhance cooperation and coordination among secretariats of the international organizations and bodies concerned with ocean-related activities. The Division for Ocean Affairs and Law of the Sea (UN-DOALOS) of the Office of Legal Affairs has been consistently recognized for its important contribution to the rational and consistent application of the Convention.

References

Borgese, Elisabeth Mann, Statement Before the Senate Committee on Foreign Relations, July 1969, Relating to S. Res. 33, a Resolution to Define and promote an International Regime for the Peaceful Uses of Ocean Space beyond the Limits of National Jurisdiction, EMB fonds, MS-2-744, Folder 177.6.

Borgese, Elisabeth Mann, 'The World Communities', *The Center Magazine*, 1971, 12.

Borgese, Elisabeth Mann, *Pacem in Maribus* (New York: Dood and Mead, 1973).

Borgese, Elisabeth Mann, *The Drama of the Oceans* (New York: Harry N. Abrams, 1975).

Chircop, Aldo, Scott Coffen-Smout, and McConnel, Moira (eds), *Ocean Yearbook* 26 (The Hague: Martinus Nijhoff, 2012).

Dupuy, R.-J. and Vignes, D., *A Handbook on the New Law of the Sea* (Dordrecht: Nijhoff, 1991), 169–70.

Ki-moon, Ban, 'Message on World Oceans Day', 2008, available at: http://www.un.org/News/Press/docs/2009/sgsm12289.doc.htm.

Lehr, Peter, 'Security Council Resolutions on Somali Piracy', in V. Popovski and T. Fraser (eds), *The Security Council as Global Legislator* (London: Routledge, 2014).

Levering, R.B. and Levering, M.L., *Citizen Action for Global Change: The Neptune Group and Law of the Sea* (Syracuse: Syracuse University Press, 1999).

Oda, Shigeru, *Fifty Years of Law of the Sea* (The Hague: Martinus Nijhoff, 2003).

Pell, Senate Res. 263, U.S. 90th Congress, 2d Sess., 114 Cong. Rec. 5181.

Resolution A/RES/60/30, http://oceansbeyondpiracy.org/sites/default/files/un_general_assembly_resolution_60-30.pdf.

Vitzthum, Wolfgang G., *Memorandum to Senior Fellows*, 6 March 1970.

Chapter 6

Marine Scientific Research and Military Survey: Law and State Practice

Stuart Kaye

Introduction

Although the United Nations Convention on the Law of the Sea[1] broke new ground with the inclusion of Part XIII dealing with marine scientific research, it has not prevented continuing contention between States. One matter in contention is whether Part XIII was intended to completely deal with matters pertaining to marine scientific research, or whether it did not encompass activities undertaken from warships, described by some as military survey. This chapter considers the arguments for and against the existence of military survey as a matter distinct from marine scientific research, as well as State practice.

Applicable Law

Part XIII of the Law of the Sea Convention regulates marine scientific research. Article 240 provides four basic principles by which marine scientific research should be conducted:

> In the conduct of marine scientific research the following principles shall apply:
>
> a. marine scientific research shall be conducted exclusively for peaceful purposes;
> b. marine scientific research shall be conducted with appropriate scientific methods and means compatible with this Convention;
> c. marine scientific research shall not unjustifiably interfere with other legitimate uses of the sea compatible with this Convention and shall be duly respected in the course of such uses;
> d. marine scientific research shall be conducted in compliance with all relevant regulations adopted in conformity with this Convention including those for the protection and preservation of the marine environment.

In addition, it provides positive obligations to cooperate with respect to the conduct and dissemination of marine scientific research, and sets up regulatory framework

1 United Nations Convention on the Law of the Sea, 10 December 1982, 1833 UNTS 3.

for coastal States to deal with marine scientific research in the territorial sea and exclusive economic zone (EEZ). In the former case, the coastal State's discretion with respect to marine scientific research is unfettered, and may only be conducted with its consent.[2] In the latter case, the coastal State may regulate the research,[3] and be informed of the results,[4] although there may be circumstances when it cannot unjustifiably refuse the right to research.[5] The coastal State also set stringent conditions on the conduct of marine scientific research:

1. States and competent international organizations when undertaking marine scientific research in the exclusive economic zone or on the continental shelf of a coastal State shall comply with the following conditions:

   a. ensure the right of the coastal State, if it so desires, to participate or be represented in the marine scientific research project, especially on board research vessels and other craft or scientific research installations, when practicable, without payment of any remuneration to the scientists of the coastal State and without obligation to contribute towards the costs of the project;
   b. provide the coastal State, at its request, with preliminary reports, as soon as practicable, and with the final results and conclusions after the completion of the research;
   c. undertake to provide access for the coastal State, at its request, to all data and samples derived from the marine scientific research project and likewise to furnish it with data which may be copied and samples which may be divided without detriment to their scientific value;
   d. if requested, provide the coastal State with an assessment of such data, samples and research results or provide assistance in their assessment or interpretation;
   e. ensure, subject to paragraph 2, that the research results are made internationally available through appropriate national or international channels, as soon as practicable;
   f. inform the coastal State immediately of any major change in the research programme;
   g. unless otherwise agreed, remove the scientific research installations or equipment once the research is completed.[6]

2 Law of the Sea Convention, Article 245.
3 Ibid., Article 246.
4 Ibid., Article 248.
5 Ibid., Article 246(3) and Article 252.
6 Ibid., Article 249(1).

If the conditions listed above are not complied with, then the coastal State may require the suspension or cessation of the marine scientific research activities.[7]

There are a number of elements in the Law of the Sea Convention's dealing with marine scientific research that distinguish it from what is asserted to be military survey. Firstly, Article 240 provides that marine scientific research be conducted for purely peaceful purposes. It is possible to envisage a situation where military survey data is collected in preparation of an armed attack. Leaving aside whether an attack might be lawful at international law, and the United Nations Charter does permit the use of force in certain circumstances, the collection of data outside of such circumstances would be inconsistent with the principle enunciated in Article 240.

Regardless of the purpose for which military survey data is collected, Article 249 imposes a range of obligations on the flag State of a vessel conducting marine scientific research in the EEZ of a coastal State which would seem inconsistent with military survey, including a right to have a presence on the vessel during the scientific research, and access to the data post-collection. It would seem unlikely that such access would be granted by the flag State of a vessel undertaking what would fall under the term military survey.[8]

---

7 Ibid., Article 253.

8 Article 249 of the Law of the Sea Convention provides:

1. States and competent international organizations when undertaking marine scientific research in the exclusive economic zone or on the continental shelf of a coastal State shall comply with the following conditions:

> (a) ensure the right of the coastal State, if it so desires, to participate or be represented in the marine scientific research project, especially on board research vessels and other craft or scientific research installations, when practicable, without payment of any remuneration to the scientists of the coastal State and without obligation to contribute towards the costs of the project;
> (b) provide the coastal State, at its request, with preliminary reports, as soon as practicable, and with the final results and conclusions after the completion of the research;
> (c) undertake to provide access for the coastal State, at its request, to all data and samples derived from the marine scientific research project and likewise to furnish it with data which may be copied and samples which may be divided without detriment to their scientific value;
> (d) if requested, provide the coastal State with an assessment of such data, samples and research results or provide assistance in their assessment or interpretation;
> (e) ensure, subject to paragraph 2, that the research results are made internationally available through appropriate national or international channels, as soon as practicable;
> (f) inform the coastal State immediately of any major change in the research programme;
> (g) unless otherwise agreed, remove the scientific research installations or equipment once the research is completed.

State Practice

Historically, some incidents involving warships or government vessels engaging in what have been described as oceanographic research or military survey have occurred. In 1968, Brazil seized the Soviet vessel *Kegostrov*. *Kegostrov* was engaged in intelligence collection some two nautical miles off the coast of Brazil when seized. The ship was engaged in satellite tracking activities, which was explained as necessary by the Soviets as the vessel 'had lost its way'. After 20 days and a Russian apology to Brazil, the vessel was released.[9]

Also in 1968, the USS *Pueblo* was seized by North Korea. *Pueblo* had, it was originally claimed by the United States, been engaged in marine scientific research, and was carrying two civilian hydrographers aboard. Under the terms of the armistice at the end of the Korean War, warships of combatants undertook not to enter the territorial seas of North or South Korea, or to hover outside. In 1968, North Korea claimed a 12 nautical mile territorial sea, and a security zone outside the territorial sea.[10] The United States claimed *Pueblo* was seized 15 nautical miles off the coast, while the North Koreans claimed it was seized 7.1 miles off the coast. In either case, the vessel appears to have been loitering in breach of the armistice provisions. It was subsequently shown that *Pueblo* possessed sophisticated electronic monitoring equipment designed to gather intelligence and declassified material from the United States National Security Agency confirms that this was the case.[11] The crew of USS *Pueblo* were interred for 11 months before being released to the United States, although the ship itself was retained by North Korea and remains moored as a museum in Pyongyang.[12]

Some maritime powers have sought to avoid the application of Part XIII to their warships by distinguishing marine scientific research from military activities. The United States has sought in its *Annotated Supplement to the Commander's Handbook on the Law of Naval Operations* to differentiate between marine scientific research and 'military survey'.[13] This distinction is important, as the reporting obligations in Part XIII would generally not be consistent with military activities. A similar attitude is taken by the United Kingdom. When challenged by

9 See M. Gorina-Ysern, *An International Regime for Marine Scientific Research* (Ardsley Park: Transnational, 2003), 240–41; J.A. Knaus, 'Development of the Freedom of Scientific Research Issue of the Third United Nations Conference on the Law of the Sea', *Ocean Development and International Law* 1 (1973): 93 at 95.

10 Gorina-Ysern, *Marine Scientific Research*, 242–4.

11 'USS Pueblo', accessed 1 October 2013, http://www.nsa.gov/public_info/_files/uss_pueblo/USS_Pueblo_AGER-2_Background_Information.pdf.

12 'North Korea's Hottest Tourist Attraction', accessed 1 October 2013, http://www.mercurynews.com/ci_23744043/north-koreas-hottest-tourist-attraction-60-year-old.

13 US Naval War College, 'Annotated Supplement to the Commander's Handbook on the Law of Naval Operations', *International Law Studies* 73 (1999): paras 2.4.2.1–2.4.2.2.

India in January 2001 while in the Indian EEZ 190 nautical miles off Diu, HMS *Scott* responded that it was engaged in military survey and did not depart the area.[14]

The US attitude appears to be that oceanographic or other research undertaken in a military context, regardless of its nature or security level, should be treated as 'military survey' and therefore be exempt from the rigours of the marine scientific research regime. While such activities have traditionally included hydrographic survey, data collected by the United States has typically been quite wide ranging, including data on ocean currents, temperature and life forms.

A number of States refuse to recognize 'military survey' as a valid activity that can be undertaken in the EEZ. Both India and China have objected to such survey activity by the United States and United Kingdom. Both States have confronted USNS *Bowditch* while it has been engaged in survey operations in 2001, with *Bowditch* reported by China as having been compelled to leave the Chinese EEZ in the Yellow Sea.[15] Similarly, in March 2009, USNS *Impeccable* was harassed over a number of days by a variety of Chinese ships and aircraft. *Impeccable* was surrounded by fishing craft and unable to manoeuvre and at one point turned its fire hose on a Chinese vessel in an attempt to clear a way forward. *Impeccable* was navigating in the Chinese EEZ, and its presence there was protested by the Chinese Government as being unlawful.[16]

The most serious recent incident occurred on 1 April 2001, with a mid-air collision between a Chinese F-8-II 'Finback' fighter and an American EP-3E Aries aircraft, off the southern coast of China. The Chinese fighter crashed into the sea, resulting in the loss of its pilot, Wang Wei, and the American EP-3E was severely damaged, and ultimately made an emergency landing at Lingshui airfield on Hainan Island in China. The aircrew of the American aircraft were arrested, and the incident sparked a diplomatic crisis. Thirteen days later the aircrew were released, as was the aircraft in June 2001, when it was airlifted from China by a leased Russian Antonov cargo aircraft.[17]

The collision followed a series of close passes and shadowing of American EP-3Es by Chinese fighters. The fighters were attempting to deter the American

---

14 See G.V. Galdorisi and A.G. Kaufman, 'Military Activities in the Exclusive Economic Zone: Preventing Uncertainty and Defusing Conflict', *California Western International Law Journal* 32 (2002): 253.

15 P. Pedrozo, 'The US-China Incidents at Sea Agreement: A Recipe for Disaster', *Journal of National Security Law and Policy* 6 (2012): 207.

16 J.G. Odom, 'The True "Lies" of the Impeccable Incident: What Really Happened, Who Disregarded International Law, and Why Every Nation (Outside of China) should be Concerned', 18 *Michigan State Journal of International Law* 18 (2010): 411; R. Pedrozo, 'Close Encounters at Sea: The USNS Impeccable Incident', *Naval War College Review* 60 (2009): 101.

17 The incident is described in S.D. Murphy (ed.), 'Contemporary Practice of the United States Relating to International Law', *American Yearbook of International Law* 95 (2001): 626; see also Galdorisi and Kaufmann, 'Military Activities', 292–4; see also 'Hainan', accessed 1 October 2013, http://home.wxs.nl/~p3orion/hainan.html.

aircraft from passing close to the Chinese coast, and utilize the EP-3E's highly sophisticated intelligence gathering capabilities. China regarded the flights as essentially 'spy flights' and considered them contrary to international law. The US attitude was that the aircraft were in international airspace, and therefore were exercising their freedom of overflight in international law. Both States had been in dispute over similar flights for a considerable period of time prior to this incident, with it being the regular practice of Chinese fighter pilots to fly at extremely close range to American planes, ostensibly to deter them from continuing. Several near misses had occurred during earlier flights prior to the collision in this incident.

The collision between the US and Chinese aircraft occurred in international airspace as recognized by both States.[18] It also took place outside a 24 nautical mile security zone claimed by China, but not recognized by the United States.[19] While the EP-3E ultimately did enter Chinese national airspace, and landed on Chinese territory, it was also not disputed by both States that this incursion was motivated entirely by the distress the aircraft was in as a result of the collision. The key issue in this context relates to the activities undertaken by the aircraft prior to the collision.

The Chinese objection to the flights centred on their purpose. China considered the activities as being overt intelligence gathering by another military power, which were designed to provide detailed information that could be used in any conflict. Such activities therefore, according to China, undermined international peace and security of the EEZ, and therefore were not lawful.[20] The Chinese Foreign Affairs Ministry stated:

---

18 China has proclaimed territorial sea baselines, which the United States has protested. The incident occurred more than 12 nautical miles from the Chinese baselines, so that its occurrence in international airspace was not in dispute. The baselines were proclaimed in 1996: *Declaration of the Government of the People's Republic of China on the baselines of the territorial sea, 15 May 1996*, accessed 1 October 2013, http://www.un.org/Depts/los/. LEGISLATIONANDTREATIES/PDFFILES/CHN_1996_Declaration.pdf. The American protest is cited in Naval War College, *Annotated Supplement to the Commander's Handbook on the Law of Naval Operations* (Newport: Naval War College, 1997), 1–77.

19 Article 13 of the *Law of the Territorial Sea and the Contiguous Zone of 25 February 1992* provides that the Chinese exercise jurisdiction over security within the contiguous zone. This is rejected by the United States as inconsistent with Article 33 of the Law of the Sea Convention, which has no reference to a security jurisdiction in respect of the contiguous zone. The 1992 US protest is cited in Naval War College, 'Commander's Handbook', para. 1.90.

20 A statement from the Chinese Embassy in Washington, DC noted: 'The surveillance flight conducted by the US aircraft overran the scope of "free overflight" according to international law. The move also violated the United Nations Convention on the Law of the Sea, which stipulates that any flight in airspace above another nation's exclusive economic zone should respect the rights of the country concerned. Thus, the US plane's actions posed a threat to the national security of China.' Reproduced at 'Surveillance', accessed 1 October 2013, http://www.chinaembassy.org/eng/9585.html.

> The act of the U.S. side constitutes a violation of the UN Convention on the Law of the Sea (UNCLOS), which provides, among other things, that the sovereign rights and jurisdiction of a coastal State over its Exclusive Economic Zone, particularly its right to maintain peace, security and good order in the waters of the Zone, shall all be respected and that a country shall conform to the UNCLOS and other rules of international law when exercising its freedom of the high seas.[21]

For China, the collision that subsequently occurred was as a result of an unlawful and unwanted activity, that the Chinese aircraft, like others before it, was doing its best to intimidate and deter without the use of force. The US view was that any activity that occurs in international airspace should be treated as legal, unless it involves hostilities against another friendly power. The use of passive systems to collect information from an area not subject to national jurisdiction is therefore entirely legitimate. The actions by the Chinese pilots in flying at close range to American aircraft in international airspace were reckless, and endangered their lives as well as those in the EP-3E's, as was tragically demonstrated on 1 April 2001.

In 2002, following the *Bowditch* and Aries incidents, China promulgated the Mapping and Survey Law of the People's Republic of China.[22] Article 2 of this law provides that all surveying and mapping activities taking place in China's territorial sea and national airspace are subject to the law's operation, as well as 'other sea areas under its jurisdiction'. This is reaffirmed in Article 7 which in part provides:

> Foreign organizations or individuals that wish to conduct surveying and mapping in the territorial air, land or waters, as well as other sea areas under the jurisdiction of the People's Republic of China shall be subject to approval by the administrative department for surveying and mapping under the State Council and the competent department for surveying and mapping of the army, and they shall observe the provisions of relevant laws and administrative rules and regulations of the People's Republic of China.

Article 7 continues by noting that survey activity must be conducted in concert with appropriate agencies and departments within the Chinese Government and that any mapping that takes place may not involve State secrets or endanger

21 'Chinese Ministry of Affairs Press Release', 3 April 2001, accessed 1 October 2013, http://www.fmprc.gov.cn/eng/9607.html.

22 'Survey and Mapping Law of the People's Republic of China', 29 August 2002, Presidential Order No. 75, accessed 1 October 2013, http://en.sbsm.gov.cn/article//LawsandRules/Laws/200710/20071000003241.shtml.

State security. This would provide a basis in Chinese domestic law to object to military survey.[23]

Specific legislation dealing with marine scientific research and hydrographic survey, like that implemented by China, is relatively unusual. Attitudes of States with respect to military survey can best be inferred from attitudes to freedom of navigation and its application to warships. If a State objects to the presence of a warship without prior authorization in its contiguous zone, then it would seem most likely that State would object to the legitimacy of military survey. Appendix 1 provides a summary of States who have such objections, and the list is not an insubstantial one, including, among others, China, Brazil and India.

Analysis

It is clear there are different interpretations favoured by States on the question of whether marine scientific research includes activities undertaken from military hydrographic and other similar vessels, or whether military survey exists as a distinct area of activity, that is unregulated under the United Nations Convention on the Law of the Sea. This is in part because the Convention does not clearly address its application to warships in all circumstances and is silent on the continued application of the law of naval warfare. This has permitted a range of interpretations to be canvassed, from the continued uninterrupted application to the law of naval warfare and rights of warships in peace time, to the complete displacement of these rules by the United Nations Convention on the Law of the

23 The tension between the United States and China over military survey and activities of United States military vessels and aircraft in the Chinese EEZ has led to calls for the conclusion by the United States and China of a similar agreement to the INCSEA agreement between the US Navy and the then Soviet Navy with respect to the avoidance of dangerous incidents at sea. There are a number of reasons why such calls are misplaced. See Agreement Between the Government of The United States of America and the Government of The Union of Soviet Socialist Republics on the Prevention of Incidents On and Over the High Seas, 25 May 1972, accessed 1 October 2013, http://www.state.gov/t/isn/4791.htm. First, one interesting point to note is that in both the cases of the incidents involving USNS *Bowditch* and USNS *Impeccable*, although these incidents led to diplomatic exchanges between the United States and China about the legality of the actions, most of the vessels and aircraft involved from the Chinese side were not military. The vessels were typically fishing vessels, apparently crewed by Chinese civilians. INCSEA was concluded between two navies, and a similar agreement would serve little purpose as the PLAN does not appear to have taken any significant role in either of these incidents. Secondly, INCSEA did not seek to address issues concerning the legality of a vessel's presence in particular waters. Its function was to try to ensure safe navigation to prevent collision. In this case, China objects to the very presence of the vessels, so questions of safety of navigation are entirely moot from the Chinese perspective: see Pedrozo, 'US-China Incidents at Sea', 207.

Sea.[24] The most widely held view appears to be that since the Convention does not prohibit military activities,[25] the only substantial restriction of such activities under the Convention is that outlined in Article 301,[26] effectively preventing activities that were aggressive and amounted to threats inconsistent with the United Nations Charter.[27]

One reason for the lack of a consensus is that the Law of the Sea Convention does not have a definition of marine scientific research. Finding a textual basis within the Law of the Sea Convention and wider international law for distinguishing marine scientific research and military survey is a challenging task. This is not least because the discussions at the Third United Nations Conference on the Law of the Sea (UNCLOS III) sought to avoid consideration of most military issues, in order to facilitate discussions.[28]

The lack of a definition of marine scientific research is not an oversight. Prior to and during the negotiation of the Convention, a number of definitions were

---

24 N. Klein, *Dispute Settlement in the UN Convention on the Law of the Sea* (Cambridge: Cambridge University Press, 2005).

25 See F. Francioni, 'Peacetime Use of Force, Military Activities and the New Law of the Sea', *Cornell International Law Journal* 18 (1985): 203 at 214; E.L. Richardson, 'Law of the Sea: Navigation and Other Traditional National Security Considerations', *San Diego Law Review* 19 (1982): 553 at 573; W.F. Doran, 'An Operational Commanders Perspective on the 1982 LOS Convention', *International Journal of Marine and Coastal Law* 10 (1995): 335; Odom, 'Impeccable Incident', 440; B. Wilson, 'An Avoidable Maritime Conflict: Disputes Regarding Military Activities in the Exclusive Economic Zone', *Journal of Maritime Law and Commerce* 41 (2010): 427.

26 Article 301 of the Law of the Sea Convention provides: 'In exercising their rights and performing their duties under this Convention, States Parties shall refrain from any threat or use of force against the territorial integrity or political independence of any State, or in any other manner inconsistent with the principles of international law embodied in the Charter of the United Nations.'

27 See the discussion in Klein, *Dispute Settlement*, 279–92.

28 That is not to suggest that there was no discussion of these matters at all. However, the Convention does little to directly address military activities. This reluctance to discuss matters did not deter the United States from stating at the conclusion of UNCLOS III in relation to the EEZ:

> [The EEZ] recognizes the interest of the coastal State in the resources of the zone and authorize it to assert jurisdiction over resource-related activities therein. At the same time, all States continue to enjoy in the zone traditional high seas freedoms of navigation and overflight and the laying of submarine cables and pipelines, and other internationally lawful uses of the sea related to these freedoms, which remain qualitatively and quantitatively the same as those freedoms when exercised seaward of the zone. Military operations, exercises and activities have always been regarded as internationally lawful uses of the sea. The right to conduct such activities will continue to be enjoyed by all States in the exclusive economic zone. (UN Doc. A/Conf 62/WS/37 reproduced in 17 *Official Records of the Third United Nations Conference on the Law of the Sea* at 244)

proposed. These appear to have fallen by the wayside in a debate over whether there should be a distinction between 'fundamental' and 'applied' research, with the latter focussed upon the exploitation of the living and non-living resources of the EEZ and continental shelf.[29] A consensus on the manner in which the Convention ought to deal with different types of research did not emerge, on differing views as to when a coastal State might withhold consent, and ultimately no definition on marine scientific research was adopted, in spite of the fact that issues on the withholding of consent by a coastal State to conduct research were subsequent addressed in Article 246.

The absence of a definition does not mean the Law of the Sea Convention is devoid of clues to indicate the character of marine scientific research. Article 87 of the Convention provides that there is a high seas freedom of marine scientific research, however that freedom is subject to Parts VI and XIII. Part XIII is devoted to marine scientific research, but Part VI deals with the continental shelf and there is no use of the term 'marine scientific research' contained within that Part at all. The only activities described in Part VI of the Law of the Sea Convention that could conceivably relate to marine scientific research pertain to exploration of the continental shelf.[30] It might be argued, therefore, that marine scientific research might be limited in scope to activities pertaining to exploration. However, this is a weak argument. The inclusion of exploration activities as part of what is encompassed by the term marine scientific research need not exclude a range of other unrelated activities falling within the term.

A stronger argument for the differentiation of military survey can be found in Article 246 of the Law of the Sea Convention. This article deals with the circumstances in which a coastal State might refuse consent for the conduct of marine scientific research in its EEZ or continental shelf. It provides in part:

1. Coastal States shall, in normal circumstances, grant their consent for marine scientific research projects by other States or competent international organizations in their exclusive economic zone or on their continental shelf to be carried out in accordance with this Convention exclusively for peaceful purposes and in order to increase scientific knowledge of the marine environment for the benefit of all mankind. To this end, coastal

29 M.H. Nordquist, ed., *United Nations Convention on the Law of the Sea 1982: A Commentary* (Dordrecht: Martinus Nijhoff, 1990), 4:432–7.

30 Law of the Sea Convention, Article 77. It provides in part:

The coastal State exercises over the continental shelf sovereign rights for the purpose of exploring it and exploiting its natural resources.

The rights referred to in paragraph 1 are exclusive in the sense that if the coastal State does not explore the continental shelf or exploit its natural resources, no one may undertake these activities without the express consent of the coastal State.

States shall establish rules and procedures ensuring that such consent will not be delayed or denied unreasonably.

2. For the purposes of applying paragraph 3, normal circumstances may exist in spite of the absence of diplomatic relations between the coastal State and the researching State.
3. Coastal States may however in their discretion withhold their consent to the conduct of a marine scientific research project of another State or competent international organization in the exclusive economic zone or on the continental shelf of the coastal State if that project:

    a. is of direct significance for the exploration and exploitation of natural resources, whether living or non-living;
    b. involves drilling into the continental shelf, the use of explosives or the introduction of harmful substances into the marine environment;
    c. involves the construction, operation or use of artificial islands, installations and structures referred to in articles 60 and 80;
    d. contains information communicated pursuant to article 248 regarding the nature and objectives of the project which is inaccurate or if the researching State or competent international organization has outstanding obligations to the coastal State from a prior research project.

Article 246 establishes a regime whereby a coastal State can withhold consent for marine scientific research in its EEZ and continental shelf, in certain limited circumstances. States may not, in normal circumstances, withhold consent unless the research falls into one of the types specified in paragraph 5. These are limited matters involving the exploration or exploitation of natural resources, drilling, activities harmful to the marine environment, the construction of artificial islands or installations, or where obligations relating to the disclosure of data had been breached in the past.

None of the categories applicable to the withholding of consent by a coastal State to the conducting of marine scientific research pertain to matters which would encompass military survey. For example, the collection of hydrographic data by a military vessel would not fall within any of the four exceptions discussed above as those where a coastal State would be able to refuse. This would seem at odds with the ability of a coastal State to refuse military survey taking place in their EEZ, as asserted by a number of coastal States.

The only possible exception under Article 246(5) could be based on Article 248, in respect of failure to provide data. Article 248 provides:

> States and competent international organizations which intend to undertake marine scientific research in the exclusive economic zone or on the continental shelf of a coastal State shall, not less than six months in advance of the expected starting date of the marine scientific research project, provide that State with a full description of:

the nature and objectives of the project;
the method and means to be used, including name, tonnage, type and class of vessels and a description of scientific equipment;
the precise geographical areas in which the project is to be conducted;
the expected date of first appearance and final departure of the research vessels, or deployment of the equipment and its removal, as appropriate;
the name of the sponsoring institution, its director, and the person in charge of the project; and
the extent to which it is considered that the coastal State should be able to participate or to be represented in the project.

It is extremely unlikely that a vessel purportedly engaged in military survey would have its activities fall within a description as that envisaged in Article 248, although in theory such a response could be made. Similarly Article 249 provides for guarantees of a number of things including coastal State access to the data collected, and a right to be on board the vessel during the research.

There are other possible grounds for distinguishing marine scientific research as a purely civilian activity. Firstly, Article IV of the Convention relative to certain Restrictions with regard to the Exercise of the Right of Capture in Naval War (Hague XI) (1907)[31] provides that vessels engaged in 'scientific missions' are exempt from capture in wartime. This would clearly not apply to a commissioned survey ship of one of the combatants, and would suggest a different status for such vessels. A similar distinction is drawn in the *San Remo Manual on International Law Applicable to Armed Conflicts at Sea*, which provides that the protection envisaged in Hague XI is limited to 'non-military scientific' vessels.[32]

There are other references in the United Nations Convention on the Law of the Sea that also refer to research and survey, rather than to incorporate survey into research. Article 19 of the Convention sets down a series of matters which are deemed to be inconsistent with the right of innocent passage. Article 19(1)(j) provides:

a. the carrying out of research or survey activities.

Similar observations can be made in respect of Article 40 of the Law of the Sea Convention in distinguishing hydrographic survey from marine scientific research. Article 40 states:

31 Convention Relative to Certain Restrictions with Regard to the Exercise of the Right of Capture in Naval War, 18 October 1907, reprinted at http://avalon.law.yale.edu/20th_century/hague11.asp.

32 L. Doswald-Beck (ed.), *San Remo Manual on International Law applicable to Armed Conflicts at Sea* (Cambridge: Cambridge University Press, 1995), Article 47(f).

> During transit passage, foreign ships, including marine scientific research and hydrographic survey ships, may not carry out any research or survey activities without the prior authorization of the States bordering straits.

Similar terminology is used in Article 21, relating to the right of a coastal State to make laws to regulate 'marine scientific research and hydrographic survey' in the territorial sea. The fact that the Convention refers to marine scientific research and hydrographic survey separately permits an inference to be drawn that the former is regulated under Part XIII, while the latter is not. This is because Articles 21 and 40 refer to survey and marine scientific research, while all references in Part XIII are to marine scientific research alone.

A further suggestion of difference can be found in Part XV of the Law of the Sea Convention dealing with dispute resolution. Article 297(2) provides for compulsory dispute resolution for marine scientific research disputes except in relation to two specific circumstances.[33] Article 298 provides that a State may choose to exempt disputes concerning military activities. This suggests that marine scientific research does not include such activities.

The issue of military activities, including surveillance, in the EEZ of another State is one not directly dealt with in the Law of the Sea Convention.[34] While the Convention makes it plain that military exercises and weaponry testing in the territorial sea of a coastal State would be contrary to the regime of innocent passage, there is no equivalent restriction articulated with respect to other maritime zones. However, neither is there any authorization with respect to such exercises, with there being no inclusion of military exercises or related activities in the list of freedoms.

---

33 Law of the Sea Convention, Article 297(2). It provides:

(a) Disputes concerning the interpretation or application of the provisions of this Convention with regard to marine scientific research shall be settled in accordance with section 2, except that the coastal State shall not be obliged to accept the submission to such settlement of any dispute arising out of:

> (i) the exercise by the coastal State of a right or discretion in accordance with article 246, or (ii) a decision by the coastal State to order suspension or cessation of a research project in accordance with article 253.

(b) A dispute arising from an allegation by the researching State that with respect to a specific project the coastal State is not exercising its rights under articles 246 and 253 in a manner compatible with this Convention shall be submitted, at the request of either party, to conciliation under Annex V, section 2, provided that the conciliation commission shall not call in question the exercise by the coastal State of its discretion to designate specific areas as referred to in article 246, paragraph 6, or of its discretion to withhold consent in accordance with article 246, paragraph 5.

34 For example see Galdorisi and Kaufmann, 'Military Activities', 253 et seq.

The lack of direct reference to military activities is not fatal to the case for the conduct of surveillance in the EEZ of another State. The rights listed in Article 87(1) are by no means an exhaustive list, and are merely specifically enunciated examples. This is explicit in the use of the phrase '*inter alia*'. Further, the freedoms of the high seas are described as being subject to the conditions set down in the Convention and 'other rules of international law'. The use of this language makes it clear that the Law of the Sea Convention is not intended to be the only source of law in relation to the use of the high seas or EEZ.

If the case for freedom to undertake military surveillance in another State's EEZ can be made, it is clearly subject to some qualification. For this the crux of the issue will essentially turn on the meaning of the phrase 'with due regard'. This qualification is applied to high seas freedoms generally in Article 87(2), and it would seem logical that one must have due regard to the rights of others while navigating through the EEZ.[35]

Undertaking surveillance of another State from that State's EEZ would not, in the ordinary course of events, be without due regard for other ships or aircraft. In the case of a ship, the act of navigating safely, with data gathering sensors deployed, would not necessarily interfere with other vessels' use of the waters, unless the use of a sensor, such as a towed array, in some way impeded fishing or navigation. With aircraft, it is submitted that the prospect of such inconvenience is even more unlikely.

One issue that could be relevant in assessing the legality of military surveillance from the EEZ or high seas relates to whether such surveillance might constitute a threat to international peace and security. The Law of the Sea Convention provides limited assistance through Article 88 which provides: 'The high seas shall be reserved for peaceful purposes.'

A wide reading of this provision would, in theory, see great limitation of the uses of warships on the high seas, and the potential circumscription on intelligence gathering. When read with the Preamble, which invokes the Convention's role in the furtherance of peace and security in the world,[36] it suggests only peaceful uses of the sea are permissible. By extension this could be drawn into the EEZ, as Article 58 adopts the high seas freedoms in the Convention, and explicitly includes

35 See Francioni, 'Peacetime Use of Force', 215, see also Nordquist, *Law of the Sea*, 553–65.

36 The Preamble states in part: 'Prompted by the desire to settle, in a spirit of mutual understanding and co-operation, all issues relating to the law of the sea and aware of the historic significance of this Convention as an important contribution to the maintenance of peace, justice and progress for all peoples of the world' and 'Believing that the codification and progressive development of the law of the sea achieved in this Convention will contribute to the strengthening of peace, security, co-operation and friendly relations among all nations in conformity with the principles of justice and equal rights and will promote the economic and social advancement of all peoples of the world, in accordance with the Purposes and Principles of the United Nations as set forth in the Charter'.

Article 88 in this list.[37] Similarly, the provisions with respect to marine scientific research under Part XIII of the Convention indicate that marine scientific research can only be undertaken for peaceful purposes.[38] A case could be made that military surveillance from the high seas or another State's EEZ were incompatible with the Law of the Sea Convention.

Such an interpretation has not been favoured by many States or publicists.[39] The *San Remo Manual on Armed Conflicts at Sea*, which sought to update and consolidate the law of armed conflict at sea, makes it clear that armed conflict at sea can take place on the high seas, and in certain circumstances in the EEZ of a neutral State.[40] The *Manual* provides that as long as belligerents have due regard to the uses to which another State may wish to put its EEZ and avoid damage to the coastal State, conflict is permissible. Clearly, if armed conflict can occur in another State's EEZ, it is difficult to assert that surveillance conducted in a passive way is contrary to international law.

Firstly, such an interpretation would be difficult to reconcile with the regime of innocent passage that is applicable to warships. Any warship may constitute a danger to States in its vicinity. By its very nature, such a ship is designed to engage in, or assist other ships to engage in, armed conflict. It may be difficult, if not impossible, to determine whether a transiting warship has activated passive sensors, and certainly inconsistent with international law to stop and board such a vessel to ascertain this, given the sovereign immune status of the vessel.

None of the above analysis undermines the legitimacy of the voyages intended to be a threat to international peace as unlawful. Certainly a ship purporting to exercise a right of innocent passage that was in another State's territorial sea for the purpose of intelligence gathering as a prelude to armed conflict would not be consistent with the Convention. An argument could also be made that a similar voyage that remained in the EEZ might also be unlawful, as its intention was to assist a manifestly unlawful act, inconsistent with the United Nations Charter. However, in such a case it is the wider behaviour and motivation that would render such a journey unlawful, not the actual act of navigation itself. Consequently, a case can be made that routine intelligence gathering flights or voyages through another State's EEZ would not of themselves be illegal, unless they formed a prelude to an unauthorized attack on another State.

---

37 Galorisi and Kaufman, 'Military Activities', 275–8.

38 Law of the Sea Convention, Article 240. It provides:

In the conduct of marine scientific research the following principles shall apply: (a) marine scientific research shall be conducted exclusively for peaceful purposes.

39 On this point see D.J. Attard, *The Exclusive Economic Zone in International Law* (Oxford: Clarendon Press, 1987), 75; F. Orrego Vicuna, *The Exclusive Economic Zone: Regime and Nature under International Law* (Dordrecht: Martinus Nijhoff, 1989), 110–13; Galdorisi and Kaufmann, 'Military Activities', 274–6.

40 Doswald-Beck, *San Remo Manual*, para. 10.

Conclusion

The issue of military survey is one which is likely to remain a matter of contention between States for some time. The Law of the Sea Convention is also probably not the vehicle to resolve the issue. The States at UNCLOS III sought to avoid clearly addressing the issue, and accepted a text which could give comfort to more than a single interpretation. In this, Part XIII dealing with marine scientific research is hardly unique.

State practice would also suggest that a resolution on these matters is unlikely in the foreseeable future. While a number of States, particularly in the developing world, have restrictions on the navigation of warships in their territorial sea, contiguous zone and beyond, and to seek to restrict certain activities that might be characterized as military survey, the presence among those States of rising powers like Brazil, China and India mean it is not a legal position that can be simply dismissed. At present, the view of these States is resisted by other maritime powers such as the United States and United Kingdom, who take the view neither the Law of the Sea Convention nor customary international law would provide a clear basis to resist the existence of military survey.

In conclusion, while there remains a difference in viewpoint on the applicable law, and that both the United States and China remained committed to the assertion of their views on the applicable law physically as well as diplomatically, the potential for further incidents like those which occurred in 2001 and 2009 to be repeated remains, with all the risk that entails.

References

Attard, D.J., *The Exclusive Economic Zone in International Law* (Oxford: Clarendon Press, 1987).

Doran, W.F., 'An Operational Commanders Perspective on the 1982 LOS Convention', *International Journal of Marine and Coastal Law* 10 (1995): 335.

Doswald-Beck, L. (ed.), *San Remo Manual on International Law applicable to Armed Conflicts at Sea* (Cambridge: Cambridge University Press, 1995).

Francioni, F., 'Peacetime Use of Force, Military Activities and the New Law of the Sea', *Cornell International Law Journal* 18 (1985): 203 at 214.

Galdorisi, G.V. and Kaufman, A.G., 'Military Activities in the Exclusive Economic Zone: Preventing Uncertainty and Defusing Conflict', *California Western International Law Journal* 32 (2002): 253.

Gorina-Ysern, M., *An International Regime for Marine Scientific Research* (Ardsley Park: Transnational, 2003).

Kaye, S., 'State Practice and Maritime Claims: Assessing the Normative Impact of the Law of the Sea Convention', in *The Future of Ocean Regime-Building: Essays in Tribute to Douglas M. Johnston*, edited by A. Chircop, T.L. McDorman and S.J. Ralston (Leiden: Martinus Nijhoff, 2009), 151–4.

Klein, N., *Dispute Settlement in the UN Convention on the Law of the Sea* (Cambridge: Cambridge University Press, 2005).

Knaus, J.A., 'Development of the Freedom of Scientific Research Issue of the Third United Nations Conference on the Law of the Sea', *Ocean Development and International Law* 1 (1973): 93.

Murphy, S.D. (ed.), 'Contemporary Practice of the United States Relating to International Law', *American Yearbook of International Law* 95 (2001): 626.

Naval War College, *Annotated Supplement to the Commander's Handbook on the Law of Naval Operations* (Newport: Naval War College, 1997).

Nordquist, M.H. (ed.), *United Nations Convention on the Law of the Sea 1982: A Commentary* (Dordrecht: Martinus Nijhoff, 1990).

Odom, J.G., 'The True "Lies" of the Impeccable Incident: What Really Happened, Who Disregarded International Law, and Why Every Nation (Outside of China) should be Concerned', *Michigan State Journal of International Law* 18 (2010): 411.

Pedrozo, R., 'The US-China Incidents at Sea Agreement: A Recipe for Disaster', *Journal of National Security Law and Policy* 6 (2012): 207.

Pedrozo, R., 'Close Encounters at Sea: The USNS Impeccable Incident', *Naval War College Review* 60 (2009): 101.

Richardson, E.L., 'Law of the Sea: Navigation and Other Traditional National Security Considerations', *San Diego Law Review* 19 (1982): 553 at 573.

Text of the *Law of the Territorial Sea and the Contiguous Zone of the People's Republic of China.*

Text of United Nations Convention on the Law of the Sea, 10 December 1982.

US Naval War College, 'Annotated Supplement to the Commander's Handbook on the Law of Naval Operations', *International Law Studies* 73 (1999): paras 2.4.2.1–2.4.2.2.

Vicuna, F. Orrego, *The Exclusive Economic Zone: Regime and Nature under International Law* (Dordrecht: Martinus Nijhoff, 1989).

Wilson, B., 'An Avoidable Maritime Conflict: Disputes Regarding Military Activities in the Exclusive Economic Zone', *Journal of Maritime Law and Commerce* 41 (2010): 427.

Appendix 1: State Practice Table[41]

State	Type of rights asserted
Bangladesh	Warships require prior authorization; CZ 18 nm Security interests
Brazil	Prohibition of the boarding, searching and of the exclusive economic zone and enact and capturing of vessels in the exclusive economic zone; military exercises and manoeuvres may be conducted in the exclusive economic zone only with the consent of Brazil
Bulgaria	24 nm ('Control rights')
Cambodia	Control of all foreign activities on the continental shelf, irrespective of their purpose; CZ 24 nm Security interests
Cape Verde	Warships require prior authorization; prohibition of 'non-innocent use' of the exclusive economic zone, including weapons exercises
China	Requires prior notice for transports of waste in TS and EEZ; warships require prior authorization; CZ 24 nm Security interests
Egypt	Warships have to announce their passage in advance; ships carrying nuclear material or other hazardous substances require prior authorization; CZ 24 nm Security interests
El Salvador	Expressed concern at UNCLOS III in respect of military activities in the EEZ
Estonia	Warships and research vessels must announce their passage 48 hours in advance; authorization must be applied for nuclear-powered ships 30 days prior to their passage
Gambia	Asserts the right to prohibit navigation in certain areas of its continental shelf
Grenada	Warships require prior authorization
Guinea	Taking photographs and transporting toxic or hazardous material are considered a criminal offence
Haiti	Passage prohibited to ships carrying waste or materials with an inherent health or environmental hazard; prohibition of the passage of all vessels carrying waste or materials that are environmentally harmful or detrimental to health; furthermore claims the right to exercise the control required in the exclusive economic zone in order to ensure navigational safety and prevent violations of financial, customs, health and environmental protection regulations; CZ 24 nm Security interests

41 Derived from S. Kaye, 'State Practice and Maritime Claims: Assessing the Normative Impact of the Law of the Sea Convention', in *The Future of Ocean Regime-Building: Essays in Tribute to Douglas M. Johnston*, edited by A. Chircop, T.L. McDorman and S.J. Ralston (Leiden: Martinus Nijhoff, 2009), 151–4.

State	Type of rights asserted
India	Warships have to announce their passage in advance; prior consent to military exercises and manoeuvres in the exclusive economic zone and on the continental shelf; CZ 24 nm Security interests
Iran	Warships, submarines, nuclear-powered ships as well as ships carrying nuclear or other hazardous materials require authorization; prohibition of 'military activities and practices' in the exclusive economic zone and on the continental shelf; CZ 24 nm Security interests
Malaysia	Prior consent to military exercises and manoeuvres in the exclusive economic zone and on the continental shelf
Maldives	Warships require prior authorization; with regard to the EEZ, acknowledge only the right of innocent passage; make entry of fishing and research vessels into the exclusive economic zone conditional upon prior consent
Mauritania	Reserves the right to restrict navigation and aviation in or above the exclusive economic zone if this is necessary for reasons of national security
Mauritius	Warships must announce their passage; apparently makes the passage of warships and submarines through the EEZ conditional upon prior approval
Myanmar	Warships require prior authorization; claims the right to restrict the freedom of navigation and overflight in its exclusive economic zone; CZ 24 nm Security interests
Nicaragua	25 nm Security interests15 days advance notification for warships and military aircraft, seven days for civilian traffic
North Korea	62 nm Military zone 50 nm seaward of the territorial sea. All ships and aircraft require prior approval.
Pakistan	Warships require prior authorization; supertankers, nuclear-powered ships and ships carrying nuclear materials are required to announce their passage in advance; claims authority to regulate transit through parts of the exclusive economic zone and enact and enforce all regulations required for controlling activities in the exclusive economic zone; CZ 24 nm Security interests
Peru	Prior consent to military exercises and manoeuvres in the exclusive economic zone and on the continental shelf
Philippines	Expressed concern at UNCLOS III in respect of military activities in the EEZ
Portugal	With regard to the exclusive economic zone, acknowledges only the right of innocent passage
Saudi Arabia	Reserves the right to regulate the passage of nuclear-powered ships; CZ 18 nm Security interests and navigation

State	Type of rights asserted
Senegal	Expressed concern at UNCLOS III in respect of military activities in the EEZ
Sri Lanka	Warships require prior authorization; CZ 24 nm Security interests
Sudan	Warships require prior authorization; the right of innocent passage may be suspended for security reasons; CZ 18 nm Security interests
Syria	Warships require prior authorization; 41 nm Security interests
United Arab Emirates	Warships require prior authorization; nuclear-powered ships and ships with nuclear or hazardous loads must announce their passage in advance; CZ 24 nm Security interests
Uruguay	Asserts the right to prohibit military exercises in the EEZ
Venezuela	15 nm National and security interests
Vietnam	Warships require authorization to be applied for at least 30 days prior to passage; passage restricted to three warships at a time; CZ 24 nm Security interests Submarines are required to navigate on the surface and to show their flag; aircraft are not allowed to land on board ships or be launched from them; on-board weapons have to be set in 'non-operational' mode prior to the entry into the zone
Yemen	Warships require prior authorization; nuclear-powered ships or ships carrying nuclear materials must announce their passage in advance; CZ 24 nm Security interests

Chapter 7
The Concept of Regional Common Heritage: Its Possible Application in the South China Sea

André Tahindro*

Introduction

The principle of the common heritage of mankind (CHM) is among the most important innovations introduced in the 1982 United Nations Convention on the Law of the Sea (UNCLOS). The CHM originated from the *Declaration of Principles Governing the Sea-Bed and the Ocean Floor, and the Subsoil Thereof, beyond the Limits of National Jurisdiction* adopted by the United Nations General Assembly in 1970, which stated that the seabed and its resources beyond the limits of national jurisdiction are the CHM.[1]

While at the time of the adoption of the 1958 Convention on the Continental Shelf it was beyond imagination that a coastal State could claim an outer edge of the continental shelf beyond 200 nautical miles (nm), however, one has witnessed in recent years an enormous expansion in the size of maritime spaces subject to jurisdictional claims by coastal States, in accordance with the relevant provisions of UNCLOS.[2]

Of the 152 coastal States, 76 have now made either partial, or full or joint submissions to the Commission on the Limits of the Continental Shelf (CLCS) in respect of the outer limits of their continental shelves beyond 200 nm.[3] Collectively, these submissions encompass already a large portion of the Area. Yet, more coastal States are expected to submit their claims to CLCS in the near future.

---

* Director General for Oceans, Ministry of Environment, Ecology, Oceans and Forestry, Madagascar.

1 UNGA Res. 2749 (XXV), 1970.

2 UNCLOS, Art. 76(4)(5)(6)(7).

3 United Nations, *Submissions, through the Secretary-General of the United Nations, to the Commission on the Limits of the Continental Shelf, pursuant to article 76, paragraph 8, of the United Nations Convention on the Law of the Sea of 10 December 1982*, http://www.un.org/Depts/los/clcs_new/commission_submissions.htm.

Such situation has the potential to affect the Area and its resources – the CHM – particularly in regions with enclosed or semi-enclosed seas, where all littoral States are entitled to claim extended continental shelves.

The question which has to be asked is the following: if all States bordering an enclosed or semi-enclosed sea, such as in the South China Sea, decide collectively to refrain from claiming the outer limits of their continental shelves, pending the settlement of maritime claim disputes between them: would the seabed and ocean floor temporarily beyond national jurisdiction be still qualified as the CHM or rather the regional common heritage of the States bordering that enclosed or semi-enclosed sea?

In an attempt to find an answer to this question, this chapter will first review briefly the legal regime of the CHM, as provided under UNCLOS. The second part will provide an overview of the geopolitical situation prevailing in the South China Sea, with particular reference to maritime disputes among littoral States. In the last part of the chapter, we will consider how the concept of a regional common heritage could be contemplated in the South China Sea within the legal framework of UNCLOS.

The Common Heritage of Mankind (CHM) under UNCLOS

Part XI of UNCLOS provides for the legal regime of the CHM.[4] In so doing, Part XI first identifies the maritime area over which the CHM applies, then the resources and activities that it intends to regulate, it identifies next the entities that are responsible for its implementation as well as those who stand to benefit from it, and finally it establishes the temporal validity of the CHM.

Ratione Loci Scope of the CHM[5]

Article 136 of the UNCLOS provides that the Area and its resources are the CHM. The Area is defined in Article 1(1) as being 'the seabed and ocean floor and subsoil thereof, beyond the limits of national jurisdiction'.

Ratione Materiae Scope of the CHM[6]

The regime of the CHM applies to the resources *in situ* in the Area, whether solid, liquid or gaseous,[7] as well as to all activities that are undertaken to explore

4 United Nations Convention on the Law of the Sea, 10 December 1982, 1833 UNTS 3, Art. 137.

5 E.D. Brown, *Sea-Bed Energy and Minerals: The International Legal Regime* (The Hague: Martinus Nijhoff, 2001), 2:3–464.

6 Ibid.

7 UNCLOS, Art. 133(a).

and exploit such resources.[8] Other marine activities, including marine scientific research (MSR), are under the purview of the regime of CHM.[9]

The CHM requires that all mining activities carried out in the Area must ensure effective protection of the marine environment and UNCLOS has mandated the International Seabed Authority (ISBA) to adopt rules and regulations to prevent damage to the fauna and flora of the Area, from harmful effects arising out of mining activities.[10] The regime of CHM imposes also an obligation on all States to preserve or dispose of all archaeological and historical objects found in the Area for the benefit of mankind as whole.[11]

Ratione Personae Scope of the CHM[12]

All States, including non-States Parties, have the obligation to treat the resources of the Area as part of the CHM. Article 137(1) stresses that no State shall claim or exercise sovereignty or sovereign rights over any part of the Area or its resources, nor shall any State or natural or juridical person appropriate any part thereof. All rights in those resources are vested on mankind as whole.[13] Article 138 requires States to act in the Area in accordance with the principles of the UN Charter and other rules of international law with a view to maintaining peace and security and promoting international cooperation and mutual understanding. ISBA organizes and controls activities in the Area,[14] and ensures the equitable sharing of benefits derived from activities in the Area.[15]

Ratione Temporis Scope of the CHM[16]

Finally, UNCLOS provides that the CHM and ISBA shall be maintained for unlimited time and could not be subject to any change by any Review Conference.[17] Moreover, Article 311(6) reminds States Parties that there shall be no amendments

---

8 Ibid., Art. 1(3).

9 Arts 140, 141 and 143.

10 Art. 145; ISBA has adopted the following rules and regulations to protect the marine environment in the Area: Regulations on Prospecting and Exploration for Polymetallic Nodules in the Area (2000); Recommendations for the guidance of contractors for the assessment of the possible environmental impacts arising from exploration for polymetallic nodules in the Area, ISBA/16/LTC/7, (2010); Regulations on Prospecting and Exploration for Polymetallic Sulphides in the Area (2010); Regulations on Prospecting and Exploration for Cobalt-Rich Crusts, ISBA/18/A/11 (2012).

11 UNCLOS, Art. 149.

12 Brown, *Sea-Bed Energy and Minerals*.

13 UNCLOS, Art. 137(2).

14 UNCLOS, Art. 157(1).

15 UNCLOS, Arts 140, 152 and 160(2)(f)(i).

16 Brown, *Sea-Bed Energy and Minerals*.

17 UNCLOS, Art. 155(2); Art. 311(6); and the Agreement relating to the Implementation

to the basic principle relating to the CHM set forth in the Convention and that they shall not be party to any agreement undermining that principle.

After this brief reminder of the legal regime of the CHM, we will have an overview of the geopolitical situation in the South China Sea, including the impacts of maritime disputes on the smooth implementation of the relevant provisions of Articles 76 and 83 of UNCLOS.

Overview of the Geopolitical Situation Prevailing in the South China Sea

An Overview of the South China Sea

The South China Sea is defined by the International Hydrographic Bureau as the semi-enclosed body of water stretching in a southwest to northeast direction and covering an area of approximately 1.2 million square miles (or 875,000 square nm). It is surrounded by Brunei Darussalam, the People's Republic of China, Indonesia, Malaysia, the Philippines, Taiwan/Province of China and Vietnam. The South China Sea can be viewed as a distinctive ecosystem due its complex coastal geography, notably the existence of numerous small islands, islets, rocks and coral reef features, as well as the striking variation in its sea floor characteristics, averaging 100 meters deep on the continental Sunda shelf and over 5,000 meters in the Philippines basin.[18]

Apart from an abundance of fishery resources and biological diversity, there is a widely held perception among littoral States that the seabed of the South China Sea holds significant oil and gas reserves. Tensions in the South China Sea began to emerge in the late 1960s, as the potential for oil and natural gas in the area unfolded.[19] The fact that a large proportion of the South China Sea's seabed lies in relatively shallow waters would make these deposits readily accessible to modern drilling technology.[20] However, the full potential of these resources would remain unrealized, as long as the current territorial and jurisdictional disputes persist in these maritime areas.[21]

---

of Part XI of the United Nations Convention on the Law of the Sea of 10 December 1982, Annex, Sect. 4.

18 David Rosenburg, 'Why a South China Sea Website?', *The South China Sea*, http://www.southchinasea.org/why-a-south-china-sea-website-an-introductory-essay/.

19 'Agora, "The South China Sea", *The American Journal of International Law* 107, no. 1 (2013): 105.

20 Clive Schofield and Ian Storey, 'The South China Disputes: Rising Tensions, Increasing Stakes', *The Jamestown Foundation*, http://www.academia.edu/2062121/The_South_China_Sea_Dispute_Rising_Tensions_Increasing_Stakes.

21 Clive Schofield, Ian Townsend-Gault, Hasjim Djalal, Ian Storey, Meredith Miller and Tim Cook, 'From Disputed Waters to Seas of Opportunity: Overcoming Barriers to Maritime Cooperation in East and Southeast Asia', The National Bureau of Asian Research, *NBR Special Report #30* (July 2011).

Sovereignty Disputes and Maritime Jurisdictional Claim Disputes in the South China Sea

Sovereignty disputes over small islands

Island territorial disputes remain the principal long-standing issue between littoral States in the South China Sea. These disputes are chiefly concerned with territorial sovereignty over certain island groups.[22] Two archipelagos of islands and reefs generally known, respectively, as the Spratly and Paracel Islands are the heart of disputes.[23] Some claims are based on history, discovery, occupation[24] or proximity.[25] Others indicated that their claims are based on the fact that the insular features concerned lie on their claimed continental shelves.[26] In the north, the Paracel Islands are claimed by both China and Vietnam. Another group of islands, the Spratly Islands, are claimed by Brunei, China, Malaysia, the Philippines and Vietnam.[27] Although the numerous islands and reefs scattered over the South China Sea may be of minimal economic value, some islands however may allow claims to offshore jurisdictions, in accordance with Article 121 of the Convention.[28]

On 1 April 2009, the Philippines notified the UN Secretary-General on the adoption of Act No. 9552 defining the Archipelagic Baselines of the Philippines, and for other purposes. The Act asserts sovereignty over the Kalayaan Island Group (KIG) and Scarborough Shoal.[29] In response to the Philippines claim, China sent on 13 April 2009 a *note verbale* to the Secretary-General stating that the islands claimed by the Philippines have been part of China since ancient time.[30]

On 6 May 2009, Malaysia and Vietnam submitted a Joint Submission to the Commission on the Limits of the Continental Shelf (CLCS) on the limits of their respective continental shelves beyond 200 nm in the southern part of the South China Sea.[31] On 7 May 2009, in reference to the Joint Submission, China sent a *note verbale* to the UN Secretary-General stating that China had indisputable

22 'Agora on the South China Sea', 119.

23 Clive Schofield and Ian Townsend-Gault, 'Brokering Cooperation Amidst Competing Maritime Claims: Preventative Diplomacy, in the Gulf of Thailand and South China Sea', *The Future of Ocean Regime-Building, Essays in Tribute to Douglas M. Johnston*, edited by Aldo Chircop, Ted L. McDorman and Susan Rolston (The Hague: Martinus Nijhoff, 2009), 645.

24 Ibid., 651–2.

25 Ibid., 653.

26 Ibid., 652.

27 Ted L. McDorman, *Central Pacific and East Asian Maritime Boundaries*, edited by David A. Colson and Robert W. Smith (The Hague: Martinus Nijhoff, 2005), 5:3447.

28 D.J. Dzurek, *Boundaries and Resources Disputes in the South China Sea, Ocean Yearbook 5* (Chicago: Chicago University Press, 1983), 271.

29 *Law of the Sea Bulletin* 70, DOALOS, United Nations, 32–5.

30 Ibid., 58.

31 United Nations, CLCS.33.2009.LOS, http://www.un.org/Depts/los/clcs_new/submissions_files/mysvnm33_09/mysvnm_clcs33_2009e.pdf.

sovereignty over the islands in the South China Sea and the adjacent waters, as well as the seabed and subsoil thereof.[32] On 8 May and 18 August 2009, in two communications to the Secretary-General, Vietnam declared that the Paracel Islands and Spratly Islands were parts of Vietnam's territory and that it had indisputable sovereignty over these archipelagos.[33] On 4 August 2009, the Philippines indicated that the Joint Submission by Malaysia and Vietnam arose controversy on territorial sovereignty over islands claimed by the Philippines.[34] On 5 April 2011, the Philippines indicated that the KIG constituted an integral part of the Philippines and that it had sovereignty and jurisdiction over the geographical features of the KIG.[35] In response, China reiterated that it had sovereignty over the islands of the South China Sea and that the KIG (called Nansha Islands by China) were entitled to territorial seas, EEZs and continental shelves, in accordance with UNCLOS and China maritime legislation.[36] On 3 May 2011, Vietnam reaffirmed its sovereignty over the Paracel and Spratly Islands.[37]

Reminding other littoral States of its status as a non-claimant State to territorial disputes in the South China Sea, Indonesia has stressed that in accordance with Article 121(3) of UNCLOS, 'rocks which cannot sustain human habitation or economic life of their own shall have no exclusive economic zone or continental shelf'.[38]

Maritime jurisdictional claim disputes

Besides sovereignty disputes over territorial features in the South China Sea, littoral States are also embroiled in maritime jurisdictional claim disputes. All claims are of very great complexity and diversity, and have been crafted to maximize the respective claimed maritime entitlements of each State.[39] In some circumstances, claims to baselines have been advanced on the basis of remarkable interpretations of established rules in UNCLOS.[40] As a result, there are now a

32 Ibid., NV No. CML/17/2009.

33 Ibid., NV No. 86/HC-2009.

34 Ibid., NV No. 000819, http://www.un.org/depts/los/clcs_new/submissions_files/mysvnm33_09/clcs_33_2009_los_phl.pdf.

35 Ibid., NV No. 000228, http://www.un.org/depts/los/clcs_new/submissions_files/mysvnm33_09/phl_re_chn_2011.pdf.

36 Ibid., NV No. CML/8/2011, http://www.un.org/Depts/los/clcs_new/submissions_files/mysvnm33_09/chn_2011_re_phl_e.pdf.

37 Ibid., NV No. 77/HC-2011, http://www.un.org/Depts/los/clcs_new/submissions_files/mysvnm33_09/vnm_2011_re_phlchn.pdf.

38 Indonesia indicated also that the so-called 'nine-dotted lines map' clearly lacked international legal basis and was tantamount to upset UNCLOS; ibid., No. 480/POL-703/VII/10, http://www.un.org/depts/los/clcs_new/submissions_files/mysvnm33_09/idn_2010re_mys_vnm_e.pdf.

39 Schofield and Townsend-Gault, 'Brokering Cooperation', 648.

40 Ibid., 650.

number of overlapping claims to maritime jurisdiction in the South China Sea.[41] Most of the disputed boundaries are the result of EEZ and continental shelf overlapping claims due to disputes over sovereignty of the islands.[42]

While there are fundamental disagreements between China and other littoral States (Vietnam, Malaysia, Brunei, the Philippines and Indonesia) on the legality of the Chinese 'Nine-Dash Line',[43] China has in turn questioned the legality of jurisdictional claims of other littoral States in the South China Sea. China has protested against the 2009 Vietnam Partial (North Area) Submission, as well as the 2009 Malaysia/Vietnam Joint Submission to CLCS on the grounds that the content of the two submissions infringed seriously on its sovereignty, sovereign rights and jurisdiction in the South China Sea. It had therefore requested the CLCS not to consider these submissions, in accordance with Article 5(a) of Annex I to the Rules of Procedure of CLCS.[44] From its part, the Philippines has indicated that the Malaysia/Vietnam Joint Submission overlapped on areas claimed by the Philippines and petitioned the CLCS to refrain from considering the Joint Submission until the Parties involved had resolved their disputes.[45] In addition, Brunei Darussalam Preliminary Submission of 12 May 2009 concerning the outer limits of its continental shelf may overlap areas covered already by the Malaysia/Vietnam Joint Submission.[46]

In order to appease concerns of neighbour States, Malaysia and Vietnam have declared that their Joint Submission was without prejudice to the question of delimitation of continental shelf between States with opposite or adjacent coasts in accordance with Article 76(10) of UNCLOS, Article 9 of Annex II of UNCLOS, Rule 46 of CLCS Rules of Procedure, and Paragraphs 1, 2 and 5 of Annex I to CLCS Rules of Procedure. The Joint Submission was also without prejudice to the position of Parties to a land or maritime disputes, in accordance with Paragraph 5(b) of Annex I to CLCS Rules of Procedure.[47] For its part, Brunei has indicated that its Preliminary Submission was made without prejudice to any future delimitation of boundaries with other States.[48]

---

41 Ibid.

42 Dzurek, *Boundaries and Resource Disputes*, 276.

43 Ibid.

44 United Nations, CML/17/2009, http://www.un.org/depts/los/clcs_new/submissions_files/mysvnm33_09/chn_2009re_mys_vnm_e.pdf; ibid., CML/18/2009, http://www.un.org/Depts/los/clcs_new/submissions_files/vnm37_09/chn_2009re_vnm.pdf.

45 Schofield and Townsend-Gault, 'Brokering Cooperation'.

46 Barbara Kwiatkowska, 'Submissions to the UN CLCS in Cases of Disputes and Undisputed Maritime Boundary Delimitations or Unresolved Land or Maritime Disputes of Developing States', in *The Law of the Sea* Series 3 (NF: Vandeplas Publ., 2012), 90.

47 United Nations, http://www.un.org/depts/los/clcs_new/submissions_files/mysvnm33_09/vnm_re__phl_2009re_mys_vnm_e.pdf; http://www.un.org/depts/los/clcs_new/submission_files/mysvnm33_09/mys_re_phl_2009re_mys_vnm_e.pdf.

48 http://www.un.org/Depts/los/clcs_new/submissions_files/preliminary/brn2009preliminaryinformation.pdf.

Initiatives to Ease Sovereignty and Jurisdictional Disputes in the South China Sea

In spite of prevailing tensions, maritime boundary delimitation agreements have been nonetheless concluded by some littoral States and regional initiatives have been conducted to ease tensions in the South China Sea.

Bilateral agreements on maritime boundary delimitations

In 1992, a Memorandum of Understanding (MOU) was signed between Malaysia and Vietnam for the Exploration and Exploitation of Petroleum in a Defined Area of the Continental Shelf involving the Two Countries, pending final delimitation of the boundary lines of their of continental shelves.[49] In 2000, China and Vietnam concluded an Agreement on the delimitation of the territorial seas, EEZs and continental shelves in the Beibu Gulf/Bac Bo Gulf. The Agreement provides for consultations in the exploitation of straddling mineral deposit across the delimitation line and in the conservation and sustainable development of living resources. The Agreement provides also for cooperative activities in the conservation, management and use of the living resources in the EEZs of the two countries in the Beibu Gulf/Bac Bo Gulf.[50] In 2003, an Agreement was concluded between Indonesia and Vietnam concerning the delimitation of their continental shelf boundary. The Agreement requires the two Parties to consult each other with a view to coordinating their policies on the protection of the marine environment and to seek to reach agreement on the exploitation of any straddling mineral deposit found across the boundary line.[51]

Regional initiatives to ease South China Sea disputes

In 2002, the 10 members of the Association of the Southeast Asian Nations (ASEAN)[52] and China adopted a Declaration on the Conduct of Parties in the South China Sea. The Declaration was considered to be a first step towards the establishment of a code of conduct in the South China Sea. The Declaration reaffirms States' commitment to the Principles of the UN Charter, UNCLOS, the Treaty of Amity and Cooperation in Southeast Asia, the 5 Principles of Peaceful

---

49 Centre for International Law, 1992 Memorandum of Understanding between Malaysia and Vietnam, http://cil.nus.edu.sg/1992/1992-memorandum-of-understanding-between-malaysia-and-the-socialist-republic-of-vietnam-for-the-exploration-and-exploitation-of-petroleum-in-a-defined-area-of-the-continental-shelf-involving-the-two-c/.

50 *Law of the Sea Bulletin* No. 63, Division for Ocean Affairs and the Law of the Sea, Office of Legal Affairs, United Nations, New York, 2007, 72–4.

51 *Law of the Sea Bulletin* No. 67, Division for Ocean Affairs and the Law of the Sea, Office of Legal Affairs, United Nations, New York, 2008, 39–40.

52 ASEAN Member States are as follows: Brunei Darussalam; Cambodia; Indonesia; Lao PDR; Malaysia; Myanmar; Philippines; Singapore; Thailand; Vietnam.

Coexistence,[53] and other universally recognized principles of international law, as the basic norms that should govern State-to-State relations. It expresses also States' resolve to explore ways and means for building trust and confidence on the basis of equality and mutual respect. Conduct of States should be aimed at reducing tensions in the territorial and jurisdictional disputes in the South China Sea by exercising self-restraint in the conduct of activities and by resorting to consultations and negotiations. The Declaration further encourages the Parties to agree on cooperative activities in less sensitive areas, such as environmental protection, marine scientific research (MSR), safety of navigation, rescue operations and transnational crimes, pending solution to their disputes in the South China Sea.[54]

In 2005, the national oil companies of China, the Philippines and Vietnam signed a Tripartite Agreement for Joint Marine Seismic Undertaking in the Agreement Area in the South China Sea. Pursuant to the Agreement, the three Parties agree to undertake joint research for petroleum resource potential in an area of the South China Sea. The three countries hailed the Agreement a success and a breakthrough for peace, stability, cooperation and development in the South China Sea.[55]

In addition to these formal approaches, Indonesia has initiated, since 1990, the Workshop Process on Managing Potential Conflicts in the South China Sea. This is an informal approach which is not intended to solve territorial disputes among various claimants, but is aimed instead at achieving three things: (1) to devise cooperative programmes with inclusive participation; (2) to promote dialogue among the directly interested Parties; and (3) to develop a confidence-building process among the Parties. The basic principles elaborated by the Worksop Process were included in the 2002 ASEAN Declaration in the Conduct of Parties in the South China Sea.

---

53 These Principles are set to govern relations among States: 1. Mutual respect for each other's territorial integrity and sovereignty; 2. Mutual non-aggression; 3. Mutual non-interference in each other's internal affairs; 4. Equality and mutual benefit; and 5. Peaceful coexistence.

54 The 2002 Declaration on the Conduct of Parties in the South China Sea, http://www.asean.org/asean/external-relations/china/item/declaration-on-the-conduct-of-parties-in-the-south-china-sea; see also Nguyen Hong Thao, 'The 2002 Declaration on the Conduct of Parties in the South China Sea: A Note', *Ocean Development and International Law* 34, no. 3–4 (2003): 279–85.

55 http://www.fmprc.gov.cn/eng/wjb/zwjg/zwbd/t187333.htm.

The Concept of Regional Common Heritage: Towards its Possible Implementation in the South China Sea

Despite efforts to address the South China Sea maritime disputes, success has been so far elusive. Due to the complexity of the problems involved, the prospects for an early settlement to the disputes seem very remote. It becomes self-evident that any regional approach that would set aside temporarily sovereignty issues and jurisdictional claims may have a better chance of success. It might be more productive for littoral States to focus on other regional marine issues that unite them than on maritime issues that divide them. Based on this assumption, a number of confidence-building measures have already been proposed at the regional level. The proposal for the seabed of the South China Sea to be declared a 'regional common heritage' is another step in that direction.

Introducing the Concept of Regional Common Heritage in the South China Sea

The concept of 'regional common heritage' *per se* does not exist in the Convention, although UNCLOS encourages a regional approach for many marine activities mandated by the Convention. As previously indicated, the legal status of the CHM applies to the Area and its resources. In regions with large Open Ocean, the outer continental shelf borders the Area, i.e., the Area begins where the outer limits of the continental shelf end. By contrast, in a region with closed or semi-enclosed seas, the outer continental shelf of a coastal State would border the outer continental shelf of another State. This would mean that the delineation by all littoral States of the outer limits of their continental shelves beyond 200 nm would convert the seabed and ocean floor into areas under national jurisdiction of all States bordering the closed or semi-enclosed sea. In that context, the principles governing the Area, including the principle of CHM, as provided under Article 137 of UNCLOS would no longer apply, since the Area would no longer exist.

In the particular case of the semi-enclosed sea of the South China Sea, should China, Brunei, Malaysia, Indonesia, the Philippines and Vietnam, in a joint submission to CLCS, delineate the outer limits of their continental shelves beyond 200 nm, in accordance with the relevant provisions of Article 76, the whole seabed of the South China Sea, or at least a very large part of it, would be under the national jurisdiction of these States. It is thus submitted that establishing a regional common heritage in the South China Sea would not be in contradiction with the principle of CHM which applies to the Area and its resources located on the 'seabed and ocean floor and subsoil thereof, beyond the limits of national jurisdiction'. Introduction of such regional common heritage is, of course, without prejudice to the enjoyment of all the freedoms recognized to all States in the exclusive economic zone, on the continental shelf and on the high seas of the South China Sea, in accordance with Articles 58, 79 and 87 of UNCLOS.

A regional common heritage, as contemplated in the South China Sea, would have more similarity with the legal regime of enclosed or semi-enclosed seas in

Part IX than that of the CHM under Part XI. Under this scenario, immediate focus would be put on cooperation on areas of common concern identified under Article 123 of the Convention rather than on issues of territorial sovereignty and maritime jurisdictional claims.

Beforehand, a number of measures aimed at building trust and reducing tensions should be adopted by all littoral States of the South China Sea. These include: (1) freezing of all current sovereignty and maritime jurisdictional claims by littoral States; (2) implementation of joint arrangements in overlapping areas; and (3) intensification of cooperation among all littoral States under the legal regime of Part IX of UNCLOS.

Freezing all claims to outer limits of continental shelves

As an important step towards the establishment of a regional common heritage in the South China Sea, all littoral States should refrain temporarily from claiming the outer limits of their continental shelves beyond 200 nm, without prejudice to their rights to do so in the future. All littoral States should bring also their current maritime areas under national jurisdiction into conformity with the relevant provisions of UNCLOS, in order to clarify the overlapping areas. This would require a review of the types of baselines used by States to establish their respective territorial seas, EEZs and continental shelves, with a view to bringing them in conformity with the relevant provisions of UNCLOS.

Most littoral States of the South China Sea have applied straight baselines and archipelagic baselines for all or parts of their jurisdictional claims.[56] Straight baselines claimed by some littoral States have been subject to international protests, since they are considered not to be in conformity with the relevant provisions of Article 7 of the Convention. In the same vein, particular attention should be given to Article 121 on the regime of islands which provides a classification of islands and the treatment to be given to them in the context of maritime boundary delimitation. In this respect, Article 121(3) grants only territorial sea to 'rocks which cannot sustain human habitation or economic life of their own'.

As stressed by legal experts, States are not free to effect *de facto* amendments to their treaty obligations under the cover of State practices. Relevant provisions of UNCLOS are totally prescriptive in respect of the nature and extent of maritime jurisdictions; and since all littoral States are parties to UNCLOS, they are under obligation to apply the relevant provisions of that legal instrument.[57]

Implementing joint developments

In the case of overlapping maritime areas, the States concerned should set aside their disputes and agree on provisional arrangements involving joint developments, pending a solution acceptable to them. Joint developments would allow claimants to set aside temporarily a boundary delimitation and to focus on

56 Schofield and Townsend-Gault, 'Brokering Cooperation', 650.

57 Ibid., 654.

the exploitation of the trans-boundary resource.[58] Provisional arrangements are particularly encouraged by UNCLOS on questions of delimitation.[59] Apart from immediate economic benefits, joint development could have the side effect of defusing tensions between States agreeing on such arrangement. While they may remain unable to agree on boundary delimitation because of their adherence to their respective claims, a joint development arrangement will generate revenue to them for a certain period of time to help to alleviate their otherwise ill-disposed relations. This can be a useful practical measure where the dispute over boundary delimitation remains deadlocked over a long period of time, as in the case of the South China Sea.[60] Examples of these joint development arrangements could be found in a number of agreements, such as the *Kuwait-Saudi Arabia Agreement of 7 July 1965*, *Iran-Sharjah Memorandum of Understanding of 29 November 1971*, *Japan-South Korea Agreement of 30 January 1974*, *Malaysia-Thailand Memorandum of Understanding of 21 February 1979*, *Australia-Indonesia Treaty of 11 December 1989*, *Malaysia-Vietnam Memorandum of Understanding of 5 June 1992*, *Colombia-Jamaica Treaty of 12 November 1993* and *Argentina-United Kingdom Joint Declaration of 27 September 1995*.[61]

The current thinking on joint development of offshore and gas dates back to the 1969 decision of the International Court of Justice (ICJ) in the *North Continental Shelf Case*, which referred to the possibility for the Parties to decide on 'a regime of joint jurisdiction, user, or exploitation for the zones of overlap or any part them'.[62] Joint development can be also part of a final agreement on boundary delimitations.

Cooperation of States Bordering Enclosed or Semi-Enclosed Seas

In accordance with Article 123 of UNCLOS, States bordering an enclosed or semi-enclosed sea are under obligation to cooperate directly or through an appropriate regional organization in the conservation and management of marine living resources (MLRs), the protection and preservation of the marine environment, and the conduct of MSR.

In the particular case of the South China Sea, regional cooperation in marine affairs on subjects listed under Article 123 has the potential to shift momentarily attention to maritime delimitation disputes and contribute to relaxing tensions, building trust and reducing the risks of confrontation among littoral States. Besides, the three areas singled out by UNCLOS for regional coordinating efforts are particularly important for the good governance of oceans.[63] In this respect,

---

58 Yacouba Cissé, *Droit des Espaces Maritimes et Enjeux Africains*, La Collection Bleue, Faculté de Droit, Section de Droit Civil (Université d'Ottawa, 2001), 261–2.

59 UNCLOS, Art. 74(3) and 83(3).

60 Ibid., 6.

61 Ibid., 6–24.

62 ICJ Reports 1969: 59, para. 101 (C) (2).

63 Ibid.

particular attention should be drawn to cooperative activities of States bordering the semi-enclosed Mediterranean Sea in the conservation and sustainable of fishery resources through the General Fisheries Commission for the Mediterranean (GFCM),[64] as well as the preservation of the marine environment and the conservation marine biodiversity, through the Convention for the Protection of the Marine Environment and the Coastal Region on the Mediterranean and its Protocols.[65]

Cooperation in the conservation, management and exploitation of MLRs

The South China Sea is known for its abundance of fishery resources.[66] Fisheries are considered to be important to the economies of littoral States. The South China Sea accounts for one-tenth of the global fisheries catch, and maintains a multi-billion dollar fishing industry.[67] According to the FAO, despite an increase in the total production of marine capture fisheries in the Western Central Pacific to 11.7 million tonnes in 2010, there were reasons for concern for the state of resources, with most stocks being either fully exploited or overfished, particularly in the western part of the South China Sea.[68] Worrisome fisheries problems in the South China Sea are the prevalence of IUU fishing and the use of destructive fishing practices.

Two regional fishery bodies (RFBs) have competence for the East Asia region, including the South China Sea: the Asia-Pacific Fishery Commission (APFIC) and the Southeast Asian Fisheries Development Centre (SEAFDEC). The two RFBs are advisory bodies with competence on both marine and inland fisheries, and are not entitled to prescribe any fisheries conservation and management measures. In addition, the geographical coverage of these RFBs is so wide that it might be difficult for them to focus on specific needs of each sub-region covered in their areas of competence. As organizations under the aegis of the FAO, they have moreover an open membership. In view of the fact that APFIC and SEAFDEC do not seem to be the appropriate regional organizations referred to under Article 123(a), within which States bordering a semi-enclosed sea could discharge their

64 See Regional Fishery Bodies summary descriptions, General Fisheries Commission for the Mediterranean (GFCM), Fishery Governance Fact Sheets, FAO Fisheries and Aquaculture Department, 27 July 2013, http://www.fao.org/fishery/rfb/gfcm/en.

65 Barcelona Convention, Protocol for the Prevention of Pollution in the Mediterranean Sea by Dumping from Ships and Aircraft, Protocol on the Protection of the Mediterranean Sea against Pollution from Land-Based Sources, Protocol Concerning Specially Protected Areas and Biological Diversity in the Mediterranean, http://www.unep.org/regionalseas/programmes/unpro/mediterranean/instruments/default.asp.

66 Dzurek, *Boundaries and Resource Disputes*, 264, 265.

67 'Fishing Wars: Competition for South China Sea's Resources', *Pac Net #57*, Pacific Forum CSIS (July 2013), http://csis.org/publication/pacnet-57-fishing-wars-competition-south-china-seas-resources.

68 Food and Agriculture Organization of the United Nations, *The State of World Fisheries and Aquaculture* 2012, http://www.fao.org/docrep/016/i2727e/i2727e00.htm.

obligations to cooperate, they may wish to establish an 'appropriate' sub-regional fishery body of their own with a clear management mandate, as a forum for their cooperation.

Cooperation in the protection and preservation of the marine environment
UNCLOS requires States bordering an enclosed or semi-enclosed sea to coordinate directly or through an 'appropriate regional organization' their actions relating to the protection and preservation of the marine environment. The East Asian Seas Programme is the UNEP regional body having competence to coordinate cooperative actions of States against marine pollution in the whole of South and East Asia.[69] The Action Plan for the Protection and Development of the Marine Environment and Coastal Areas of the East Asian Seas Region (the East Asian Seas Action Plan) is steered by the Coordinating Body on the Seas of East Asia (COBSEA). COBSEA has been instrumental to initiating a project of direct interest to the South China Sea, called 'UNEP GEF project on Reversing Environmental Degradation Trends in the South China Sea and Gulf of Thailand (SCS)'.[70] Such project addressing specifically South China Sea issues would have the potential to bring littoral States together and could assist in easing tensions. States bordering the South China Sea should explore also regional programmes for the implementation of Sustainable Development Strategy for the Seas of East Asia (SDS-SEA) initiated by the Partnerships in the Environmental Management for the Seas of East Asia (PEMSEA), which could contribute to strengthening cooperation and building trust among littoral States. They may wish to adopt an Action Plan applicable only to the South China Sea, through a convention that would cement their cooperation. Note should be made of the fact that one of the objectives of PEMSEA is 'to build confidence among partners through collaborative projects and programmes'.[71]

Cooperation on MSR
Article 123(a) requires States bordering enclosed or semi-enclosed seas to cooperate on MSR, including through joint programmes. MSR could include research programmes of a littoral State in areas under the national jurisdiction of another littoral State, in accordance with the provisions of Article 246, or joint programmes of research in areas under the national jurisdiction of a littoral State of the South China Sea, under the conditions stipulated in Article 249 or on the high seas, pursuant to Article 257. Such States should also adopt measures to facilitate MSR in areas under their national jurisdiction, in accordance with

69 'About Regional Seas', UNEP, http://www.unep.org/regionalseas/about/default.asp.

70 'About COBSA: Achievements', UNEP, http://www.cobsea.org/aboutcobsea/achievements.html.

71 PEMSEA, Partnerships in Environmental Management for the Seas of East Asia, http://www.pemsea.org.

Article 255. All these activities would have strong added value in terms of building trust and confidence among littoral States in the South China Sea.

Conclusion

This brief overview has given us some insight on the complexity of the situation in the South China Sea. Disputes are rooted on sovereignty claims and complicated by mistrust and mutual suspicion. Although UNCLOS is of no assistance in resolving sovereignty claims to land features, its legal framework offers numerous options for the resolution of maritime disputes. Recent experience seems to show however that third party dispute settlement procedures are of little assistance in the case of the South China Sea disputes. The situation in the South China Sea is such that the search for a solution to the maritime disputes requires the prior adoption of measures to defuse tensions and build trust and confidence among littoral States. Introducing a concept of regional common heritage starting with the temporary freezing of all seabed claims beyond 200 nm and engaging littoral States in joint developments for overlapping areas are measures aimed at defusing tensions in the South China Sea. Regional common heritage would not purport to solve territorial sovereignty and maritime jurisdictional disputes in the South China Sea. It may however instil a better sense of regional identity and induce a possible joint stewardship in the conduct of marine activities in the South China Sea, pending a solution to maritime disputes.

References

Brown, E.D., *Sea-Bed Energy and Minerals: The International Legal Regime* (The Hague: Martinus Nijhoff, 2001), 2:3–464.

Centre for International Law, 1992 Memorandum of Understanding between Malaysia and Vietnam, http://cil.nus.edu.sg/1992/1992-memorandum-of-understanding-between-malaysia-and-the-socialist-republic-of-vietnam-for-the-exploration-and-exploitation-of-petroleum-in-a-defined-area-of-the-continental-shelf-involving-the-two-c/.

Cissé, Yacouba, *Droit des Espaces Maritimes et Enjeux Africains*, La Collection Bleue, Faculté de Droit, Section de Droit Civil (Université d'Ottawa, 2001), 261–2.

Dzurek, D.J., *Boundaries and Resources Disputes in the South China Sea, Ocean Yearbook 5* (Chicago: Chicago University Press, 1983), 271.

Food and Agriculture Organization of the United Nations, *The State of World Fisheries and Aquaculture*, 2012, http://www.fao.org/docrep/016/i2727e/i2727e00.htm.

Kwiatkowska, Barbara, 'Submissions to the UN CLCS in Cases of Disputes and Undisputed Maritime Boundary Delimitations or Unresolved Land or

Maritime Disputes of Developing States', in *The Law of the Sea*, Series 3 (NF: Vandeplas Publishing, 2012), 90.

McDorman, Ted L., *Central Pacific and East Asian Maritime Boundaries*, edited by David A. Colson and Robert W. Smith (The Hague: Martinus Nijhoff, 2005), 5:3447.

Nguyen, H.T., 'The 2002 Declaration on the Conduct of Parties in the South China Sea: A Note', *Ocean Development and International Law* 34, no. 3–4 (2003): 279–85.

Rosenburg, David, 'Why a South China Sea Website?', *The South China Sea*, http://www.southchinasea.org/why-a-south-china-sea-website-an-introductory-essay/.

Schofield, Clive and Storey, Ian, 'The South China Disputes: Rising Tensions, Increasing Stakes', *The Jamestown Foundation*, http://www.academia.edu/2062121/The_South_China_Sea_Dispute_Rising_Tensions_Increasing_Stakes.

Schofield, Clive and Townsend-Gault, Ian, 'Brokering Cooperation Amidst Competing Maritime Claims: Preventative Diplomacy, in the Gulf of Thailand and South China Sea', *The Future of Ocean Regime-Building, Essays in Tribute to Douglas M. Johnston*, edited by Aldo Chircop, Ted L. McDorman and Susan Rolston (The Hague: Martinus Nijhoff, 2009), 645.

Schofield, Clive, Townsend-Gault, Ian, Djalal, Hasjim, et al., 'From Disputed Waters to Seas of Opportunity: Overcoming Barriers to Maritime Cooperation in East and Southeast Asia', The National Bureau of Asian Research, *NBR Special Report #30* (July 2011).

Text of the 1982 United Nations Convention on the Law of the Sea (UNCLOS).

Text of the 2002 Declaration on the Conduct of Parties in the South China Sea.

United Nations, *Submissions, through the Secretary-General of the United Nations, to the Commission on the Limits of the Continental Shelf, pursuant to article 76, paragraph 8, of the United Nations Convention on the Law of the Sea of 10 December 1982*, http://www.un.org/Depts/los/clcs_new/commission_submissions.htm.

United Nations, http://www.un.org/depts/los/clcs_new/submissions_files/mysvnm33_09/vnm_re__phl_2009re_my_vnm_e.pdf;http://www.un.org/depts/los/clcs_new/submission_files/mysvnm33_09/mys_re_phl_2009re_mys_vnm_e.pdf.

PART III: Practices of UNCLOS and the South China Sea

Chapter 8
Trouble Over the Starting Line: State Practice Concerning Baselines in the South China Sea

Clive Schofield

Introduction

It has long been understood in international law terms that 'the land dominates the sea'.[1] That is, sovereignty over land territory is a necessary prerequisite for claims to maritime jurisdiction extending offshore. This, in turn, provokes the seemingly straightforward question: where does the land end and the sea begin? The straight forward answer is 'the coast'. However, in practical terms the coast generally consists of an inter-tidal zone rather than a specific line. Legally, the land/sea interface, is represented by a coastal State's baselines along the coast. Baselines are significant not only because they mark the outer 'edge' or limit to land territory but because they provide the 'starting line' for the measurement of maritime claims offshore. Additionally, baselines are often critical to the delimitation of maritime boundaries.

The definition of baselines is, however, frequently a challenging task both legally and technically and their designation can have significant implications for the classification of offshore features. That is, whether a particular feature can be considered to be an island, a rock, a reef, a low-tide elevation or merely an entirely sub-surface component of the seabed. Such distinctions have significant implications for the capacity of insular features to be used as basepoints to generate claims to maritime jurisdiction and potentially their treatment in the delimitation of maritime boundaries.

The United Nations Convention on the Law of the Sea (UNCLOS)[2] allows for multiple types of baseline. The baselines claims advanced by many the littoral States of the South China Sea have been a source of contention thanks to the questionable nature of aspects of this practice, especially with respect to straight

1 See, for example, Prosper Weil, *The Law of Maritime Delimitation – Reflections*, (Cambridge: Grotius, 1989), at 50.

2 United Nations Convention on the Law of the Sea, Dec. 10, 1982, 1833 U.N.T.S. 397 (hereinafter UNCLOS).

baselines.[3] This chapter outlines the role of baselines in the definition of the limits of claims to maritime jurisdiction with particular reference to the provisions of UNCLOS as well as their potential role in the delimitation of maritime boundaries. A number of notable issues and uncertainties are highlighted in this context. The baselines practice of the South China Sea littoral States is then examined. The chapter concludes by addressing some of the technical, legal and political issues arising from the baselines practice of the South China Sea States.

Baselines and Claims to Maritime Jurisdiction

While often termed 'territorial sea baselines', such baselines are relevant to the definition of the outer limits of all other maritime zones, since the contiguous zone, exclusive economic zone (EEZ) and continental shelf are all measured from relevant baselines.[4] Further, within baselines lie either land territory, internal waters or historic waters (see below and Figure 8.1).[5]

More specifically, baselines provide the basepoints from which the 'envelope of arcs' defining the outer limit to a maritime zone of a particular breadth is defined.[6] This is illustrated in Figure 8.2.[7]

As noted above, baselines are also frequently crucial to the delimitation of maritime boundaries. This is the case because the majority of maritime boundaries concluded to date have been based on equidistance,[8] and baselines are fundamental to the construction of a strict equidistance or median line.

---

3 This chapter deals with the coastal States and entities that border the South China Sea 'proper', that is, China/Taiwan, the Philippines, Brunei Darussalam (hereinafter: 'Brunei'), Malaysia, Indonesia and Vietnam. States bordering the Gulf of Thailand extension of the South China Sea (Cambodia and Thailand) are not dealt with here.

4 This issue is more complex as the outer limits of 'extended' or 'outer' continental shelf areas are under consideration. Nonetheless, distance measurements from baselines, especially the 200 and 350 nautical miles limits remain crucial in this context.

5 Where straight baselines and closing lines are applied internal waters will exist landward of the defined baseline. Where, for example, a closing line is defined for a historic bay, however, historic internal waters will exist landward of that closing line.

6 C.M. Carleton and C.H. Schofield, 'Developments in the Technical Determination of Maritime Space: Charts, Datums, Baselines, Maritime Zones and Limits', *Maritime Briefing* 3, no. 3 (2001): 62.

7 For source information, see International Hydrographic Organization (with the International Oceanographic Commission and the International Association of Geodesy), *A Manual on Technical Aspects of the United Nations Convention on the Law of the Sea, 1982*, special issue, no. 51, 5th edn (Monaco: International Hydrographic Bureau, 2014) (hereafter *TALOS Manual*, 2014), figures 5.4 and 5.6, at chapter 5, pp. 6 and 8.

8 For example, with respect to delimitations between opposite coastal States it has been estimated that 89 per cent of agreements concluded were based on some form of equidistance. The figure does, however, drop to 38 per cent when adjacent State

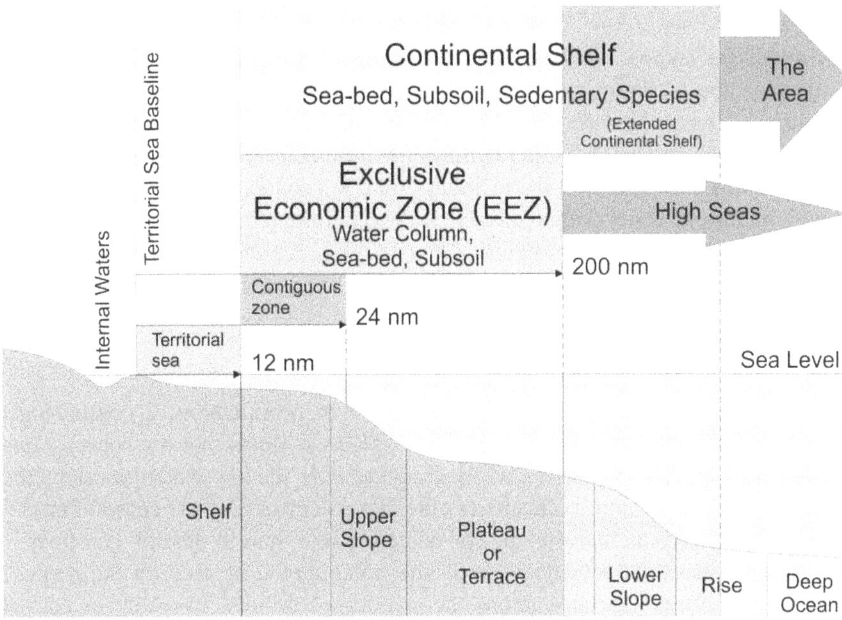

Figure 8.1 Baselines and claims to maritime jurisdiction
Source: Adapted from Schofield and Arsana, 2009.

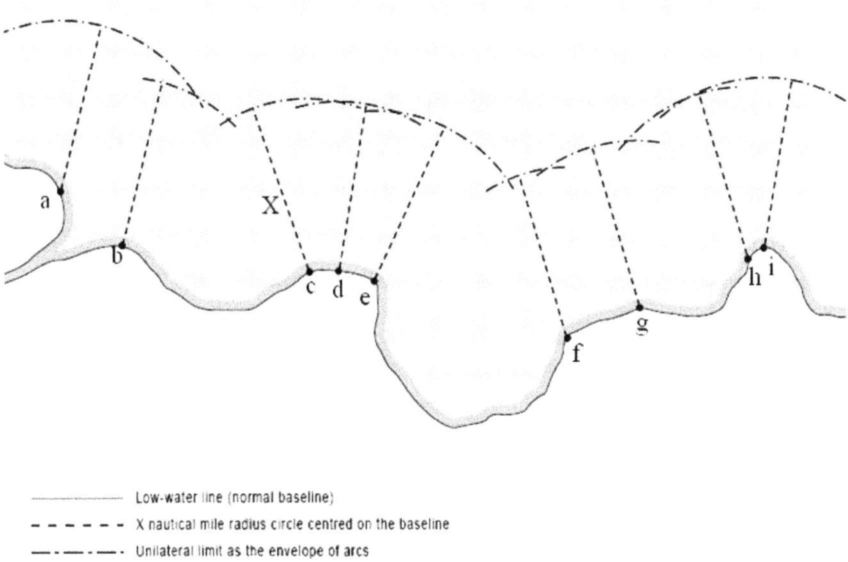

Figure 8.2 Defining the outer limits of maritime claims through an 'envelope of arcs'
Source: Adapted from Technical Aspects of the Law of the Sea (TALOS) Manual, 2014.

UNCLOS provides the generally accepted framework for maritime jurisdictional claims, including the definition of baselines.[9] All of the South China Sea coastal States are parties to the Convention.[10] Accordingly, the baseline provisions as provided for by UNCLOS are applicable to the South China Sea States. As noted above, UNCLOS allows for various different types of baseline to be applied by coastal States. In the South China Sea context four types of baselines are of direct relevance: normal baselines; the baselines of reefs; straight baselines; archipelagic baselines.

Normal Baselines

Under usual circumstances and in the absence of other claims, a coastal State will have 'normal' baselines. Article 5 of UNCLOS states that the coastal State will possess 'normal' baselines, which coincide with 'the low-water line along the coast as marked on large-scale charts officially recognized by the coastal State'.[11] Normal baselines can therefore be considered to be a State's 'default' baselines.[12]

Article 5 does not articulate which low-water should be used for the purpose of defining normal baselines among the myriad possibilities. In reality, as coastal States tend to rely on nautical charting for the depiction of low-water lines and therefore normal baselines, this issue is left up to chart-making authorities. In this context it is worth noting that the primary purpose of charts is safety of navigation. Consequently, charting agencies tend to use a particularly low low-water line so

delimitations are considered. See L. Legault and B. Hankey, 'Method, Oppositeness and Adjacency, and Proportionality in Maritime Boundary Delimitation', in *International Maritime Boundaries*, vol. I, edited by J.I. Charney and L.M. Alexander (The Hague: Martinus Nijhoff, 1993), 214.

9 At the time of writing UNCLOS had 166 parties comprising 165 States plus the European Union. See, United Nations, Division for Ocean Affairs and the Law of the Sea, Office of Legal Affairs, *Chronological List of Ratifications of, Accessions and Successions to the Convention and the Related Agreements as at 10 October 2014* (United Nations, Division for Ocean Affairs and the Law of the Sea, Office of Legal Affairs, 2014), http://www.un.org/Depts/los/reference_files/chronological_lists_of_ratifications.htm#TheUnitedNationsConventionontheLawoftheSea.

10 Ibid. The exception to the rule among the South China Sea coastal States, broadly defined, is Cambodia, which is, at the time of writing, not a party to UNCLOS. However, as noted above, this chapter concentrates on the baselines claims of the States bordering the South China Sea 'proper' rather than its Gulf of Thailand extension. Within the South China Sea itself it can be noted that Taiwan is not a party to UNCLOS as a consequence of its anomalous political status meaning that it is not a full member of the United Nations.

11 This represents a near verbatim repetition of Article 3 of the 1958 Convention on the Territorial Sea and Contiguous Zone.

12 See J.R.V. Prescott and C.H. Schofield, *The Maritime Political Boundaries of the World* (Leiden and Boston: Martinus Nijhoff, 2005), 94–7.

that the chart in question illustrates all conceivable hazards to navigation. This is achieved by opting for a particularly conservative, or low, reference level, termed the vertical datum, or 'zero line' from which depths and heights of tide can be measured.[13] A frequently used, very low, vertical datum used by charting authorities is the Lowest Astronomical Tide (LAT). The LAT can be defined as: 'the lowest level which can be predicted to occur under average meteorological conditions and under a combination of astronomical conditions.'[14]

From a maritime jurisdictional perspective the choice of an especially low vertical datum is advantageous as the lower the low-water line selected, the further down the incline of the coast and thus the further seaward the normal baseline will lie. The impact of selecting a lower vertical datum will be accentuated by the morphology of the coastline, that is, if the coastline shelves particularly gently. Where the gradient on a coastline is especially shallow even relatively minor changes in the choice of vertical datum may result in dramatic horizontal shifts in the location of the low-water line.[15] This can have significant knock-on effects in terms of which near low-water level features will be accorded the status of low-tide elevations and which will simply be sub-surface features, which can, in turn, have significant impacts in terms of the limits of maritime claims.[16]

In the South China Sea context normal baselines are of particular relevance to those parts of the surrounding mainland and main island coastlines that have not had straight and archipelagic baselines applied to them. As the straight and archipelagic baseline systems claimed by the South China Sea littoral States are extensive (see below), normal baselines apply to only limited portions of the surrounding coasts, notably to the coast of Brunei as well as China and Vietnam's coastlines fronting the Beibu Gulf/Gulf of Tonkin (see Figure 8.3).[17] That said, normal baselines may yet be relevant to coasts fronted by claims to straight baselines, especially where such claims are excessive. This is because such excessive claims may be rolled back in future or, where opposing States

13 See Carleton and Schofield, 'Developments in the Technical Determination', 21–5.

14 *TALOS Manual*, 2014, chap. 2, p. 19.

15 C.H. Schofield and I.M.A. Arsana, 'Climate Change and Maritime Jurisdiction', in *Climate Change and the Oceans: Gauging the Legal and Policy Currents in the Asia Pacific Region*, edited by C.H. Schofield and R. Warner (Cheltenham: Edward Elgar, 2012), 136–7, 127–52

16 For example, Dorst and Elema note that a change in depth of 'a few decimetres' can result in changes in baseline position horizontally of several kilometres. See L. Dorst and I. Elema, 'The Effects of Changing Baselines on the Limits of the Netherlands in the North Sea' (presentation, Advisory Board on the Law of the Sea (ABLOS) Conference on Difficulties in Implementing the Provisions of UNCLOS, Monaco, 15–17 October 2008), http://www.gmat.unsw.edu.au/ablos/ABLOS08Folder/ablos08_papers.htm. See also, Prescott and Schofield, *The Maritime Political Boundaries of the World*, 94–7.

17 Beibu Gulf being the Chinese name for the body of water in the north-western South China Sea while Gulf of Tonkin is the Vietnamese name for the same area.

each claim questionable straight baselines, such claims may essentially cancel one another out, leading to a reversion to the use of normal baselines.

Normal baselines also apply to the South China Sea's insular features. Just as for parts of the mainland coast, islands, by default, will possess normal baselines comprising the low-water line along the coast as marked on officially recognized charts, consistent with Article 5 of UNCLOS. The significance issue here is different types of insular features have radically differing capacities to generate claims to maritime jurisdiction. For example, while an island may, in accordance with UNCLOS Article 121(2), generate a full suite of maritime zones in an identical fashion to mainland coasts, a low-tide elevation, as provided by Article 13, may be used as a territorial sea basepoint, but only if it is proximate to an above high-tide piece of territory. Specifically, low-tide elevations may be utilized as basepoints only if they fall wholly or partially within the breadth of the territorial sea measured from the normal baseline of a State's mainland or island coasts. A low-tide elevation's value for maritime jurisdictional claims is therefore geographically restricted to coastal locations,[18] something that has led them to being termed 'parasitic basepoints'.[19]

An important consideration regarding the practical application of normal baselines is the fact that coastlines are dynamic. That is, coastlines progressively shift location over time, meaning that normal baselines, since these are coincident with the low-water line along the coast, can likewise progressively change or 'ambulate', potentially significantly. This, in turn, can have an impact on the location of the outer limits of claims to maritime jurisdiction.[20] This potential instability in the limits of maritime claims is problematic from a maritime enforcement perspective. The status of insular features – whether they are above high or low tide levels – is also potentially susceptible to change. These issues are likely to become more pressing in the context of global sea level rise.[21]

It can also be observed that the South China Sea also poses especially acute problems concerning the definition of low-water lines and therefore the

---

18 See Carleton and Schofield, 'Developments in the Technical Determination', 38.

19 C.R. Symmons, 'Some Problems Relating to the Definition of "Insular Formations" in International Law: Islands and Low-Tide Elevations', *Maritime Briefing*, vol. 1, no. 5 (Durham: International Boundaries Research Unit, 1995), 7.

20 M.W. Reed, *Shore and Sea Boundaries: The Development of International Maritime Boundary Principles through United States Practice* (Washington, DC: US Department of Commerce, 2000), 185; Prescott and Schofield, *The Maritime Political Boundaries of the World*, 100–101.

21 See, for example, C.H. Schofield, 'Rising Waters, Shrinking States: The Potential Impacts of Sea Level Rise on Claims to Maritime Jurisdiction', *German Yearbook of International Law 2010* 53 (2011): 189–231; and, Schofield, C.H. and Freestone, D. (2013), 'Options to Protect Coastlines and Secure Maritime Jurisdictional Claims in the Face of Global Sea Level Rise', pp. 141–65 in Gerrard, M. and Wannier, G. (eds), *Threatened Island Nations: Legal Implications of Rising Seas and a Changing Climate*, (Cambridge: Cambridge University Press, 2013).

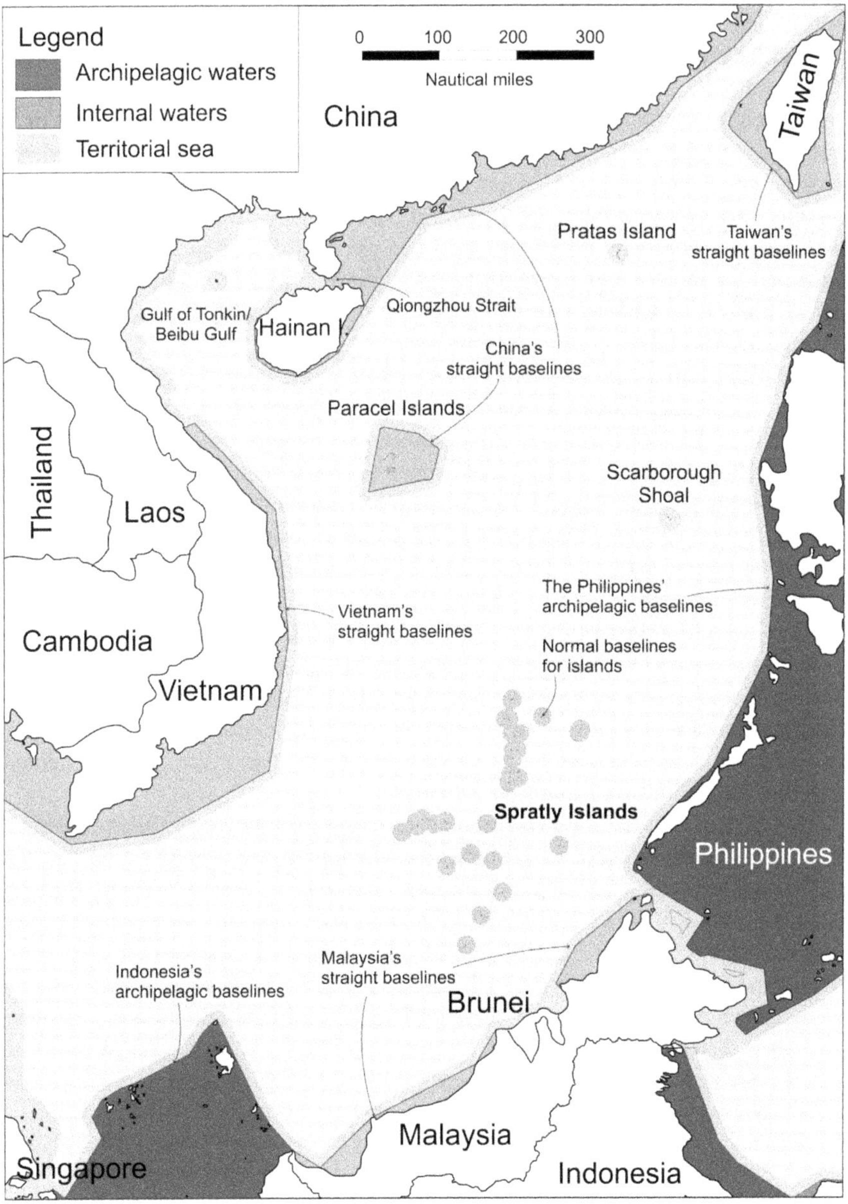

Figure 8.3 Baseline claims in the South China Sea

normal baselines of islands in particular. This is due in part to limitations and misunderstandings regarding hydrographic information related to disputed insular features in the South China Sea.[22] Additionally, the South China Sea boasts an especially complex and variable tidal regime making the calculation of a particular vertical datum and thus the definition of the low-water line particularly problematic.[23] Indeed, Lyons refers to the tides in the South China Sea as being 'among the most complex in the world', pointing to 'extraordinary features' including varying bathymetry and an ocean circulation system that traverses the equator.[24] In the context of multiple low-lying features of negligible elevation above high or indeed low water levels this has been aptly characterized as a 'particularly critical yet complex' issue.[25]

A further important consideration in relation to the normal baselines of South China Sea islands relates to land reclamation efforts and island-building and the significant distinctions that exist between these activities. There has been a long-standing acceptance that coastal states have the right to defend and extend their coastlines. Accordingly, reclaiming around and extending an existing insular feature would constitute land reclamation and, in principal, the State with sovereignty over that feature could then extend its maritime claims from its reclaimed coastline. Such a feature would, however, need to already fulfil the terms of Article 121(1) of UNCLOS, that is, it should be a naturally formed area of land, surrounded by water and above water at high tide. An immediate concern here is, of course, that sovereignty over many South China Sea features is disputed. Further, even if sovereignty issues were to be resolved, it is not necessarily the case that neighbouring States would necessarily accept the use of the 'new' reclaimed coastlines in delimiting a maritime boundary.

Artificial island-building represents a different case, however. Where features that are naturally wholly or periodically submerged,[26] are elevated above the high water mark as a consequence human intervention, they constitute artificial islands. UNCLOS draws a sharp distinction between such features and islands as defined in Article 121(1). Indeed, UNCLOS is explicit in stating that such man-made structures do *not* possess the status of islands, have no territorial waters of their own and their presence does not impact on the delimitation of maritime

22 See D. Hancox and J.R.V. Prescott, 'A Geographical Description of the Spratly Islands and an Account of Hydrographic Surveys Amongst those Islands', *Maritime Briefing*, vol. 1, no. 6 (Durham: International Boundaries Research Unit, 1995). See also, C.H. Schofield, 'Dangerous Ground – A Geopolitical Overview of the South China Sea', in *The South China Sea: Towards a Cooperative Management Regime* (London: Routledge, 2009), 7–25.

23 Y. Lyons, 'Prospects for Satellite Imagery of Insular Features and Surrounding Marine Habitats in the South China Sea', *Marine Policy* 45 (2014): 146–55.

24 Ibid.

25 Ibid.

26 A low-tide elevation which is submerged at high tide but which emerges above water at low tide represents an example of such a periodically submerged feature.

boundaries.[27] At most artificial islands can be used to generate a 500 m safety zone.[28] Legal difficulties that arise concerning the construction of artificial islands in the South China Sea context are include the fact that the right to construct artificial islands, installations and structures arises from a coastal State's rights over its zones of maritime jurisdiction which with respect to large parts of the South China Sea are contested as a direct consequence of the above-mentioned sovereignty disputes over islands. A further consideration here is whether major land reclamation and island-building efforts achieved for instance by dredging up material from the sea floor and depositing this on the top of reef structures in order to build them up is consistent with general obligation of parties to UNCLOS to protect and preserve the marine environment.[29]

Reefs

UNCLOS provides provisions that are specific to reefs. These rules are clearly relevant to the South China Sea, which hosts numerous coral reef structures. As is the case for normal baselines, the determination of the location of the low-water line is vitally important. Article 6 of UNCLOS, dealing with reefs, refers to 'islands situated on atolls' and 'islands having fringing reefs'. From this phrasing it is clear that an island, that is, a feature that is a naturally formed area of land surrounded by water and above water at high tide,[30] is a prerequisite for the application of Article 6. The article goes on to state that where such islands on atolls or fringing reefs exist:

> the baseline for measuring the breadth of the territorial sea is the seaward low-water line of the reef, as shown on the appropriate symbol on charts officially recognised by the coastal State.

An oddity concerning Article 6 is that it makes no mention of closing lines in relation to reefs. This is surprising as atolls and reefs commonly have passages or connections through them linking the largely enclosed lagoon waters of the reef and the open ocean. However, this apparent oversight has not proved to be problematic in practice as where such closing lines have been declared, international protests have not been forthcoming.[31]

---

27 UNCLOS, Article 60(8).

28 Ibid., Article 60(5).

29 Ibid., Article 192.

30 In keeping with Article 121(1) of UNCLOS.

31 Prescott and Schofield, *The Maritime Political Boundaries of the World*, 105–6. See also, Peter B. Beazley, 'Coral Reefs and the 1982 Convention on the Law of the Sea', in *Maritime Boundaries*, edited by Gerald H. Blake (London/New York: Routledge, 1993), 59–72.

Straight Baselines

The objective of straight baselines is to deal with especially complex coastal geography. In particular, straight baselines are designed to address the scenario of a 'highly irregular' configuration of normal baselines that could result in a similarly convoluted pattern of maritime spaces comprising part of the territorial sea and pockets lying beyond territorial sea limits.[32] The straight baseline provisions contained in Article 7 of UNCLOS have, however, been subject to substantial criticism due to their lack of objective tests and thus capacity to be interpreted, to put it politely, in a flexible fashion. Indeed, as has been pointedly noted by Prescott, 'the imprecise language [of Article 7] would allow any coastal country, anywhere in the world, to draw straight baselines along its coast'.[33]

In particular, the key, operative, paragraph of Article 7, that is, paragraph 1, states that straight baselines may be applied in localities 'where the coastline is deeply indented and cut into, or if there is a fringe of islands along the coast in its immediate vicinity'.[34] However, how many and how deep the indentations need to be to constitute a 'deeply indented and cut into' coastline, how many and how close the islands need to be to one another in order to form a 'fringe' of islands and at how far offshore such a fringe of islands may be and still fulfil the requirement that they be in the coastline's 'immediate vicinity' is not specified and provides a source of uncertainty. Further, Article 7 of UNCLOS also refers to concepts and terms such as 'highly unstable' coasts,[35] the 'general direction of the coast' and the need not to depart from this direction to 'an appreciable extent' such that enclosed sea areas be 'sufficiently linked to the land domain to be subject to the regime of internal waters',[36] and allows for straight baselines to take account of 'economic interests peculiar to the region concerned'.[37] None of these terms and phrases are defined, giving rise to significant scope for varied interpretation. That being said, such excessive straight baseline claims have been met with protests

---

32 *TALOS Manual*, chap. 4, 6.

33 J.R.V. Prescott, *The Maritime Political Boundaries of the World* (London: Methuen, 1985), 64. See also, Prescott and Schofield, *The Maritime Political Boundaries of the World*, 162–4.

34 The United Nations Group of Technical Experts on Baselines concluded that Article 7(1) was the key, operative paragraph upon which the rest of the provisions of Article 7 rest. Thus, Article 7(2) of the UNCLOS is 'subordinate to paragraph 1, and is not an alternative to it' such that 'for paragraph 2 to apply the coastline of the delta must satisfy the conditions set out in paragraph 1'. *Baselines: An Examination of the Relevant Provisions of the United Nations Convention on the Law of the Sea* (New York: Office for Ocean Affairs and the Law of the Sea, United Nations, 1989), 24.

35 UNCLOS, Article 7(2).

36 Ibid., Article 7(3).

37 Ibid., Article 7(5).

internationally, especially on the part of the United States.[38] Here it is also notable that the US Department of State has issued guidelines on the application of Article 7.[39] Moreover, it should be emphasized that when the International Court of Justice was called on to deal with the question of straight baselines in the *Qatar/Bahrain Case*, its response was clear-cut, stating that the method of straight baselines in accordance with Article 7 of UNCLOS 'must be applied restrictively'.[40]

Several of the South China Sea littoral States have defined straight baselines that front large sections, indeed the vast majority, of their coastlines (see Figure 8.3). These claims to systems of straight baselines are difficult to characterize as anything other than excessive. These straight baselines claims are outlined below with certain potentially problematic issues highlighted.

China

China promulgated a law relating to its baselines in 1992[41] and subsequently enacted this legislation through the partial yet extensive definition of a system of straight baselines along most of its mainland coast and around the Paracel group of islands in the South China Sea in 1996.[42] A detailed analysis of this baseline system by the US Department of State was critical of the system on the grounds that most of China's coastline does not meet the UNCLOS criteria for applying straight baselines.[43] Overall, there would seem to be little substance in China claiming that almost its entire mainland coastline meets the criteria for employing straight baselines. Nonetheless, large sections of relatively smooth coastline generally devoid of fringing islands are fronted with straight baselines.[44] These baselines

38 See J.A. Roach and R.W. Smith, *United States Responses to Excessive Maritime Claims*, 3rd edn (The Hague: Martinus Nijhoff, 2012).

39 As the US Guidelines themselves state, however, they "do not have international standing as benchmarks" for testing the legality of straight baselines systems. See, United States Department of State, "Developing Standard Guidelines for Evaluating Straight Baselines", *Limits in the Seas*, No. 106 (Bureau of Oceans and International Environmental and Scientific Affairs, U.S. Department of State, Washington DC: 31 August 1987).

40 *Case concerning Maritime Delimitation and Territorial Questions between Qatar and Bahrain (Qatar v. Bahrain)* (Merits) [2001] ICJ Rep 40, para. 212, http://www.icj-cij.org/docket/files/87/7027.pdf (hereinafter, the *Qatar/Bahrain Case*).

41 *Law on the Territorial Sea and Contiguous Zone*, 25 February 1992, http://www.un.org/Depts/los/LEGISLATIONANDTREATIES/PDFFILES/CHN_1992_Law.pdf.

42 *Declaration of the Government of the People's Republic of China on the Baselines of the Territorial Sea*, 15 May 1996, http://www.un.org/Depts/los/LEGISLATIONAND TREATIES/PDFFILES/CHN_1996_Declaration.pdf.

43 U.S. Department of State, Bureau of Oceans and Environmental and Scientific Affairs, 'Straight Baseline Claim: China', *Limits in the Seas*, no. 117 (1996): 3, http://www.state.gov/documents/organization/57692.pdf.

44 Ibid., 4–8.

stretch for 1,734.1 miles and vary in length from 0.1 miles to 121.7 miles.[45] Some of the straight baseline segments that have been defined therefore appear to be overly long as well as linking small and isolated features (including low-tide elevations and even sub-surface features) located at considerable distances offshore.[46] Moreover, the straight baseline closing off the eastern entrance to the Qiongzhou Strait between Hainan and the Chinese mainland is particularly objectionable in view of both its method of drawing and the implications for the freedom of navigation. In any case China has expressed the position that international shipping does not have a right of innocent passage in this strait.[47]

Further, the enclosing of the Paracel Islands by China with apparent straight baselines would seem to be clearly contrary to international law. There is no provision in the UNCLOS for baselines around mid-ocean archipelagos that are not part of an archipelagic State (as opposed to a mainland or continental State such as China).[48] Consequently, China has argued that these baselines are not archipelagic baselines but straight baselines.[49] However, even if these baselines are straight rather than archipelagic ones, they remain problematic in character, linking as they do a number of very small and dispersed insular features so as to enclose a considerable maritime space as internal waters.[50] Finally, sovereignty over the Paracel Islands is also claimed by Vietnam which, unsurprisingly, does not accept China's right to define a system of baselines of any sort applicable to these islands. These features of China's claimed straight baselines have led to international protests.[51]

---

45 Ibid., 4.

46 For example, points 12 and 13 of China's straight baselines system located on rocks around 60 nm offshore the mainland coast while point 9 is located on a low-tide elevation located over 12 nm from the nearest above high tide feature and point 9 is located above a submerged part of the seabed. Ibid., 6–7.

47 Ibid., 17. See also D.J. Dzurek, 'The People's Republic of China Straight Baseline Claim', *Boundary and Security Bulletin* 4, no. 2 (1996): 77–89.

48 In the course of the Third United Nations Conference on the Law of the Sea a number of mainland coastal States did argue that the special rules applicable to archipelagos should also be applicable to their offshore island possessions, these proposals did not prove successful. See H.W. Jayewardene, *The Regime of Islands in International Law* (Dordrecht: Martinus Nijhoff, 1990), 140–42 and M.B. Tsamenyi, C.H. Schofield and B. Milligan, 'Navigation through Archipelagos: Current State Practice', in *Freedom of the Seas, Passage Rights and the 1982 Law of the Sea Convention*, edited by M.H. Nordquist, T.B. Koh and J.N. Moore (Leiden and Boston: Martinus Nijhoff, 2009), 413–54.

49 Chen Degong, 'China and the Law of the Sea', *Occasional Paper* (Canberra: Northeast Asia Program, Research School of Pacific and Asian Studies, Australian National University, December 1996), 23.

50 U.S. Department of State, 'Straight Baseline Claim: China', 8.

51 Ibid.

Malaysia

Malaysia appears to have utilized straight baselines for a considerable period of time. This has been apparent from an examination of official Malaysian maps, despite the absence of a formal claim or definition of the coordinates of the turning points defining a system of straight baselines on the part of the Malaysian government.[52] In particular the Malaysian Directorate of National Mapping issued a map on 21 December 1979 illustrating Malaysia's agreed maritime boundaries and the limits of Malaysia's unilateral territorial sea and continental shelf claims.[53]

Although no baselines are shown on these maps, some of Malaysia's claimed territorial sea limits are depicted with straight lines, something that is only possible if they are drawn from straight baselines. The location of these baselines can then be inferred by drawing lines parallel to the straight outer limits of the Malaysian territorial sea claim but transposed 12 nautical miles in a landward direction.[54] The origins of this system appear to lie in the negotiations between Indonesia and Malaysia on a continental shelf boundary between the two countries, concluded in 1969, when Malaysia appears to have sought to define baselines to 'balance' or 'match' the archipelagic baselines claimed by Indonesia.[55]

Malaysia's inferred straight baselines connect small, isolated islands located far from the mainland coast.[56] It is therefore questionable, to say the least, whether Malaysia's apparent straight baseline claims are in keeping with the terms of UNCLOS Article 7. However, these straight baselines have apparently not led to international protests although this is likely to be in large part because of their unofficial, undeclared character rather than because they are necessarily acceptable to other States. In short, the apparent lack of international protests against Malaysia's straight baselines stems from the absence, officially at least, of excessive practice to protest against.

---

52 K. Kittichaisaree, *The Law of the Sea and Maritime Boundary Delimitation in South-East Asia* (Oxford: Oxford University Press, 1987), 17–18.

53 The *Peta Menunjukkan Sempadan Perairan dan Pelantar Benua Malaysia* or 'Map Showing the Territorial Waters and Continental Shelf Boundaries of Malaysia', often referred to as the *Peta Baru* ['New Map'], published by the Malaysian Directorate of National Mapping in two sheets.

54 See C.H. Schofield and M. Tan-Mullins, 'Claims, Conflicts and Cooperation in the Gulf of Thailand', *Ocean Yearbook* 22 (Leiden and Boston: Martinus Nijhoff, 2008), 75–116. http://www.brill.nl/default.aspx?partid=210&pid=30432, 86–7 and M.J. Valencia, 'Validity of Malaysia's Baselines and Territorial Sea Claim in the Northern Malacca Strait', *Marine Policy* 27 (2003): 367–73.

55 See U.S. Department of State, 'Continental Shelf Boundary: Indonesia-Malaysia', *Limits in the Seas*, no. 1 (Washington, DC: Bureau of Intelligence and Research, 21 January 1970), 2.

56 It has been noted that in one part of the Malacca Strait, Malaysia's claimed limit of territorial sea is more than 59 nautical miles from the nearest Malaysia land territory. See M.J. Valencia, *Malaysia and the Law of the Sea* (Kuala Lumpur: ISIS Malaysia, 1991), 20.

Subsequently, on 1 May 2007, Malaysia passed the Baselines of Maritime Zones Act 2006.[57] This legislation provides for the declaration of geographical coordinates of basepoints for the purpose of determining the territorial sea baselines of Malaysia and for other associated matters. However, no geographical coordinates are specified or have been subsequently issued at the time of writing. Intriguingly, at least some of Malaysia's straight baselines have been depicted on an official map. In particular, straight baselines fronting the Malaysian Provinces of Sarawak and Sabah were shown on a map accompanying Malaysia and Vietnam's joint submission to the United Nations Commission on the Limits of the Continental Shelf (CLCS).[58] The baselines involved consist of lengthy segments fronting the entirety of the predominantly smooth coastlines of Sabah and Sarawak.

Taiwan

As noted above, Taiwan is not a party to UNCLOS. Nevertheless, Taiwan has made claims to maritime jurisdiction which are broadly consistent with the jurisdictional framework set out in the Convention. Taiwan defined an extensive system of straight baselines around the main island of Taiwan and associated islands and Pratas Island in 1999.[59] Despite appearances these baselines are not archipelagic in character as Taiwan, as the Republic of China, claims to represent China as a whole. The straight baselines which entirely surround and enclose the main island of Taiwan generally use overly long baseline segments to connect small and widely separated islands located at a considerable distance from the coast of Taiwan itself.[60] For example, a straight baseline over 109 nautical miles in length connects a point on Taiwan's north-western coast to a low-tide elevation in the northern part of the Pescadores group of islands and the baselines system then connects to other small offshore features off Taiwan's south-western coast rather

---

57 V.L. Forbes, 'The Territorial Sea Datum of Malaysia', *MIMA Bulletin* 14, no. 4 (2007): 3–8, at 7–8.

58 *Joint Submission to the Commission on the Limits of the Continental Shelf pursuant to Article 76, paragraph 8 of the United Nations Convention on the Law of the Sea 1982 in respect of the southern part of the South China Sea*, Executive Summary, 6 May 2009, http://www.un.org/Depts/los/clcs_new/submissions_files/submission_mysvnm_33_2009.htm.

59 US Department of State, 'Taiwan's Maritime Claims', *Limits in the Seas No. 127* (Washington, DC, 15 November 2005), http://www.state.gov/documents/organization/57674.pdf.

60 The US State Department study notes that the islands used as turning points in Taiwan's claimed straight baselines system off its southeast coastline (Lu Tao and Lan Yu) are respectively 17 and 34 nautical miles offshore while the Pescadores islands off the west coast are approximately 25 nautical miles off the mainland coast. It was also observed that over half of the straight baseline segments defined around Taiwan are over 24 nautical miles in length. Ibid., 10.

than directly connecting the Pescadores to the mainland of Taiwan as a group of fringing islands.[61] In the view of the US State Department, therefore:

> For the most part, the waters enclosed by the straight baseline system do not have the close relationship with the land as needed, but rather reflect the characteristics of the territorial sea or high seas.[62]

Consequently, it was suggested that normal rather than straight baselines would have been appropriate for much of the coastline of Taiwan. Taiwan's baselines claim relating to Pratas Island, involving a 6.9 nautical mile long closing line for the semi-circular reef on which the island is situated, can be considered to be less problematic. However, Taiwan also claims normal baselines with respect to Macclesfield Bank even though this feature is an entirely and permanently sub-surface one which therefore has no low-water line and therefore no normal baselines.[63]

Vietnam

Vietnam's straight baselines, claimed in 1977,[64] were implemented in 1982.[65] These claimed straight baselines stretch for approximately 850 nautical miles and enclose the entirety of Vietnam's mainland coast south of the Gulf of Tonkin by connecting a number of small, scattered islands which are also predominantly distant from the mainland coast.[66] The US State Department's assessment of Vietnam's claimed straight baselines is critical, pointing out that the turning points used to define the straight baselines are, on average, 39.4 nautical miles offshore, with five of the nine turning points being more than 50 nautical miles offshore and the most distant being 80.7 nautical miles offshore.[67] As a result Vietnam claims an area of approximately 27,000 nm^2 (93,000 km^2) as internal waters, landward

61 Ibid., 10–13.

62 Ibid., 15.

63 For example, the relevant British Admiralty sailing directions or Pilot refers to Macclesfield Bank as a 'below-water atoll' with a least depth of water of 9.1 m over it. See, United Kingdom Hydrographic Office (UKHO), *China Sea Pilot*, Vol. 1, 8th edition, Admiralty Sailing Directions (Taunton: UKHO, 2010), 68–9.

64 By means of Vietnam's *Statement on the Territorial Sea, the Contiguous Zone, the Exclusive Economic Zone and the Continental Shelf*, 12 May 1977, http://www.un.org/Depts/los/LEGISLATIONANDTREATIES/PDFFILES/VNM_1977_Statement.pdf.

65 *Declaration on Baseline of Territorial Waters*, 12 November 1982, http://www.un.org/Depts/los/LEGISLATIONANDTREATIES/PDFFILES/VNM_1982_Statement.pdf.

66 US Department of State, 'Straight Baselines: Vietnam', *LIS*, no. 99 (Washington, DC: Bureau of Intelligence and Research, 12 December 1983), 5.

67 Ibid., 5–6.

of its straight baselines.[68] Consequently, Vietnam's straight baselines claims have been subject to international protest, notably on the part of the United States[69] and Thailand.[70]

Archipelagic Baselines

Straight baselines are not to be confused with archipelagic straight baselines that are subject to different, and significantly more robust, rules. Firstly, and fundamental to archipelagic State claims to archipelagic baselines and archipelagic waters, Article 47(1) provides that an archipelagic State may draw baselines joining 'the outermost points of the outermost islands and drying reefs of the archipelago'.

Five key conditions are then laid down in Article 47: that the claimant state's 'main islands' must be included within the archipelagic baseline system;[71] that the ratio of water to land within the baselines must be between 1:1 and 9:1;[72] that the length of any single baseline segment must not exceed 125 nautical miles;[73] that no more than 3 per cent of the total number of baseline segments enclosing an archipelago may exceed 100 nautical miles;[74] and, that such baselines 'shall not depart to any appreciable extent from the general configuration of the archipelago'.[75]

---

68 Ibid.

69 The US note of protest stated that 'there is no basis in international law for the system of straight baselines provided in the declaration of November 12, 1982'. J. Ashley Roach and Robert W. Smith, *Excessive Maritime Claims*, 3rd edn (The Hague: Martinus Njihoff, 1996), 102.

70 The Thai note, dated 9 December 1985, stated that between points 0 and A7, Vietnam's claimed straight baselines were 'at variance with the well-established rules of international law', referring to both the 1958 and 1982 Conventions, and concluded that: 'the Government of Thailand reserves all its rights under international law in relation to the sea areas in question and the airspace above them.' See *UN Law of the Sea Bulletin* 7 (April 1986): 111.

71 UNCLOS, Article 47(1).

72 Ibid., Article 47(1).

73 Ibid., Article 47(2).

74 Ibid. It is worth noting that as it is the coastal State that constructs the archipelagic baseline system and as there is no restriction on the number of baselines that an archipelagic State might draw, it is usually possible to adjust the baseline system to overcome the no more than 3 per cent of baseline segments exceeding 100 nautical miles in length restriction and thus conform to the UNCLOS requirements. See UN Division for Ocean Affairs and the Law of the Sea, *Handbook on the Delimitation of Maritime Boundaries* (New York: United Nations, 2000), 8.

75 For a more detailed analysis of claims to archipelagic baselines and archipelagic waters see M.B. Tsamenyi, C.H. Schofield and B. Milligan, 'Navigation through Archipelagos: Current State Practice', in *Freedom of the Seas, Passage Rights and the 1982 Law of the Sea Convention*, edited by M.H. Nordquist, T.B. Koh and J.N. Moore (Leiden and Boston: Martinus Nijhoff, 2009), 413–54.

In combination these conditions amount to a substantially more exacting test for the legitimate application of archipelagic baselines as compared with the ambiguous provisions of Article 7 of the UNCLOS dealing with straight baselines.

The 125 nm length limitation coupled with the ratio calculation represent the critical tests of the validity of a system of archipelagic baselines. The intent of the latter provision appears to be to exclude both coastal States dominated by a few large islands, such as the United Kingdom, and those whose islands are particularly dispersed, such as Kiribati, from enclosing broad maritime spaces with archipelagic baselines. Article 47(7) provides clarification as to what may be reasonably regarded as water and land in order to aid in the computation of the crucial water to land ratio, providing that for this purpose 'land areas may include waters lying within the fringing reefs of islands and atolls, including that part of a steep-sided oceanic plateau which is enclosed or nearly enclosed by a chain of limestone islands and drying reefs lying on the perimeter of the plateau'.[76]

Indonesia

Indonesia's archipelagic baselines claims are long-standing, having been first advanced in 1960.[77] Indonesia has subsequently progressively refined its archipelagic baselines, notably through Act No. 6 of 8 August 1996 regarding Indonesian Waters and related implementing regulations dating from 2002[78] and 2008.[79] Indonesia's archipelagic baselines fronting the south-western South China Sea principally encompass the Natuna Island group, have aroused no diplomatic protests internationally and can be considered to be compliant with the terms of Article 47 of UNCLOS. Indeed, it can be suggested that Indonesia's extensive system of archipelagic baselines provided the model for the provisions ultimately contained in UNCLOS.

---

76 For a discussion of how the 1 to 1 and 1 to 9 ratios were arrived at, see Jayewardene, *The Regime of Islands*, 145.

77 Indonesia, Act Concerning Indonesian Waters, Article 1, 20 January 1960. Reproduced in *The Geographer* (1971) 'Straight Baselines: Indonesia', *Limits in the Seas*, no. 35 (Washington, DC: Bureau of Intelligence and Research).

78 See *Peraturan Pemerintah* (PP) [Government Regulation] No. 61 of 1998, on the List of Geographical Coordinates of the Base Points of the Archipelagic Baselines of Indonesia in the Natuna Sea, United Nations Division of Ocean Affairs and the Law of the Sea website, http://www.un.org/Depts/los/LEGISLATIONANDTREATIES/PDFFILES/IDN_1998_Regulation61.pdf.

79 See C.H. Schofield and I.M.A. Arsana, 'Closing the Loop: Indonesia's Revised Archipelagic Baselines System', *Australian Journal of Marine and Ocean Affairs* 1, no. 2 (2009): 57–62.

Philippines

The Philippines established baselines through Republic Act No. 3046 of 17 June 1961,[80] and subsequently amended them through Republic Act No. 5446 of 18 September 1968.[81] While this system of baselines certainly appears to be archipelagic in character, enclosing as they do the approximately 7,000 islands that constitute the Philippines, the relevant Philippines legislation refers to 'straight baselines'. Additionally, it is worth noting that one of the baseline segments defined by the Philippines, that closing the Moro Gulf, measures approximately 141 nautical miles – a configuration that would breach the maximum archipelagic baseline segment length limit of 125 nautical miles set out in UNCLOS Article 47(2). Additionally, in accordance with the Philippines Constitution of 1973,[82] the waters landward of these baselines were claimed to be the internal waters of the Philippines rather than archipelagic waters. However, in 2009 the Philippines revised its baselines and brought them into line with UNCLOS.[83] The Philippines now claims archipelagic baselines around its main archipelago and applies the 'regime of islands' to outlying islands claimed such as Scarborough Shoal and those Spratly Islands claimed by the Philippines.[84]

Reflections and Conclusions

In one sense baseline issues are secondary in the South China Sea. As noted at the outset of this chapter, the land dominates the sea. Resolution of the territorial disputes, that is, the sovereignty disputes over islands that beset the South China Sea, is a necessary precursor to serious consideration of baseline issues at least in the context of the delimitation of maritime boundaries. Nonetheless, baseline issues remain important in the South China Sea, partially because, despite the region's reputation for conflict, by no means everything is disputed. Thus, baselines are important with respect to territories that are not subject to competing

80 See Republic Act No. 3046 of 17 June 1961, http://www.un.org/Depts/los/LEGISLATIONANDTREATIES/PDFFILES/PHL_1961_Act.pdf.

81 An Act to Amend Section One of the Republic Act Numbered Thirty Hundred and Forty-Six, Entitled 'An Act to Define the Baselines of the Territorial Sea of the Philippines', http://www.un.org/Depts/los/LEGISLATIONANDTREATIES/PDFFILES/PHL_1968_Act.pdf.

82 *Constitution of the Republic* (in force since 17 January 1973), Article 1, http://www.un.org/Depts/los/LEGISLATIONANDTREATIES/PDFFILES/PHL_1973_Constitution.pdf.

83 See Republic Act No. 9522, An Act to Amend Certain Provisions of Republic Act No.3046 as Amended by Republic Act No.5446, to Define the Archipelagic Baselines of the Philippines, and for Other Purposes, 10 March 2009, *Law of the Sea Bulletin*, no. 70 (2000), 32.

84 Ibid.

sovereignty claims and this, of course, comprises the majority of the mainland (or main island) coasts bordering this large semi-enclosed sea. The baselines along uncontested coasts are therefore important as they provide the 'starting line' for the measurement of claims to maritime jurisdiction which extend into the South China Sea. This, in turn, has a bearing on the scope of maritime claims and helps to explain why certain baselines have been subject to diplomatic protests among the South China Sea States.

Further, consideration of baselines is linked to the status of insular features which has a direct bearing on the ongoing sovereignty disputes. This is the case in particular in that many of the apparently 'islands' do not, in fact, appear to be islands at all within the meaning of Article 121 of UNCLOS. That is, many of the myriad features of the Spratly Islands for example are not above water at high tide. As such they do not constitute territory that is capable of being subject to a sovereignty claim. In this context the complexities and peculiarities of ascertaining the high and low water line in the South China Sea and thus what features qualify as being above high water in order to be properly accorded the status of island/rock under Article 121 of UNCLOS bear consideration. Similarly, determining the position of the low-water line is significant not only for defining the starting point for maritime claims around islands but also such that insular features can be categorized as low-tide elevations or entirely sub-surface features. Here it can be observed that substantial and ongoing land reclamation activities and artificial island building activities in the South China Sea is likely to make the task of distinguishing between different types of insular feature significantly harder.

With respect to the straight baselines practice of the South China Sea States, it is clear from the foregoing review that straight baselines have not been applied restrictively in the South China Sea and can generally be considered to be excessive in character. This is illustrated by the international diplomatic protests that they have prompted. That said, the impact of straight baselines on the scope of maritime claims should not be overstated.

In particular, it should be noted that the islands often used as turning or anchoring points in the construction of the straight baselines system can themselves be used to generate claims to maritime jurisdiction.[85] Thus, concerning territorial sea claims, for example, the coastal State will 'only' gain additional territorial sea measured from straight baselines beyond 12 nautical miles from valid normal baselines, as illustrated in Figure 8.4. Additionally, while expansive straight baseline claims may translate into impressive apparent gains in terms of claimed internal waters and 'extra' territorial sea areas, this does not necessarily mean that continental shelf and EEZ claims are similarly enhanced. If the island anchoring the straight baselines system are themselves capable of generating EEZ rights then EEZ gains as a result of claims to straight baselines will be minimised. This

85 See R. Lavalle, 'Not Quite a Sure Thing: The Maritime Areas of Rocks and Low-Tide Elevations Under the U.N. Law of the Sea Convention', *IJMCL* 19 (2004), no. 1: 57–64.

reflects the geometric reality that the greater the breadth of the maritime zone being measured, the fewer the basepoints will be required such that the impact of straight baselines is likely to be reduced further offshore. This is, however, dependent on whether the features in question can themselves be considered to be islands capable of generating claims to continental shelf and EEZ rights in accordance with UNCLOS Article 121(2) or whether they are, in fact, 'rocks' incapable of generating such claims, in line with Article 121(3). Additionally, many coastal States are located in close proximity to their maritime neighbours, restricting their opportunity to claim full 200 nautical mile breadth maritime zones.

It can further be observed that while many of the straight baselines claimed by the South China Sea coastal States are arguably problematic, these States are hardly alone in this type of practice. Indeed, many other straight baseline claims in the region fit this trend such that it has been observed that 'almost all the states of the Asia-Pacific region have adopted straight baseline systems that are inconsistent with international law'.[86]

Straight baselines may also have a role to play in maritime boundary delimitation. This is perhaps not of immediate concern in a maritime area characterized by multiple overlapping sovereignty and maritime claims.[87] Caution is, however, required when discussing the potential impact of straight baselines on the delimitation of maritime boundaries. Straight baselines will not necessarily have an impact on the course of a final maritime boundary line. As straight baselines are unilaterally defined by States, they are not binding on other States. The use, or otherwise, of straight baselines in the delimitation of a maritime boundary is therefore not automatic. The consent of neighbouring State(s) is required for their application and this is often a subject of negotiation.[88] For example, in their 1997 maritime boundary agreement in the Gulf of Thailand,[89] Thailand and Vietnam

86 J. Ashley Roach and Robert W. Smith, 'Straight Baselines: The Need for a Universally Applied Norm', *Ocean Development and International Law*, 31 (2000), 47–80, 66.

87 See Prescott and Schofield, *The Maritime Political Boundaries of the World*, 156–7.

88 N.M. Antunes, *Towards the Conceptualisation of Maritime Delimitation: Legal and Technical Aspects of a Political Process* (Leiden: Martinus Nijhoff, 2003), 300–301. Antunes (2003, 301) notes that 'taking into account the bilateral nature of delimitation, since straight baselines stem from unilateral decisions of states, their use vis-à-vis other states depends on consent' and backs this interpretation up by reference to the *Libya/Malta Case*, the *Guinea/Guinea-Bissau Arbitration*, the *Eritrea/Yemen Arbitration* and the *Qatar/Bahrain Case* (ibid., 300–1).

89 *Agreement between the Government of the Kingdom of Thailand and the Government of the Socialist Republic of Vietnam on the Delimitation of the Maritime Boundaries between the Two Countries in the Gulf of Thailand*, August 1997 (entry into force: 27 February 1998), http://www.un.org/Depts/los/LEGISLATIONANDTREATIES/PDFFILES/TREATIES/THA-VNM1997MB.PDF. See also, J.I. Charney and R.W. Smith,

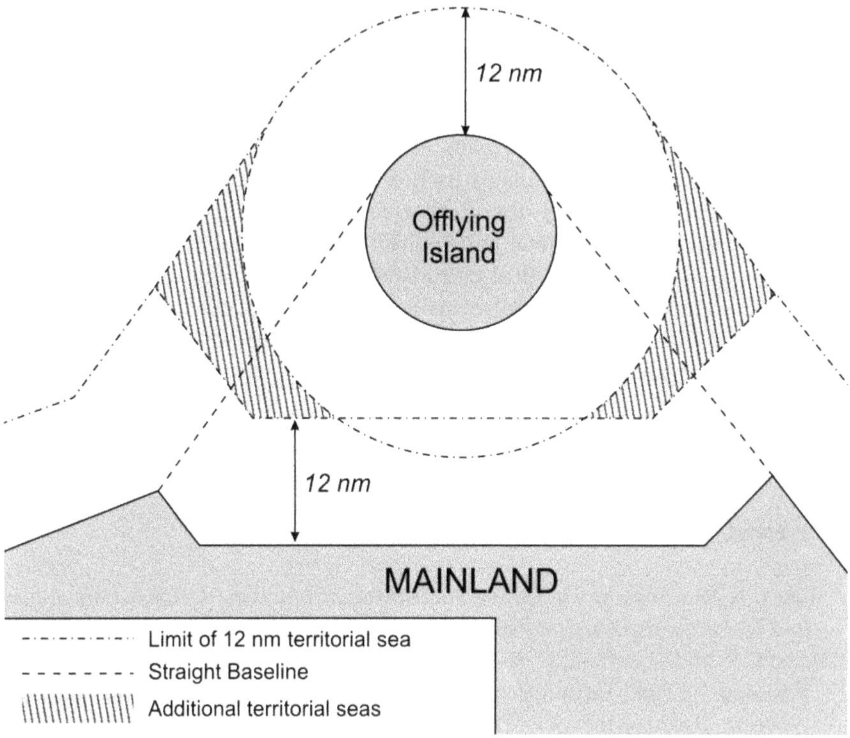

Figure 8.4 Additional maritime areas gained as a result of the application of straight baselines

Source: Adapted from Bateman and Schofield, 2008.

delimited a boundary line utilizing the normal baselines of islands,[90] rather than the extensive, and arguably excessive, systems of straight baselines claimed by each State.

Overall, significant issues exist concerning baselines in the South China Sea across a variety of distinct types of baselines. The issues and uncertainties that arise are of technical, legal and political character. Such uncertainties over baselines necessarily have impacts in terms of the limits and spatial extent of maritime jurisdictional claims and with respect to potential future maritime boundary delimitation. Their resolution will require technical and scientific cooperation, for

R.W. (eds.), *International Maritime Boundaries*, Vol. IV (Dordrecht: Martinus Nijhoff, 2002), 2,692–4.

90 N.H. Thao, 'Vietnam's First Maritime Boundary Agreement', *Boundary and Security Bulletin* 5, no. 3 (Autumn 1997): 75–7. See also Schofield and Tan-Mullins, 'Claims, Conflicts and Cooperation', 98–101.

example, concerning the definition of normal baselines in a geomorphologically and hydrographically complex arena where sovereignty over insular features is subject to dispute. Uncertainty also arises because certain South China Sea States have seemingly been reluctant to fulfil their obligations with respect to providing due publicity to their baseline claims as provided for under Article 16 of the UNCLOS – something that arguably undermines their claims.

With respect to arguably excessive claims to straight baselines, it would seem unlikely that these claims will be 'rolled back' in the foreseeable future, primarily for the sake of political considerations. That said, as demonstrated in bilateral maritime boundary agreements reached in the South China Sea region, potentially problematic straight baseline claims can be overcome in the context of a negotiation. Overall, while defining the 'starting line' can therefore prove to be a troublesome task, legally, technically and politically, it should not be considered to be an impossible one.

References

Antunes, N.M., *Towards the Conceptualisation of Maritime Delimitation: Legal and Technical Aspects of a Political Process* (Leiden: Martinus Nijhoff, 2003).

Bateman, S. and Schofield, C.H. 'State Practice Regarding Straight Baselines in East Asia – Legal, Technical and Political Issues in a Changing Environment', Advisory Board on the Law of the Sea (ABLOS) on *Difficulties in Implementing the Provisions of UNCLOS*, International Hydrographic Bureau Monaco, 16–17 October 2008.

Beazley, P.B., 'Coral Reefs and the 1982 Convention on the Law of the Sea', in *Maritime Boundaries*, edited by Gerald H. Blake (London/New York: Routledge, 1993), 59–72.

Carleton, C.M. and Schofield, C.H., 'Developments in the Technical Determination of Maritime Space: Charts, Datums, Baselines, Maritime Zones and Limits', *Maritime Briefing* 3, no. 3 (2001): 62.

Charney, J.I. and Smith, R.W. (eds.), *International Maritime Boundaries*, Vol. IV (Dordrecht: Martinus Nijhoff, 2002).

Degong, C. 'China and the Law of the Sea', *Occasional Paper* (Canberra: Northeast Asia Program, Research School of Pacific and Asian Studies, Australian National University, December 1996), 23.

Dzurek, D.J., 'The People's Republic of China Straight Baseline Claim', *Boundary and Security Bulletin* 4, no. 2 (1996): 77–89.

Forbes, V.L., 'The Territorial Sea Datum of Malaysia', *MIMA Bulletin* 14, no. 4 (2007): 3–8, at 7–8.

Hancox, D. and Prescott, J.R.V., 'A Geographical Description of the Spratly Islands and an Account of Hydrographic Surveys Amongst those Islands', *Maritime Briefing*, vol. 1, no. 6 (Durham: International Boundaries Research Unit, 1995).

ICJ, *Case Concerning Maritime Delimitation and Territorial Questions between Qatar and Bahrain (Qatar v. Bahrain)* (Merits) [2001] ICJ Rep 40, para. 212, http://www.icj-cij.org/docket/files/87/7027.pdf.

International Hydrographic Organization (with the International Oceanographic Commission and the International Association of Geodesy), *A Manual on Technical Aspects of the United Nations Convention on the Law of the Sea, 1982*, special issue, no. 51, 5th edn (Monaco: International Hydrographic Bureau, 2012).

Jayewardene, H.W., *The Regime of Islands in International Law* (Dordrecht: Martinus Nijhoff, 1990).

Kittichaisaree, K., *The Law of the Sea and Maritime Boundary Delimitation in South-East Asia* (Oxford: Oxford University Press, 1987).

Lavalle, R., 'Not Quite a Sure Thing: The Maritime Areas of Rocks and Low-Tide Elevations Under the U.N. Law of the Sea Convention', *IJMCL* 19 (2004), no. 1: 57–64

Law on the Territorial Sea and Contiguous Zone, 25 February 1992, http://www.un.org/Depts/los/LEGISLATIONANDTREATIES/PDFFILES/CHN_1992_Law.pdf.

Legault, L. and Hankey, B., 'Method, Oppositeness and Adjacency, and Proportionality in Maritime Boundary Delimitation', in *International Maritime Boundaries*, vol. I, edited by J.I. Charney and L.M. Alexander (The Hague: Martinus Nijhoff, 1993), 214.

Lyons, Y., 'Prospects for Satellite Imagery of Insular Features and Surrounding Marine Habitats in the South China Sea', *Marine Policy* 45 (2014): 146–55.

Prescott, J. R.V., *The Maritime Political Boundaries of the World* (London: Methuen, 1985).

Prescott, J.R.V. and Schofield, C.H., *The Maritime Political Boundaries of the World* (Leiden and Boston: Martinus Nijhoff, 2005).

Reed, M.W., *Shore and Sea Boundaries: The Development of International Maritime Boundary Principles through United States Practice* (Washington, DC: U.S. Department of Commerce, 2000).

Roach, J.A. and Smith, R.W., *Excessive Maritime Claims*, 3rd edn (The Hague: Martinus Njihoff, 1996).

Roach, J.A. and Smith, R.W., 'Straight Baselines: The Need for a Universally Applied Norm', *Ocean Development and International Law*, 31 (2000), 47–80.

Roach, J.A. and Smith, R.W., *United States Responses to Excessive Maritime Claims*, 3rd edn (The Hague: Martinus Nijhoff, 2012).

Schofield, C.H., 'Dangerous Ground – A Geopolitical Overview of the South China Sea', in *The South China Sea: Towards a Cooperative Management Regime* (London: Routledge, 2009), 7–25.

Schofield, C.H., 'Rising Waters, Shrinking States: The Potential Impacts of Sea Level Rise on Claims to Maritime Jurisdiction', *German Yearbook of International Law 2010* 53 (2011): 189–231.

Schofield, C.H. and Arsana, I.M.A., 'Extending Indonesia? Opportunities and Challenges related to Indonesia's Claims to Extended Continental Shelf Rights', in *Indonesia Beyond the Water's Edge: Managing an Archipelagic State*, edited by R. Cribb and M. Ford (Singapore: Institute of Southeast Asian Studies Press, 2009), 74.

Schofield, C.H. and Arsana, I.M.A., 'Closing the Loop: Indonesia's Revised Archipelagic Baselines System', *Australian Journal of Marine and Ocean Affairs* 1, no. 2 (2009): 57–62.

Schofield, C.H. and Arsana, I.M.A., 'Climate Change and Maritime Jurisdiction', in *Climate Change and the Oceans: Gauging the Legal and Policy Currents in the Asia Pacific Region*, edited by C.H. Schofield and R. Warner (Cheltenham: Edward Elgar, 2012), 136–7, 127–52

Schofield, C.H. and Freestone, D. 'Options to Protect Coastlines and Secure Maritime Jurisdictional Claims in the Face of Global Sea Level Rise', in Gerrard, M. and Wannier, G. (eds), *Threatened Island Nations: Legal Implications of Rising Seas and a Changing Climate* (Cambridge: Cambridge University Press, 2013), 144–65.

Schofield, C.H. and Tan-Mullins, M., 'Claims, Conflicts and Cooperation in the Gulf of Thailand', *Ocean Yearbook* 22 (Leiden and Boston: Martinus Nijhoff, 2008), 75–116.

Symmons, C.R., 'Some Problems Relating to the Definition of "Insular Formations" in International Law: Islands and Low-Tide Elevations', *Maritime Briefing*, vol. 1, no. 5 (Durham: International Boundaries Research Unit, 1995), 7.

Thao, N.H., 'Vietnam's First Maritime Boundary Agreement', *Boundary and Security Bulletin* 5, no. 3 (Autumn 1997): 75–7.

Tsamenyi, M.B., Schofield, C.H. and Milligan, B., 'Navigation through Archipelagos: Current State Practice', in *Freedom of the Seas, Passage Rights and the 1982 Law of the Sea Convention*, edited by M.H. Nordquist, T.B. Koh and J.N. Moore (Leiden and Boston: Martinus Nijhoff, 2009), 413–54.

United Kingdom Hydrographic Office (UKHO), *China Sea Pilot*, Vol. 1, 8th edition, Admiralty Sailing Directions, (Taunton: UKHO, 2010).

United Nations, *United Nations Convention on the Law of the Sea*, 10 December 1982, Publication no.E97.V10, (United Nations, New York, 1983). See also, 1833 U.N.T.S. 397.

United Nations, Division for Ocean Affairs and the Law of the Sea, Office of Legal Affairs, *Chronological List of Ratifications of, Accessions and Successions to the Convention and the Related Agreements* as at 10 October 2014 (United Nations, Division for Ocean Affairs and the Law of the Sea, Office of Legal Affairs, 2014), http://www.un.org/Depts/los/reference_files/chronological_lists_of_ratifications.htm#TheUnitedNationsConventionontheLawoftheSea.

US Department of State, 'Continental Shelf Boundary: Indonesia-Malaysia', *Limits in the Seas*, no. 1 (Washington, DC: Bureau of Intelligence and Research, 21 January 1970), 2.

US Department of State, 'Straight Baselines: Vietnam', *LIS*, no. 99 (Washington, DC: Bureau of Intelligence and Research, 12 December 1983), 5.

US Department of State, 'Developing Standard Guidelines for Evaluating Straight Baselines', *Limits in the Seas*, No. 106 (Bureau of Oceans and International Environmental and Scientific Affairs, US Department of State, Washington, DC: 31 August 1987).

Valencia, M.J., *Malaysia and the Law of the Sea* (Kuala Lumpur: ISIS Malaysia, 1991).

Valencia, M.J., 'Validity of Malaysia's Baselines and Territorial Sea Claim in the Northern Malacca Strait', *Marine Policy* 27 (2003): 367–73.

Weil, P. *The Law of Maritime Delimitation – Reflections* (Cambridge: Grotius, 1989).

Chapter 9
UNCLOS Navigational Regimes and their Significance for the South China Sea

Donald R. Rothwell

Freedom of the Seas and Navigational Rights and Freedoms in the South China Sea

A feature of the modern law of the sea as it has evolved through the 1958 Geneva Conventions, UNCLOS,[1] and state practice into the twenty-first century has been a capacity to balance the rights and interests of coastal states with those of maritime states. Initially, when the territorial sea was developed the interests of coastal states were conceived in terms of national security and the limited assertion of state sovereignty over a narrow band of adjacent waters. However those interests have now expanded to include concerns over the marine environment, health of marine living resources, threats posed by non-state actors such as terrorist groups, and the management of ocean space extending from the territorial sea out through adjacent maritime zones to the edge of the continental shelf. Accordingly, whilst UNCLOS sought to ensure a careful balance between the interests of coastal states and maritime states in the innocent passage regime through the territorial sea, as the concerns of coastal states over the security of the territorial sea expanded so too does the potential for increased interference with innocent passage.[2] The tension, which has arisen in the past for some coastal states over innocent passage by foreign warships,[3] has in recent decades been extended to include vessels that are deemed to constitute an unacceptable environmental risk.[4] These constraints however do not end at the limits of the territorial sea, and one of the contemporary

1 1982 United Nations Convention on the Law of the Sea (UNCLOS), 1833 UNTS 397.

2 See discussion in Sam Bateman, Donald R. Rothwell and David VanderZwaag, 'Navigational Rights and Freedoms in the New Millennium: Dealing with 20th Century Controversies and 21st Century Challenges', in Donald R. Rothwell and Sam Batemen (eds), *Navigational Rights and Freedoms and the New Law of the Sea* (Martinus Nijhoff, The Hague: 2000) 314, 317–18.

3 See Keyuan Zou, 'Innocent Passage for Warships: The Chinese Doctrine and Practice' (1998) 29 *Ocean Development and International Law* 195–223.

4 Jon M. Van Dyke, 'Sea Shipment of Japanese Plutonium under International Law' (1993) 24 *Ocean Development and International Law* 399–430.

challenges of the current law is ensuring that there are reasonable limits to coastal state regulation of an ever expanding array of activities within the adjoining exclusive economic zone (EEZ). Whilst some of these initiatives, including the creation of maritime identification zones, may be considered benign or consistent with coastal state rights created under a loose amalgam of United Nations Security Council resolutions and new conventional law dealing with maritime security, the impact of these measures upon the traditional freedom of the seas beyond the limits of the territorial sea needs to be carefully considered.

The International Court of Justice summed up the process of balancing these various rights and interests in the *Nicaragua Case* in 1986, just four years after the conclusion of UNCLOS. The court observed that:

> Since freedom of navigation is guaranteed, first in the exclusive economic zones which may exist beyond territorial waters (Art. 58 of the Convention), and secondly, beyond territorial waters and on the high seas (Art. 87), it follows that any State which enjoys a right of access to ports for its ships also enjoys all of the freedom necessary for maritime navigation.[5]

This statement encapsulates some of the key principles upon which this body of the international law of the sea is based and which continues to have an impact.

The question of the freedom of the seas and the exercise of navigational rights and freedoms are becoming increasingly significant in the South China Sea. Traditionally an area in which the United States has sought to exercise its navigational freedoms for the benefit of the US Navy, with the rise of China as a significant military power and the contested nature of the waters within the South China Sea, navigational rights and freedoms within the region are becoming increasingly contested. This has especially been the case given the constant vigilance of the United States in protesting the assertion of maritime claims which it considers to go beyond the limits of the law of the sea and impact upon the freedom of navigation. These protests take place at both a diplomatic level and also by way of the US Freedom of Navigation (FON) programme, and are made against all states, including those with which it enjoys close relations. In the South China Sea, these issues have especially been contentious given variable interpretations of the law of the sea with respect to the navigational rights and freedoms of naval vessels and military operations at sea more generally.

This chapter will address these issues by assessing the freedom of the seas and navigational rights and freedoms under the modern law of the sea. Consideration will be given to how these rights are recognized in the territorial sea, within international straits, within archipelagic waters, the exclusive economic zone (EEZ), and the high seas. Particular attention will be given to the navigational rights of warships.

---

5 *Case Concerning Military and Paramilitary Activities in and Against Nicaragua* (*Nicaragua v. United States of America*) Merits Judgement ICJ Reports 1986, p. 14 [214].

Territorial Sea

A contemporary assessment of the navigation regime within the territorial sea requires a sound appreciation of the rights and interests that the coastal state has within that area. It is important therefore to recall that UNCLOS, Article 2 makes clear that the sovereignty of the coastal state extends 'beyond its land territory and internal waters' to the territorial sea and that sovereignty includes both the air space above as well as the bed and subsoil beneath the water column. The sovereignty of the coastal state therefore is as complete as that which pertains in and over the land and internal waters, contingent only in the qualification that it is 'subject to this Convention and to other rules of international law'.[6]

Whilst the innocent passage regime of UNCLOS therefore represents a concession on the part of the coastal state towards foreign ships which results in practical terms in a diminution of state sovereignty, it may be noted that the right is reciprocal so that coastal states acquire navigational rights in the territorial seas of other states. Importantly for the South China Sea, the focus of the innocent passage regime vis-à-vis the coastal state is entirely directed towards foreign flagged ships exercising the right of innocent passage. The coastal state, consistent with its sovereignty, is entitled to regulate its own flagged shipping within the waters of the territorial sea, extending to the exercise of both criminal and civil jurisdiction, however with respect to navigational safety within the territorial sea often uniform laws and regulations will be applied as between domestic and foreign flagged vessels.[7] This is especially significant for small intra-coastal, cross-strait and inter-island craft which may operate for commercial purposes, in addition to small inshore fishing vessels used by both recreational and commercial fishers.

The Right of Innocent Passage

The key provisions in UNCLOS dealing with the right of innocent passage and how it is to be exercised are found in Part II, Section 3, subsection A dealing with the rules applicable to all ships contained within Articles 17–20. Consistent with the historical development of the law of the sea, the right of innocent passage through the territorial sea in Article 17 exclusively applies to the ships of all states, whether coastal or land-locked. Innocent passage, because it is a right recognized under both treaty and customary international law, does not require express

6 UNCLOS, Article 2(3).

7 This is reflected in the 1972 Convention on the International Regulations for Preventing Collisions at Sea (COLREG), 1050 UNTS 18, under the International Regulations for Preventing Collisions as Sea 1972, Part A, Rule 1 which makes clear that 'These Rules shall apply to all vessels upon the high seas and in all waters connected therewith navigable by seagoing vessels'. The Regulations then go on to distinguish between the capacity of the coastal state to make special rules for internal waters such as roadsteads and harbours.

recognition in the laws of coastal states for it to be exercised consistently with international law.

The physical act of navigation by way of passage through the territorial sea is defined in Article 18, with three types of passage provided for:

1. traversing the territorial sea without entering internal waters or calling at a roadstead or port facility outside of internal waters, in which case the ship is effectively traversing the territorial sea and using it as a maritime highway;
2. proceeding to or from internal waters or after having called at a roadstead or port facility outside internal waters, in which case the ship will have called at either a port or other facility within the coastal state in order to off-load or load cargo, disembark or embark passengers, or required bunkering or related shipping services;[8]
3. stopping or anchoring within the territorial sea when rendered necessary by *force majeure* or distress to the ship, or to other persons, ships or aircraft in danger of distress,[9] or when incidental to ordinary navigation, which would include the taking onboard of a pilot to assist with navigation within the territorial sea or in order to enter a port.

With the exception of the third type of passage, the activity is to be continuous and expeditious and accordingly ships undertaking innocent passage should do so with due speed, taking into account their capacity and navigational conditions. Consistent with the history of innocent passage, the act of hovering by a foreign ship is not legitimate passage. Likewise, a foreign flagged cruise ship which sails within the territorial sea between the coast and adjacent islands providing its passengers with scenic views would not be engaged in passage,[10] whilst the same cruise ship sailing by the most expeditious route through the territorial sea between two ports in the same coastal state would be engaged in passage.

The act of innocent passage is fully expanded upon in Article 19(1), which retains the core language of the Convention on the Territorial Sea and Contiguous Zone and states that:

8 Which the ICJ has described as being part of a 'customary right of innocent passage in territorial waters for the purposes of entering or leaving internal waters': *Case Concerning Military and Paramilitary Activities in and Against Nicaragua* (*Nicaragua v. United States of America*) Merits Judgement ICJ Reports 1986, p. 14 [214].

9 This is consistent with a general duty to render assistance to persons in danger at sea, UNCLOS, Article 98.

10 Scenic cruising by regularly scheduled cruise ships within the territorial sea of a coastal state is permissible if granted in advance by the coastal state; common examples would be cruises undertaken in the Mediterranean Sea and along the coast of Alaska.

> Passage is innocent so long as it is not prejudicial to the peace, good order or security of the coastal State. Such passage shall take place in conformity with this Convention and other rules of international law.

The right of innocent passage is therefore conditional upon the foreign ship not engaging in acts which pose a threat to the adjacent coastal state, adherence to other relevant provisions in UNCLOS, and other relevant international laws. Masters of vessels exercising innocent passage therefore need to be conscious of how their actions may be interpreted by the coastal state, whilst also being mindful of any other obligations they have under the Convention and international law more generally.[11] Here an obvious difficulty with the definition of innocent passage in Article 19(1) is that it is capable of subjective assessment by the coastal state, possibly resulting in the denial of innocent passage for acts that would otherwise be considered benign and posing no threat to the coastal state. To address this issue, Article 19(2) provides a non-exhaustive but nonetheless detailed list of actions that would be deemed to be considered prejudicial to the peace, good order and security of the coastal state if engaged in by a foreign ship.[12] This list effectively identifies categories of accepted 'non-innocent' passage.[13]

The list includes:

- any threat or use of force against the coastal state, or in violation of international law principles embodied in the United Nations Charter;[14]
- weapons exercises;
- acts aimed at collecting information to the prejudice of the defence or security of the coastal state;
- acts of propaganda that affect the defence or security of the coastal state;
- the launching, landing or taking on board of any aircraft or military device;

11 Relevant rules of UNCLOS would include adherence to navigational safety provisions allowing for the coastal state to declare sea lanes, UNCLOS, Article 22; while more general rules of international law would include the COLREG; and 1973/78 International Convention for the Prevention of Pollution from Ships, as modified by the Protocol of 1978 Relating Thereto (MARPOL 73/78), 1340 UNTS 62.

12 Cf. USA-USSR Joint Statement on the Uniform Interpretation of Rules of International Law Governing Innocent Passage, (1989) 14 Law of the Sea Bulletin 13, para. 3 asserting that 'Article 19 of the Convention on 1982 sets out in paragraph 2 an exhaustive list of activities that would render passage not innocent'.

13 The 1930 Hague Conference draft used the term passage that is 'not innocent': Satya N. Nandan and Shabtai Rosenne (eds), *United Nations Convention on the Law of the Sea 1982: A Commentary* Vol. II (Martinus Nijhoff, Dordrecht: 1993) 166 (hereafter 'Virginia Commentary').

14 This is effectively a restatement of UN Charter, Article 2(4); see also UNCLOS, Article 301; cf. *Corfu Channel Case* [1949] ICJ Reps p. 4, 30–31 where the ICJ accepted that though the British warships were at action stations whilst passing through the strait this was consistent with innocent passage.

- the loading or unloading of any commodity, currency or person contrary to relevant laws and regulations of the coastal state;
- wilful and serious pollution contrary to UNCLOS;[15]
- fishing activities;
- research and survey activities; or,
- any act aimed at interfering with communications or other facilities or installations of the coastal state.

In addition, 'any other activity not having a direct bearing on passage'[16] is included as a matter considered prejudicial to the interests of the coastal state. Reference to an 'activity' suggests a positive act by the vessel whilst in passage, rather than an omission.[17] The phrasing here is troubling and potentially open to abuse by a coastal state which deems that an activity of a foreign vessel whilst in passage is not directly related to passage, however there is little state practice to suggest that this provision has been abused.

Whilst the Article 19(2) list is clearly helpful, some difficulty arises in assessing what test is to be applied in determining whether the actions of a ship are contrary to its provisions.[18] This is especially relevant given the sensitivity associated with the right of innocent passage for some coastal states, and the potential for over-generous interpretations of the Article 19(2) list resulting in questionable limitations being placed upon the freedom of territorial sea navigation. It is possible to envisage a number of scenarios where subjective interpretations by a coastal state could result in denial of innocent passage contrary to the intention of the Convention.[19] In order to address any potential disagreements that may have arisen over the interpretation of Article 19(2), the United States and former USSR in 1989 issued a Joint Statement on the Uniform Interpretation of Rules of International Law Governing Innocent Passage, which provided as follows:

> A coastal State which questions whether the particular passage of a ship through its territorial sea is innocent shall inform the ship of the reason why it questions the innocence of the passage, and provide the ship an opportunity to clarify its intentions or correct its conduct in a reasonably short period of time.[20]

---

15 Which needs to be read with UNCLOS, Article 1 and Part XII.

16 UNCLOS, Article 19(2)(l).

17 K. Hakapää and E.J. Molenaar, 'Innocent Passage – Past and Present' (1999) 23 *Marine Policy* 131, 132.

18 William K. Agyebeng, 'Theory in Search of Practice: The Right of Innocent Passage in the Territorial Sea' (2006) 39 *Cornell International Law Journal* 371, 382.

19 For example, Article 19(2)(d) prohibits an act of propaganda, however difficulty would arise in objectively interpreting such an act in the context of passage through the territorial sea; see Donald R. Rothwell, 'Coastal State Sovereignty and Innocent Passage: The Voyage of the *Lusitania Expresso*' (1992) 16 *Marine Policy* 427.

20 USA-USSR Joint Statement on the Uniform Interpretation of Rules of International Law Governing Innocent Passage, para. 4.

Such an approach essentially gives the foreign vessel the benefit of the doubt and, reflecting international comity and the very particular nature of the right of innocent passage within the territory of another state, gives to the foreign vessel the opportunity to rectify any potentially delinquent behaviour.[21]

Coastal State Rights and Duties Regarding Innocent Passage

Prevention of passage

UNCLOS outlines the rights and duties of a coastal state with respect to innocent passage in Articles 24 and 25. Closely aligned with the Article 19 criteria for determining that a ship was not engaged in innocent passage, Article 25 permits coastal states to take 'the necessary steps' to prevent passage which is not innocent. In the case of ships proceeding to internal waters or a territorial sea port facility, the coastal state is also entitled to take similar measures to prevent a breach of any relevant conditions of admission to those waters or facilities. Article 25 is broadly drafted and gives to the coastal state considerable scope for a variety of responses depending on the circumstances. This could include an exchange of communications requesting a delinquent ship to refrain from certain acts, a request that the ship leave the territorial sea immediately, the positioning of vessels to prevent the ship from continuing its passage, the intervention of state authorities such as a Coast Guard or Maritime Police in order to board the vessel to direct it away from the territorial sea, or, subject to the threat posed to the coastal state by the delinquent ship, the use of armed force.[22] UNCLOS is intentionally silent on this issue as ultimately it goes to the question of state sovereignty and how a state may choose to protect itself from what may be perceived or actually is a threat to the interests of the coastal state. Nevertheless, a permissible response would ultimately depend upon the circumstances and, as the International Tribunal for the Law of the Sea observed in *The M/V Saiga (No 2) Case*, would be subject to general principles of international law such as necessity and proportionality.[23]

A related right of protection for the coastal state is the capacity to temporarily suspend innocent passage in specific areas of the territorial sea for the protection

21 See discussion in Vaughan Lowe, 'Uniform Interpretation of the Rules of International Law Governing Innocent Passage' (1991) 6 *International Journal of Estuarine and Coastal Law* 73.

22 See for a description of the practice of 'bumping off' delinquent vessels within the territorial sea, J.C. Hilt Jr, 'Oceans Law and Superpower Relations: The Bumping of the Yorktown and Caron in the Black Sea' (1989) 29 *Virginia Journal of International Law* 713–43.

23 In *The M/V 'Saiga' (No 2) Case* (*Saint Vincent and the Grenadines v. Guinea*) ITLOS Case No. 2 (1 July 1999) [155], where ITLOS observed as follows: 'Although the Convention does not contain express provisions on the use of force in the arrest of ships, international law, which is applicable by virtue of article 293 of the Convention, requires that the use of force must be avoided as far as possible and, where force is unavoidable, it must not go beyond what is reasonable and necessary in the circumstances.'

of its security.[24] Such a right of temporary suspension, which can extend to the conduct of weapons exercises, can only take effect after having been duly published thereby preventing ad hoc suspensions of passage.[25] Some states expressly allow for suspension of innocent passage within their national legislation.[26] This right of the coastal state would extend to the capacity to suspend innocent passage in cases of internal unrest requiring police or military operations to quell that unrest.[27] It is also broad enough in scope to deal with military exercises which may be conducted by the coastal state either on its own or in conjunction with military allies requiring the closure of the territorial sea on a temporary basis. What constitutes a 'temporary' closure is undefined in UNCLOS, and how that term is interpreted may depend upon the circumstances, including whether the events justifying the closure were anticipated, as would be the case with military exercises, have arisen with little notice, or require an ongoing response.[28]

Regulation of passage

An additional right of the coastal state, consistent with its sovereignty over the territorial sea and capacity to adopt and enforce laws and regulations against its own flagged vessels, is the capacity under Article 21 to adopt laws and regulations relating to innocent passage by foreign flagged vessels. Such laws can extend to a wide array of activities related to passage, including navigational safety and the regulation of maritime traffic, conservation of living resources, preservation of the marine environment including the prevention of pollution, marine scientific research and surveying, and customs, fiscal, immigration and sanitary matters. Foreign ships exercising a right of innocent passage are expected to comply with these coastal state laws.[29] In this respect there are clear correlations between activities considered non-innocent under Article 19 and activities subject to legitimate regulation under Article 21. Two of the most relevant for many vessels are those relating to pollution prevention and those addressing fishing. In addition

24 UNCLOS, Article 25(3).

25 See United Nations Division for Ocean Affairs and the Law of the Sea, 'Suspension of Innocent Passage' at www.un.org/Depts/los/convention_agreements/innocent_passages_suspension.htm (27 September 2009) listing notifications of suspensions of innocent passage within the territorial sea received by the United Nations Secretary-General.

26 Maritime Zone Act 2005 (Mauritius), Article 10(4); Law No. 28 (8) 2003 (Syria), Article 13.

27 Cf. exclusion zones which have been declared on security grounds; in May 1990 Papua New Guinea declared a 50 nautical mile exclusion zone around the island of Bougainville, in response to a secession movement on that island, Australia protested this claim and the exclusion zone was revoked: (1992) 13 *Australian Year Book of International Law* 297.

28 In the case of where internal civil disturbance is taking place, it may be possible to justify suspension of innocent passage for a considerable period of time in order to ensure the safety of foreign vessels within those waters.

29 UNCLOS, Article 21(4).

to an act of wilful and serious pollution constituting non-innocent passage, the coastal state is also able to regulate other forms of pollution within the territorial sea which foreign vessels may be responsible for. Any such laws, however, must be consistent with both UNCLOS and other relevant provisions of international law.[30] Likewise in addition to not fishing within the territorial sea, the coastal state can also legislate to prevent the infringement of fisheries laws and regulations, which may for example extend to the stowing of fishing gear while foreign fishing vessels undertake innocent passage.[31]

Duty to not hamper innocent passage

The duties of the coastal state with respect to ships undertaking innocent passage are expressed as being not to 'hamper' passage through the territorial sea.[32] This is consistent with the intention of UNCLOS to permit the free flow of international maritime commerce through the territorial sea providing that passage is innocent. Prima facie therefore ships exercising the right of innocent passage are not to be denied the right of passage, and whilst undertaking passage are not to be subject to interference. One area of contention has been whether a coastal state may legitimately require that all ships take on board a pilot while navigating through the territorial sea. In the absence of international recognition by a body such as the IMO that the waters of the territorial sea were either particularly hazardous or particularly sensitive thereby requiring the services of a pilot to ensure safe passage,[33] compulsory pilotage enforced by way of coastal state laws and regulations would be considered to hamper innocent passage.

In order to distinguish between the legitimate application of certain coastal state laws and regulations with the obligation to not hamper passage, laws which have the practical effect of denying or impairing the right of innocent passage, or which discriminate against ships from certain states or which are carrying certain cargoes are not permissible.[34] A related duty of the coastal state is to publicize dangers to navigation within its territorial sea, of which it has knowledge. No

30 Erik Jaap Molenaar, *Coastal State Jurisdiction over Vessel-Source Pollution* (The Hague, Kluwer Law International: 1998) 199–240.

31 Alex Oude Elferink, 'Rules of Navigation of Ships through the Territorial Sea and the Internal Waters of Estonia' (1993) 8 *International Journal of Marine and Coastal Law* 422, 424 referring to Estonian practice.

32 UNCLOS, Article 24(1).

33 Michael White, 'Navigational Rights in Sensitive Marine Environments: The Great Barrier Reef', in Donald R. Rothwell and Sam Bateman (eds), *Navigational Rights and Freedoms and the New Law of the Sea* (The Hague, Martinus Nijhoff: 2000) 230 discussing compulsory pilotage within the waters of the Great Barrier Reef.

34 Likewise, UNCLOS, Article 21(2) makes clear that laws and regulations of the coastal state relating to design, construction, manning or equipment of foreign ships are only applicable if they reflect generally accepted international rules and standards. See also UNCLOS, Article 227 regarding non-discrimination against foreign vessels in Part XII.

charges may be levied against ships engaged in innocent passage, other than for services rendered to the ship.[35]

The Rights of Foreign Flagged Vessels

Other than the broad right of innocent passage in Article 17, UNCLOS does not provide much more express detail as to the precise rights of foreign flagged vessels whilst engaged in innocent passage. The broad statement as to what constitutes innocent passage in Article 19 is clearly capable of wide interpretation, and though assisted by the listing of non-innocent acts outlined in Article 19(2), still gives to the coastal state a firm basis upon which to revoke passage if it so determines.[36] The duty of the coastal state to not hamper passage outlined in Article 24 gives foreign vessels some confidence in their capacity to enjoy innocent passage, but UNCLOS is silent as to what a foreign vessel can do if its innocent passage rights have been denied or improperly terminated. The gap which exists in UNCLOS is an indication of an evidentiary standard as to whether a vessel is undertaking non-innocent passage, and in particular whether an objective or subjective standard is applicable. When this question arose in the *Corfu Channel Case*, the ICJ focused more on the manner in which the passage of the British warships was being conducted than the actual motive of the passage.[37]

International Straits

UNCLOS devotes considerable attention in Part III to the regime of straits used for international navigation. Reference is made to a 'regime of passage through straits used for international navigation'[38] established in Part III of the Convention, suggesting that the intention was to create a comprehensive legal framework for such straits. This is what is ultimately achieved by the transit passage regime, which is a separate regime within UNCLOS for straits used for international navigation. However, there are many potential categories of straits which, depending on their history, geographic configuration and usage, may be subject to different

35 UNCLOS, Article 26. However, this would permit the levying of charges for pilotage services in those parts of the territorial sea where this would be necessary to ensure safe navigation.

36 Ngantcha emphasizes that the coastal state's subjective appraisal of passage as non-innocent should be limited by the objective requirement that any violation which is alleged to have occurred have taken place while the vessel is in passage; Francia Ngantcha, *The Right of Innocent Passage and the Evolution of the International Law of the Sea* (Pinter, London: 1990) 51.

37 *Corfu Channel Case* [1949] ICJ Reps p. 4, 30 stating that 'It remains, therefore, to consider whether the manner in which the passage was carried out was consistent with the principle of innocent passage'.

38 UNCLOS, Article 34(1).

characterizations for the purposes of the law of the sea. The International Court in the *Corfu Channel Case* hinted that a variety of factors may need to be taken into account in determining which navigational rights applied within a particular strait. Accordingly, one of the initial issues that needed to be addressed in UNCLOS was distinguishing between various navigational regimes that apply in the different bodies of water that may comprise a strait. One of those factors is clearly the width of the strait and surveys have estimated that there are 52 international straits less than 6 nm in width, 153 international straits between 6 and 24 nm in width, and 60 other international straits in excess of 24 nm.[39]

Categories of Straits

The starting point for an analysis of Part III is its title – 'Straits Used for International Navigation' – a descriptor repeated in various articles found within this Part of the Convention. This immediately raises for consideration what the Convention classifies as a strait used for international navigation. Using terminology similar to that found in the *Corfu Channel Case*, by the ILC, and in the Geneva Convention on the Territorial Sea and Contiguous Zone, this phrase suggests both a geographical and functional element. The geographical element relates to a strait being a body of water which lies between two areas of land, either continental land masses,[40] a continent and an island,[41] or two islands.[42] However, there is no guidance as to how proximate the bodies of land must be to one another, or at which point the width of the body of water which separates the two areas of land is no longer considered a strait but rather a sea or an ocean.[43] For practical purposes this distinction may not be of great relevance as most bodies of water that separate sufficiently proximate areas of land are referred to as straits, or have equivalent titles.[44] Nevertheless, the recognition of a body of water as a strait is an important starting point in the application of the Part III legal regime.

39 A.R. Thomas and James C. Duncan (eds), 'Annotated Supplement to The Commanders Handbook on the Law of Naval Operations' (1999) 73 *International Legal Studies* 207–8, Table A2-5.

40 An example is the Bering Strait separating continental Asia and North America.

41 The Dover Strait lies between the continent of Europe and an island comprising Great Britain.

42 The Cook Strait separates the North and South Island of New Zealand.

43 R.R. Baxter, *The Law of International Waterways* (Harvard University Press, Cambridge, MA: 1964) 3–4. George K. Walker, 'Definitions for the 1982 Law of the Sea Convention – Part II: Analysis of the IHO Consolidated Glossary' (2003) 33 *California Western International Law Journal* 219, 298, observes that 'The geographic definition of a strait is a narrow passage of water between two land masses or islands, or groups of islands connecting two sea areas'.

44 Of which the term 'channel' is in state practice used as an alternate to 'strait', as in the Corfu Channel; alternate terms which are used include 'Belt', 'Mouth' and 'Sound'.

In addition to the geographical criterion, in the *Corfu Channel Case* the ICJ placed emphasis on the strait being one that was 'used for international navigation'.[45] While there was no analysis as to what volume of navigation through the strait would be required to meet the usage requirement, reference was made to the volume of navigation through the strait between 1936 and 1937, which in the view of the Court assisted it in determining that the Corfu Channel had been 'a useful route for international maritime traffic'.[46] Therefore, while this functional element remains a feature of UNCLOS, it is unclear as to what level of international navigation is required for a strait to be appropriately classified as an 'international strait'. However, it is doubtful whether infrequent or irregular use of a strait would suffice to meet the functional criterion. Likewise, the strait must have been used by foreign flagged vessels; and not only by through or cross-strait local vessel traffic.

The principal focus of Part III is upon straits used for international navigation between different parts of the high seas and EEZ, and the regime of transit passage which applies within those straits.[47] However, Part III also makes reference to other categories of straits. These include the following:

- straits which are regulated in whole or in part by long-standing international conventions;[48]
- straits where there exists a route through the high seas or EEZ of similar convenience;[49]
- straits which exist between the mainland and an island where there exists seaward of the island a route through the high seas or EEZ of similar convenience;[50]
- straits used for international navigation between one part of the high seas or EEZ and the territorial sea of a foreign state.[51]

All of these categories of straits are ones in which the principal regime of transit passage as created under UNCLOS does not apply, but in its place alternate navigation regimes are recognized. In the case of straits that are subject to long-standing international conventions, there are a number of instances of such straits including the Turkish Straits, Danish Straits, Strait of Magellan and the Aaland Straits.[52]

45 *Corfu Channel Case* [1949] ICJ Reps p. 4, 28.

46 *Corfu Channel Case* [1949] ICJ Reps p. 4, 28.

47 UNCLOS, Article 37.

48 UNCLOS, Article 35(c).

49 UNCLOS, Article 36.

50 UNCLOS, Article 38(1).

51 UNCLOS, Article 45.

52 Hugo Caminos, 'Categories of International Straits Excluded from the Transit Passage Regime under Part III of the United Nations Convention on the Law of the Sea', in

Where there is a high seas or EEZ route through a strait, providing that the route is of similar convenience with respect to navigational and hydrographical circumstances, then Part III of UNCLOS does not apply.[53] In theory this includes all straits that are broader than 24 nm, although in marginal cases such as where the breadth of the waters barely exceeds 24 nm at its narrowest point, it may be arguable as to whether a narrow channel through the EEZ is one of 'similar convenience'. This will especially be the case if the traffic through the strait is heavy and needs to be separated through the use of sea lanes for safety reasons. The related exemption applies in the case of where the strait is formed by a mainland and an island and there exists a route of similar convenience with respect to navigational and hydrographical characteristics seaward of the island. In this instance UNCLOS is essentially stating that if international navigation has a choice of route of similar convenience, then that which exists through the high seas or EEZ is to be preferred. If on the other hand international shipping prefers to pass between the mainland and the island then a right of innocent passage applies in the place of transit passage, though the right of innocent passage cannot be suspended.[54] Examples of straits that fall within this exception are the Strait of Messina (Italy), Pemba Channel (Tanzania), Georgia (Canada), Hainan (China), and The Solent (United Kingdom).[55] However care needs to be taken in applying this exception because even within a strait the presence of islands within a strait may create a number of navigational options with the effect that there exists a number of geographical straits within a much larger strait.[56]

The Regime of Transit Passage

The regime of transit passage which exists between straits used for international navigation between one part of the high seas and EEZ and another part of the high seas and EEZ is one which all ships and aircraft enjoy.[57] That transit passage is

---

Tafsir Malick Ndiaye and Rűdiger Wolfrum (eds), *Law of the Sea, Environmental Law and Settlement of Disputes* (Martinus Nijhoff, Leiden: 2007) 583, 583–4; Thomas and Duncan, 'Annotated Supplement to The Commanders Handbook on the Law of Naval Operations', 205, Table A2-3 lists five straits: Bosporus, Dardanelles, Magellan, Oresund and Store Belt (Storebaelt).

53 UNCLOS, Article 36.

54 UNCLOS, Article 45.

55 Thomas and Duncan, 'Annotated Supplement to The Commanders Handbook on the Law of Naval Operations', 204–5, Table A2-2 listing 22 straits that fall into this category.

56 An example is Bass Strait formed between the Australian continent and the island of Tasmania where within the strait there are two significant islands (Flinders Island and King Island) plus a number of smaller island chains which in themselves form straits: Donald R. Rothwell, 'International Straits and UNCLOS: An Australian Case Study' (1992) 23 *Journal of Maritime Law and Commerce* 461.

57 UNCLOS, Article 38(1).

also open to aircraft as well as ships is an important point of distinction with the regime of innocent passage in the territorial sea, and a contemporary recognition that freedom of overflight within an international strait has significant implications for the freedom of movement of peoples and for government aircraft. The right of transit passage is also one that is not to be 'impeded',[58] implying that the strait state must not bar or suspend transit passage or otherwise engage in activities that may have the practical effect of doing so.

The act of transit

Article 38(2) of UNCLOS goes on to outline the physical act of transit passage which includes the freedom of navigation and overflight 'solely for the purpose of continuous and expeditious transit of the strait', which reflects the objective of ensuring that the regime facilitates the movement of vessels and aircraft physically through the strait from an entrance to an exit point. These provisions build upon the ICJ's notion in *Corfu Channel* of a strait being an 'international highway'.[59] Allowance is also made in the case of where passage through the Strait is undertaken for the purpose of 'entering, leaving or returning from a State bordering the strait',[60] thereby facilitating ships or aircraft which are seeking to dock or land at a facility within a state adjoining a strait, of which Singapore is one of the most prominent examples.[61] Transit passage is therefore enjoyed by ships and aircraft which seek to pass through the strait, or which are entering or exiting the strait after having stopped at or on their way to a state which borders the strait.

Duties of ships and aircraft in transit

Once engaged in transit passage, under Article 39 of UNCLOS ships and aircraft have certain duties that are reflective of some of the elements of innocent passage, though these are by no means as extensive. They include the requirement to proceed without delay, to refrain from any use or threat of force against the sovereignty, territorial integrity or political independence of the strait state, or in any other manner in violation of the principles of international law found in the United Nations Charter, and to refrain from activities other than those which are incidental 'to their normal mode' of transit, unless rendered necessary by *force majeure* or distress.

These duties of ships and aircraft engaged in transit passage reflects an important balancing of rights and interests within the straits regime. On the one hand transit passage was developed to permit the free and unimpeded passage of

58 UNCLOS, Article 38(1).

59 *Corfu Channel Case* [1949] ICJ Reps p. 4, 29.

60 UNCLOS, Article 38(2).

61 The only way in which Singapore can be approached by ship is via either the Straits of Malacca and Singapore, or the Straits of Jahore; similarly for an aircraft making an approach by sea and not overflying the territory of adjoining states, these Straits provide the only means of air access.

ships and aircraft through international straits, thereby ensuring the continuation of important guarantees of the freedom of navigation and overflight that had historically developed through the law of the sea within certain bodies of water. On the other hand, strait states have legitimate security concerns relating to the presence of foreign ships and aircraft within or above their territorial sea in what may be relatively confined waters, and accordingly must be protected from any acts that may constitute a threat to their sovereignty or territorial integrity. Balancing those competing rights and objectives, especially in the case of military vessels and aircraft, has at times proven to be a major challenge.[62]

In addition to these generic duties, ships in transit passage are to comply with generally accepted international regulations and procedures dealing with safety of life at sea and the 1972 Convention on the International Regulations for Preventing Collisions at Sea (COLREG), and also with generally accepted international regulations for the prevention, reduction and control of pollution.[63] Aircraft shall observe the Rules of the Air established by the International Civil Aviation Organisation (ICAO), and related measures for the safety of air navigation, and also monitor radio frequencies for the purpose of air traffic control.[64]

Obligations of strait states

Article 44 of UNCLOS makes clear that strait states are not to 'hamper' transit passage and are to give appropriate notification of any dangers to navigation or overflight within or over the strait of which they may be aware, which would extend to cases of shipwreck blocking parts of the strait or to severe weather conditions. It is also made clear that strait states are not to suspend transit passage. Here one of the important distinctions that exists between the regime of transit passage in an international strait and innocent passage within the territorial sea is made clear – while transit passage cannot be suspended by the strait state, a coastal state may temporarily suspend innocent passage.[65] Therefore, even if a strait state has concerns regarding its national security because of the potential for transiting traffic to be caught up in internal disturbances, it may not seek to suspend the right of transit passage. However, it may seek to issue a warning to ships of the potential hazards that exist within its waters at any particular point in time.[66] The obligation upon the strait state not to 'hamper' transit passage suggests that no obligations or requirements may be imposed upon ships or aircraft that

62 See the discussion below.

63 UNCLOS, Article 39(2).

64 UNCLOS, Article 39(3); the later requirement is especially significant for state aircraft, in particular military aircraft, which may not otherwise be subject to such requirements.

65 UNCLOS, Article 25(3).

66 Note that UNCLOS, Article 44, refers to 'any danger to navigation or overflight within or over the strait of which they have knowledge', which is a direct reference to the issues that arose in *Corfu Channel* regarding whether Albania did or did not have

create a burden for them. One traditional interpretation of this requirement is that the strait state may not impose tolls or any other fees in return for a right of passage.[67] However, some strait states have expressed concerns about the financial burdens they face in maintaining navigational aids and other safety and marine environmental protection measures within the waters of an international strait without receiving any recompense and have argued there should be an entitlement to charge tolls or at least a fee-for-service that relates directly to the benefits they provide to international shipping that passes through the strait.[68] Related issues have arisen with respect to whether the imposition of compulsory pilotage in some international straits is an imposition which amounts to the hampering or impairment of transit passage, or is instead a legitimate measure to reduce the risk of marine environmental damage.[69]

Regulation of transit passage

Within the limits of the above obligations imposed upon strait states, they enjoy the capacity to enact laws and regulations relating to transit passage. For ships such laws can extend to the safety of navigation and regulation of maritime traffic, the prevention, reduction and control of pollution by giving effect to applicable international regulations, the stowage of gear on fishing vessels, and the loading or unloading of any commodity, currency or person contrary to customs, fiscal, immigration or sanitary laws.[70] Such laws are not to have the effect of discriminating between foreign ships, which are expected to comply with such laws subject to appropriate publicity having been given to their enactment.[71] However, consistent with the limitations that are reflected in Article 44 such laws are also not to 'have the practical effect of denying, hampering or impairing the right of transit passage'.[72]

Closely related to these measures and the initiatives which the strait state can take to ensure the safety of navigation, UNCLOS Article 41 permits the designation of sea lanes and traffic separation schemes within straits. A strait state that wishes to

knowledge as to the existence of mines in the strait: see *Corfu Channel Case* [1949] ICJ Reps p. 4, 22–3.

67 UNCLOS, Article 26; *Virginia Commentary*, Vol. II, 161, 236.

68 Mark J. Valencia and Abu Bakar Jaafar, 'Environmental Management of the Malacca – Singapore Straits: Legal and Institutional Issues' (1985) 25 *Natural Resources Journal* 195–232.

69 R.C. Beckman, 'PSSAs and Transit Passage – Australia's Pilotage System in the Torres Strait Challenges the IMO and UNCLOS' (2007) 38 *Ocean Development and International Law* 337; Donald R. Rothwell, 'Compulsory Pilotage and the Law of the Sea: Lessons Learned from the Torres Strait', in Shicun Wu and Keyuan Zou (eds), *Securing the Safety of Navigation in East Asia: Legal and Political Dimensions* (Chandos, Cambridge: 2013) 51–72.

70 UNCLOS, Article 42(1).

71 UNCLOS, Article 42(2), (3), (4).

72 UNCLOS, Article 42 (2).

designate a sea lane needs to take into account the views of a relevant international organization, of which the IMO is considered to be the leading authority in this particular field. This will not only impact upon how a sea lane has been designated, but also the navigational rules and safety standards which will apply within the sea lane. The COLREGs deal with safety of navigation, and Rule 10 addresses the behaviour of vessels in or near a traffic separation scheme (TSS) within which certain sea lanes operate. The first formal TSS was established in the Straits of Dover in 1967 on a voluntary basis, but following several maritime incidents in 1971 the IMO's Maritime Safety Committee recommended that the observance of all TSS become mandatory and this was endorsed by the IMO Assembly and is now reflected in COLREGs. A TSS seeks to separate vessel traffic in opposite directions by the use of a separation zone, or a lane, or by other means. A sea lane which exists within a TSS is predominantly designed to facilitate safe one-way through traffic of shipping. The lanes or zones may or may not be marked by buoys or other navigational aids, though a coastal state does have the legal capacity to install such devices. The operation of the sea lane is principally divided between through traffic, 'local' or 'coastal traffic', and crossing vessels which are seeking to move from one sea lane to another. Vessels engaged in through traffic within a sea lane are to proceed in the general direction of the traffic flow, as far as practicable keep clear of a traffic separation line, only join the lane at designated points or in such a manner as to merge with the general flow of traffic, and avoid crossing traffic lanes. Compliance with navigational rules within a sea lane will depend upon the relevant laws of the strait state, which may extend its laws to all vessels including those which are foreign-flagged.

Enforcement of strait state laws and regulations

One aspect of the transit passage regime which is not made clear in UNCLOS is the level of enforcement action a strait state may undertake against a delinquent vessel purportedly exercising a right of transit passage. One scenario arises when a vessel is not complying with the requirements of transit passage and its actions are in breach of Article 39 such that it is posing a threat to the strait state or it is not engaging in 'normal mode' passage. A strait state retains its capacity of self-defence under international law and could rely upon that right in the face of a hostile act by a transiting ship or aircraft. It also has the capacity, consistent with UNCLOS, to prohibit passage by a ship or aircraft which is not engaging in transit passage in conformity with Part III. Accordingly, even if the ship or aircraft poses no threat to the national security of the strait state, a delinquent ship could be prevented from continuing its passage.

Another enforcement scenario arises when a ship, or an aircraft, legitimately engaging in transit passage in compliance with its Article 39 duties breaches the laws and regulations of the strait state. Part III is silent on the actual enforcement capacity of the strait state in such circumstances, which raises issues as to how a strait state may go about seeking to enforce its law in a manner that does not have the practical effect of hampering or impairing transit passage. Nevertheless, Article

34 of UNCLOS makes clear that the Part III regime dealing with straits used for international navigation does not in other respects affect the legal status of the waters of the strait with regards to the coastal state's sovereignty and jurisdiction. This would extend to the coastal state's criminal and civil jurisdiction within the territorial sea of the strait. This view is supported by the text of Articles 27 and 28 which respectively deal with coastal state criminal and civil jurisdiction in the case of 'a foreign ship passing through the territorial sea'. These provisions make clear that in the case of criminal jurisdiction there is a limited right to board a ship and effect an arrest whilst that ship is within the territorial sea, which would also extend to a ship engaged in transit passage.

Archipelagic Navigation

One of the major achievements of the Third United Nations Conference on the Law of the Sea was the recognition accorded to archipelagic states via Part IV of UNCLOS. As of 2014, there were a total of 22 states that had asserted the status of archipelagic states,[73] of which two of those states fall within the South China Sea region: Indonesia and the Philippines.

One of the principal goals of UNCLOS III once agreement was reached on the definition of an archipelago was to determine the various navigation regimes which existed within archipelagic waters. In this regard, it was important to not only focus upon waters on the landward side of the archipelagic baselines but to also consider waters that fell within the potential maritime zones that an archipelagic state could assert, of which the territorial sea was the most significant from a navigational perspective.

Whilst UNCLOS provided that archipelagic states were able to claim sovereignty over the waters within the limits of the archipelagic baselines which also extended to the air space,[74] the sovereignty of the archipelagic state was to be exercised in conformity with Part IV of the Convention, which made express allowance for a range of navigational regimes within archipelagic waters. Article 50 makes clear that within archipelagic waters, subject to certain exceptions, the ships of all states enjoy the right of innocent passage and that this right is to be applied in accordance with the relevant articles found in Part II dealing with innocent passage.[75] Therefore, for the purposes of navigation within archipelagic waters the innocent passage regime effectively applies in the same way as it does within the territorial sea. Hence ships of all states have the right of passage through archipelagic waters irrespective of whether they are calling at a local port, or simply passing through from an entry to an exit point, provided that the

73 See discussion in J. Ashley Roach and Robert W. Smith, *Excessive Maritime Claims*, 3rd edn (Martinus Nijhoff, Leiden: 2012) 206–8.

74 UNCLOS, Article 49.

75 UNCLOS, Articles 17–32.

passage is innocent and not prejudicial to the peace, good order and security of the archipelagic state and in conformity with any relevant laws and regulations the archipelagic state may have adopted. Notwithstanding Article 23 of UNCLOS, which permits innocent passage by foreign nuclear-powered ships or those which are carrying nuclear or other dangerous or toxic substances providing appropriate documentation is being carried and precautionary measures are being observed, a number of archipelagic states have objected to the presence of such vessels within their waters.[76]

Innocent passage within archipelagic waters

Innocent passage within archipelagic waters is the default navigation regime for those ships not otherwise undertaking archipelagic sea lanes passage and is subject to only two qualifications.[77] First, like the innocent passage regime within the territorial sea, the archipelagic state may temporarily suspend innocent passage within specified areas of the archipelagic waters 'if such suspension is essential for the protection of its security'.[78] Such suspension is to only take effect after having been duly published. Accordingly, an archipelagic state may from time to time, and with appropriate notice, completely close areas of its archipelagic waters to international shipping. UNCLOS places few limitations on this right other than it be non-discriminatory, and a temporal and notification requirement, thereby providing the archipelagic state with considerable latitude in how it interprets this provision,[79] including its capacity to suspend navigation in waters which are at a considerable distance from any of the islands that fall within archipelagic baselines.

Second, the innocent passage regime is without prejudice to the ability of the archipelagic state to draw closing lines for the delimitation of internal waters within the archipelago.[80] Nevertheless, innocent passage may still be enjoyed between archipelagic waters and the internal waters of the archipelago where a ship is proceeding to or from those internal waters, such as in the case of a port

---

76 Mohamed Munavvar, *Ocean States: Archipelagic Regimes in the Law of the Sea* (Martinus Nijhoff, Dordrecht: 1995) 166.

77 This is made clear by UNCLOS, Article 52(1), which states that the right of innocent passage is '[s]ubject to article 53 [right of archipelagic sea lanes passage] and without prejudice to article 50 [delimitation of internal waters]'. In the case of Indonesia, Government Regulation No. 37 on the Rights and Obligations of Foreign Ships and Aircraft Exercising the Right of Archipelagic Sea Lanes Passage through Designated Sea Lanes (28 June 2002) (2003) 52 *Law of the Sea Bulletin* 20, Article 13 contemplates the exercise of the right of innocent passage within an archipelagic sea lane.

78 UNCLOS, Article 52(2).

79 The equivalent provision in UNCLOS, Article 25(3), provides that the coastal state may temporarily suspend innocent passage 'if such suspension is essential for the protection of its security, including weapons exercises'. The omission of a reference to weapons exercises in Article 52(2) does not appear significant.

80 UNCLOS, Article 50, 52(1).

facility.[81] In addition to the right of innocent passage within archipelagic waters, innocent passage also applies within the territorial sea of an archipelagic state, which lies on the seaward side of the normal baselines and archipelagic baselines. Therefore, foreign ships which enter into the territorial sea of an archipelagic state would enjoy an ongoing right of innocent passage as they passed from the territorial sea into archipelagic waters and then passed through the archipelago back out into the territorial sea.

Archipelagic Sea Lanes Passage

The most significant distinctive navigational regime that applies within archipelagic waters is that of archipelagic sea lanes passage (ASLP) which is outlined in Article 53 but which borrows heavily from the transit passage regime in Part III of UNCLOS, even to the extent of applying some of the provisions of the transit passage regime *mutatis mutandis*.[82] ASLP is exercised within and above archipelagic waters, which is an area over which the archipelagic state enjoys sovereignty extending to both the air space, seabed and the subsoil.[83] Within archipelagic sea lanes all ships and aircraft enjoy a right of ASLP in sea lanes and air routes.[84] The right is one that can be exercised for the purpose of 'continuous, expeditious and unobstructed transit' between one part of the high seas or an EEZ and another part of the high seas or an EEZ.[85] The omission of a reference to transit through the territorial sea at the perimeter of the entrance and exit from archipelagic waters is intentional, as the sea lanes through which ASLP is enjoyed traverse through the archipelagic waters and the adjacent territorial sea.[86] ASLP therefore duplicates key aspects of the transit passage regime within international straits in that it is designed to facilitate the passage of both ships and aircraft through and

---

81 Using the language and the provisions found in UNCLOS, Article 18(1)(b).

82 UNCLOS, Article 54.

83 UNCLOS, Article 49. Upon signature and subsequent ratification of UNCLOS, the Philippines lodged a Declaration under UNCLOS, Article 310, which in part provided 'The provisions of the Convention on archipelagic passage through sea lanes do not nullify or impair the sovereignty of the Philippines as an archipelagic State over the sea lanes and do not deprive it of authority to enact legislation to protect its sovereignty, independence and security': United Nations Division for Ocean Affairs and the Law of the Sea, 'Declarations and Statements', www.un.org/Depts/los/convention_agreements/convention_declarations.htm (7 November 2009).

84 UNCLOS, Article 53(2). Writing in 1991, Barbara Kwiatkowska and Etty R. Agoes, *Archipelagic Waters Regime in the Light of the 1982 United Nations Law of the Sea Convention and State Practice* (ICLOS, UNPAD, Bandung: 1991) 43, asserted the right of 'non-suspendable archipelagic sea lanes passage of all ships and aircraft … is alongside with the innocent passage of warships the most controversial element of [*sic*] archipelagic state regime'.

85 UNCLOS, Article 53(3).

86 UNCLOS, Article 53(4).

over the waters of the archipelagic state so that they can freely move through the archipelago as they continue their journey. In this respect, emphasis is given to the regime being one which promotes continuous and expeditious transit. Vessels that seek to call at a port within archipelagic waters therefore do not exercise ASLP, but rather revert to the innocent passage regime noted above.[87] Indonesia, as the first archipelagic state to designate archipelagic sea lanes consistent with the processes outlined in Article 53 of UNCLOS, in 2002 adopted Government Regulation No 37 dealing with the rights and obligations of foreign ships and aircraft in passage.[88] The Indonesian Regulation directly refers to the right of archipelagic sea lane passage by foreign ships and aircraft as being a right recognized under Indonesian law by Act No 6 regarding Indonesian Waters.[89]

Navigation in 'normal mode'

The right of ASLP is one that is to be exercised in the 'normal mode', which again duplicates language found in the transit passage regime.[90] As in the case of transit through an international strait, ASLP in the normal mode through an archipelagic sea lane can raise significant issues especially in the case of warships,[91] where an archipelagic state may have a legitimate sensitivity to the presence of such ships within the waters which in effect comprise the state. Likewise, it is arguable that because passage through an archipelago along an archipelagic sea lane may be a lengthy voyage that could take many hours then 'normal modes' of operation for warships should be allowed a more flexible interpretation, especially in the case of submarines and aircraft carriers.

---

87 UNCLOS, Article 38(2), which anticipates a vessel or aircraft in transit passage entering, leaving or returning from a state which borders a strait, does not have an equivalent provision in the ASLP regime. This is understandable given that within archipelagic waters there exists a mixed regime of innocent passage for some ships and ASLP for other ships.

88 Indonesian Government Regulation No. 37 on the Rights and Obligations of Foreign Ships and Aircraft Exercising the Right of Archipelagic Sea Lanes Passage through Designated Sea Lanes (28 June 2002) (2003) 52 *Law of the Sea Bulletin* 20.

89 Act No. 6 of 8 August 1996 regarding Indonesian Waters (Indonesia); see also Indonesian Government Regulation No. 37 on the Rights and Obligations of Foreign Ships and Aircraft Exercising the Right of Archipelagic Sea Lanes Passage through Designated Sea Lanes, Article 2.

90 UNCLOS, Article 53(3); cf. 39(1)(c).

91 Kwiatkowska and Agoes, *Archipelagic Waters Regime*, 44, 54; Munavvar, *Ocean States*, 168. Upon its signature of UNCLOS in 1983, Sao Tome and Principe lodged a declaration consistent with UNCLOS, Article 310, which in part provided 'The Government of the Democratic Republic of Sao Tome and Principe reserves the right to adopt laws and regulations relating to the innocent passage of warships through its territorial sea or its archipelagic waters and to take any other measures aimed at safeguarding its security'. United Nations Division for Ocean Affairs and the Law of the Sea 'Declarations and Statements', www.un.org/Depts/los/convention_agreements/convention_declarations.htm (7 November 2009).

Navigation within archipelagic sea lanes

Unlike the transit passage regime, where the coastal state has little capacity to influence where ships and aircraft exercise the right of transit other than in designated sea lanes, the right of ASLP is one which UNCLOS conferred significant rights upon the archipelagic state so as to designate sea lanes within which ASLP can be exercised. The sea lanes and air routes must include 'all normal passage routes used as routes for international navigation and overflight' and in the case of ships 'all normal navigational channels'.[92] Recognizing that the waters within many archipelagic states would previously have been either high seas, or straits within which a right of international navigation prevailed, the clear intent of UNCLOS is to preserve these previously existing navigation routes and this is emphasized by repeated use of the word 'normal' in the context of the passage routes and channels. The effect of this foundational provision as to where ASLP may be enjoyed is that UNCLOS sought to retain the status quo with respect to navigation routes that existed through some of the major archipelagos prior to the conclusion of UNCLOS, and accordingly for major straits such as Sunda and Lombok within the Indonesian archipelago, the entry into force of ASLP provisions should not have had a major impact upon traditional navigation routes. Nevertheless, irregularly used routes such as those which may be selected by foreign yachts undertaking a pleasure cruise through an archipelago would not fall into the category of a 'normal' route. The archipelagic sea lanes are also to include 'all normal navigational channels' with an exception arising in the case of where there may have previously existed a number of duplicate routes of similar convenience. The effect here is that only one sea lane is required for designation within any one particular body of water. In addition, the designation of particular sea lanes may also need to take into account the harmonization of foreign ships undertaking ASLP with local commercial navigation moving within the archipelago.[93]

Obligations while undertaking archipelagic sea lanes passage

Whilst Part IV outlines in some detail the regime of ASLP, many of the rights, duties and obligations of both the user state and archipelagic state are left silent. The exception is Article 54, which makes clear that the provisions of Articles 39, 40, 42 and 44 apply *mutatis mutandis* to ASLP, which is a further reinforcement of the linkage between the transit passage and ASLP regimes. Accordingly, both ships and aircraft engaged in ASLP are required to proceed without delay and to refrain from any threat or use of force against the sovereignty or territorial

92 UNCLOS, Article 53(4).

93 Jay L. Batongbacal, 'Barely Skimming the Surface: Archipelagic Sea Lanes Navigation and the IMO', in Alex G. Oude Elferink and Donald R. Rothwell (eds), *Oceans Management in the 21st Century: Institutional Frameworks and Responses* (Martinus Nijhoff, Leiden: 2004) 49, 65.

integrity of the archipelagic state.[94] Article 39(1)(c) reinforces that passage is to be undertaken in the normal mode. Ships and aircraft also have obligations to comply with appropriate safety at sea and marine environmental provisions, and for civil aircraft to comply with ICAO Rules of the Air and for state aircraft to have due regard to the safety of navigation, whilst also monitoring designated air traffic control authorities. Foreign ships engaged in ASLP are also not to undertake marine scientific research, including any survey activities, without prior authorization.[95] There is likewise an obligation upon foreign ships and aircraft to comply with the relevant laws and regulations of the archipelagic state which may have been adopted which in the case of ships may deal with safety of navigation, pollution control, stowage of fishing gear, and activities contrary to customs, fiscal, immigration or sanitary laws and regulations.[96] That the same category of laws and regulations which apply to ships in transit passage also apply in ASLP is a significant concession to international maritime traffic given the comparative length of time ships may spend within archipelagic waters as opposed to the territorial sea whilst in transit passage.

Obligations of the archipelagic state

The obligations of the archipelagic state with respect to ASLP are likewise transposed from Article 44 within Part III and as such they are to not hamper transit passage, give appropriate publicity to any danger of which they have knowledge, and to not suspend ASLP. These obligations upon the archipelagic state are further reinforced with the Article 53 reference to ASLP being 'unobstructed'. Accordingly, other than for permissible laws and regulations which the archipelagic state may enact consistent with UNCLOS, an archipelagic state must permit ASLP to be enjoyed by all vessels and aircraft other than those not acting in conformity with their Article 39 obligations, in which case they are not legitimately undertaking ASLP and could have their continued right of navigation or overflight revoked by intervention from the archipelagic state. The obligation to give publicity to any dangers to navigation and overflight is potentially significant, given the size of some archipelagic states, and is only qualified to the extent that it applies only to those dangers of 'which they have knowledge'. In the past decade both Indonesia and the Philippines have faced internal disruption as a result of the actions of insurgent groups and these have had the potential to pose dangers to navigation and

94 UNCLOS, Article 39(1)(a)(b). This is reflected also in Indonesian law; Indonesian Government Regulation No. 37 on the Rights and Obligations of Foreign Ships and Aircraft Exercising the Right of Archipelagic Sea Lanes Passage through Designated Sea Lanes, Articles 4, 6.

95 UNCLOS, Article 40.

96 UNCLOS, Article 42(1). The safety of navigation and regulation of maritime traffic provisions cross-refer back to Article 41, which would also apply in the case of ASLP which makes allowance for the possible designation of a traffic separation scheme within an archipelagic sea lane.

overflight.[97] In the 1990s and throughout the 2000s there have also been reports of pirate attacks within the waters of both archipelagos.[98] Not only do these events trigger obligations to warn, but may also result in the need to adjust sea lanes in order to ensure safe passage. Bearing in mind that ASLP cannot be suspended, in the case of significant ongoing threats, especially to ships, there may be a need to substitute designated sea lanes with other sea lanes on a temporary basis.[99]

One of the clearest obligations which archipelagic states have with respect to ASLP is not to suspend passage and this duplicates a similar obligation of strait states with respect to transit passage within international straits. The obligation is significant as it means that at all times the waters within the archipelago will be subject to navigation and overflight through the sea lanes such that there will always be a foreign presence within the waters of the archipelagic state. This dual nature of the non-suspendable ASLP regime and the suspendable innocent passage regime within archipelagic waters perhaps inevitably will lead to confusion as to which regime applies in essentially the same body of water, especially as ships engaging in innocent passage may legitimately have the need to enter and exit archipelagic waters via an archipelagic sea lane, or to intersect a sea lane whilst moving from one part of the archipelago to the other. In 1988 Indonesia temporarily closed the Sunda and Lombok Straits to navigation in order to conduct weapons exercises. This action brought about diplomatic protests from several countries, including the United States, West Germany and Australia.[100] Whilst at the time Indonesia had ratified UNCLOS the Convention had yet to enter into force, creating challenges in assessing the content of Indonesia's obligations under both treaty law and customary international law to give effect to the ASLP regime. Whilst Indonesia has not attempted to close passage through these or other straits in recent years, this incident did highlight the sensitivity associated with how UNCLOS sought to balance the interests of maritime states wanting to maintain the freedom of navigation in the Convention with the rights and interests of archipelagic states.[101]

---

97 In the case of the Philippines these incidents have included the 2000 bombing of the inter-island ferry *MV Our Lady of Mediatrix*, and bombing of the *MV SuperFerry 14* in Manila Bay in 2004: Mary Ann Palma, 'The Philippines as an Archipelagic and Maritime Nation: Interests, Challenges and Perspectives' (2009) *RSIS Working Paper* No. 182, 21.

98 Rendi A. Witular, 'Java Sea, Lombok Strait Becoming More Dangerous, Government Says', *The Jakarta Post*, 3 August 2005, p. 13.

99 Some allowance is made for the need to substitute sea lanes in UNCLOS, Article 53(7).

100 Nayan Chanda and Nigel Holloway, 'Troubled Waters: Indonesia's Neighbours Consider Responses to Closure of Straits', *Far Eastern Economic Review*, 10 November 1988, p. 18.

101 Donald R. Rothwell, 'The Indonesian Straits Incident: Transit or Archipelagic Sea Lanes Passage?' (1990) 14 *Marine Policy* 491–506.

Navigation within the Exclusive Economic Zone

Whilst the EEZ was developed as a distinctive regime to sit between the territorial sea and high seas with a predominant focus upon coastal state sovereign rights over living and non-living natural resources, there was an immediate appreciation during UNCLOS III negotiations of the need to make significant allowances for navigational freedoms within the EEZ. If not, then the recognition of this new and very highly significant maritime zone would have been impossible. Accordingly, Part V of UNCLOS makes clear that all states, both coastal and land-locked, enjoy similar freedoms within the EEZ as those outlined in Article 87, which includes the freedom of navigation.[102] However, unlike the manner in which navigational freedoms may be capable of exercise on the high seas, within the EEZ another dynamic exists and Article 58(3) notes that in the exercise of their rights 'States shall have due regard to the rights and duties of the coastal State and shall comply with the laws and regulations adopted by the coastal State in accordance with the provisions of this Convention and other rules of international law'. While not strictly necessary, some states have enacted municipal laws which recognize the freedom of navigation of foreign flagged vessels within their EEZ.[103]

In many respects any balancing of the rights and interests of the coastal state within its EEZ and those of other states seeking to navigate within those waters should not be the cause of conflict. The freedom of navigation for foreign vessels does not prima facie include a freedom to fish such that there would be a clear incompatibility with coastal state laws and regulations dealing with fishing activities. Likewise, marine scientific research is a separate activity and can be regulated by a coastal state consistent with UNCLOS without interference with navigation. If the coastal state were to construct artificial islands and installations, then navigational freedoms would be subject to minor constraints, but of no greater inconvenience than similar structures in the territorial sea.[104] Therefore, in principle the Part V EEZ rights of a coastal state should not have significant impact upon the freedoms of navigation being exercised by other states. Nevertheless, some coastal states concerned about the transhipment of hazardous cargoes have sought to impose prior notification requirements upon vessels seeking to transit their EEZ. The controversy raised by the voyages of the *Akatsuki Maru* and

102 UNCLOS, Article 58(1).

103 China's Law on the Exclusive Economic Zone and the Continental Shelf is an example: Keyuan Zou, 'Navigation of Foreign Vessels within China's Jurisdictional Waters' (2002) 29 *Marine Policy and Management* 351, 364.

104 Cf. the issues that arose in the *Arctic Sunrise Case* following the protest activities of Greenpeace International within the EEZ of the Russian Federation: *The Arctic Sunrise Case* (*Kingdom of the Netherlands v. Russian Federation*) Provisional Measures (2013) ITLOS Case No. 22; Alex G. Oude Elferink, 'The Arctic Sunrise Incident: A Multi-Faceted Law of the Sea Case with a Human Rights Dimension' (2014) 29 *International Journal of Marine and Coastal Law* 244–89.

Pacific Pintail also saw some states prohibit the transit of those vessels through their EEZs.[105]

The right of transit of fishing vessels across the EEZ has attracted controversy because of the fear that such vessels may use the opportunity to illegally engage in fishing activities.[106] A fishing vessel with its gear stowed and operating in a manner that does not attract suspicion that it is intending engage in fishing should be permitted to transit the EEZ without interference. However, this would not prevent the coastal state undertaking visual surveillance of the fishing vessel, or requiring it to comply with maritime identification procedures while it is within the EEZ.

High Seas Navigation

The modern articulation of the freedom of the seas is to be found in Part VII of UNCLOS dealing with the high seas. While prima facie these provisions apply to those parts of the sea not included within the territorial sea or the EEZ, or the archipelagic waters of an archipelagic state,[107] there is the capacity for a number of the high seas freedoms to also have application within the EEZ to the extent that they are not incompatible with the rights and duties that exist therein.[108] Article 87 sets out thc contemporary framework for the freedom of the seas as originally developed by Grotius, and in addition to the freedom of navigation, also extends to the freedom of overflight, the laying of submarine cables and pipelines, construction of artificial islands and installations, fishing, and marine scientific research. Freedom in this context needs to be qualified by an appreciation that several of these activities are subject to extensive regulation in other parts of UNCLOS, and in the case of high seas fishing by other related international instruments. The freedom of navigation is not, however, so qualified other than that it is exercised subject to conditions found in UNCLOS and other rules of international law.

The freedom of high seas navigation is open to all states: both coastal and land-locked.[109] This reflects the ongoing position within the law of the sea that the high

---

105 Molenaar, *Coastal State Jurisdiction over Vessel-Source Pollution*, 379–80. See Netherlands (1996) making clear in its UNCLOS Declaration that 'Nothing restricts the freedom of navigation of nuclear-powered ships or ships carrying nuclear or hazardous waste in the [EEZ], provided such navigation is in accordance with the applicable rules of international law': UNDOALOS, United Nations Convention on the Law of the Sea: Declarations.

106 Roach and Smith, *Excessive Maritime Claims*, 395 referring to United States protests against the actions of Costa Rica requiring prior notification of EEZ transit.

107 UNCLOS, Article 86.

108 UNCLOS, Articles 58(2), 86.

109 UNCLOS, Article 87(1).

seas is *res communis* and open for all states to use and enjoy. With respect to land-locked states, Article 87 is consistent with the rights granted to those states in Part X, and especially Article 125 which makes clear that such states 'have the right of access to and from the sea for the purpose of exercising … the freedom of the high seas'. A key term in this context is 'navigation'; which is inexorably linked with the notion of the freedom of the seas. Whilst navigation is not defined in Part II of UNCLOS, its context when referred to with respect to innocent passage clearly suggests some act of physical movement through the water, whether on the surface or beneath.[110] Article 90 refers to a 'Right of navigation' but avoids any precise definition as to what the act of navigation is, instead relying upon 'sail' as being a broad enough maritime term to encompass all means of vessel propulsion at sea.[111]

The freedom of high seas navigation is only lightly regulated under UNCLOS. Ships are expected to fly a flag reflecting a grant of nationality by a flag state[112] and are subject to the jurisdiction of the flag state whilst on the high seas,[113] which may result in the ships being bound to conform with a number of relevant international conventions such as those dealing with safety of life at sea (SOLAS), collisions (COLREG) and marine pollution (MARPOL). Certain ships enjoy immunity on the high seas, including warships[114] and state vessels on government non-commercial service.[115] In order to avoid some of the controversy that arose from the *Lotus Case* where the Permanent Court of International Justice recognized certain rights by a non-flag state following a high seas collision,[116] Article 97 outlines procedures for penal jurisdiction arising from collisions or other navigational incidents on the high seas. Other than the enforcement related provisions of UNCLOS dealing with the right of visit and hot pursuit, the only other limitations which exist under UNCLOS upon the freedom of high seas navigation are those which relate to the transportation of slaves,[117] piracy,[118] drug trafficking,[119] and unauthorized high seas broadcasting.[120]

---

110 UNCLOS, Article 20, stating that 'submarines and other underwater vehicles are required to navigate on the surface'.

111 The term 'sail' is also referred to in the context of UNCLOS, Article 92(1): 'Ships shall sail under the flag of one State'; cf. the French language version of UNCLOS which in Article 90 uses the term 'naviguer'.

112 UNCLOS, Articles 91, 92.

113 UNCLOS, Article 94.

114 UNCLOS, Article 95.

115 UNCLOS, Article 96.

116 *The Case of the S.S. 'Lotus'* (1927) PCIJ Reports Series A No. 10.

117 UNCLOS, Article 99.

118 UNCLOS, Articles 100–107.

119 UNCLOS, Article 108.

120 UNCLOS, Article 109.

Navigational Rights and Freedoms by Military Vessels

The foundation upon which military operations at sea rests is the freedom of navigation. Although growth in air power since the mid twentieth century has permitted an ever expanding range of military operations by air over the oceans, the extent of these operations cannot in any way be compared to the military power that can be projected by naval operations.[121] During this time there has not only been an expansion in the capability of navies, but also their capacity, raising a number of issues for the law of the sea of which nuclear-powered and armed warships is but one. It was because of the fundamental importance of the freedom of navigation to naval operations that the breadth of the territorial sea was so contentious, and the associated navigational regimes of innocent passage, transit passage, and archipelagic sea lanes passage were so crucial to the development of the international law of the sea at UNCLOS I and III. The outcomes of these negotiations are all reflected in the regimes agreed upon in UNCLOS.

The influence of the *Corfu Channel* decision on the development of the law in this regard should not be underestimated.[122] The ICJ's finding that the freedom of navigation is enjoyed by warships in peacetime was subsequently reflected in deliberations at both the First and Second UN Conferences on the Law of the Sea, in both the Geneva Conventions and UNCLOS.[123] That it was considered a general principle further elevates its significance and needs to be taken into account when interpreting the international law of the sea concerning navigation by warships.

Innocent Passage by Warships

Part II, Section 3 of UNCLOS dealing with innocent passage in the territorial sea makes clear that the ships of all states enjoy the right of innocent passage. Whilst subsection C encompassing Articles 29–32 address some issues which are particular to warships, they do not go to the right of innocent passage. Accordingly, UNCLOS is clear that warships enjoy a right of innocent passage which may be exercised in the same manner as merchant ships. Nevertheless, there are three particular types of constraints in the innocent passage regime that have relevance

121 Robert McLaughlin, *United Nations Naval Peace Operations in the Territorial Sea* (Martinus Nijhoff, Leiden: 2009) 46–7, referring to the 'manifest usefulness of navies'; and generally Charles E. Pirtle, 'Military Uses of Ocean Space and the Law of the Sea in the New Millennium' (2000) 31 *Ocean Development and International Law* 7.

122 See generally Karine Bannelier, Theodore Christakis and Sarah Heathcote (eds), *The ICJ and the Evolution of International Law: The Enduring Impact of the Corfu Channel Case* (Routledge, New York: 2012).

123 See also the discussion of these principles in the *Case Concerning Military and Paramilitary Activities in and Against Nicaragua* (*Nicaragua v. United States of America*) Merits, Judgment [1986] ICJ Reports 14, 111–12 with respect to the freedom of communications and maritime commerce.

for warships. The first is that warships need to take particular care that whilst in passage they do not engage in acts which are considered non-innocent under Article 19. A number of limitations on passage found in Article 19(2) have particular application to warships including that they not engage in actions considered to constitute any threat or use of force against the coastal state, any form of weapons exercise, acts aimed at collecting information to the prejudice of the defence or security of the coastal state, acts of propaganda, research or survey activities, acts aimed at interfering with the communications systems of the coastal state, and the launching, landing or taking on board of any aircraft or military device. This is clearly an extensive list of requirements, which if complied with will ensure that the possible security threats to coastal states posed by foreign warships are neutralized as far as possible whilst they are within the territorial sea. In contrast to the transit passage and archipelagic sea lanes passage regimes, there is no reference in the right of innocent passage to 'normal mode' of navigation, therefore precluding warships undertaking activities which would otherwise be permissible in other settings. A clear limitation in this respect is the inability of aircraft carriers to launch or receive aircraft whilst undertaking innocent passage, as such activity conflicts with Article 19(2)(f). However, some aspects of warship operations remain ambiguous, such as the activation of radar whilst in passage. Radar is clearly an aid to navigation for all vessels and as such also promotes safety at sea, but also may be used for defensive purposes.[124] By way of contrast, there is nothing in the innocent passage regime, UNCLOS, or general international law which suggests that warships do not enjoy the right of self-defence whilst within the territorial sea of a foreign state.[125] This issue has been highlighted since the October 2000 terrorist attack on the USS *Cole* whilst in port at Aden, Yemen and the subsequent US response to ensuring security of its warships whilst within potentially hostile waters.[126]

The second constraint relates to compliance by warships with the laws and regulations of a coastal state relating to innocent passage that may have been adopted under Article 21 of UNCLOS. In the case of warships, relevant provisions would be those relating to the safety of navigation and regulation of maritime traffic, the preservation of the environment and the prevention of pollution. UNCLOS makes clear that '(f)oreign ships exercising the right of innocent passage … shall comply' with such laws and regulations.[127] Whilst coastal states would encounter difficulty in applying their civil and criminal laws to warships because of the

124 John Astley and Michael N. Schmitt, 'The Law of the Sea and Naval Operations' (1997) 42 *Air Force Law Review* 119, 131.

125 See discussion in A.V. Lowe, 'Self-Defence at Sea', in William E. Butler (ed.), *The Non-Use of Force in International Law* (Martinus Nijhoff, Dordrecht: 1989) 185–202.

126 See Department of Defense USS Cole Commission (United States) *USS Cole Commission Report* (Washington, Department of Defense, 2001).

127 UNCLOS, Article 21(4).

principles of sovereign immunity,[128] UNCLOS in recognition of this legal reality makes clear in Article 30 that if a non-compliant warship disregards a request for compliance the coastal state may require the warship to leave the territorial sea with the effect that the right of innocent passage has been lost. The third restraint found in UNCLOS relates to the particular situation of submarines, which under Article 20 are 'required to navigate on the surface and show their flag'.[129]

A number of issues arise from these provisions. One is the capacity of the coastal state to interpret UNCLOS unilaterally and determine that either the mere presence of a warship within the territorial sea constitutes a threat to its security, or that the actions of the warship whilst engaged in passage are not innocent. There is a widely held view that a presumption of innocence exists, which can only be rebutted by proof from the coastal state, relying upon the objective and specific criteria in Article 19, of a non-innocent act.[130] While maintaining a balance between a coastal state's sovereign rights and its duty to respect innocent passage would suggest that only an objective standard would be acceptable when interpreting Article 19,[131] this is made challenging by the existence of terms such as 'propaganda' which are difficult to define and assess objectively when national interests are at stake. Even if such a wide discretion is acknowledged, commentators such as Ngantcha emphasize that the coastal state's subjective appraisal of passage as non-innocent should be limited by the objective requirement that any violation which is alleged to have occurred has taken place while the vessel is in passage.[132]

Another contentious issue is whether coastal states may insist on prior authorization or prior notification by warships prior to undertaking innocent passage through the territorial sea. Whilst there was debate on this issue at the Third UN Conference on the Law of the Sea, it was never included in UNCLOS, however a number of state parties made clear through Declarations their intention to require prior authorization or prior notification.[133] State parties which require prior authorization include Albania, Algeria, Antigua, Barbados, Cape Verde, China,

128 UNCLOS, Article 32.

129 *Virginia Commentary*, Vol. II, 183, observing the use of the term 'are required' is unusual, leaving open the possibility that the coastal state may waive the requirement.

130 F.D. Froman, 'Uncharted Waters: Non-Innocent Passage of Warships in the Territorial Sea' (984) 21 *San Diego Law Review* 625, 658; J.W. Rolph, 'Freedom of Navigation and the Black Sea Bumping Incident: How "Innocent" Must Innocent Passage be?' (1992) 135 *Military Law Review* 137, 159.

131 Gerald Fitzmaurice, 'Some Results from the Geneva Conference on the Law of the Sea' (1959) 8 *International and Comparative Law Quarterly* 73, 96–7.

132 Ngantcha, *The Right of Innocent Passage*, 51.

133 See UNCLOS Declarations made by Bangladesh (2001), China (1996) Egypt (1983), Croatia (1995), Iran (1982), Malta (1993), Montenegro (2006), Oman (1983), United Nations Division for Ocean Affairs and the Law of the Sea (UNDOALOS), 'United Nations Convention on the Law of the Sea: Declarations Made Upon Signature, Ratification, Accession or Succession or Anytime Thereafter', at www.un.org/Depts/los/convention_agreement/convention_declarations (27 September 2009).

Congo, Grenada, Maldives, Myanmar, Oman, Pakistan, Philippines, Romania, St Vincent, Seychelles, Somalia, Sri Lanka, Sudan, Syria, Vietnam and Yemen.[134] Prior notification of the passage of warships is required by Bangladesh, Croatia, Denmark, Egypt, Estonia, Guyana, India, Libya, Malta, Mauritius, Nigeria, Serbia and Montenegro, and South Korea.[135] A number of state parties responded to these claims in their UNCLOS Declarations, with Germany, Italy and the Netherlands all making clear that a requirement either for consent or notification of passage by warships was inconsistent with the Convention.[136] The United States, though a non-party to UNCLOS, has also protested these consent and notification requirements for warships, and in some instances actively asserted the right of innocent passage as part of its freedom of navigation programme.[137]

There is some evidence to suggest these differing interpretations of UNCLOS on prior notification and consent represent a divide between the West and Asia,[138] which with the growing rise of China as an economic and military power has the potential to become a future flashpoint. In 1989 the United States and Soviet Union, the two most significant naval powers of the time, issued a 'Joint Statement on the Uniform Interpretation of Rules of International Law Governing Innocent Passage' which provided as follows:

> All ships, including warships, regardless of cargo, armament or means of propulsion, enjoy the right of innocent passage through the territorial sea in accordance with international law, for which neither prior notification nor authorization is required.[139]

This 1989 Statement, which also went on to address common interpretations of other key provisions of UNCLOS dealing with innocent passage, reflects the US and Russian position on these issues into the twenty-first century. The People's

---

134 Robin R. Churchill, 'The Impact of State Practice on the Jurisdictional Framework Contained in the LOS Convention', in Alex G. Oude Elferink (ed.), *Stability and Change in the Law of the Sea: The Role of the LOS Convention* (Martinus Nijhoff, Leiden: 2005) 112–13.

135 Churchill, 'The Impact of State Practice', 113. Some states which previously required prior notification have now abandoned that practice: Hakapää and Molenaar, 'Innocent Passage – Past and Present', 131, 138.

136 See UNCLOS Declaration by Germany (1994), Italy (1995) and Netherlands (1996) in UNDOALOS 'Declarations Made Upon Signature, Ratification, Accession or Succession or Anytime Thereafter'.

137 Roach and Smith, *Excessive Maritime Claims*, 243–51; Agyebeng, 'Theory in Search of Practice', 371, 398.

138 Dale G. Stephens, 'The Impact of the 1982 Law of the Sea Convention on Conduct of Peacetime Naval/Military Operations' (1999) 29 *California Western International Law Journal* 283, 306.

139 Joint Statement on the Uniform Interpretation of Rules of International Law Governing Innocent Passage, para. 2.

Republic of China, on the other hand, made clear at the time of its 1996 ratification of UNCLOS that the Convention did not 'prejudice the right of a coastal State to request … a foreign State to obtain advance approval from or give prior notification to the coastal State for the passage of its warships through the territorial sea'.[140] This position was consistent with Chinese practice prior to becoming a party to UNCLOS, but has been the subject of criticism from Chinese scholars based outside China.[141]

Transit Passage by Warships

Given the issues and sensitivities associated with innocent passage by warships, it is not surprising that similar and even more acute issues arise in the context of transit passage through international straits. This is illustrated by the pre-UNCLOS codification efforts in relations to straits, and the ongoing sensitivities associated with naval navigation through pivotal 'choke points' which have persisted. The 1936 Montreux Treaty[142] is a prominent illustration of a pre-UNCLOS initiative to address questions of navigation through an international strait by warships containing a range of measures which made distinctions between different types of naval vessels depending on their capacity and size, flag of origin, and overall maximum aggregate tonnage of a naval force exercising passage. A right of transit through the straits could be enjoyed with or without significant limitations and constraints, though any transit was to be preceded by notification to Turkey.[143] The ICJ's decision in *Corfu Channel* is another prominent example in this respect given the court directly endorsed the innocent passage by warships through an international strait without prior authorization.[144] With an obvious reference to the Montreux Treaty, the court observed that: 'Unless otherwise prescribed by an international convention, there is no right for a coastal State to prohibit such passage through straits in time of peace.'[145]

These pre-UNCLOS precedents need to be measured against the impact of the Convention recognizing the legitimacy of a 12 nm territorial sea and the impact of that upon the high seas corridor which would have once existed through a number of international straits around the world. The effect of the 12 nm territorial sea was that 116 international straits potentially became enclosed within a territorial

140 UNDOALOS, 'United Nations Convention on the Law of the Sea: Declarations'.

141 Zou, 'Innocent Passage for Warships' and 'Navigation of Foreign Vessels'.

142 Convention Regarding the Regime of the Straits, 173 LNTS 213.

143 Convention Regarding the Regime of the Straits, Article 13; see further discussion in Nihan Űnlü, *The Legal Regime of the Turkish Straits* (Martinus Nijhoff, The Hague: 2002) 87–100.

144 *Corfu Channel Case* (*United Kingdom v. Albania*), Judgment of April 9th, 1949 [1949] ICJ Reps 4, 28.

145 *Corfu Channel Case* (*United Kingdom v. Albania*), Judgment of April 9th, 1949 [1949] ICJ Reps 4, 28.

sea which even though subject to the regime of innocent passage had the potential to place considerable constraints upon the freedom of military operations and especially the capacity of navies to speedily move from one maritime domain to another.[146] Particularly sensitive strategic 'choke points' where maritime traffic converges to move from one ocean or sea to another include the Straits of Gibraltar, Dover, Hormuz, Malacca, Sunda, Lombok, and Formosa (Taiwan).[147]

UNCLOS makes clear that transit passage is a right enjoyed by 'all ships' with respect to straits used for international navigation where warships pass through the territorial sea between one part of the high seas or EEZ and another part of the high seas or EEZ.[148] Warships whilst engaged in transit passage are bound by the same constraints as merchant ships. Two particular constraints apply to warships. The first is that they are to refrain from any activity constituting a threat or use of force against the coastal state, and likewise refrain from any activities not incidental to their normal mode. The second of these is that they are to comply with generally accepted international rules and regulations regarding safety of life at sea and pollution prevention.

Of particular significance here is what constitutes 'normal mode' of operations for a warship and when would such operations be considered to cross the boundaries so as to constitute a threat to the coastal state? In the *Virginia Commentaries* to UNCLOS, the observation has been made that 'it is clear from the context and from the negotiating history that the term was intended to refer to that mode which is normal or usual for navigation for the particular type of ship ... making the passage in given circumstances. In the case of surface ships, this means navigation on the surface in ordinary sailing conditions'.[149] Some guidance on this point can again be found in *Corfu Channel*, where the ICJ was satisfied that even when the British warships passed through the channel with crews at action stations, and ready to retaliate if fired upon, this was consistent given the tensions that then existed between Albania and the United Kingdom at the time with the right of passage.[150] It is doubtful, however, whether this would be an acceptable mode of navigation on all occasions as the court gave weight to the context of when the passage was being exercised and its manner. At the other end of the spectrum, in the case of the actions of the British warships several weeks later when minesweeping operations were conducted in the strait, the ICJ did not accept those actions as being legitimate under either the law of the sea or other general principles of

146 Ken Booth, *Law, Force and Diplomacy at Sea* (Allen & Unwin, London: 1985) 97–119.

147 Booth, *Law, Force and Diplomacy at Sea*, 98–9.

148 UNCLOS, Article 38(1).

149 *Virginia Commentary* Vol. II, 342.

150 *Corfu Channel Case* (*United Kingdom v. Albania*), Judgment of April 9th, 1949 [1949] ICJ Reps 4, 31.

international law.[151] For modern warships, the normal mode for surface vessels would extend to the launching and recovering of aircraft and the deployment of radar, sonar and depth finding devices. For submarines, navigation through the strait could be submerged.[152] The conduct of weapons exercises, however, would not be consistent with normal mode as such an activity would constitute a threat of the use of force against the coastal state.

The second constraint is the expectation that all ships, including by implication warships, also comply with legitimate coastal states laws and regulations relating to transit passage. Laws of particular relevance would be those relating to safety to navigation, including passage through sea lanes and traffic separation schemes, and pollution control.[153] In recognition of the immunities enjoyed by warships and the difficulties therefore associated with the enforcement of any coastal state laws against warships, UNCLOS makes clear that the flag state will bear international responsibility for any loss or damage that may arise as a result of the warship acting contrary to those laws and regulations.[154]

Archipelagic Sea Lanes Passage by Warships

There is overlap in the issues which arise concerning the rights of passage by warships through international straits and archipelagic sea lanes due to the similarity of these two passage regimes. Given the strategic significance of straits that fell within archipelagic states such as Indonesia and the Philippines, and the very significant US naval presence in East and Southeast Asia and the western Pacific, the negotiation of Part IV of UNCLOS dealing with archipelagic states raised particular sensitivities for military operations. The outcome in Part IV sought to balance the rights and interests of archipelagic states and the naval powers, making the important concession in Article 53(3) that archipelagic sea lanes passage was the exercise in accordance with the convention 'of navigation … in the normal mode' for 'continuous, expeditious and unobstructed transit' through the archipelago from one part of the EEZ or high seas to another. This was a right enjoyed by all ships, without qualification. The use of the term 'normal mode' was crucial for warships and duplicates the entitlements enjoyed when undertaking transit passage through an international strait. Similar issues therefore arise as to what constitutes normal mode, including for aircraft carriers, the rights of submarines to navigate submerged, and 'security streaming' for a naval task force.[155]

151 *Corfu Channel Case* (*United Kingdom v. Albania*), Judgment of April 9th, 1949 [1949] ICJ Reps 4, 33–5.

152 *Virginia Commentary* Vol. II, 342–3; Astley and Schmitt, 'The Law of the Sea and Naval Operations', 133.

153 UNCLOS, Article 42.

154 UNCLOS, Article 42(5); see also Article 236.

155 Stephens, 'The Impact of the 1982 Law of the Sea Convention', 291; Thomas and Duncan, 'Annotated Supplement to The Commanders Handbook', 127.

There are three important aspects of archipelagic sea lanes passage for warships. The first is that the right is non-suspendable, and can therefore be enjoyed by warships without fear of closure. The second is that the right can only be enjoyed within the designated sea lanes, or those sea routes which are 'normally used for international navigation'.[156] As the archipelagic state is entitled to designate traffic separation schemes for the purpose of safe passage through narrow channels within the archipelagic sea lane, an issue arises as to whether foreign warships are bound by these constraints given their entitlement to sovereign immunity or rather because of the practical importance of safe navigation through narrow shipping channels they elect to follow the designated shipping route. The third issue is that as the conduct of archipelagic sea lanes passage may see a foreign warship within the waters of an archipelagic state for a considerable period of time, not only would there be heightened sensitivity that the warship not engage in any actions during that time which would pose a threat to the archipelagic state, but also that the warship not pollute the marine environment. Whilst a warship retains its rights of sovereign immunity within archipelagic waters, there remains an expectation that the warship comply with those generally accepted international regulations concerning the prevention, reduction and control of pollution.

EEZ Navigation by Warships

The EEZ is a zone of coastal state resource sovereignty and jurisdiction, but it is not a zone which gives to a coastal state extensive capacity to regulate navigation. This is confirmed by Articles 58 and 90 of UNCLOS which provide that every state has a right to sail ships flying its flag on both the high seas and adjacent EEZ, subject only to recognizing the lawful uses by the coastal state of the EEZ. It therefore follows that warships enjoy a freedom of navigation within the EEZ of coastal states. However, at the time of the conclusion of the convention some states took a position on the interpretation of Article 301 providing for the peaceful use of the oceans which suggested they may place some limitations on the activities of foreign warships. Brazil, for example, asserted in a Declaration lodged with its 1988 ratification of UNCLOS that Article 301 applied 'in particular to the maritime areas under the sovereignty or jurisdiction of the coastal State',[157] whilst also asserting that within the EEZ other states were not to conduct 'military exercises or manoeuvres'. This is an interpretation which has been contested by the United States.[158] The United States likewise protested provisions of the Iranian Marine Areas Act 1993,[159] which sought to place limitations upon foreign warships within

156 UNCLOS, Article 53(12).

157 UNDOALOS, 'United Nations Convention on the Law of the Sea: Declarations'.

158 Roach and Smith, *Excessive Maritime Claims*, 381–2.

159 Act on the Marine Areas of the Islamic Republic of Iran in the Persian Gulf and the Oman Sea 1993 (Iran), reprinted in (1993) 24 *Law of the Sea Bulletin* 10–15.

the EEZ on the grounds that the freedom of navigation by foreign warships was being constrained.[160]

Military survey activities

An aspect of naval operations in the EEZ which has been contentious has been military survey activities. These are surveillance or scientific research activities undertaken by military or naval auxiliary vessels within the EEZ of third states. Often these activities may be designed to gather oceanographic or other data, or they may be undertaken to secure other forms of intelligence with a national security dimension. These activities raise a range of issues under UNCLOS, including whether they constitute legitimate marine scientific research under Article 246, or whether they are generic research activities which fall within the reach of Article 87 high seas freedoms which are also enjoyed within the EEZ.

The United States has been involved in several incidents within China's claimed EEZ involving military survey operations. In March 2001 the unarmed hydrographic survey ship USNS *Bowditch* was confronted by a Chinese naval frigate and ordered to leave the EEZ. The *Bowditch* complied with the Chinese request, but returned to the area a few days later accompanied by an armed US naval escort.[161] In a similar incident in March 2009, the USNS *Impeccable*, a US Navy ocean surveillance vessel operating 75 nm south of China's Hainan island within the Chinese claimed EEZ, was surrounded by five Chinese vessels including a naval intelligence ship and a government-operated fisheries patrol vessel and subjected to significant harassment necessitating the taking of avoidance action to avoid collision.[162] The *Impeccable* withdrew but returned to the area the next day under the escort of a US guided-missile destroyer.[163] The United States protested to China following the 2009 incident, however China responded by asserting that the *Impeccable* was operating illegally within the Chinese EEZ in violation of both international and Chinese law.[164] The point of distinction between the Chinese and United States position on these issues is whether a non-resource related activity in the EEZ such as military marine data collection is a form of marine scientific research subject to coastal state regulation or whether this is a legitimate freedom of the seas. Providing these military activities fall beyond the scope of Article 246 marine scientific research and there is no direct threat posed to the coastal state

160 Roach and Smith, *Excessive Maritime Claims*, 383; generally on military operations within the EEZ see Jon M. Van Dyke, 'Military Ships and Planes Operating in the Exclusive Economic Zone of Another Country' (2004) 28 *Marine Policy* 29.

161 Raul Pedrozo, 'Close Encounters at Sea: The USNS *Impeccable* Incident' (Summer 2009) 62, No. 3 *Naval War College Review* 101, 101.

162 Pedrozo, 'Close Encounters at Sea', 101; John R. Crook (ed.), 'Contemporary Practice of the United States Relating to International Law' (2009) 103 *American Journal of International Law* 349–50.

163 Pedrozo, 'Close Encounters at Sea', 102.

164 Crook, 'Contemporary Practice of the United States', 350–51.

which would legitimately activate the right of self-defence then military-related survey activities in the EEZ are consistent with UNCLOS and international law.

Concluding Remarks

The UNCLOS navigational regimes have immense significance for the South China Sea. They are the foundation upon which navigational rights and freedoms are based within the region and are a pivotal driver to economic growth throughout Southeast and East Asia. Most importantly they benefit both coastal and maritime states within the region and beyond, and this is an important consideration for those South China Sea states which have aspirations beyond the region. In the absence of the settlement of maritime rights and entitlements throughout the South China Sea it is inevitable that some tensions will remain throughout the region, however UNCLOS does provide a high degree of certainty with respect to the navigational rights within the territorial sea, international straits, the EEZ and high seas. Given the regional dynamics noted above, it would appear to be in the best interests of all South China Sea states to respect those navigational rights and freedoms.

Greater uncertainty exists with respect to certain aspects of the navigational rights of warships and other military vessels and clashes have occurred previously in the region where the United States has sought to assert certain navigational rights. While the United States remains the only true global naval superpower, there are increasing question marks over whether it will eventually face significant constraints upon the freedom of navigation that its navy enjoys. Over the past decade a number of incidents have occurred in which the United States has been challenged over its interpretation of the law of the sea, principally by China. These issues were highlighted in March 2009 by the USNS *Impeccable* incident. This highlighted the legal uncertainty arising from the fact the United States remains a non-party to UNCLOS. While the United States supported UNCLOS in the 1970s, in 1981 the Regan Administration withdrew that support based on objections to provisions dealing with the deep seabed. Notwithstanding 1984 modifications designed to directly address some of those concerns, the United States has continued to reject the Convention. This is notwithstanding support for UNCLOS from both the Bush and Obama Administrations and ongoing efforts in recent years to build momentum for a US Senate vote on accession.

The US position on the law of the sea and UNCLOS is creating unnecessary tension in the South China Sea. That President Obama and former Secretary of State Clinton have referred over the past two years to the respect for the freedom of navigation and settlement of South China Sea disputes consistently with international law has only served to highlight how equivocal the US position is on the law of the sea. Part of the objections that have resonated in the US Senate rest on national security grounds and fears that undue restraints may be placed upon US naval freedoms. However, as has been demonstrated, the freedom of navigation is deeply embedded in the Convention, partly due to vigorous US advocacy during the negotiations in the 1970s. Much would therefore be gained if the United States was to move towards adoption of the Convention. Uncertainty would immediately be removed as to the rights and duties of the United States under the law of the sea and it would be on a level playing field in terms of the basic legal framework that exists between it and China. In the context of the South China Sea this would have the effect of depriving some states from arguing that the United States as a non-party to the Convention was not entitled to enjoy certain navigational rights and freedoms. An agreed interpretation on key components in the law of the sea between the two maritime powers would assist in bringing about stability and confidence in their relations in the South China Sea, and diminish contentious matters escalating into major disputes which would have ramifications not only for both states but also the region.

References

Act on the Marine Areas of the Islamic Republic of Iran in the Persian Gulf and the Oman Sea 1993 (Iran). Reprinted in *Law of the Sea Bulletin* 24 (1993).

Agyebeng, William K. 'Theory in Search of Practice: The Right of Innocent Passage in the Territorial Sea'. *Cornell International Law Journal* 39 (2006).

Astley, John and Michael N. Schmitt. 'The Law of the Sea and Naval Operations'. *Air Force Law Review* 42 (1997).

Bannelier, Karine, Theodore Christakis and Sarah Heathcote, eds. *The ICJ and the Evolution of International Law: The Enduring Impact of the Corfu Channel Case.* New York: Routledge, 2012.

Bateman, Sam, Donald R. Rothwell and David VanderZwaag. 'Navigational Rights and Freedoms in the New Millennium: Dealing with 20th Century Controversies and 21st Century Challenges', in Donald R. Rothwell and Sam Batemen, eds. *Navigational Rights and Freedoms and the New Law of the Sea.* The Hague: Martinus Nijhoff, 2000.

Batongbacal, Jay L. 'Barely Skimming the Surface: Archipelagic Sea Lanes Navigation and the IMO', in Alex G. Oude Elferink and Donald R. Rothwell, eds. *Oceans Management in the 21st Century: Institutional Frameworks and Responses*. Leiden: Martinus Nijhoff, 2004.

Baxter, R.R. *The Law of International Waterways*. Cambridge, MA: Harvard University Press, 1964.

Beckman, R.C. 'PSSAs and Transit Passage – Australia's Pilotage System in the Torres Strait Challenges the IMO and UNCLOS'. *Ocean Development and International Law* 38 (2007).

Booth, Ken. *Law, Force and Diplomacy at Sea*. London: Allen & Unwin, 1985.

Caminos, Hugo. 'Categories of International Straits Excluded from the Transit Passage Regime under Part III of the United Nations Convention on the Law of the Sea', in Tafsir Malick Ndiaye and Rűdiger Wolfrum, eds. *Law of the Sea, Environmental Law and Settlement of Disputes*. Leiden: Martinus Nijhoff, 2007.

Chanda, Nayan and Nigel Holloway. 'Troubled Waters: Indonesia's Neighbours Consider Responses to Closure of Straits'. *Far Eastern Economic Review* 10 (November 1988).

Churchill, Robin R. 'The Impact of State Practice on the Jurisdictional Framework Contained in the LOS Convention', in Alex G. Oude Elferink, ed. *Stability and Change in the Law of the Sea: The Role of the LOS Convention*. Leiden: Martinus Nijhoff, 2005.

Crook, John R., ed. 'Contemporary Practice of the United States Relating to International Law'. *American Journal of International Law* 103 (2009).

Department of Defense USS Cole Commission (United States) *USS Cole Commission Report*. Washington, DC: Department of Defense, 2001.

Elferink, Alex G. Oude. 'The Arctic Sunrise Incident: A Multi-Faceted Law of the Sea Case with a Human Rights Dimension'. *International Journal of Marine and Coastal Law* 29 (2014).

Elferink, Alex G. Oude. 'Rules of Navigation of Ships through the Territorial Sea and the Internal Waters of Estonia'. *International Journal of Marine and Coastal Law* 8 (1993).

Fitzmaurice, Gerald. 'Some Results from the Geneva Conference on the Law of the Sea'. *International and Comparative Law Quarterly* 8 (1959).

Froman, F.D. 'Uncharted Waters: Non-Innocent Passage of Warships in the Territorial Sea'. *San Diego Law Review* 21 (1984).

Hakapää, K. and E.J. Molenaar. 'Innocent Passage – Past and Present'. *Marine Policy* 23 (1999).

Hilt Jr, J.C. 'Oceans Law and Superpower Relations: The Bumping of the Yorktown and Caron in the Black Sea'. *Virginia Journal of International Law* 29 (1989).

Indonesian Government Regulation No. 37 on the Rights and Obligations of Foreign Ships and Aircraft Exercising the Right of Archipelagic Sea Lanes Passage through Designated Sea Lanes (28 June 2002). *Law of the Sea Bulletin* 52 (2003).

Kwiatkowska, Barbara and Etty R. Agoes. *Archipelagic Waters Regime in the Light of the 1982 United Nations Law of the Sea Convention and State Practice*. Bandung: ICLOS, UNPAD, 1991.

Lowe, A.V. 'Self-Defence at Sea', in William E. Butler, ed. *The Non-Use of Force in International Law*. Dordrecht: Martinus Nijhoff, 1989.

Lowe, Vaughan. 'Uniform Interpretation of the Rules of International Law Governing Innocent Passage'. *International Journal of Estuarine and Coastal Law* 6 (1991).

McLaughlin, Robert. *United Nations Naval Peace Operations in the Territorial Sea*. Leiden: Martinus Nijhoff, 2009

Molenaar, Erik Jaap. *Coastal State Jurisdiction over Vessel-Source Pollution*. The Hague: Kluwer Law International, 1998.

Munavvar, Mohamed. *Ocean States: Archipelagic Regimes in the Law of the Sea*. Dordrecht: Martinus Nijhoff, 1995.
Nandan, Satya N. and Shabtai Rosenne, eds. *United Nations Convention on the Law of the Sea 1982: A Commentary* Vol. II. Dordrecht: Martinus Nijhoff, 1993.
Ngantcha, Francia. *The Right of Innocent Passage and the Evolution of the International Law of the Sea*. London: Pinter, 1990.
Palma, Mary Ann. 'The Philippines as an Archipelagic and Maritime Nation: Interests, Challenges and Perspectives'. *RSIS Working Paper* No. 182 (2009).
Pedrozo, Raul. 'Close Encounters at Sea: The USNS *Impeccable* Incident'. *Naval War College Review* 62 (Summer 2009).
Pirtle, Charles E. 'Military Uses of Ocean Space and the Law of the Sea in the New Millennium'. *Ocean Development and International Law* 31 (2000).
Roach, J. Ashley and Robert W. Smith. *Excessive Maritime Claims* 3rd edn. Leiden: Martinus Nijhoff, 2012.
Rolph, J.W. 'Freedom of Navigation and the Black Sea Bumping Incident: How "Innocent" Must Innocent Passage Be?' *Military Law Review* 135 (1992).
Rothwell, Donald R. 'Coastal State Sovereignty and Innocent Passage: The Voyage of the *Lusitania Expresso*'. *Marine Policy* 16 (1992).
Rothwell, Donald R. 'Compulsory Pilotage and the Law of the Sea: Lessons Learned from the Torres Strait', in Shicun Wu and Keyuan Zou, eds. *Securing the Safety of Navigation in East Asia: Legal and Political Dimensions*. Cambridge: Chandos, 2013.
Rothwell, Donald R. 'The Indonesian Straits Incident: Transit or Archipelagic Sea Lanes Passage?'. *Marine Policy* 14 (1990).
Stephens, Dale G. 'The Impact of the 1982 Law of the Sea Convention on Conduct of Peacetime Naval/Military Operations'. *California Western International Law Journal* 29 (1999).
Thomas, A.R. and James C. Duncan, eds. 'Annotated Supplement to The Commanders Handbook on the Law of Naval Operations'. *International Legal Studies* 73 (1999).
UNCLOS Declarations made by Bangladesh (2001), China (1996) Egypt (1983), Croatia (1995) Iran (1982), Malta (1993), Montenegro (2006), Oman (1983), United Nations Division for Ocean Affairs and the Law of the Sea (UNDOALOS), 'United Nations Convention on the Law of the Sea: Declarations Made Upon Signature, Ratification, Accession or Succession or Anytime Thereafter', 27 September 2009. www.un.org/Depts/los/convention_agreement/convention_declarations.
United Nations Division for Ocean Affairs and the Law of the Sea 'Declarations and Statements', 7 November 2009. www.un.org/Depts/los/convention_agreements/convention_declarations.htm.
United Nations Division for Ocean Affairs and the Law of the Sea 'Suspension of Innocent Passage'. www.un.org/Depts/los/convention_agreements/innocent_passages_suspension.htm.

USA-USSR Joint Statement on the Uniform Interpretation of Rules of International Law Governing Innocent Passage. Law of the Sea Bulletin 14 (1989).

Valencia, Mark J. and Abu Bakar Jaafar. 'Environmental Management of the Malacca – Singapore Straits: Legal and Institutional Issues'. *Natural Resources Journal* 25 (1985).

Van Dyke, Jon M. 'Sea Shipment of Japanese Plutonium under International Law'. *Ocean Development and International Law* 24 (1993).

Walker, George K. 'Definitions for the 1982 Law of the Sea Convention – Part II: Analysis of the IHO Consolidated Glossary'. *California Western International Law Journal* 33 (2003).

White, Michael. 'Navigational Rights in Sensitive Marine Environments: The Great Barrier Reef', in Donald R. Rothwell and Sam Bateman, eds. *Navigational Rights and Freedoms and the New Law of the Sea.* The Hague: Martinus Nijhoff, 2000.

Witular, Rendi A. 'Java Sea, Lombok Strait Becoming More Dangerous, Government Says'. *The Jakarta Post*, 3 August 2005.

Zou, Keyuan. 'Navigation of Foreign Vessels within China's Jurisdictional Waters'. *Marine Policy and Management* 29 (2002).

Zou, Keyuan. 'Innocent Passage for Warships: The Chinese Doctrine and Practice'. *Ocean Development and International Law* 29 (1998).

Chapter 10
Historic Waters and Historic Rights in the South China Sea: A Critical Appraisal

Clive R. Symmons

Introduction

The topic of 'historic claims' to, or in, maritime areas has long been an arcane and unsatisfactory subject in the law of the sea on which little comprehensive analysis has been done in the past.[1] This is unfortunate as this aspect of the law of the sea is dependent for its rules on international customary law, with all the lack of clarity that can attend such a source of law; and indeed, as this writer has found, when the supposed rules are analysed in depth, they are found to be wanting. This deficiency is exemplified in UNCLOS which has at most only three references to historic issues *ex nomine*: mentioning 'so-called "historic bays"' in Art. 10(6) (the bays provision), 'historic title' (in the context of territorial sea delimitation (Art. 15)); and the exclusion of disputes involving 'historic bays or titles' from compulsory dispute settlement procedures in Art. 298(1).[2] No attempt is made in any of these references to elucidate the meaning of these differing terms or the rules attached to them. However, it may be noted that the very phrase 'historic *title*' was used by

1 My book, *Historic Waters in the Law of the Sea: A Modern Reappraisal* (Leiden: Nijhoff, 2008) is the only book published on this subject in recent years. The only other books on the subject (by A. Gioia, *Titoli Storici e Linee di Base de Mer Territoriale* (Padova: Edizioni Cdeam, 1990) and M. Wesley Clark, *Historic Bays and Waters: A Regime of Recent Beginnings and Continued Usage* (New York: Oceana, 1994)) have now a dated historical ring to them and have been hardly cited in the now increasing periodical literature on the topic in connection with the SCS dispute.

2 A matter now of potential importance in the pending Philippines Notification and Statement of Claim of January 2013 requesting arbitration, stating (at para. 40) that its claims did not fall within the PRC's declaration of 25 August 2006, because they did not 'involve historic bays or titles within the meaning of the relevant provisions of [UNCLOS]'. This is not to say that the arbitral tribunal may still not look at the *substance* of the PRC claim pleading, as the dispute potentially involves the PRC's claimed historic title to the waters therein (see below nn. 234 et seq.). The meaning of 'historic title' in Art. 15 (in the context of territorial sea delimitation per se) cannot be the *only* intended meaning of the *second* mention of this phrase in UNCLOS Art. 298. The recent US *Limits in the Seas* publication (*infra* n. 116) sees these references as now containing the only permissible instances of historic waters in the law the sea (see below n. 50).

the ICJ in 1951 to describe 'historic waters'.[3] In the light of such limited reference, resort must be had to the UNCLOS preamble for guidance relating to matters not dealt with within the Convention; and these are said to be governed by customary international law.[4] This is, of course, of no interpretative assistance on the relevant terminology here, and this omission only adds to the vagueness as to the meaning of the various 'historic' concepts mentioned (including those possibly implied) in the Convention[5] and the rules that are presumed to exist relating to them. Such lack of precision has, unfortunately, the inherent danger of encouraging states to make historic maritime claims 'of increasing scope' – as may now be evident in the South China Sea (SCS) dispute.[6]

More generally, another of the unsatisfactory elements in respect of historic claims to, or in, maritime areas is that there is no consistent terminology used in state practice here.[7] For example 'historic claims' (to use a broad and neutral phrase) may firstly include 'historic title' (as specifically mentioned in UNCLOS). This latter term in turn seems essentially to comprehend both 'historic waters' (and within that concept the narrower phenomenon of 'historic bays') and possibly also the separable issue of 'historic rights' on the other (though then very word 'title' implies perhaps some claim to sovereignty as in a land-based analogy[8]).

3 See below n. 8; and, for example, F. Dupuy and P.-M. Dupuy, 'A legal analysis of China's historic rights claim in the South China Sea', *AJIL* 107 (2013), 124 (the 'term "historic rights" (sometimes confusingly used in this context in combination with other germane notions such as *historic waters* and *historic title*) has often been imbued with a certain degree of confusion and controversy in international law'. M. Valencia rightly argues that the fact that the Convention does not refer to historic title, historic rights or historic waters only means that the Convention does not touch on these matters and leaves them to customary law. This is so in a substantive sense, at any rate. He adds nonetheless that the PRC's claim of 'historic rights' is a distinct one from the other two: see 'The South China Sea dispute: what China could say', nautilus.org, 29 June 2013, http:nautilus.org/napset/napset-policy-forum/the-south-china-sea-what-china-could-say.

4 Zou, K., 'Historic rights in international law and China's practice', *ODIL* 32 (2001), 149, 152. See also the same author, 'Historic rights in the South China Sea' in the Conference Proceedings of 'The South China Sea: UNCLOS and State Practice', 24–25 October, Haikou, China, organized by the National Institute for South China Sea Studies, 2013, 50, 55 ('it is obvious that [UNCLOS] deliberately avoids the issue of "historic rights" or "historic waters"').

5 Such as whether historic title can attach to internal waters enclosed by the expansive straight baseline system endorsed in Art. 7 of UNCLOS: see Symmons, *supra* n. 1, at pp. 23–6.

6 Clark, *supra* n. 1, at p. 9.

7 See, e.g., Zou, *supra* n. 4, at p. 152; and Franckx and Benatar, *infra* n. 14, at p. 95; also Dupuy and Dupuy, *supra* n. 3, at p. 124.

8 Zou, *supra* n. 4, at p. 152. The ICJ in *Tunisia/Libya* used the phrases 'historic rights' and 'historic title' completely interchangeably: see [1982] ICJ Reports, 18, p. 73, para. 100. Gao and Jia (*infra* n. 11, at p. 122) comment that the tribunal in the *Eritrea/Yemen Case* did not distinguish between 'historic rights' and 'historic title', but 'indicated

Indeed, these two types of 'rights' – historic waters and historic rights – differ in important respects, even if the supposed legal rules underpinning both of them are the same or similar;[9] this difference being essentially because the former implies a claim to sovereignty (of whatever form) in the specified waters, whereas a claim to 'historic rights' implies merely a (lesser) jurisdictional claim in certain (often international) waters.[10] Thus in the *Eritrea/Yemen Arbitration* the tribunal described certain 'historic rights' which 'accrued in favour of both parties through a process of historical consolidation as a sort of "servitude internationale" *falling short of territorial sovereignty*'.[11]

Other differences are that whilst the former notionally applies '*erga omnes*' (i.e., against all nations), historic rights (normally historic fishing rights[12]) seemingly apply only on a more subjective '*quoad hunc/hos*' basis (i.e., applying only between a *particular* state or states) as claimant(s) and against a 'servient

by its [statement that] it accepted the notion of historic rights as something falling short of territorial sovereignty'.

9 See, e.g., Symmons, *supra* n. 1, at p. 4.

10 For a more detailed discussion, see C.R. Symmons, 'Rights and jurisdiction over resources and obligations of coastal States: validity of historic rights claims', a paper given at the 5th International Workshop on The South China Sea: Co-operation for Regional Security and Development, 11–12 November 2013, Hanoi, Vietnam (Diplomatic Academy of Vietnam). Zou, *supra* n. 4, at p. 152, mentions historic rights covering 'special rights' without a claim of full sovereignty, such as historic fishing rights which a state may have acquired 'in particular areas of the high seas'; and A. Gioia, in 'Tunisia's claims over adjacent seas and the doctrine of "historic rights"', *Syracuse Jnl of Intl Law & Commerce* 11 (1984), 327, at pp. 328–9, distinguishes 'historic rights' according to their content: that is to say according to the 'extent of *imperium* due to the state which has acquired the right in question'. She says that if these amount to 'full sovereignty', then the situation is covered by historic waters (ibid., at p. 328), of which one aspect is historic bays (ibid., at p. 329). She adds that historic rights also cover 'those special rights a State may acquire, in derogation of existing general rules relating to exercise of limited authority over certain portions of the high seas, without at the same time involving a claim to full sovereignty' (ibid., at p. 329): one example of this being historic fishing rights in a particular area of the high seas (ibid.). Dupuy and Dupuy, *supra* n. 3, also (at p. 137) confirm that historic *rights* (as opposed to historic title) include rights *falling short of sovereignty* such as fishery rights.

11 Award, para. 126. This passage is cited by Z. Gao and B. Jia, in 'The nine-dash line in the South China Sea :history,status and implications', 107 *AJIL* (2013),98, at p. 121, as supporting an 'additional claim' to the 'amenities of the sea' within the line based on 'historic title'.

12 L. Barnard, 'The effect of historic fishing rights in maritime boundaries delimitation' (*LOSI* Conference paper, Seoul, Korea (2012)), points out that the jurisprudence of international courts and tribunals indicates not only a reluctance to recognise such regional claims (p. 13), but also they have all concerned specificity as to type of fishery, e.g., pearls (*Bahrain/Qatar*) or flying fish (*Barbados/Trinidad* (Award, para. 247, p. 4)).

state' (or states) in a similar fashion to a prescriptive right in municipal law.[13] In this writer's opinion, however, the supposedly more objective character as to inter-state applicability of the separable doctrine of *historic waters* may, on closer analysis, be more apparent than real as it is possible to argue that even the latter doctrine works on an 'opposability' basis.[14]

It may be added here that this aspect of maritime rights is relevant in the SCS dispute, where *several* neighbouring states claim traditional fishery rights in the insular waters, so that China has no monopoly in this regard.[15] In such shared fishery instances, a possible result has been that – either by bilateral delimitation agreement (as between India/Sri Lanka[16]) or by international decision (as in the *Eritrea/Yemen Arbitration*[17]) – both such states' fishermen may have continuing reciprocal rights of fishing both sides of any fixed maritime boundary line.[18]

It may be also argued that whereas historic waters must necessarily be *adjacent* to the claimant's land territory (on an analogy with the territorial sea regime), historic rights need not be; and may indeed be exercised far from the shores of the state whose nationals exercise such rights.[19] It should be noted, however, that such is the looseness of terminology in this area that even the phrase 'historic *rights*' may generically cover other aspects of historic maritime claim such as even historic (internal) *waters*;[20] as such phrases are 'often used interchangeably in maritime contexts'.[21] It seems mistaken, however, to argue that there are 'no definitive [rules] in international law which govern the status of historic *rights*'.[22]

13 See the quotation above n. 11. It may be noted here that where both disputing states in an arbitration have shared this right,(as in the above-mentioned case) the tribunal has 'recognised the historic rights of both sides' (Zou, *supra* n. 4, at p. 155).

14 See Symmons, *supra* n. 1, at pp. 229–300. Other commentators have taken this up in an approving fashion: see, e.g., E. Franckx and M. Benatar, 'Dots and lines in the South China Sea: insights from the law of map evidence', *Asian Jnl of Intl Law* 2 (2012), 89, at p. 97, where they cite the views of Scovazzi and myself on this issue.

15 See, e.g., D. Huy, 'China's u-shaped line in the South China Sea', *Asia Sentinel Consulting*, 19 September 2012, at pp. 2–3.

16 The 1974 Sri Lanka/India agreement, according to the USA Office of the Geographer (No. 66 (12 December 1973), at p. 5) divides the Bay of Palk by a modified equidistance line, preserving the traditional fishing rights of both parties on both sides of the line, seemingly recognizing past Sri Lankan pearl and chank fisheries, as the treaty preamble implies by referring to 'historical evidence' having been 'taken into account'.

17 Phase 1, 9 October 1998, http://www.pca-cpa.org/ER-YEAwardTOC.htm.

18 Award, para. 526.

19 See Symmons, *supra* n. 1, at p. 6.

20 Ibid., at pp. 4–5.

21 Zou, *supra* n. 4, at p. 152.

22 Ibid., at p. 163. Cf., for example, T. Thuy, Center for East Sea (South China Sea) Studies, Diplomatic Academy of Vietnam (30 September 2012), who opines that although such rights are not a 'well-recognised concept in international law', they nonetheless have the requirements for historic waters claims as a 'prerequisite'.

There very arguably are; and they are seemingly similar to those relating to historic waters claims; though there are again corresponding elements of ambiguity here.[23]

Added terminological confusion comes because similar, if not identical, rights may exist in the law of the sea corresponding to all, or at least most of, the above-mentioned types of historic claim, and which do not even attract the epithet 'historic'. For example, Art. 51(1) of UNCLOS enjoins an archipelagic state to recognize 'traditional fishing rights'; the same phrase as used in the *Eritrea Yemen Arbitration*;[24] whereas the phrase 'established rights' was used in the *Fisheries Jurisdiction Case* to describe similar rights:[25] and notably circumlocutory phraseology is utilized in Art. 62(3) of UNCLOS (concerning rights (such as fishing) which have been 'habitually' exercised in an area of seas). It was pointed out by Judge Oda in the *Gulf of Fonseca Case* that even in the case of one of the classic 'historic bays' – the Gulf of Fonseca – the Central American Court in 1917 merely described it as being 'possessed of the characteristics of *an enclosed sea*' rather than being an 'historic bay' per se.[26] All this terminological incertitude is now evident in the supposed Chinese historic claim in the SCS, as discussed below.

Historic Rights

Of the two basic 'historic' types of maritime rights mentioned, only 'historic *waters*' is of real continuing importance in the contemporary law of the sea. For in the context now of UNCLOS, only *indirect* reference seems to be made to 'historic *rights*' as such; so this is not *eo nomine*: namely the reference in Art. 62(3) to possible prioritized access to surplus stocks of fish by other states in a particular foreign-owned EEZ applying to 'States whose nationals have habitually fished in the zone'. It may be noted here, then, that there is not even a reference to 'historic' rights as such, though they may be inferred.[27] The implication in Art. 62(3) of UNCLOS is that historic fishing rights are now overtaken by the expansive

---

23 See Symmons, *supra* n. 1, at pp. 4–5.

24 Ibid., at p. 4. The phrase 'traditional fishing rights' (relative to UK fishermen) was also used by the ICJ in the *Fisheries Jurisdiction Case* (1974) ICJ Rep. p. 30, para. 69. However, other judges such as de Castro in his Sep. Op. (at p. 98 para. 7) did specifically categorize the British rights off Iceland outside the 12 nm limit as 'historic' ('account should be taken of the historic rights of countries with historic sea fishing'; and, he said, such long usage 'should be respected' (ibid.)). See also Judge Petren, Diss. Op. (p. 162), who said that the Court had based its judgment 'solely on considerations concerning *historic rights*' of the UK (emphasis added). It was stated in the parallel case, *Germany v. Iceland* (p. 197, para. 57) that Iceland had actually admitted the Applicant's '*historic* and special interests in fishing the disputed waters' (emphasis added).

25 Symmons, *supra* n. 1, at p. 5.

26 Symmons, *supra* n. 1, at p. 15.

27 There may be an implication of a *preferential* Chinese fishery claim in the SCS dispute: see Huy, *supra* n. 15, at p. 3. It is there argued that such rights beyond 12 nm have

economic rights of a coastal state recognized in its EEZ; so that, worldwide, such third state rights have been phased out of supervening EEZ regimes which may enclose them.[28] And insofar as they may have been exercised in the past outside an accepted territorial sea distance *off but adjacent to*, the shoreline of a particular coastal state by that same State, these rights are now to be interpreted in terms of a supervening *juridical*, rather than 'exceptional' (i.e., historic) exercise of rights off its coast.[29]

In a similar way, past alleged historic claimed *seabed* rights (such as sedentary fisheries[30]) adjacent to coastal states may now be more properly viewed as being, in an inter-temporal sense, subsumed under the modern-day continental shelf doctrine, as is discussed further below. As will be seen, this is of importance in the SCS dispute, where the supposed Chinese claim to historic fishing rights has no necessarily direct relevance to a claim to 'historic *waters*' as such.

---

been properly acquired as historic rights *before* UNCLOS and so could be 'the types that are preserved by that convention' (ibid., at p. 2).

28 But cf. the *Eritrea/Yemen arbitration* (Second Stage) (Maritime Delimitation) (1999), paras 62–71 (available in WorldCourts.com/International Case Law Database). T. McDorman opines that the award indicates that 'an historic fishing right ascribed to foreign fishers within the waters of a coastal State does not trump coastal State sovereignty', but that still the award 'supports the view that that historic fishing rights by a third State in waters otherwise under the jurisdiction of a coastal State are not necessarily extinguished by [UNCLOS]': see 'Rights and jurisdiction over resources in the South China Sea: UNCLOS and the "Nine-Dash Line"', in *The South China Sea Disputes and the Law of the Sea*, edited by S. Jayakumar, T. Koh and R. Beckman (Cheltenham: Edward Elgar, 2014), 144, 158). It may be noted that even the obligation under Art. 51(1) of UNCLOS on an archipelagic state to 'recognise traditional fishing rights' of immediately adjacent states in its *archipelagic waters* is subject, in any exercise of such rights, to 'terms and conditions'; so even such limited 'historic' rights as are preserved under UNCLOS are not necessarily equal to those that preceded it. Similarly it may be noted that where any historic fishing rights may be claimed on the *high seas* outside any other state's EEZ, the UN Convention on Conservation and management of Straddling Fish Stocks and Highly Migratory Fish Stocks (set out in 1995 A/CONF.164/37 (1 September 1995)) makes no mention of historic rights in this context; and, indeed, it is implicit in, e.g., Arts 7(1) and 8(1) of the Convention that the obligation to co-operate on measures to conserve straddling fish stocks in 'adjacent high seas areas' to coastal states applies equally to any state claiming 'historic rights' in the area concerned. The caselaw of the ICJ supports the thrust of Art. 62(3) of UNCLOS: for in the *Gulf of Maine Case* (1984), an ICJ Chamber noted that the advent of EEZ-based fisheries jurisdiction within a 200 nm zone overrode any prior usage and rights of other states within that zone: see *Delimitation of the Maritime Boundary in the Gulf of Maine* (Canada//USA) 1984 ICJ Rep. 246, paras 233, 235. This is cited in the US *Limits in the Seas* publication (*infra* n. 116, at p. 20).

29 See *infra* n. 69; and Symmons, *supra* n. 1, at p. 195.

30 Gioia (*supra* n. 10, at p. 364, n. 135) says that many writers have explained *sedentary* fishing rights as acquired *pursuant to the law, rather than in derogation of it.*

Furthermore, such alleged rights seem, since the advent of the EEZ regime, to have had little or no application in practice to *delimitation* of maritime zones.[31] For example, it is regionally significant that in negotiating a maritime boundary with the PRC in the Gulf of Tonkin Vietnam abandoned its former claim to the Gulf as being historic.[32]

One of the reasons for such contemporary downgrading of historic fishing rights generally may be the limited *jurisdictional* nature of such rights, as seen above.[33] Indeed, for example, in the SCS situation, rights of fishing conducted by other regional states were not (at least until recently) interfered with by the PRC; and so that the latter's fishery rights were not, in the past, considered 'exclusive'.[34] The only example of bilateral delimitation agreements where historic rights issues may have been expressly taken into account is to be seen in the maritime delimitations between India and Sri Lanka.[35]

Despite, indeed, the mention of 'historic title' in Art. 15 of UNCLOS in the context of the delimitation of the *territorial sea*, this factor has had minimal effect in state practice in delimitation of territorial seas just as in other maritime areas,[36] whether in terms of historic rights or historic waters claims.

---

31 See, e.g., the cases of *Bahrain/Qatar*, *Libya/Tunisia* and *Eritrea/Yemen* (*supra* n. 17): Symmons, *supra* n. 1, at p. 46. Zou (*supra* n. 4, at p. 156) talks of the 'rather conservative attitude' of international tribunals on historic rights; and see most recently the *Barbados/Trinidad Delimitation Arbitration* (cited in N. Hong, *UNCLOS and Ocean Dispute Settlement: Law and Politics in the South China Sea* (London: Routledge, 2012), at p. 63; see also (at p. 64) her reference to the *Grisbardana arbitration*).

32 The Vietnamese claim to historic waters had been made in 1982 in its Statement on the Territorial Sea Baseline of Vietnam.

33 See *supra* n. 10 et seq.; and Bernard, *supra* n. 12, at p. 19.

34 Zou, *supra* n. 4, at p. 162, citing H. Thao. Cf. the practice of sponge fishing off Tunisia in the case of which Judge Arechaga in the *Libya/Tunisia Case* (*supra* n. 8, at p. 124, para. 83) validly pointed out that the fact that mostly foreigners carried out the sponge fishing (outside a territorial sea) did not mean that 'sovereign rights' were not involved as they got the rights through the granting of fishery 'concessions' from Tunisia outside its (then) territorial sea limits.

35 According to 'Limits in the sea: historic waters boundary: India-Sri Lanka' (Office of Geographer, USA, No. 66 (December 12, 1973)), the 1974 agreement divides, with a modified equidistance line, 'the historic waters and seabed of Palk Bay, preserving the traditional fishing rights of both parties on both sides' (in Art. 6) (ibid., p. 5). Thus the India/Sri Lanka delimitation agreements (including the related 1976 one in the Gulf of Manaar) seemingly take historical evidence into account; and here the modified median lines may have recognized past Sri Lankan pearl and chank fisheries in the Gulf of Manaar and Palk Bay: see Symmons, *supra* n. 1, at p. 47.

36 Judge Oda in his Diss. Op. in *Libya/Tunisia* (*supra* n. 8, at p. 211, para. 88) stated that there was no suggestion at the 1958 Conference that there should be an exemption to the median line delimitation method (because of historic title) in the case of continental shelf delimitation. As seen (above n. 32), the Vietnamese claim to the Gulf of Tonkin was

Historic Waters

As seen, this term most particularly may include 'historic bays' as are expressly mentioned in Art. 10(6) of UNCLOS,[37] though there is no definition of such geographical features there laid down; and, indeed, the there-preceding epithet – 'so-called' – casts some doubt on their very nomenclature in the law of the sea.[38] Historic *waters* as such (which are not, as seen, mentioned *in specie* in UNCLOS[39]), have been succinctly and judicially described as 'waters which are treated as internal waters, but which would not have that character if it were not for the existence of historic title'.[40] Despite the lack of treaty definition, which like the rules relating thereto is still dependent on customary law (as, as seen, implied from the UNCLOS preamble, and as confirmed by the ICJ in the *Libya/Tunisia Case*),[41] it seems that such bays fail the requirements of geographical configuration, as now settled in Art. 10, most particularly in not conforming to the 'semi-circle' test or exceeding the maximum width of mouth.[42]

Permissible Types of Historic Waters

The phrase 'historic waters', although (as seen) not a term used in UNCLOS as such, may be applied, by implication at least, to other areas of coastal waters (apart from bays[43]) which may, like bays, be geographically enclosed *and connected to an adjacent landmass*,[44] such as internal waters in the case of an enclosed a *coastal*

---

ignored in subsequent delimitation there with the PRC (see Zou, *supra* n. 4, at p. 161) because the PRC refused to recognize this claim.

37 Symmons, *supra* n. 1, and Zou, *supra* n. 4, at p. 152.

38 See Symmons, *supra* n. 1, at p. 21.

39 See the ICJ in *Tunisia/Libya, supra* n. 8, at p. 73, para. 100 (UNCLOS does not contain 'any detailed provisions on the "regime of historic waters"', there being neither a 'definition of the concept' nor any 'elaboration' of the 'juridical regime of 'historic waters' or 'historic bays'. There are, however, said the Court (ibid., at p. 74), 'references [in UNCLOS] to "historic bays" or "historic titles" or historic reasons in a way amounting to a reservation to the rules set forth therein' which continue to be governed by customary law. The judicial reference here to 'historic reasons' is puzzling, as it simply adds to the existing terminological confusion in the law of the sea, as no such term exists in UNCLOS).

40 *Anglo-Norwegian Fisheries Case* [1951] ICJ Reports,116, at p. 130.

41 Symmons, *supra* n. 1, at p. 22.

42 Ibid., at pp. 19–20.

43 Obviously, in the SCS case, the nine-dash claim could not be a claim to *bay* waters. See, e.g., T. Thuy, 'China's u-shaped line: possible interpretations, asserting actions and reactions from outside', a paper presented at a Conference on 'The practices of the UNCLOS and the resolution of the South China Sea Dispute', 3–4 September 2012, Taipei, Taiwan.

44 Symmons, *supra* n. 1, at p. 18 (though the *UN Juridical Regime* (*infra* n. 126) seems to argue otherwise (ibid., at p. 25)).

archipelago under (now) Art. 7 of UNCLOS which concerns an expansive straight baseline system (as was seemingly accepted to be the case by both the parties in the *Anglo-Norwegian Fisheries* case[45]); though examples of this are rare.[46] One such example was the case of the Alaskan claim to historic waters within the Alexander Archipelago in *Alaska v. US*.[47] Unlike in the case of bays (Art. 10(6)), there is no express proviso in UNCLOS allowing for claims to *historic waters* under Art. 7 and coastal archipelagos; though this may be said to be still implicit.[48] However, recent state practice is not inclined to favour such expansive claims, particularly because of freedom of navigation issues: one of the more recent 'non-bay' historic claims – that of Canada to 'historic waters' within its decreed straight baselines around its distant offshore Arctic islands archipelago – was immediately protested against by the EU in 1986.[49] All these types of enclosed and encloseable waters, may, then, potentially generate internal waters landward of their baselines as a form of 'historic waters', provided the zones so claimed are not simply part of the open seas.[50]

This geographical aspect is, of course, important in the case of any Chinese claim to historic waters within the SCS archipelago where the disputed islets are far from its mainland territory;[51] so that it cannot be based on 'bay-like'

---

45 *Supra* n. 24: see Symmons, *supra* n. 1, at p. 25.

46 Ibid., at p. 18.

47 See ibid., at p. 26.

48 See ibid., at pp. 24–5. Dupuy and Dupuy (*supra* n. 3, at p. 137) comment that *neither* Art. 7 nor 10 'define historic waters'; but at least Art. 10 does expressly refer to *historic bays* as a proviso to the juridical rules (albeit without any definition of same), whereas *Art. 7 makes no reference at all to any sort of historic waters*; except that Art. 7(5), in mentioning regional 'economic interests' which are 'clearly evidenced by long usage', may be implicitly referring to relevance of *historic* (fishing) claims in determining particular baselines; i.e. a more limited purpose.

49 Note that some mention of historicity comes in Art. 46(b) of UNCLOS in *defining* an 'archipelago' as meaning a group of islands so inter-related that, *inter alia*, they have been *historically* regarded as an intrinsic geographical,economic and political entity,: see Symmons (*supra* n. 1, at pp. 23–4 (emphasis added)), and *CAB v. Island Airlines* 235 F.Supp.990 (discussed ibid., at p. 24).

50 Zou, *supra* n. 4, at p. 151. See now the US position in its *Limits in the Seas* publication, *infra* n. 116, at p. 19 ('Apart from a narrow category of "historic bays" (Art. 10) and "historic title" in the context of territorial sea boundary delimitation, the modern international law of the sea does not recognise history as the basis for maritime jurisdiction'; thus a Chinese claim in the SCS would 'encompass areas distant from the Chinese-claimed features', and thus implicate the UNCLOS position on the EEZ, continental shelf and possibly even the high seas).

51 At least 500 nms away. Y. Song and P. Yu in 'China's "historic waters" in the South China Sea: an analysis from Taiwan, ROC', *American Asian Review* 12 (1994), 83, make the obvious point that historic waters and historic bays are not 'synonomous', as historic waters are wider in scope. They also mention the possibility of a Chinese claim to 'historic archipelagic waters' which is not an explicit UNCLOS III concept; on which see

claims as has been the norm. So here the adjacency element of historic claim can only be supplied by a valid Chinese claim to the *individual islands* in the distant archipelago.

Other supposed types of historic waters such as an 'historic territorial sea' have not been of past importance, no doubt because of the fluidity of past state practice on the optimal maximum extent of such zones; and thus the greater uncertainty as to whether such a claim is in essence exceptional (and so historic) or simply 'juridical' (such as the Scandinavian four-mile league as a territorial sea distance) in the light of past diversity of state practice.[52] It is certainly the case that the ICJ has stated in the *Tunisia/Libya Case* that general international law did not provide for 'a particular regime for each of the concrete, recognised cases of "historic waters" or "historic bays"'.[53] The Court thus endorsed a potential particularized regime for each historical claim, and so for some *diversity of types* of historic regimes. This factor was repeated by the ICJ in the *Gulf of Fonseca Case*,[54] there emphasizing the necessity for the Court to investigate 'the particular history of the Gulf of Fonseca',[55] and finding that the waters were internal in terms of modern law, and so not a territorial sea subject to a special regime.[56] The Chinese claim to the Quiongzhou (Haikou) Strait as historic internal waters indicates that the PRC does not view historic waters as being confined to bays.[57] However, for obvious reasons, any claim to straits waters as being historic is controversial.[58]

Another possibly qualifying historic waters zone has been a *historic fishing zone*; but herein lie problems relating to the past history of such zones and their initial varying widths and relating to relevant acts of sovereignty therein. Here the *commensurate exercise of jurisdiction rule*[59] exists as an important sub-rule to the 'effective exercise of jurisdiction' rule discussed below to evidence a proper historic waters claim as traditionally understood. As to establishing this above-mentioned type of zone, modern authority, such as it is, seems to indicate that enforcement of fishery regulations in a claimed offshore area may not be a meaningful assertion of sovereignty to found any more general historic claim as discussed below, particularly where it only concerns exploiting a limited species

---

also M. Valencia, J. Van Dyke and N. Ludwig, *Sharing the Resources of the South China Sea* (Hawaii: University of Hawaii Press, 1999), at p. 28, who comment that historic waters may have a unique status covering archipelagic waters.

52 Symmons, *supra* n. 1, at p. 36. One such example in more recent times is that of Sri Lanka claimed by presidential proclamation in 1977 relating to the territorial sea in the Gulf of Manaar (*infra* n. 135).

53 Symmons, *supra* n. 1, at p. 22.

54 *Supra* n. 40.

55 Ibid., at p. 22.

56 Symmons, *supra* n. 1, at p. 37.

57 Zou, *supra* n. 4, at p. 157.

58 See Symmons, *supra* n. 1, at pp. 32–5.

59 See ibid., at pp. 174–81.

of fish;[60] and so not constitute a valid claim to 'historic *waters*' as normally understood.[61] The latter issue brings up also the relationship of such waters with the more modern development of the EEZ, and even with the continental shelf; insofar as some past historic claims have concerned *seabed fishery rights*, as in the *Libya/Tunisia Case* and a claimed Tunisian right to exploit offshore *sedentary* species of fish. This aspect may be relevant in the SCS dispute as detailed below.

Application of Particularized Historic Claims to the SCS Dispute

The issue of locational qualification for 'historic waters' status seems important in the case of the present supposed Chinese claim to historic waters in the SCS, as recent Chinese statements and even recent Chinese legislation on the EEZ/continental shelf seem to hint at possible historical claims to extensive zones extending from the islands within the nine-dashed line (and even possibly beyond). This is in contrast to China's claims to historic *bays* elsewhere off the Chinese coast: as under a 1959 pamphlet concerning 'internal bays'; and in its Declaration on the Territorial Sea of 1958, when the PRC *expressly* declared both Bohai Gulf and Qiongzhou Strait to be *internal (historic) waters*,[62] giving as a rationale long actual control and international recognition; and importance for its economy and defence. Interestingly, though, *this* declaration did not mention the nine-dashed line claim (then in existence in the SCS) as similarly containing internal waters on historic grounds, when it might have been expected to do so.

Can there be a Historic EEZ/Continental Shelf Claim in Contemporary International Law?

One commentator has stated, in one passage, that China's claim in its EEZ law is 'not unusual'; and that, because it is embedded in its EEZ law, it could only make

60 Gioia, *supra* n. 10, at p. 373, points out that Tunisia's historic rights only related anyway to protection and control over *a narrow range of natural resources* – sponge and octopus fisheries; whereas an UNCLOS-based EEZ gives a coastal state full sovereign rights of exploring and exploiting *all the natural resources of the sea and seabed.* This should arguably rule out a state unilaterally claiming the whole area of its past 'historic rights' as part of its EEZ. Judge Oda in his Diss. Op. in the *Libya/Tunisia Case* (*supra* n. 8, p. 202, para. 73) stated restrictively that any legal doctrine prior to 1958 which might have been derived from 'long usage' of *sedentary fisheries* 'could [in any case] only give rise to a claim to historic rights *to those specific fisheries*' (emphasis added).

61 See, e.g., Clark, *supra* n. 1, at pp. 101, 201 ('such an assertion of dominion, to be meaningful, must be commensurate with the scope of that sovereign's enforcement mechanism').

62 Zou, *supra* n. 4, at p. 156.

the SCS waters an EEZ or continental shelf claim:[63] but in another,[64] he states that in the sense that the above claim does not fit *either* of the historic waters rights categories, it is thus is an 'historic claim equivalent to EEZ and/or the continental shelf' which is 'apparently new in state practice, since no similar claim has yet been made by other State'. This commentator goes so far as to dub these zones as a new form of extensive historic claim – 'historic rights with tempered sovereignty' – which may, he argues, be the prototype of a new customary rule in the law of the sea.[65] He seems to view such waters as being grounded on historic fishing rights, so as to give the area the *same status* as an EEZ/continental shelf under UNCLOS,[66] but possibly even beyond the 200 nm mark; and possibly with a regime differing from an EEZ (as seen, a so-called 'tempered' regime, whatever this may mean).[67] Similarly another commentator on the SCS dispute has claimed that the Chinese claim is 'an *historic* EEZ', which has same status as an EEZ in UNCLOS.[68]

---

63 Ibid., at p. 160. See also Zou, K., 'The traditional maritime boundary in the South China Sea and its legal consequences for the resolution of the dispute over the Spratly Islands', *IJMCL* 14 *(*1999), at p. 47, where he opines that the 200 metre line was 'historically intended to define the continental shelf of the islands'. Similarly, Z. Gao and B. Jia in 'The nine-dash line in the South China Sea: history, status and implications', *AJIL* 107 (2013), 98, at p. 108, comment controversially that in addition to rights conferred by UNCLOS within the nine-dashed line, China can assert 'historic rights' within the line, in respect not just of fishing, but also navigation and 'exploration and exploitation of resources'.

64 Zou, *supra* n. 4, at p. 160 (emphasis added). Most recently, similar assertions are made by Zou, K. and L. Xinchang in 'The legal status of the u-shaped line in the South China Sea and its legal implications for sovereignty, sovereign rights and maritime jurisdiction' forthcoming in the *Chinese Jnl of International Law* (2015), http:/chinesejil.oxfordjournals.org/, published on April 5, 2015.

65 Ibid., at p. 160. See also Zou, K., *Law of the Sea in East Asia: Issues and Prospects* (London/NY: Routledge, 2005), at p. 170 (it is obvious that 'such a claim to historic rights is not only a right to fisheries, but to other resources and activities as well' (he here uses again the strange phrase 'historic rights with *tempered* sovereignty' (emphasis added)). For my critique on this viewpoint, see Symmons, *supra* n. 1, at pp. 7–13. H. Nong also refers to a supposed trend in 'historic claims' despite the advent of the EEZ/continental shelf regimes which, she claims, 'may eventually help to codify the rules of historic rights and/or historic waters in general international law': see 'Interpreting the u-shaped line in the South China Sea', www.chinausfocus:com/…./interpreting-the-u-shaped-line-in-the-South-China-Sea (China/US Forum, 15 May 2012). She cites in this regard the dictum of the ICJ in the *Libya/Tunisia Case* (see *supra* n. 8) as making the Chinese historic claim one of such 'particular cases' which may stand up in international law.

66 Ibid., at p. 162.

67 Ibid.

68 J. Yongke, 'No question of re-demarcation in the South China Sea', *Ocean Development and Management* (2000), 17, at p. 52 (emphasis added), cited by Dupuy and Dupuy, *supra* n. 3, at p. 136. See also Franckx and Benatar, *supra* n. 14, at p. 101, citing Yonke regarding the PRC's 'historic proprietary title' (EEZ/historic EEZ), so having

There are several reasons why such viewpoints are untenable for evidencing *an historic claim*; but most particularly because *any such modern-day zonal claims* cannot be intertemporarily backdated to an earlier period in history. For they are now (even in the case of past claimed seabed rights beyond a territorial sea, such as sedentary fisheries) to be interpreted as solely dealing with *juridical* rights in the contemporary law of the sea (where land appropriately dominates the sea) under the relevant provisions of UNCLOS; and where, as seen, Art. 62 effectively phases out any surviving third state historic *fishing* rights.[69]

The very creation worldwide of exclusive fishery zones from the 1950s onwards can be seen in retrospect as 'part of a well-known process which aimed at extending the rights of coastal states beyond the external limit of their territorial seas',[70] a process which ultimately culminated in the EEZ regime at UNCLOS. This point was, in effect, argued analogously by Libya in the *Tunisia/ Libya* case[71] – in respect of the continental shelf doctrine involving '*ipso jure*' attachment to the adjoining landmass as an inherent right.[72] As was there stated by the Court: 'It is clearly the case that, basically, the notion of historic rights over waters and that of the continental shelf are governed by distinct legal regimes in customary international law', the first being based on 'acquisition or occupation' and the second on 'the existence of rights "*ipso facto* and *ab initio*"'; so that any coincidence of the two can only be 'fortuitous'.[73]

---

the same status under UNCLOS provisions; and P. Dutton in 'Three disputes and three objectives: China and the South China Sea', *Naval War College Review* (2011), 64, 42, at p. 44, who argues that the combination of the Chinese 1992 Territorial Sea Law and its 1998 Law 'assert an EEZ'; and (at p. 51) that Chinese historic rights are *not relinquished* by creation of an EEZ/continental shelf under UNCLOS.

69 R. Beckman (MIMA Conference on the South China Sea: 'Recent developments and implications towards peaceful dispute resolution', 12–13 December 2011, Kuala Lumpur, Malaysia), at p. 10, merely states that it is arguable that when states become parties to UNCLOS, they in effect give up any rights to fish in the waters of other states. He also argues (ibid., and controversially in this writer's opinion) that '*historic rights*' would not be excluded by the Chinese declaration under Art. 298 'as claims to historic r*ights* are very different than claims to *historic bays or titles or claims to historic waters*' (emphasis added) (see my discussion *infra* n. 249). By contrast, he uncontroversially adds that 'another issue is whether disputes relating to "historic *waters*" would fall within the exclusion in Art. 298 of disputes relating to "historic bays or titles"'; and concludes that it is reasonable to assume they would (ibid., at p. 7). He also asserts (ibid., at p. 7) that the fact that the terms 'historic bays and titles' appear in Pt. 2 of UNCLOS on *territorial sea*s 'suggest the terms are used to refer to maritime space that is similar to internal waters or territorial sea'. More broadly, the latter point may be an additional interpretative reason why there cannot be claims to '*historic EEZ*s' under UNCLOS. See *infra* n. 87.

70 See Goia, *supra* n. 10, at p. 357.

71 See Symmons, *supra* n. 1, at p. 46.

72 Zou, *supra* n. 4, at p. 154.

73 *Supra* n. 10, at p. 74, para. 100. Libya had argued that the fishing practice of one state could not 'in principle prevail over the inherent and *ab initio* rights of another State

As Professor Zou himself admits,[74] the continental shelf doctrine of 'inherency' 'should be viewed as deliberately aimed against the operation of any historic rights previously acquired'. As against this stands the (somewhat isolated) Dissenting Opinion of Judge Arechaga in the *Tunisia/Libya Case*: to the effect that 'a new legal concept consisting in the notion introduced in 1958 that continental shelves are inherent or "*ab initio*", cannot by itself have the effect of abolishing or denying acquired or existing rights'.[75] However, in my opinion any doctrine of 'acquired rights' in this respect must, on an analogy with the fate of historic *rights* more generally, be subservient to any such *supervening juridical* claim, even if such

in respect of its natural prolongation'; and queried whether such a claim amounted to an 'exercise of sovereignty': ibid., at p. 72, para. 98.

74 *Supra* n. 4, at p. 162, citing O'Connell (*infra* n. 87), at p. 713. In the *Tunisia/Libya Case*, Tunisia did indeed try to draw a parallel between the modern recognition of the rights of a coastal state over the continental shelf and the asserted recognition by third states of its rights over banks and shoals off her coasts which *were capable of being exploited centuries before the continental shelf doctrine became of economic and legal significance.*

75 As he stated (*supra* n. 10, at p. 124, para. 82), such abolition of rights would be contrary to the 'basic principles of intertemporal law': however, he added that such rights were 'assimilated into the new doctrine'. He also added (ibid., at p. 123, para. 123) that the '*ab initio*' doctrine only appeared in 1958: see Gioia, *supra* n. 10, at p. 370. Tunisia admitted before the ICJ that the new law of the sea included its 'fishing rights' in an EEZ; but claimed that this factor could not cut off *its acquired rights* since time immemorial despite the high seas regime then being outside 3 nms (Tunisian Reply, at p. 29). Libya contested the view that these claimed rights amounted to sovereignty over the seabed, which in any case could not 'deprive a neighbouring State of a shelf area which, according to the law, appertains to it *de jure* and *ab initio*'. The ICJ avoided a decision on the question of whether Tunisia's claimed historic rights were relevant to the delimitation of a continental shelf (at pp. 370–71), though asserting that such rights should be respected and preserved as they always have been by long usage. Thus (ibid., at p. 371), the ICJ seems to have 'denied the relevance of any existing historic rights' since 'basically the notion of historic rights or waters and that of the continental shelf are governed by distinct legal regimes in customary international law'. As the ICJ stated (supra n. 8, at p. 74): 'While it may be that Tunisia's historic rights and titles are more nearly related to the concept of the EEZ, Tunisia has not chosen to base its claims upon that concept': see Gioia, *supra* n. 10, at p. 371. But cf. Judge Arechaga (Sep. Op. at p. 122) (relevance of historic rights relating to sponge fisheries was 'decisive' in the case because this constitutes *a form of exploitation of one of the natural resources of the continental shelf* according to Art. 2 of the CSC 1958 – an exploitation of continental shelf resources 'long antedating the Truman declaration'. Thus he found (ibid., at p. 72, para. 72) that Tunisia's historic rights (over parts of the seabed) were derived from 'long established interests and activities of its population in exploiting the *fisheries of the bed and waters* off its coasts' – amounting to the 'exercise of sovereign rights' by the Tunisian authorities, and 'coupled with at least the tacit toleration and recognition thereof by third States' (emphasis added)).

rights developed before UNCLOS.[76] Other recent commentators[77] argue against what more broadly might be dubbed an 'anti-historic-characteristic' perspective, on an analogy with the *existing* rules relating to historic waters: namely that the 'suggestion that waters situated hundreds of nautical miles away from the coast of China could be considered its historic waters blatantly contradicts the very concept of historic waters – a special category of either internal waters or territorial sea – *as always pertaining to waters close to the coast of the interested State*'. For on such a basis, even if the PRC has good title to the SCS islands, part of the claimed waters would be far more than 12 nms from them.[78] As another critic has pertinently stated, 'international law has never recognised claims of historic waters that extend so far out to sea', but those which would normally be '*enclosed by baselines rather than lie outside them*'.[79]

---

76 This 'pre-UNCLOS' aspect to the supposed Chinese claim to 'historic rights' in the SCS seems to underpin Gao and Jia's argument (*supra* n. 11, at p. 123) ('China's historic title and rights, *which preceded the advent of UNCLOS by many years*, have a continuing role to play' (emphasis added)). This view also has been expressed in official PRC statements: see, e.g., J. Ku, 'China's Judge Xue Hanqin publicly defends China's non-participation in the UNCLOS Arbitration' (blog on Opinio Juris: lawprofessors.typepad.com/.../chinas-icj-judge-xue-hanqin-publicly-defends (21 November 2013)). The recent US *Limits in the Seas* publication strongly supports a non-retroactive argument, maintaining that the fact that China that the fact China's supposed historic claims predated UNCLOS 'does not provide a basis under [UNCLOS] or international law for derogating from [UNCLOS]': see *infra* n. 116, at p. 22. The recent publication by Zou and Xinchang (*supra* n. 64) repeats this 'pre-UNCLOS' and historical viewpoint (ibid., at para. 34) ('It is clear and logical that when a coastal state extends its maritime zones outward from the coast, that state *should respect the existence of historic rights and waters which have already existed in the high seas*' (emphasis added)).

77 Dupuy and Dupuy, *supra* n. 3, at p. 139.

78 Ibid., at p. 139. See also the Paracel and Spratly Islands Forum: Song and Yu, *supra* n. 51, at p. 84 . They claim that the map was of January 1948, 'arbitrarily' drawn, and cite (at p. 3) Hamzah as saying that at 'no stretch of the imagination' can the SCS be considered as 'internal waters or historic lake'.

79 See Huy, *supra* n. 15, at p. 2 (emphasis added) (historic waters have been normally enclosed by 'straight baselines', as officially declared elsewhere by the PRC to date); also (ibid.), a PRC note of 2011 indicating that the SCS islands were fully entitled to a territorial sea, EEZ/continental shelf generated by the archipelago could indicate such claims as being *confined to inside the dashed line*, and the line being the limit of this: the 1948 line being too far from the isles for a permissible claim to such zones *at that time* (the 1948 map did not mention such '12nm-plus' claims). Also it may be said that lines encircling historic waters are normally *solid* lines linking with basepoints on land and completely enclosing a specific area. The Chinese 'dashes' are not only separated but are not even enclosed at the top (north sections) on the 'cow's tongue'. See also T. McDorman in Koh et al., *supra* n. 28 ('Such a claim beyond near-shore waters would be exceptional and inconsistent with the history of the law of the sea where, until recently, what existed were narrow bands of national waters along a coast'); and M. Myoshi, 'China's u-shaped line claim in the South China Sea: any

Even some Chinese commentators seem to accept that an 'historical EEZ' is a doctrine too far.[80] The historic 'EEZ-claim' viewpoint also seems to ignore the precedents of history on exaggerated claims in the past; as even in the nineteenth century one of the most pretentious illegal claims to erstwhile high seas (by Czar Alexander in his ukase of 1815 concerning a 100 mile 'no-go' zone off Alaska) was stymied at birth by immediate protests from the major powers, causing it to be almost immediately withdrawn.[81]

The same supposed historic waters principles – such as they are – if applied *pari passu*, as in any other historic claim, to a supposed historic EEZ, immediately meet a legal obstacle: namely, as seen, that a mere claim to *control one jurisdictional aspect* such as fisheries is not enough to support 'a claim to full sovereignty';[82] and particularly where it only concerns a *limited* type of fishery such as *sedentary* fisheries.[83] However it may be arguable that a claim to historic fishing rights might be a relevant factor in delimiting an EEZ boundary with a neighbouring state,[84] where, of course, a key sovereign right element concerns exploitation of natural resources such as fisheries in the water column; but not in the case of a continental shelf delimitation.[85]

---

validity under international law?', *ODIL* 43 (2012), 1, at p. 3. The above-mentioned deficit relating to the lack of solidity of closing lines in the alleged Chinese historic claim has not been rectified by the most recent Chinese map published in 2014 which now applies *10* dashed segments around the SCS islands: see 'Notes' to the announcement in the *South China Sea Bulletin*, vol. 2, No. 8 of 1 August 2014: and *infra* n. 158.

80 See L. Jinming and L. Dexia, 'The dotted line on the Chinese map of the South China Sea', *ODIL* 34 (2003), 287, at p. 292 (cited in Dupuy and Dupuy, *supra* n. 3, at n. 60).

81 See Symmons, *supra* n. 1, at pp. 72–3. Franckx and Benatar (*supra* n. 14, at pp. 94–5) comment that to judge the 1947/8 map *in an intertemporal way* makes the Chinese claim seem even more exorbitant; as historic claims *normally relate to bays or other territorial waters*.

82 Clark, *supra* n. 1, at p. 114, n. 242, at p. 347. Gioia (*supra* n. 10, at p. 347) alleges that a 'state cannot claim a vast area of sea as internal water on the sole basis of "historic rights" previously acquired for fishing purposes, unless it is possible to consider that those "historic rights" were in fact *indicative of a right to full sovereignty*' (emphasis added): the manner in which the rights are being exercised is vital, as it is 'another thing entirely to claim exclusive rights for limited purposes over the high seas'.

83 Gioia (*supra* n. 10, at p. 375) asks regarding Tunisia's past claims to historic rights over sedentary fisheries whether this was a claim to *full sovereignty*; and whether creation of *such exclusive fishery zones* should be 'regarded as part of the process which culminated in the affirmation of the EEZ' in UNCLOS.

84 Zou, *supra* n. 4, at p. 154, citing Gioia. Gioia queries whether historic rights could be a 'special circumstance' in EEZ/continental shelf delimitation (*supra* n. 10, at p. 373) – as an 'equitable solution' under Arts. 74 and 83 of UNCLOS.

85 But cf. the ICJ in *Tunisia/Libya* (*supra* n. 8, at p. 75, para. 102), which noted that Tunisia's historic rights could 'be relevant to the case in a number of ways'; but that its delimitation line would leave Tunisia 'in full and undisturbed exercise of such rights'. Judge Arechaga in his Separate Opinion (at p. 122, para. 79) stated that 'basically speaking,

In the case of the PRC's claim in the SCS, then, the argument that the (now)-67-year-old line, pre-dating UNCLOS by some 34 years, is exempt from the UNCLOS EEZ rules,[86] and thus has not been superceded,[87] is a flawed one. It seems to be in any case a strained treaty interpretation, as it is implicit in UNCLOS that the essential substantive references *concerning historic claims apply only to the territorial sea provisions* (including particularly waters landward of their baselines such as bays). Therefore it is only in this limited zonal context now that historic waters can exist: essentially in the *internal waters* landward of the baselines;[88] and likewise any past-claimed historic rights must now be squared with the EEZ provisions of UNCLOS. For such reasons it seems perverse to state

---

the existence of historic fishery rights is a circumstance which is relevant to continental shelf delimitation', *even though UNCLOS only referred to 'historic rights' in the context of territorial sea delimitation* (ibid., at p. 123, para. 80). Thus he stressed the 'sedentary fisheries' aspect *of the continental shelf doctrine*, saying the relevance of Tunisian sponge fishing was 'decisive' in the case, because the 'taking of sponges adhering to the seabed *constitutes a form of exploitation on one of the natural resources of the shelf* (emphasis added) (as in Art. 2(4) of the CSC 1958), describing it as much a 'form of exploitation' as in the case of 'the exploitation of oil or gas': ibid., at p. 123, para. 81.

86 See the Tunisian argument in *Tunisia/Libya* (*supra* n. 8, para. 99), where Tunisia invoked the parallel between the modern recognition of rights of the coastal state over its natural extension which were capable of being exploited 'centuries before the continental shelf became of economic and legal significance'.

87 This argument has featured in some recent PRC justificatory claims. Gioia (*supra* n. 10, at p. 372) comments: 'It follows that, insofar as the area of "historic rights" claimed by a coastal state over the sea-bed might overlap with the area of the continental shelf appertaining to a neighbouring state, these "historic rights" might only survive if it were proved that they have in fact continued to be exercised with the acquiescence of the state concerned *after* the establishment of the customary rules on the continental shelf' (emphasis added). Cf. Judge Arechaga's dictum in *Libya/Tunisia* (*supra* n. 8, at pp. 123–4), and *supra* n. 75. D.P. O'Connell, The International Law of the Sea (Oxford University Press: 1982–4, vol. 2, at p. 372) views customary rules on the continental shelf *as being deliberately aimed against the survival of previously acquired rights* insofar as they encroach on a continental shelf of a neighbouring state (and thus can only be reacquired by *later acquiescence* of that state):id, at p. 482 ('the doctrine of historic rights or acquisitive acquisition would not be available' to prioritize any claimed seabed rights on another state's continental shelf). Cf. R. Beckman, 'China, UNCLOS and the South China Sea', *Asian Socy of Intl Law*, 3rd Biennial Conference, Beijing, 27–28 August 2011, 1, at p. 12, where he says that the PRC's 1998 legislation 'seems intended to preserve its historic rights beyond the territorial sea', and to preserve 'certain [other] "historic rights in the SCS"' (ibid., at p. 12); but that this is doubtful, as the PRC gave up 'whatever historic rights it had to the natural resources in areas that are now the EEZ or continental shelf of other States'.

88 Zou, *supra* n. 4, at p. 152. Beckman, *supra* n. 87, at p. 12, similarly states that there are serious doubts that the PRC by a provision 'in its domestic legislation' could preserve Chinese rights outside a territorial sea as a continental shelf and EEZ, as an such extensive rights are now superceded by the UNCLOS provisions.

that a supposed claim to 'historic rights is not only a right to fisheries, but also other resources and activities as well';[89] or as one Chinese commentator has put it, that the waters in the u-shaped line should be considered as 'China's special EEZ or historic EEZ'.[90]

There seems to be some substance in the view that possibly the PRC's 'historic EEZ' idea has been belatedly raised because the PRC may now be 'back-pedalling' from the idea that the waters in the nine-dashed line are '*internal or territorial sea*' historic waters (now seen as untenable); and is thus deviating opportunistically towards an alternative historic EEZ/continental shelf claim.[91] Indeed, some recent Chinese commentators have interpreted the 1998 EEZ *legislative* insertion (dealing with continental shelf/EEZ rights *alone*) as in itself indicating that China no longer even regards the waters *within* the line as historic *in the traditional sense*.[92]

Added to all this is an obvious matter of practical politics: namely that no neighbouring state of a claimant to historic waters (or even historic rights) *of such magnitude* is likely to acquiesce in such a claim – a feature which has been fully evidenced in the case of the SCS dispute after the PRC reference to the nine-dashed line map in 2009 in the context of continental shelf claims.[93] Thus to argue that the PRC's claim in the latter sense can be regarded as a particular case which may stand up in international law as doctrine evolves over time seems totally unrealistic, given the fact that neighbouring states have immediately protested such claims (see below). No new type of historic waters genus could possibly

---

89 Zou, *supra* n. 4, at p. 160. See Gao and Jia (*supra* n. 11, at p. 108) who mention that the Chinese historical claim within the line has 'an additional Chinese claim of historical rights of fishing, navigation, *and other marine activities* (*including the exploration and exploitation of resources, mineral or otherwise*), on the islands *and in their adjacent waters*' (emphasis added). The addition of the italicised words is controversial.

90 Cited by Zou, *supra* n. 4, at p. 161, from J. Yonke (*supra* n. 68, at p. 52). It may be noted that in the *Tunisia/Libya Case*, the ICJ remarked that 'while it may be that Tunisia's historic rights are more nearly related to the concept of the [EEZ] … Tunisia has chosen not to base its claims on that concept': *supra* n. 8, at p. 74, para. 100.

91 Zou, *supra* n. 4, at p. 163.

92 Jinming and Dexia, *supra* n. 80, at p. 293. See also T.T. Thuy, 'China's u-shaped line in the South China Sea possible interpretations, asserting activities and reactions from outside', who opines that historic waters cannot extend beyond internal waters (paper presented at the Conference on the 'Practices of the UNCLOS and the resolution of the South China Sea dispute', 3–4 September 2012, Taipei, Taiwan).

93 See M. Malek, 'A legal assessment of China's historic claims in the South China Sea', *Australian Jnl of Maritime and Ocean Affairs* 5 (2013), 28, at p. 33: mentions that it is doubtful that the PRC can claim 'historic status' over the continental shelf or EEZ as both regimes are fairly modern concepts (the EEZ even more modern); and that there is (ibid.) no mention of historic title regarding delimitation of an EEZ/continental shelf in UNCLOS. See also ibid., at p. 34 (it is 'unlikely that [from limited state practice, and case law and UNCLOS provisions which refer to historic claims] that vast areas of EEZ/high seas/continental shelf could be claimed under this [historic] concept'; as the international community would not acquiesce to such 'an unreasonable or excessive claim').

come into existence in the post-UNCLOS period without at the very least the acquiescence of third states,[94] a test which lies at the heart of all valid historic claims. For the rules on historic waters, such as they are, still apply with all their force to any new or novel claim as an exception to the general (and juridical) rules, including all the sub-rules (discussed below) relating to historic claims: such as clear formal declaration, publicity, and description of geographical extent, which all seem to be clearly unfulfilled in any such instance.

In sum, the concept of any new and extensive type of historic waters regime is essentially obsolete because of the advent of the EEZ and continental shelf doctrines;[95] so there is no risk of this developing through state practice into a *general historic waters* doctrine. Furthermore, the historic waters doctrine developed historically with reference to maritime zones that were *well-known to the past* and, as such, purported claims *had sufficient historicity behind them to mature*. The same is not true of more modern maritime zones established in the law of the sea.[96] As seen, historic waters have normally constituted *internal* waters just as in the case of juridically enclosed waters *within baselines*;[97] and, as will be seen, this causes additional legal problems for any potential Chinese historic waters claim in the SCS. As one recent Chinese commentator has aptly stated, it is clear from China's stance that it seeks to 'enjoy *historic privileges of some kind* in the SCS' – on one view based on a 'quasi-territorial sea or as historical waters with some modifications'.[98] However, as will be seen, the most rational 'historic' interpretation of any such Chinese maritime claim is that it directly derives from its 'territorial claim' including thus potentially therefrom an EEZ and continental shelf.[99]

---

94 One Chinese commentator concludes that the PRC historic claim in the SCS is 'non-exclusive' as it does not block other states' rights to navigation, flight, and laying cables and pipelines under UNCLOS, so implying a valid *lesser* Chinese claim to fisheries and seabed rights there: see T. Qifang, 'On the dotted line: law and history support China's claims over the South China Sea', 7 February 2013, www.bjreview.com.cn, at p. 2.

95 Zou, *supra* n. 4, at p. 164. See, e.g., Song and Yu, *supra* n. 51, at p. 91, commenting that the advent of the EEZ and continental shelf doctrines may lead to the gradual phasing out and even *elimination of historic claims*.

96 Dupuy and Dupuy, *supra* n. 3 at p. 135, rightly say that the main problem with an alleged historic EEZ claim is 'the *inherent contradiction* here of speaking about "historic waters"', which are by definition either internal or territorial waters '*in relation to the EEZ or continental shelf*' (emphasis added).

97 Symmons, *supra* n. 1, at p. 39.

98 Hong, *supra* n. 31, at p. 69 (emphasis added).

99 Dupuy and Dupuy, *supra* n. 3, at p. 127.

Supposed Historic Claims in the South China Sea

Historic Rights?

Such rights – in their broadest sense – have been defined as rights possessed by a state over maritime areas that would not normally accrue to it under the general rules of international law, such as are evidenced in the wording in Art. 62 of UNCLOS, such rights having been acquired by that state 'through a process of historical consolidation';[100] and also which are 'acquired vis-à-vis one or more states'.[101] Though such rights differ from claims to *historic waters* (as seen), nonetheless supposedly the rules underpinning these rights are based on similar principles to those relating to historic waters, most particularly requiring a length of time factor, continuous exercise of same, and relevant State acquiescence.[102] Several regional states, including China, may have claims to *historic fishing rights* in the SCS. It may be noted that the PRC's Law on the EEZ and Continental Shelf, of 26 June 1998, mentions the gist of this very phrase (but without specific reference to 'fishing') in Art. 14 thereof: which provides that 'the provisions of this Law shall not affect *historic rights* enjoyed by the [PRC]'.[103] One commentator claims that the 'most convincing rights' that the PRC could enjoy in the SCS would be 'fishing rights'[104] since Chinese fishers have been fishing there since ancient times. He concludes, however, with a 'thin-end-of the-wedge-type' argument: namely that a broad historic rights claim may give PRC 'greater flexibility of pushing forward its claim from historic rights to historic waters, if necessary'.[105]

As already seen, in the light of the above-mentioned contemporary overtaking of these rights by *juridically* based provisions in UNCLOS,[106] such rights –

100 Y. Blum, 'Historic Rights' in *Encyclopaedia of International Law* (instalment 7) (1984), at p. 147.

101 G. Sperduti, 'Sul regime guiridico di mari', *Rivista di International* 143 (1960), 59, at p. 72.

102 See, e.g., Symmons, *supra* n. 1, at pp. 111–16.

103 See Zou, *supra* n. 4, at p. 149 (emphasis added). It may be noted that the phrase used is 'historic *rights*' rather than 'historic *waters*' here. See also Zou and Xinchang, *supra* n. 63 at para. 48 ('The historic rights reserved in the 1998 Law are related to the EEZ and continental shelf … without reference to the territorial sea').

104 bid., at p. 162.

105 Ibid., at p. 163. See generally Malek, *supra* n. 93, at p. 32 (a discussion of 'historic rights'); also N.-D. Thang and N.H. Thao, 'Chinese nine-dotted line: the 2011 exchange of diplomatic notes between the Philippines and China', ODIL, 50 (2012), 35 at p. 46, who mention that *historic rights* may simply be a 'fall-back' option.

106 Dupuy and Dupuy (*supra* n. 3, at p. 137) comment that the entry into force of UNCLOS has considerably reduced uncertainties on the legal status of the seas, and has, to that extent, 'limited the practical relevance of historic waters'.

particularly in the light of these rights often being regionally shared anyway[107] – bestow little in the way of rights of value in any area; for example, as the basis for any alleged incipient claim to a 200 nm EEZ radiating from the Spratly Islands where ownership of the islands and rocks is currently in dispute. Such rights, as seen, have little or no relevance in the contemporary law of the sea since the advent of the 200 nm EEZ. UNCLOS does not even use the phrase 'historic rights' *as such* (though such rights *might still* be includable under the actually used and vague phrase 'historic *title*'). This suggests that any supposed *historic*, rather than juridical, claim by China of possible present-day *meaningful legal importance*, in a maritime sense, would necessarily be one to *historic waters*,[108] any lesser 'historic rights' claim having been downgraded post-UNCLOS, as seen, by the wording of Art. 62.

Hereby hangs the initial 'interpretative' problem: namely that China until recently at least has not characterized its (maritime) claim as essentially 'historic'; as will be further discussed below.[109] As this writer has stated elsewhere, it is arguable that any such claim should use the word 'historic' *eo nomine* when it is first formally made, if only to inform other states that an 'exceptional' type of claim has been made and to put them on notice of it for a possible protest.

For example, as a US protest to Australia in 1991 aptly stated, the 'persistent failure by Australia to identify the particular bays *as historic* when the opportunity arose several times in the twentieth century', did not amount to an 'open and notorious claim'.[110] Similarly, for example, the Japanese protest to Russia over its historic claim to Peter the Great Bay (of 17 January 1958) complained that past Russian assertion of jurisdiction had not referred to it as being *historic*.[111] As will be further discussed below, such a requirement may be linked to the broader aspect of lack of clarity of a claim; as well as to consequent lack of knowledge of the claim by other states as being of an *exceptional* nature (as was brought up by Libya in its pleadings in the *Libya/Tunisia Case* concerning the Gulf of Gabes, where

107 Gioia points out (*supra* n. 10. at p. 363) that Tunisia's past-claimed historic rights were essentially the exploitation of 'sedentary fisheries' (at p. 359) such as sponge/octopus fisheries which rights, Libya, in the *Libya/Tunisia Case* (Libyan Counter Memorial, at p. 44) pointed out, *never purported to exclude foreigners from exploitation of these fisheries*; however after the 1951 decree, the purpose was to control *all biological resources* (ibid., at p. 365) in a reserved zone.

108 Jinming, 'Behind the dotted line in the Chinese map of the South China Sea', 17 June 2013, http://blog.chinadaily.com.cn/?1057682, at p. 2.

109 It may be noted, however, that recent Chinese comments on the newly published map of the 'u-shaped' line in 2014 (*infra* n. 158) indicate that the new *10*-dash line *does* highlight China's 'historic title' within it: see *South China Sea Bulletin* vol. 2, No. 8, 1 August 2014; and that the zone contained within the dashed lines should be defined as 'China's historic waters', K. Fu et al., http://scinxmu.edu.cn/show.asp?id=2006.

110 Symmons, *supra* n. 1, at p. 105.

111 See ibid., at p. 104.

allegedly Tunisia had never, until 1973, classified this bay as 'historic'[112]). Thus even a *late reference* to alleged 'historicity' of claim may be fatal to such claim.

Historic Waters in the SCS?

Effect of Omission from Listings by Commentators

The lack of mention in any existing official 'listings' of any supposed historic waters claim (whether compiled by the UN, academics or in relevant international litigation to date)[113] may be *prima facie* evidence against the objective existence of any 'historic waters' claim. A recent article by Franckx and Benatar[114] on the alleged PRC historic claim in the SCS has perceptively commented that in my book[115] I failed to discuss *at all* the supposed Chinese claim to historic waters in the South China Sea. In fact, the reason for this omission was simple: I did not know *at the time of writing* that this PRC claim was allegedly 'historic': as having consulted all the main published listings of alleged historic waters throughout the world, I found no mention of any Chinese claim to such waters.[116]

Omission from such listings has been mentioned in at least one past protest (that of the United States to Australia mentioned above);[117] and it also arose as an important factor in *Alaska v. US* (in which I was involved) concerning the Alaskan claim to historic waters in the Alexander Archipelago off the west coast of Alaska: where similarly there was no mention of *this* alleged historic claim in any listings – a matter which the Special Master (judge) in the case commented on: in

112 Ibid., at pp. 104–5. See below n. 142 and accompanying text.

113 See Symmons, *supra* n. 1 at p.11.

114 See E. Franckx and M. Benatar, 'Dotted lines in the South China Sea: fishing for (legal) clarity', in Diplomatic Academy of Vietnam, 'The South China Sea: Towards a Recognition of Peace Security and Co-operation', ed. T. Thuy (Vietnam: Gioi Publishers, 2011), at p. 211 ('it is therefore not surprising to note that a recent treatise on historic waters does not find it necessary to make any reference to the historic claim to the nine-dotted line').

115 See above n. 1.

116 This was despite the fact that in 1992 Professor Zou had written an article indicating this claim *could* be historic. It may be noted, by the same token, that the purported Chinese historic waters claims in respect of Bohai Bay and Qiongzhou Strait (see above n. 57) do not seem to appear on any such listings either. The same point (relating to omission of discussion of any PRC *historic* claim to SCS waters in this writer's book on historic waters, *supra* n. 1) is made tellingly in the recent US commentary on the PRC's historic claims in the SCS (the book there being described as a 'comprehensive study' of historic waters): see *Limits in the Seas*, No. 143: 'China: Maritime Claims in the [SCS]' (Washington, DC: Bureau of Oceans and Environmental and Scientific Affairs, US Department of State, 5 December 2014) at p. 19.

117 See above n. 109.

terms that the alleged claim was not contained in any 'published list of the world's historic waters'. He added that 'even if publication is not required, the absence of publication [in such lists] has significance in disagreements about historic waters claims'.[118] And, as I have argued, such non-listing may have an important effect in estopping a claimant state in making such a claim where it has never publicly complained of such omission in the past.[119]

Supposed Requirements for a Valid Claim to Historic Waters

Because, as seen, such rights are not defined or elaborated in UNCLOS, resort here can only be had to customary law where three requirements have been traditionally laid down; namely (in essence) formal claim, continuous and effective exercise of jurisdiction and international acquiescence.[120] However commentators have unfortunately tended to make little or no reference to the abundance of 'sub-rules' which, on closer study, flesh out these rules; and which intrinsically interrelate not only with themselves but with the supposed main rules.

Indeed, the tendency here, as in the case of 'listings' of supposed claims to historic waters mentioned above (and a substantial repetition of previous lists of commentators), has been an approving repetition in parrot-like fashion of the above-mentioned supposed three main rules in a 'synoptic approach' to the subject;[121] so that commentaries on the subject tend to take the form of 'self-perpetuating and recycled information',[122] without any proper critical analysis. International tribunals, such as the ICJ in the *Gulf of Fonseca Case*, have also tended to gloss over the 'legal requirements' issue on historic waters,[123] whilst accepting at face value the basic, but vague, requirements of past formulations.[124] Several of the burgeoning number of commentaries on the possible PRC historic claim to the waters within the nine-dashed line have similarly lacked incisiveness by repeating the *supposed* main rules without much more.

The true situation is, however, that when the three supposed elements relevant to maritime historic title are *closely* analysed, they need inevitably (as already indicated) to be further substantiated by a series of interlocking sub-rules.[125] Even the much-cited and excellent two UN studies have, in parts and on close reading,

118 Symmons, *supra* n. 1, at p. 14.

119 Ibid., at pp. 14–15.

120 See ibid., at pp. 111–16.

121 Ibid., at pp. 11–12.

122 See ibid., at p. 11. M. Wesley Clark's book on historic waters (*supra* n. 1) tends, for example, to be in this category, with a plethora of continual quotations from previous authors throughout the text.

123 Symmons, ibid., at p. 11.

124 Ibid., at p. 111.

125 Ibid., at pp. 113–16 .

somewhat contradictory or vague elements in them.[126] To make matters worse, even the supposed main rules have *intrinsically vague* aspects and serious interpretative ambiguities contained in them: which, in fact, absent any detailed treaty-based clarification or *incisive* case law interpretation by international tribunals, are essentially insoluble in any logical manner. Despite this, an attempt will be made to analyse the legality of the possible PRC claim to historic waters within the nine-dashed line in the same broad context as I tried to take in my book; in the present case by asking a series of questions.

a. Was there ever a *clear formal* Chinese *historic* claim to these waters?

An alleged historic claim must be made in the appropriate manner,[127] involving normally an unequivocal assertion to such waters by an appropriate organ of the claimant state (usually its executive branch – the department of foreign affairs[128]); in other words, there must be a 'State-orientated "declaration"'.[129] Strohl, for example, asserts that such declarations must be made by the 'competent authorities'.[130] This will usually involve official decrees or legislation,[131] as confirmed by the *UN Juridical Regime*. Hence it seems disputable to say[132] that 'the

126 See *The Juridical Regime of Historic Waters, including Historic Bays* (study prepared for the UN Secretariat): UN Doc.A/CN.4/143 (9 March 1962 (hereafter '*UN Juridical Regime*')); and Memorandum by the UN Secretariat, 'Historic Bays' (Preparatory Document No. 1): A/CONF.3.1, 30 September 1957.

127 Symmons, *supra* n. 1, at p. 117.

128 Ibid., at p. 121. See, e.g., the US *Limits in the Seas* publication *supra* n. 116 at p. 18 ('with respect to the [SCS], there appears to be no Chinese law, declaration, proclamation or other official statement putting the international community on notice to a historic claim within the dashed line').

129 Symmons, ibid., at p. 118. For such a reason, it is unclear how *government-*endorsed is the new Chinese map of 2014 (see *infra* n. 158) indicating a 10-dash line around the Spratly Islands, published *by a local Chinese publishing house* named Hunan Maps Press. For example, one Chinese commentator (Professor Lee Yunglung of Xiamen University, has described the central Government in Beijing as 'testing the waters' by 'letting a *provincial level publisher* put out [this] map' (emphasis added) (as has also happened on previous occasions) to see how other nations react: abcnews.go.com>international, 27 June 2014; and one commentator on the new map of 2014 has described the publisher, Hunan Maps Press, as being merely a 'government-*approved*' press (emphasis added): see M.Florenz@ibtimes.com (25 June 2014). E. Graham (*infra* n. 153) maintains, though, that the publisher of a previous map of the SCS of June 2013, 'SinoMaps Press', 'is under the jurisdiction of the State Bureau of Mapping' – thus seemingly a governmental body. And several commentators have described the new map as 'official': see, e.g., H. Kaziounis, 'China's Ten Red Lines in the [SCS]', nationalinterest.org/.../chinas-south-china-sea-strategy-win-the perception (28 June, 2014).

130 Symmons, ibid., at p. 120.

131 Ibid.

132 As do Jinming and Dexia, *supra* n. 80, at p. 292.

Chinese Government has continuously reasserted *through domestic legislation*' its historic claims; as the first and so far the only possible *legislative* evidence of historic claim in the PRC came in 1998 (see below); and even that was vague and unspecific;[133] and previous to that the alleged claims arose from maps produced by mere Chinese *mapping agencies*.[134]

Looking at this matter globally, for example, the legislation of several states does give the president or the government *express competence to declare historic waters* offshore.[135] In the case of Australia, s. 8 of its Seas and Submerged Lands Act 1973 provides that when the Governor-General is satisfied that a bay is an historic one, he may, by proclamation, declare a bay to be so historic and define its seaward limits. Thus, under Australia's Seas and Submerged Land (Historic Bays) Proclamation, 2006, a previous proclamation of 1987 was revoked and the same four bays were confirmed to be historic with updated coordinates.[136] Several states even without such prior legislative empowerment have, of course, made claims by governmental decree in more recent times to historic waters.

This factor inter-relates with other 'sub-rule' issues such as the question of when 'historic time' begins to run (see below[137]); and the need for publicity of a

133 See Qifang, *supra* n. 94, who cites the 1958 PRC law; but there *was in fact no legislative reference* to historic waters *there* in relation to the SCS islands. Franckx and Benatar (*supra* n. 14, at p. 107) comment that the 'deliberate vagueness' is exacerbated by failure as yet by the PRC to '*pass legislation* giving the U-line any effect in its domestic order' (emphasis added). Gao and Jia (*supra* n. 11, at p. 108) comment indeed that the 'consistent line of Chinese legislation since 1958' has shown that the nine-dashed line 'is not intended to assert an *historic* title of sovereignty over the sea areas, as enclosed by those lines, beyond what is allowed in international law'.

134 See above n. 129.

135 E.g., Sri Lanka under s. 9 of its Maritime Zones Law No. 22 of 1976; which by a 1977 presidential proclamation claimed historic internal waters in the Palk Strait and an historic territorial sea in the Gulf of Manaar (so incidentally constituting one of the few, if not the only, historic *territorial sea* claims in recent times). In the case of Seychelles, s. 8, its law states that the President may by order specify the limits of historic waters. Mauritius, in its Maritime Zones Act (No. 1 of 2005), empowers the Prime Minister to prescribe by regulations (under s. 11) the historic waters of Mauritius. India in its Territorial Waters and Continental Shelf, EEZ and other Maritime Zones Act (1976), s. 8, similarly empowers the Indian Central Government to 'specify the limits of [historic waters] adjacent to its land territory'. Also Kenya continues to claim Ungwana Bay as historic in its Maritime Zones Act s. 3(3): and, on 11 April 2006, Kenya transmitted a note verbale to the UN S-G specifying geographical coordinates of its so-claimed straight baselines there. The Minister is empowered to declare other bays or waters as historic by notice in the Government Gazettte: see A. Chircop, D. Dzidzornu, J. Geurreiro and C. Grilo, 'The maritime zones of East African States in the Law of the Sea: benefits gained, opportunities missed', 16 *RADIC* (2008) 121, 137.

136 F2006L00526.

137 Symmons, *supra* n. 1, at p. 114.

claim (particularly where such claim arises entirely domestically within a state,[138] as some past protests have evidenced[139]). And indeed, arguably there should be an accompanying explanation or rationale of the grounds of the claim[140] – a matter that arose in the case of the Italian claim to the Gulf of Taranto (as protested by the United States);[141] and a factor clearly lacking in the case of the SCS dispute.

Arguably, also, as seen, it should be made clear that the claim is *historic* by express use of the epithet at the time of declaration,[142] though this admittedly leads to logical difficulties of analysis unless implying retroactivity.[143] Both these issues of timing (when the 'historic clock' starts ticking) and non-articulated 'historicity' of claim, caused problems in the *Alaska v. US* case[144] where there was a dispute not only as to *when* the so-called historic claim to inland waters was first made, but also as to *whether this was an historic or juridical claim*. The problem underlying this latter possible requirement for valid historic claim is, as seen, that non-use of the word 'historic' at the time of declaration or claim may disguise the fact that the alleged claim is 'exceptional' rather than simply based on *juridical* grounds (i.e., to indicate a title which was in origin an 'illegal situation' and which is 'subsequently validated'[145]); with the possible result that other states may consequently be lulled into a false sense of security and so fail to protest. For any such lack of protest may be a sign that states are convinced that a claim 'conforms with existing law, rather than implying acquiescence to an exceptional and unjustified claim'[146] – a matter of no little importance in the SCS dispute.

---

138 Ibid., at pp. 114, 125. See also P. Dutton, 'Three disputes and three objectives: China and the South China Sea', *Naval War College Review* 64 (2011), 42, at p. 44, who says that the 1947 map was based on a 1935 *internal* government report (at pp. 50–51). See also the recent US *Limits in the Seas* publication (*supra* n. 116, at p. 18) which claims that the 1947 Chinese map not only made no historic claim, but also lacked 'notoriety' as it was a *domestic publication in the Chinese language*.

139 Symmons, ibid., at p. 117.

140 See Zou (*supra* n. 63, at p. 47) ('Beijing has ever kept silent and offered no express statement on the line').

141 See Symmons, *supra* n. 1, at p. 118.

142 Zou (*supra* n. 4, at p. 162) comments that it is clear from China's stance that it seeks to enjoy 'historic privileges of some kind'. Dupuy and Dupuy (*supra* n. 3, at p. 128) comment on the PRC's 'occasional' reference only to 'historic waters'.

143 See Symmons, *supra* n. 1, at p. 102.

144 Ibid., at pp. 118–19.

145 *UN Juridical Regime*, *supra* n. 126, at p. 13. Dupuy and Dupuy (*supra* n. 3, at p. 130) mention the Chinese notes and failure to provide any legal justification to explain the (then) nine-dashed map. They comment that as since the 1930s China had given publicity several times to the geographical scope of its islands, this confirms that the 'limits of its sovereignty must be assessed by reference to historical evidence'.

146 Gioia, *supra* n. 10, at p. 340. It is for such reasons that the United States has not specifically protested any Chinese historic claim in the SCS, as, in its view, no such action is necessary until the claim is clarified: see *supra* n. 116, at p. 22.

If, indeed, the Chinese 'historic' claim was made in the 1947/1948 era[147] – as seems a reasonable date supposition – then arguably the time (several decades) that has elapsed since then measures up to the excessively vague 'historicity' requirement as to passage of time[148] that underlies historic claims in customary international law;[149] but, of course, the *interlinking* requirement of continuous and effective exercise of relevant jurisdiction also *over this period* is absent in the case of the SCS dispute.[150]

b. Is the clarity/consistency requirement satisfied?

The need for clarity of claim[151] is obvious, and has been mentioned as necessary by several commentators for similar reasons to those mentioned above: namely to put other states on proper notice of an historic claim.[152] Thus, ideally, the initial claim should make clear (as seen) that it is 'historic' and give reasons

147 This dating is repeated in the Chinese comment on the latest SCS map of 2014: see, e.g., the comment at http:/usa.chinadaily.com.cn/opinion/2014-07-04, which concludes: 'China has a long history of exploring and exploiting the [SCS], which is proven by the nine-dash u-shaped line *marked on official maps since the 1940s*' (emphasis added).

148 See, e.g., Symmons, *supra* n. 1, at p. 156 et seq.

149 The *UN Juridical Regime* (*supra* n. 126, at p. 63) mentions the need for 'prolonged' and 'continuous' periods of claim: see generally Symmons, *supra* n. 1, at pp. 151–2 and pp. 156–9. Zou, *supra* n. 63, comments (at p. 59) that although it may be difficult for the PRC to justify the nine-dashed line as historic *waters*, its existence for over half a century may suffice to evidence a claim to historic *rights*. See also Thang and Thao, *supra* n. 105, who mention, as seen, that *historic rights* may be a 'fall-back' option. However, this is disputable, as the legal requirements of *both* doctrines are very similar, including not just the time factor.

150 See *infra* n. 224 et seq.; and see Symmons, *supra* n. 1, at pp. 152–6. This point of 'no continuous authority' being displayed in the SCS by China is emphasized in the US *Limits in the Seas* publication, *supra* n. 116, at p. 21.

151 Both aspects of the clarity requirement are inter-related with the separable requirements of knowledge and acquiescence by other nations: see Symmons, *supra* n. 1, at p. 133.

152 Ibid., at pp. 128–9. Hence, intentional ambiguity is the very antithesis of a true historic claim. The point is well made by E. Graham (see 'China's new map: just another dash', https://www.rusi.org>downloads>assets>201309 (13 September 2013)) as regards the most recent Chinese maps of the SCS claim, that although the dashes are supposedly in the same location, the addition 'of new shading [which has the visual effect of projecting China's claims in the SCS, however defined, closer to the coastlines of the Philippines, Malaysia and Vietnam], plus the fact that the space in between is marked (in diminutive characters ...) as "boundary not defined" indicate*s China seeks to maintain some ambiguity around the status of the dashed line, to minimise controversy while preserving room for manoeuvre*' (emphasis added).

therefor.[153] Thus historical inconsistency of claim, as well as initial ambiguity of official position over such status, may be fatal to an historic claim.[154] Indeed, in the *Gulf of Fonseca Case*, the ICJ endorsed its previous dictum in *Libya/ Tunisia* that 'historic titles ... must be preserved as they always have been by long usage', implying, incidentally perhaps, that *subsequent inconsistent actions* regarding them may destroy such claims.[155] There may, though, be a fine line between a 're-statement of an existing claim and [making] a new claim'.[156] Thus, for example, the very recent practice of Australia (mentioned above) in re-specifying by decree the exact claimed limits of several of its *past*-claimed historic bays may be an acceptable precedent as a technical clarification of its historic claim.[157]

This issue also arises in the case of the SCS dispute in the light of a new map published in August 2014 (by Hunan Maps Press)[158] aimed at supposedly indicating more clearly the main Chinese-claimed maritime areas; where a 10-dashed line (instead of *nine*-dashed as previously) now indicates the so-enclosed SCS area in a vertical appendage to the main Chinese cartography rather than as before as a separate inset map.[159] The main aim, then, of the map, according to Internet comments from China, seems to be giving what is described as an 'historic waters'

153 See, e.g., Gioia (*supra* n. 10, at p. 345), who points out that neither the 1973 Tunisian law nor the 1973 Tunisian decree provided any justification for the closure of the Gulf of Gabes.

154 See, e.g., Symmons, *supra* n. 1, at pp. 128–9. See above, n. 152.

155 *Supra* n. 65, at p. 589, para. 384. Cf., e.g., the notorious 'Bayard letter' in *Alaska v. US* (ruling out any US claim to historic water in the Alexander Archipelago) which was central to the Supreme Court's rejection of a supposed Alaskan state historic claim to the waters of the Alexander Archipelago); Symmons, *supra* n. 1, at p. 130. See most recently the US *Limits in the Seas* publication (*supra* n. 116, at p. 18) ('the various maps published by China ... lack the precision, clarity and consistency that could convey *the nature and scope* of such a [historic] claim, even if [China] had asserted one' (emphasis added)); and ibid., at p. 7 (the 1947/48 map is 'cartographically inconsistent with other Chinese published maps', and the dashed lines published in more recent maps of 2013/4 do 'not seem to be in the same locations').

156 Zou, *supra* n. 4, at p. 160.

157 In its 'Seas and Submerged Lands (Historic Bays) Proclamation 2006', revoking the previous 1987 proclamation. This '*again declares* these bays to be historic bays' with updated geographical baseline coordinates (emphasis added). See above, n. 134. By contrast, the Panamanian Law No. 83 of June 1996, confirming Panama's claim to the Gulf of Panama as an historic bay (DOD 2005.1-M.) seems to be simply a *repetition* of an earlier claim; when, on ratifying UNCLOS in July 1996, Panama appended to its deed of ratification a declaration reiterating its claim to the Gulf of Panama as being historic.

158 It is unclear what *official* status this seemingly provincial mapping agency has in China: see above n. 129. .

159 See, e.g., Chinese Government spokesman Huya Chunying who commented (on 25 June 2014) that older maps with insets of the islands made the claim look like a mere 'appendage': see below, n. 161.

claim (the 'outer limit of China's historic waters in the SCS') better publicity, including domestically in China, largely by including the SCS islands on one map and depicting them on the same (i.e., larger) scale as Chinese land areas.[160] The map has been described as 'official' in several Internet comments, but an official government spokesman has denied it changes the original claim.[161] Whether the latter is true is difficult to assess in the light of continuing lack of published coordinates[162] to indicate the locations of the 10 dashes, the added number being at least one change to the preceding claim;[163] but on balance it seems essentially to be merely a reiteration of the previous claim, with a more formal title of constituting the 'u-shaped line'.[164]

Added to the matter of clarity as to historical status is that of *geographical clarity* as to the limits of the historically claimed area, which both initially at time of declaration and thereafter, must be clear and consistent;[165] and a depictive chart

---

160 See comment by M. Florenz who states that the new map was 'designed to fully illustrate what China has always claimed in previous versions'. See also comment *infra* n. 164 ('China's new vertical map gives extra play to disputed [SCS] territories').

161 See the statement of the Chinese Foreign Ministry spokesman, Huya Chunying, saying that not too much should be read into the new map; and that the Chinese position in respect of the claim had not changed, being 'consistent and clear': www.southchinasea.org.maps/territorial-claims-maps (25 June 2014).

162 As one Philippine commentator has said, the new map shows no co-ordinates in the SCS; which thus are 'moveable': 'New map boosts China's maritime claims' (blog.geogarage.com/2014/.../new-map-boosts-chinas-maritime-claims.ht).

163 As one commentator has stated, such a tenth dash does not in fact expand on China's existing claims as it 'subsumes the identical claim of Taiwan' in the SCS: see https://www.rusi.org>downloads>assets>201309_NB_Graham (13 September 2013).

164 Comment by K. Fu and Hong Chang in http://scsi.xmu.edu.cn?show.asp?id+2006 (cf. (ibid.) other Chinese comment that the 'official name of the historic waters boundary line should be the "nine dash line"'). Graham, *supra* n. 152, comments that the new maps provide 'the most expansive accounting to date of the features [some 130] claimed within it'. This, he says, had not been had apparent on previous maps which seemingly only featured the bigger islands in the SCS. See also the comment of the Philippines on the new map of 2014 which alleged an 'expanded claim' was made in the SCS, in that the dashes were allegedly 'closer to the land mass of the Philippines,Malaysia and Vietnam': 'Philippines says China's new map shows unreasonable expansive claim', 26 June 2014: www.eaglenews.ph>philippines-says-chinas-new-official-map-shows; and see the recent US *Limits in the Seas* publication (*supra* n. 116, at pp. 6–7) (this shows the inconsistencies in some detail between the map of 1947/8 and the later ones (e.g., dash 7 of the 1947/8 map is said to be slightly larger and nearer to the Philippines (Palawan Island) and certain other coasts (Brunei/Malaysia)). Furthermore (ibid., at p. 7) this commentary points out that, in turn, the map dashes on the 2009 Chinese map are not in the identical geographic locations as the dashes shown on the 2013–14 maps .

165 Symmons, *supra* n. 1, at pp. 132–3.

accompanying the claim may be desirable for this purpose.[166] This again is because other states should know the intended *areal extent* of the alleged claim in the light of considering a possible protest. In the SCS dispute, for example, much ink has been spilt by recent commentators on the true *geographical basis*, in maritime terms, of the drawing of the nine-dashed (or now 10-dashed) line by China. For example, was it supposed to be a median (or delimitation) line between the outer SCS islands and neighbouring states?[167] If so, it has been commented that even if the dashed line was intended to be so equidistant, it 'has not functioned as such in practice'.[168] The fact, however, that the PRC in its 1996 Statement on the Baselines of Territorial Waters claimed specified straight baselines around the separate insular group of the Paracel Islands, *and not round the Spratly Islands*, might imply that the PRC considered such a 'baseline' announcement concerning the latter islands would have been essentially superfluous and as in any case detrimentally affecting the status of the dashed line there.[169] The line is also intermittent, and not a solid

166 Ibid., at p. 135. This ties in with the publicity duty under Art. 16 of UNCLOS: see M. Read, 'An attempt to unravel charting and publicity requirements imposed by UNCLOS Article 16', in *Selected Contemporary Issues in the Law of the Sea*, edited by C.R. Symmons (Leiden: Nijhoff, 2011), at pp. 3, 10, 11. Dupuy and Dupuy (*supra* n. 3, at p. 131) ask whether the PRC's production of the map in 2009 was 'an attempt to clarify the scope of that claim'. They conclude not, as it only casts additional doubts on its *geographical scope*.

167 Jinmimg and Dexia (*supra* n. 80, at p. 290) comment that the boundary line was drawn as a median line between the Spratly Islands and adjacent states. See also N. Thang and N. Thao, 'China's dotted line in the South China Sea: the 2011 exchange of diplomatic notes', *ODIL* 43 (2012), 35, at p. 45, regarding the argument by PRC commentators that the line is an equidistance line. They refute this (at p. 46), as the lines do not correspond with equidistance lines drawn from outermost features of the Spratlys and their opposite coasts (ibid., at p. 47), adding that the PRC neither 'approves nor disapproves' *any* interpretation of its line. See also Gao and Jia (*supra* n. 7, at p. 108) who claim that the nine-dashed line may 'have a *residual function as potential maritime delimitation boundaries*' (emphasis added). See most recently the US *Limits in the Seas* publication (*supra* n. 116, at p. 5) which points out (with maps) the distances of some of the dashes from 'land features'; and which comments (at p. 6) that the dashes are generally closer 'to the surrounding coats of neighboring States than they are to the closest islands in [the SCS]'. Also (ibid., at p. 14) this detailed US commentary adds that the dashed lines lack 'other important hallmarks of a maritime boundary, such as a published list of geographic co-ordinates and a continuous, unbroken line that separates the maritime space of two countries'.

168 Jinming, *supra* n. 108, at p. 2. In the Nautilus Institute's 'The South China Sea: evolution or disregard for International La', H. Duong and T. Pham (NAPsnet Policy Forum, 25 June 2013 (http:/nautilus.org/napsnet/napsnet-policy-forum/the-south-china-sea-evolution-of-or-disregard-for-international-law)) (in response to a previous assertion by M. Valencia), similarly argue (at p. 3) that the nine-dashed lines lie beyond an equidistance line between the islands and adjacent states; and so are arbitrary and excessive.

169 But the matter is unclear: cf. Zou, *supra* n. 63, at p. 52 (the provisions for straight baselines for the Paracels in 1996 indicated that 'China did not consider the traditional line the maritime boundary in the [SCS]'). See also Jinming, *supra* n. 108, at p. 3.

line as one would normally expect in the case of maritime delimitation; and it is open-ended at its northern side.[170]

Most significant, though, is that *if* the intent behind the nine-dashed map was to illustrate the PRC's geographical extent of claim in the SCS, it cannot stand as a maritime delimitation line when it is *lacking coordinates*[171] and it is drawn in such a rough and approximate way,[172] the intermittence[173] and thickness of the dashes on the line giving rise to added imprecision.[174] On top of all this is the later inconsistency when in 1953 the number of dashes was changed from 11 to nine.[175]

---

170 See 'Eight experts: how should we look on the nine-dash line in the South China Sea?' (31 July 2012, http://chinaelectionsblog.net/?p=20579, at p. 1); and M. Miyoshi, 'China's "u-shaped" line claim in the South China Sea: any validity under international law?' 43 ODIL (2012),1, at p. 3 ('a boundary line, of any other line for that matter, must be a continuous one'). For comment on this aspect, see again Graham, *supra* n. 152.

171 For comment on it not being a standard method of delimiting waters as by a median line, see Dupuy and Dupuy, *supra* n. 3, at p. 132. However, one of the original authors of the map reportedly described it as 'the national boundary line drawn as the median line between China and the adjacent States' (Jinming and Dexia, *supra* n. 80, at p. 290). Some members of a Taiwan commission viewed the lack of coordinates on the nine-dashed map as fatal for determining historic waters: Jinming, *supra* n. 108, at p. 2.

172 See Jinming and Dexia, ibid., at p. 291 (citing H. Djalal, 'Spratley dispute needs democratic settlement', *Jakarta Post*, 2 January 1995). K. Saito (*infra* n. 178) says the map shows (at p. 75) 'special historic waters and the sphere of a semi-enclosed sea'; but that (ibid., at n. 23) the respective dashed lines of the ROC and PRC are not identical, with the ROC's seeming to be a little further north in comparison with the PRC's nine-dot line. Even the fact that the lines are dashed gives an impression of provisionality. As seen, the new Chinese SCS map of 2014 adds little further clarity as to the exact *extent* of the alleged Chinese claim in the SCS running through 10 shaded dashes, though Chinese commentators seem to think it does.

173 For example, it is not even clear also how the intermittent dashes join up together.

174 Dupuy and Dupuy, *supra* n. 3, at p. 134. Franckx and Benatar (*supra* n. 14, at p. 109) state that the dotted line roughly follows the 200 m isobath; but that (ibid., at p. 110) there are also inconsistencies in PRC maps, with endpoints of different segments varying from 1 to 5 nms, sometimes at variance with the attached Annex 1 map, which is also on a very small scale. The recent US *Limits in the Seas* publication, *supra* n. 116, at p. 4, further adds that no numbers are assigned to the dashes which 'are not uniformly distributed and separated from each other'.

175 B. Than ('Nine-dotted line: a vague claim', baobinthnan.com.vn/en/default.aspex?cat_id=6977news_9d) cites Chinese commentators, such as P. Shiying, claiming that the PRC has claimed the entire area of waters within the line (p. 2); and notes the Chinese researcher Li Linghua as saying that mapping predecessors invented the line 'without specific longitudes and latitudes, as well as without legal evidence' (ibid., at p. 2). He refers also to the inconsistency of the maps (ibid., at p. 3), with later map editions having only nine dots. Franckx and Benatar (*supra* n. 14, at p. 106) add that portrayals of a nine-dotted line are 'not consistent', including a new *electronic map* of the PRC of 21 October 2010, with a *new 10th segment added*. As seen, the tenth dash (inheriting Taiwan's claim) is now on the new map of 2014.

Application of the Chinese Maps to the SCS Dispute

All the above issues have direct relevance and importance in the supposed PRC claim to historic waters within the nine-dashed line; but, as regards the matter of a formal official declaration – and consequently the 'critical date' of the start of an historic claim[176] (a matter which in many instances is no easy matter to determine where several possible dates could qualify[177]) – a brief history of the 'map claim' must be analysed. The first depiction of the line in essence occurred in the early 1930s[178] when maps showing the lines were drawn up by a Chinese department, seemingly for the purpose of clarifying the SCS islands to which China claimed title. This was prepared by the Territory Division of the then Ministry of Home Affairs, showing the location of 'Chinese Islands in the [SCS]', with the dashed line enclosing them.[179] Thus it is important to note there was no reference *at this time* to any *maritime claim*; and certainly no mention of it being an 'historic' one.[180] Additionally, the Chinese body that issued the maps was essentially a geographical institution, not an executive branch of government.[181] Indeed, it has been commented that 'the source and author' of it remain 'unknown'.[182]

176 See Symmons, *supra* n. 1, at pp. 101, 109; and Malek, *supra* n. 93, at p. 28 (the 'origin and the basis of the interrupted line itself [have] never been satisfactorily explained').

177 See Symmons, ibid., at p. 106. It may also be argued that if a state *at a late date* suddenly alleges that some of its waters are 'historic', it should have labelled them so at an earlier time in history when the rights *realistically* started: see ibid., at p. 109, n. 45. See, e.g., as regards the appropriate (late) starting date to the Tunisian claim to the Gulf of Gabes, Gioia (*supra* n. 10, at p. 349) (the 1973 Tunisian legislation could 'at best be regarded as the beginning of a process aimed at the formation of a new "historic title" which would allow Tunisia to qualify the Gulf of Gabes as internal waters').

178 See K. Saito, 'China's frontier: issues concerning territorial claims at sea – security implications in the East China and South China Sea' (pt. 2), 71, at p. 75. He says that the line was unofficially drawn by Hu Jinjie in 1914 and officially drawn on a map by Bai Meichu in 1947 and 1953. He adds that it is unclear whether Bai had 'full knowledge' of the law of the sea when he drew up the map; and that (ibid.) Chinese logic on historic waters 'does not conform to the general definition of the international law of the sea'.

179 See, e.g., Jinming, *supra* n. 108, at p. 2. A detailed history of the 1930s map is given in Jinming and Dexia, *supra* n. 80, at p. 289. It was first published in the journal of the Land and Waters Maps Committee in 1935; a second map in 1936 marked national boundary lines showing islands inside were Chinese-claimed.

180 Franckx and Benatar, *supra* n. 14, at pp. 90–91, discuss the mapping of line; and (ibid., at p. 92) the Chinese submission to the UN Secretary-General of the map in 2009, but with no specific reference to historic waters as such.

181 This problem of the exact *official* status of the Chinese map-publisher still continues in the case of the new map of 2014: see above nn. 129, 138.

182 Dupuy and Dupuy, *supra* n. 3, at p. 131.

In 1948, the Geographical Department of the Chinese Ministry of Internal Affairs published a map showing an 11-dashed line;[183] but it was still not described as containing 'historic waters'. This was followed in 1953 by a further map of dashes (eliminating two in the Gulf of Tonkin) seemingly following the line of older maps[184] after the PRC was set up. This period has been viewed by many commentators as indicating the beginning of a possible Chinese formal claim to the SCS area;[185] but this is disputable. For example, it seems it was only in 1993 that the Taiwan authorities issued policy guidelines clearly suggesting the u-shaped/nine-dashed line was 'the historic waters limit in the maritime area under the jurisdiction of the Republic of China'.[186] Despite this, in Taiwan's 1998 Law on the Territorial Sea and Contiguous Zone, even the provision on historic waters was dropped before promulgation of the legislation.[187] This in itself could be of some significance in conjunction with those Chinese commentators doubtful of the claim in the PRC: as it may be that internal division on the valid existence of an historic claim may be relevant to proof of it.[188] In the past, several Chinese scholars have indeed used a variety of phrases to describe China's maritime claims in the area, including 'historic rights', historic title' and 'historic waters',[189] as have official Chinese spokesmen – as in the case of the latest SCS map of 2014;[190] but on any objective assessment, a key issue remains whether the then nine-dashed line was intended to articulate 'territorial claims, maritime claims or both'.[191]

183 According to Jinming and Dexia (*supra* n. 80, at p. 290), the first map (issued during the Kuomingtang period) was introduced by the Department of Border Management under the Ministry of Home Affairs in February 1948; and according to Thang and Thao (*supra* n. 156, at p. 2), it originated from a private map by Bai Meichu. It was then nicknamed the 'bulls tongue' because it resembled such a tongue licking down into the sea. In 1947 the nine-dotted maps had been endorsed by a Chinese government department (Geography Department in Ministry of Internal Affairs) (see again Jinming and Dexia, ibid., at p. 290) and published.

184 Jinming and Dexia, ibid., at p. 290.

185 Some commentators, however, see the 1953 date as the official start of any Chinese historic claim.

186 Zou, *supra* n. 4, at p. 161. See also Franckx and Benatar (*supra* n. 14, at p. 94) who cite ROC policy guidelines for the SCS.

187 Zou, ibid., at p. 161.

188 See, e.g., Clark, *supra* n. 1, at p. 200, who points out, for example, in the case of the USSR, that no Soviet jurist prior to 1957 considered the waters of Peter the Great Bay to be historic.

189 Several commentators (e.g., Dupuy and Dupuy, *supra* n. 3, at pp. 134–5) comment that even Chinese commentators are divided on interpretation of the map as showing 'historic waters'.

190 In this case Chinese Foreign Ministry spokesman Hua Chunying described (on 25 June 2014) the new map as maintaining Chinese 'maritime rights'.

191 Dupuy and Dupuy, *supra* n. 3, at p. 128.

In all instances of the older-published maps there has been no explanatory *verbal* claim accompanying them, as well as no reference to any historic *maritime* claims. Arguably, then, the maps do not in any event amount to a formal declaration of historic waters (as discussed above) such as international law requires.[192] It is for such reasons that numerous recent commentators have dubbed the supposed Chinese historic claim as being generally ambiguous[193] or even deliberately ambiguous.[194]

The most recent developments on the Chinese claim came in the years 1998, 2009 and 2014 (as in the case of the newly published Chinese map discussed above). In the Chinese EEZ law (Art. 14) of 1998 there was no explanation as to why the 'historic rights' proviso was inserted and to what sea area(s) it referred; and certainly there was no map depiction.[195] Then, the PRC sent a much-discussed *note verbale* to the UN Secretary-General on 7 May 2009 (reportedly unsigned[196]), objecting to the joint submission of Malaysia and Vietnam to the CLCS at the time; and referring to a map in an appendix.[197] This was seemingly the first time the nine-dashed map (for such it *then* was) had been attached to an official communication to the UN. It has been claimed that in referring to 'adjacent areas' 'and 'relevant waters'[198] in the note itself, the communiqué does not *specifically* say the attached map 'demarcates any of these areas'.[199] It can, though, be reasonably assumed to

192 As R. Beckman says in 'The UNCLOS dispute settlement and the South China Sea' (MIMA Conference on the [SCS], December 2011, Malaysia, at p. 8), 'the publication of a map is not a clear notification of a claim to historic waters *without a formal declaration*' (emphasis added).

193 See, e.g., Dupuy and Dupuy, *supra* n. 3, at p. 131 (the Chinese position remains 'essentially ambiguous'; and the meaning the PRC attaches to 'historic' remains obscure).

194 See, e.g., Dupuy and Dupuy, ibid., at p. 124 (the 'vagueness of the legal terminology used by China raises the issue of whether the very vagueness is being used as an element of political strategy'). See above comment at n. 152.

195 Zou, *supra* n. 63, at p. 160 (the PRC 'chose the more softened term "historic rights"').

196 See 'China's u-shaped line in the South China Sea', *Nam Viet Times*, at p. 1.

197 R. Beckman, 'South China Sea: how China could justify its claims', RSIS Commentaries, No. 116/2010 (16 September 2010), at p. 1, notes that it was sent in an attached file and not in a direct document.

198 As to the meaning of the phrase used in the note – 'see adjacent map' – T. McDorman interprets this as referring to the immediately preceding phrase 'sovereign rights and jurisdiction over the relevant waters as well as the seabed and subsoil thereof' (*supra* n. 79, at p. 514). Other commentators interpret these words as including claims to sovereignty both over the islands and adjacent waters in the SCS. See below n. 229. Gao and Jia (*supra* n. 11, at p. 109), while admitting that the 'precise meaning' of the references to these phrases 'has never been defined by China', nonetheless assert that 'its claim over such waters – in view of China's ratification of UNCLOS – is necessarily conditioned by the Convention's relevant provisions'.

199 See 'China's u-shaped line in the South China Sea: possible interpretations, asserting actions, and reactions from outside', a paper presented at the conference on

have been intended to relate to a claim to all the waters within the nine-dashed line;[200] indeed, the fact that a similar proviso was not made in the earlier *Chinese legislation on the territorial sea* has been interpreted as an additional reason for considering it as a purported EEZ claim.[201] At least, however, on this occasion there was arguably some 'verbalization' of a claim and not just production of a bare map.[202]

Later Developments in the PRC on the Question of the Dashed Line

There was to be no further clarification in the later PRC's revised Law of Environmental Protection (1999) where Art. 2 refers enigmatically to it applying in 'other sea areas under the jurisdiction [of the PRC]': in other words in zones apart from the conventional zones.[203] The omission in all these earlier legislative provisions to mention the word 'historic' *specifically* in relation to the SCS is deafening; and the absence of any reference to the (then) nine-dashed line in the PRC's later *note verbale* of 4 April 2011 just adds further ambiguity.[204] In the course of *this* exchange of notes, the PRC referred to 'abundant historical and legal evidence' of the PRC's sovereignty 'and related rights'; but nowhere is

---

'The practices of the UNCLOS and the resolution of the South China Sea dispute', Taipei, Taiwan, 3–4 September 2012, at p. 3 (alleging that the u-shaped line is *the limit or basis* of such claims). Dupuy and Dupuy (*supra* n. 3, at pp. 124–5) state that the two Chinese notes to the UN, including the map of 7 May 2009, 'essentially' echoed 'repeated assertions made by China since the 1950s'. Gao and Jia (*supra* n. 11, at p. 109) comment that there is 'evidence' that the dashed lines were designed at a time with the 'nascent notion of the continental shelf in mind'; and that they might be dictated by the 'geographical reality' of the SCS as the 200 metre isobath runs close to the shores of the coastal states; and the lines may serve a 'potential delimitation purpose' as median lines.

200 Jinming and Dexia (*supra* n. 80, at p. 293) add that the PRC 'has *continuously reasserted through domestic legislation* that the islands are part of Chinese territory' (emphasis added), citing (ibid.) the 1998 EEZ/CS law. This is plainly untenable; and even they admit that this later law does not interpret the term 'historic rights'.

201 Zou, *supra* n. 4, at p. 163.

202 As has been commented, the phrase 'see attached map' indicates that it is a cartographic illustration of what the note asserts in writing (Dupuy and Dupuy, *supra* n. 3, at p. 132). By contrast, 'claim' verbalization *was* evident in the case of the PRC's *historic bay claims*: see Malek (*supra* n. 93, at p. 30) who refers to the PRC's past experience in claiming historic title, including its claim to Bohai Bay as an historic bay.

203 Zou, *supra* n. 4, at p. 160. He adds that this may reinforce the argument that the PRC's claim in the SCS may be to 'historic waters rather than historic rights' (ibid.). The same author (*supra* n. 145, at p. 59) also comments that it would be naive to think that the PRC's present silence on the 'line' is 'tantamount to tacit abandonment of the line'.

204 See above n. 150; and Dupuy and Dupuy, *supra* n. 3, at p. 130. Franckx and Benatar (*supra* n. 14, at p. 93) comment that despite the note, the PRC claim remains 'hazy', the new letter of 2011 referring to (as seen) 'abundant historical and legal evidence' (ibid.), *but with no reference now to any 'map'* (possibly indicating abandonment of claim?).

the latter phrase defined.[205] However, one set of commentators in discussing the PRC's 2011 *note verbale* interpret it as possibly using the 'exceptional doctrine of historic rights to defend its claims in the [SCS]'; as the phrase 'related rights' seems to refer to 'historic rights'.[206] In sum, the first of the texts of these two Chinese *notes verbales* (of 7 May 2009) completely failed to refer to any Chinese historical rights or 'historical factors';[207] whilst the second note of 2011 did refer vaguely to 'historical factors', but without any accompanying map.[208] A similar situation of ambiguity (possibly intentional), as seen, still pertains in relation to the latest Chinese map of the SCS claim in 2014.[209]

c. Was there sufficient publicity of claim?

The PRC note of 2011 claimed that since the 1930s, the Chinese Government had 'given publicity several times to the geographical scope' of the Chinese Nansha Islands;[210] and that the line has been in use for over 60 years during which time internationally over 200 atlases and maps have marked the line:[211] thus allegedly

205 In this PRC note of 2011, as seen, the phrase 'related rights' is used rather than 'sovereign rights': so the 'abundant and legal evidence' is not only related to sovereignty, but possibly to 'related rights' and 'jurisdiction' as well; so these could be possibly 'historic rights': see Malek, *supra* n. 93, at p. 44.

206 Thang and Thao, *supra* n. 156, at pp. 43–4.

207 Dupuy and Dupuy, *supra* n. 3, at p. 132.

208 Dupuy and Dupuy, ibid., at p. 133. Franckx and Benatar (*supra* n. 14, at p. 107) cite a variety of interpretations by legal scholars as well as the 2009 note: e.g., noting that the references to 'relevant waters' and 'adjacent waters' are not terms used in UNCLOS.

209 See above n. 160 and accompanying text. Furthermore, the objection by China to Vietnam's late intervention in the ongoing arbitral proceedings – instigated by China's 'position paper' published on 7 December 2014 – throws no further legal light on the supposed Chinese historic waters claim: see 'Beijing rejects Hanoi's legal challenge on the Spratley, Paracel Islands dispute', *South China Morning Post*, 12 December 2014 . It would seem that this Chinese move was intended to unofficially indicate to the tribunal the gist of its possible pleading on jurisdiction; and so to this extent the tribunal could and, indeed has taken cognisance of it by issuing a dossier of 26 questions (on December 14, 2014) seemingly based on China's position paper for the Philippines to respond to See *infra* n. 221.

210 Cited by Thang and Thao, *supra* n. 156, at pp. 44–5. They say (ibid., at p. 45) that this was intended to 'define the geographical scope of China's claim in the SCS in general'. A. Espina (RCAPS Working Paper Series 'Dojo', 'Implications of the submission of claims for extended continental shelf in the South China Sea' (21 January 2013, at p. 14)) makes a critical note of China's nine-dashed map claims.

211 Qifang, *supra* n. 94, at p. 2. See also Song and Yu (*supra* n. 51, at p. 2). They claim that the map was 'officially published' in January 1948, and first became available to the public then; but the line was drawn 'arbitrarily', and received no protests to it.

leading to broad acquiescence or recognition of the line internationally.[212] As against this, other commentators have denied this constituted sufficient publicity as China only allegedly circulated maps of the nine-dashed line 'internally'; and the 1992 Law of the PRC concerning the Territorial Sea and Contiguous Zone (as already seen) made no mention of 'historic waters'.[213]

It seems clear that in general terms certain 'internal' government actions or statements may not be sufficient to 'put foreign governments on notice of a claim',[214] a matter which, of course, is best effected by diplomatic notification to the international community, including notification to the UN.[215] This matter is still a problem with the latest Chinese map of 2014 because of its provincial publication, although Chinese comment has claimed this map gives the SCS claim better publicity by its larger and more prominent projection.[216]

d. Has there been acquiescence/lack of protest?

Several commentators raise the question whether other states have acquiesced to the supposed Chinese claim by their past silence.[217] The (formerly) nine-dashed

212 Jinming (*supra* n. 108, at p. 2) comments that since publication in 1947, the line did not incur any challenges, being included in 'the Atlas of the Administrative Areas of the Republic of China circulated throughout the world and observed by most countries' and included in foreign maps. Jinming claims that the lack of neighbouring protests and from the international community signified 'tacit recognition' until the 1990s (ibid.).

213 H. Duong, 'South China Sea disputes: how can China reassure its neighbours?', East Asia Forum, 13 July 2013, at p. 3. As seen, even in the case of the latest Chinese map of the SCS in 2014, it was published by 'a provincial level publisher', as also was the case with previous versions: comment of Prof. Lee Yunglung (*supra* n. 129); and the *US Limits in the Seas* publication comment (*supra* n. 138).

214 See Symmons, *supra* n. 1, pp. 147–8 citing the *Alabama & Mississippi Boundary Case*.

215 See ibid., pp. 146–7.

216 See above n. 164. The notes attached to the *SCS Bulletin* cited above n. 109 (by K. Fu and Hong Chang: see http://scsi.xmu.edu.cn/show.asp?id+2006) allege that the *previous* English-based descriptions of the Chinese SCS claim conveyed the idea that the dashed line was 'informal' and was demarcated 'randomly', making for 'abundant interpretations on the complex issue of its legal attribute[s]', which was '*unfavourable to China in its publicity efforts*' (emphasis added).

217 E.g., Dupuy and Dupuy, *supra* n. 3, at p. 132 (citing Jinming and Dexia, *supra* n. 80) (on declaration of the nine-dashed line 'the international community at no time expressed dissent'; and adjacent states did not make diplomatic protest; so that they argue that this silence in the face of 'public declaration' may be said to 'amount to acquiescence' and recognition for 'half a century'). See also Jinming and Dexia (*supra* n. 80, at p. 290) who comment that when the 'boundary line' was drawn between the Spratly Islands and adjacent states, no adjacent states protested; and that it was (allegedly) recognized for half a century thereafter.

line has belatedly been most strongly protested by the Philippines,[218] Vietnam (in May 2010 via notes to the UN); and Malaysia, Brunei and Indonesia (July 2010) have also protested.[219] Thus, for the first time, *regional* states have issued diplomatic protests, even if arguably the (former) nine-dashed line (and whatever it might have signified legally) was seemingly undisputed between 1948 and 2010. The Vietnamese protest in 2010 was the most comprehensive. This said that Vietnam would not 'recognise any so-called "historical interests" which are not consistent with international law and violate the sovereignty and sovereign rights of Vietnam';[220] and in response to the PRC's 2009 *note verbale*, Vietnam claimed that the map attached had 'no legal, historical or factual basis'.[221] Other Vietnamese

218 The Philippines in its 'Notification and Statement of Claim' to the arbitral tribunal (22 January 2013, Dept. of Foreign Affairs No. 13-0211, para. 6), claimed that 'China's claims based on its "nine-dash" line are inconsistent with [UNCLOS] and therefore invalid'. The Philippines by diplomatic note of 21 November 2012, had declared, as it had on previous occasions, that it could 'not accept the validity of the "nine-dash line" or China's claims based thereon' (see para. 27 of the Philippine's Arbitration Notification of 2013). The Department of Foreign Affairs of the Philippines has stressed that the Philippines does not accept the validity of the nine-dashed line which amounts to an excessive declaration of maritime space in international law. In its recent arbitration request, the Philippines wants the tribunal to declare the nine-dashed line to be 'invalid' and 'unlawful'. At the time of writing,the Philippines has reportedly (in March 2015) submitted a 3,000 page supplementary memorial to the arbitral tribunal in response to the tribunal's 26-question dossier submitted to it for clarifications on December 16, 2014 (the questions being seemingly based on issues raised in the previous Chinese 'position paper' in December 2014).The Philippines have claimed that their supplementary dossier has left no doubt that the tribunal has jurisdiction over the case, including, in particular, in its arguments about the *illegality of the 'nine-dash line'* which were 'well-founded in fact and law': see Shannon Tiezzi, 'Philippines counters China in new [SCS] case submission', March 18, 2015.

219 A good account of these developments is set out in Gao and Jia's article (*supra* n. 11, at pp. 105–8).

220 Ibid., at p. 113. Zou states (*supra* n. 4, at p. 162) that this makes it difficult for the PRC to allege acquiescence to its historic rights claim due to 'Vietnam's opposition'.

221 Ibid., at p. 113. This has been followed up most recently by Vietnam belatedly 'intervening' (on 5 December 2014, just before the tribunal-ordained 'cut-off' date for any Chinese pleadings on 15 December 15) in the on-going arbitration proceedings brought by the Philippines: when a Vietnamese statement to the arbitral tribunal indicated that the nine-dash line claim of China was 'without legal basis'. As a Vietnamese Foreign Affairs spokesman, Le Hai Binh, stated, Vietnam had expressed its position to the tribunal to 'protect its legal rights and interests' which might be 'affected in the [SCS] arbitration case'; and Vietnam 'fully' rejected 'China's claims of "historic rights" to the waters and seabed within the "dotted line" unilaterally stated by China': see E.T. Tordesillas, 'Vietnam supports its position: UN tribunal has jurisdiction on the [SCS] dispute', Yahoo Philippines News (blog), 12 December 2014. This falls short of an official and conventional 'third party' intervention, and the statement has no official standing to the proceedings as such (the unconventional procedure being described by Professor Thayer as a 'cheap way of getting

actions have included protests against interference with Vietnamese vessels inside the line.[222] Additionally, there was *early* implicit rejection of the claim also by the United States in its reiteration of freedom of navigation in the SCS area.[223] Japan also has impliedly rejected this claim as being against the provisions of international law.[224] Such protests have continued with the publication of the new Chinese map in 2014 and later.[225]

The question thus arises as to whether such explicit protest has come too late to cancel out possible former acquiescence to an alleged historic claim, insofar, as seen, arguably the Chinese claim originated in 1947/8. Interconnected with this matter are several sub-rules, one of which is that publicity to an alleged historic title must not come too late in time;[226] and, as seen, another is the importance of affected states at least having knowledge and understanding of the claim as being 'historic'

---

into the backdoor [of the case] without joining the Philippines case' (ibid.)). It remains to be seen what weight, if any, the tribunal will give the statement. See above n. 209.

222 Ibid., at p. 114.

223 M. Valencia in his comment 'The South China Sea: what China could say to clarify its claims and actions' (http:/nautilus.org/napset-policy-forum-the-south-cvhina-sea-whatchina-could-say (7 May 2013) at p. 2), interprets US insistence that claims to maritime jurisdiction in the SCS *must be from land* implies that the historic claim is seen by the United States as invalid. On 10 February 2014, the US Assistant Secretary of State for East Asian and Pacific Affairs, Mr D. Rinsel, testified before a House of Representatives Committee on Foreign Affairs, that under international law, maritime claims 'must be derived from land features'; and that any of the nine-dash line claim to maritime rights not based on claimed land areas was 'inconsistent with international law': see 'Home/ Connections/East Asia Beat' by P. Pondurai (09/022014). This later US statement was seen as the first US *explicit* rejection of the legality of the (then) nine-dash line (see www.globalsecurity.org/military/world/war/south-china-sea.htm). The more recent US rejection can be seen in the US *Limits in the Seas* publication, *supra* n. 116, which in the preamble states that the study 'represents the views of the US Government' on the matters specifically discussed. This study has been described as representing the 'most developed and detailed' US positions on historic Chinese claims in the SCS: see Sean Mirski, 'The US and China's nine-dash line', Lawfare, 7 January 2015.

224 See, e.g., 'Japan gets involved in [SCS] territorial dispute' by Michelle Florcruz (March 11, 2015).

225 According to reports, this new map has evoked strong reactions from Vietnam and the Philippines who have criticized China's 'unreasonably expansive claim': see, e.g., Junming Wang, 'New map boosts China's claim in sea', www.chinadaily.com.cn/opinion/2014-07-04/content_17646555 (4 July 2014). E. Graham, though (*supra* n. 152), has commented that Asian reaction to such more recent maps has been 'subdued, at least publicly'; even though, for example, China's western-most dash 'clearly bisects [Indonesia's] own gas-rich [EEZ] off the Natuna Islands', in the case of which Indonesia has reportedly 'not made official objection' to such a map.

226 See Symmons, *supra* n. 1, at p. 144.

since alleged 'publicity' was given to it in 1948.[227] As has been aptly stated in US caselaw, the adequacy of an historical claim has to be 'measured internationally'; and so an 'assertion of sovereign authority over waters must give foreign nations realistically accessible notice';[228] and as Bouchez has stated, 'other States must be in a position to raise objections'.[229] Thus time can only run adversely against other states from the moment they receive meaningful knowledge of an historic claim.[230] This principle is particularly applicable where an alleged historic claim, even if publicized, is so bizarre[231] or ambiguous as to raise no concerns on the part of other states as affecting their interests. As has been commented in the case of the Chinese claim, the 'strange u-shape was so abnormal and so exorbitantly outside reality ... that it is not conceivable that by way of acquiescence with regard to map claims a (tacit) recognition' by foreign states would be given to such 'extremely irregular pretensions'.[232]

Thus, it is only possible to make a protest once a claimant state has made an 'official and intelligible claim';[233] and indeed, if relevant jurisdictional interferences are not occurring with third state shipping, etc., in the claimant's

---

227 See, e.g., Malek, *supra* n. 93, at p. 34 ('the need for publicity of the extent and nature of the claim so as to enable other states to know what they are protesting or acquiescing to').

228 In the *Cook Inlet Case*: see Symmons, *supra* n. 1, at pp. 145–6. See also ibid., the Japanese protest to the United States in 1962 relating to the Shelikov Strait which allegedly had 'never been proclaimed' by the United States to be internal waters.

229 See Symmons, ibid., at p. 148. Malek comments (*supra* n. 93, at p. 30) that whether in the 1940s there was 'effective notice to the international community of such a map so as to elicit a response is debateable'. Franckx and Benatar (*supra* n. 14, at p. 229) cite other commentators on there being allegedly no international dissent for half a century in the face of a 'public declaration'; but (at p. 230) they rightly claim it is only possible to 'act by way of protest once the opposing State has made an official and intelligible claim'.

230 See Clark, *supra* n. 1, at p. 130.

231 C. Schofield and I. Townsend-Gault describe the nine-dotted line as 'one of the most extraordinary assertions of jurisdiction anywhere' in 'Brokering cooperation amidst competing maritime claims: preventative diplomacy in the Gulf of Thailand and the [SCS]', in *The Future Ocean-building Regime: Essays in Tribute to Douglas M. Johnston*, edited by A. Chircop, T. Dorman and S. Ralston (Leiden: Nijhoff, 2009), 643, 652. Malek (*supra* n. 93, at p. 33) comments: 'There is no precedent or similar circumstance of a historic waters/rights claim that mirrors China's claim by way of the nine-dashed line ... [anywhere in the World]'.

232 Franckx and Benatar, *supra* n. 14, at p. 112, citing Strupp; but they also cite Blum (ibid.) to the effect that 'on the whole, it seems to emerge that States will be imputed with knowledge of each other's domestic activities and other acts done under their authority'. This is a dubious proposition: see Symmons, *supra* n. 1, at p. 216. See also Jinming and Dexia, *supra* n. 80, at p. 290 (the silence which was 'in the face of a public declaration' amounts to 'acquiescence').

233 Franckx and Benatar, ibid., at p. 114. This, as seen, is the general US position in its *Limits in the Seas* publication, *supra* n. 116.

waters, the need to protest does not arise in any case;[234] and it may be that it is only when a *jurisdictional escalation* occurs in practice that states may feel the need to protest.[235] This ties in with Judge Oda's Dissenting Opinion in the *Gulf of Fonseca Case* when he implied that it is only possible to protest once a historic claim is in being, and acknowledged, albeit through late realization, as having such 'special status'.[236] Arguably then in the SCS situation, it has only been possible to object to comprehensible Chinese u-shaped-line assertions in the area when instances occur (as in the 2009 PRC letter). Thus Vietnam's diplomatic ripostes to the Chinese SCS claim seem to have been timely and well-publicised, *in the particular circumstances*.[237]

Additionally it may be argued that the consent or opposition of *neighbouring* states is particularly important in gauging international acceptance (and so existence) of an historic claim, as they may be most affected by the claim and thus most vociferous in protest; and such states can now be seen to be wholly in opposition to the Chinese claim in the SCS.[238] The recent move by the Philippines over referring adjudication of the status of the nine-dashed line to the tribunal may be seen as an additional and effective means of preventing any maturation of a Chinese historic claim.[239]

e. Was there exercise of relevant jurisdiction within the nine-dashed line?

---

234 Song and Yu (*supra* n. 51, at p. 8) add, after noting lack of Chinese enforcement jurisdiction, that 'states whose interests would be acted [*sic*] by the claim need not respond nor take action to invalidate the ROCs claims' (ibid., at p. 9). Malek (*supra* n. 93, at p. 34) is rightly doubtful if states which have traversed SCS sea lanes for centuries would acquiesce to any historic waters claim there. See, for example, Japan's protest note to Russia in January 1958 that it had no knowledge of Russia's claimed fishery regulations in Peter the Great Bay: cited in Clark, *supra* n. 1, at p. 183.

235 For example, Gioia (*supra* n. 10, at p. 348) points out that until 1973 Tunisia had never claimed full sovereignty over the Gulf of Gabes, simply sovereign rights for the 'limited purpose of exploiting the natural resources of the sea and the seabed'; and whenever Tunisia had attempted to infer from exclusive fishery rights the 'territoriality' of the Gulf, 'third states had expressed their dissent'. See also Clark, *supra* n. 1, at p. 129, who emphasizes that exercise of sovereign acts can have no meaning unless the exercise is 'public'; so that states most likely to be affected the claim 'would know (or reasonably should know) of the acts represented to be committed in support of the waters' appropriation'. This latter factor strongly underlies the US position on lack of past protest by itself to the Chinese SCS claim (in its *Limits in the Seas* publication, *supra* n. 116).

236 See Symmons, *supra* n. 1, at p. 144.

237 See, e.g., Biendong.Net, 'China has no historical rights in the nine-dotted line' (December 30, 2013) for reference to the Vietnamese note sent to the UN in May 2009.

238 See Symmons, *supra* n. 1, at pp. 240, 241; Clark, *supra* n. 1, at pp. 134, 144, 155.

239 See, e.g., Clark, ibid., at p. 152.

Many commentators have pointed out the past lack of exercise of jurisdiction by the Chinese authorities in the nine-dashed line in the SCS which has been 'infrequent since promulgation of line by either Taiwan or PRC'; and where freedom of navigation and fishing seems to have been 'unaffected'.[240] For such reasons, one commentator has claimed that China's claim to historic rights is distinct from the concept of historic waters as the latter regime does not permit freedom of navigation or overflight whereas the former does.[241] More recently the PRC does seem to have exercised *some* jurisdictional rights within the line.[242] However, if this is so, it has come too late in time for historic title purposes; and in any event it has been subject, as seen, to protest by the most affected states.[243]

---

240 E.g. Zou, *supra* n. 4, at p. 161. Jinming and Dexia (*supra* n. 80, at p. 292) comment regarding internal waters and the territorial sea status, that China has since 1947 'seldom practised this kind of exclusive rights over waters within line' (the doctrine of proportional jurisdiction); and that foreign ships still fish or sail in the waters without control (ibid.). Jinming (*supra* n. 108, at p. 2) states similarly that since the map's publication, neither the ROC or PRC has exercised jurisdiction in waters within the line affecting freedom of navigation or fishing (citing Z. Mei, *Jnl of China's SE Asian Studies*, vol. 4, 1995). See also: Zou (*supra* n. 144, at p. 171) (PRC/ROC exercise of authority over the SCS area has been 'infrequent'); Franckx and Benatar (*supra* n. 14, at p. 96) (only infrequent acts displaying sovereignty, thus no 'effectiveness'); and Song and Yu (*supra* n. 51, at p. 7) who conclude that the waters of the SCS are not internal because they were never claimed as such, and also have been continuously and freely navigated without protest from the ROC: foreign aircraft have been flying over the SCS since 1948; and shipping has exercised freedom of navigation (ibid., at p. 7); and Gao and Jia (*supra* n. 11, at pp. 119–20), citing Art. 11 of the 1998 Law on the EEZ and Continental Shelf.

241 See Valencia *supra* n. 223, at p. 2.

242 See 'Maritime territorial disputes in East Asia: issues for Congress', 30 January 2013 (www.fas.org/sgp/row/R42930.pdf, at p. 9). This points out that the PRC has taken unilateral actions in 1999 by imposing a fishing ban in the northern part of the SCS, which has been re-imposed annually; and its ships have detained foreign fishermen and their boats, etc. (ibid., p. 10). Taiwan has generally refrained from interdicting ships entering the SCS. Beckman (*supra* n. 79, at p. 12) cites the PRC's guarantee of freedom of navigation in the area (as recently as 21 June 2011) (ibid., at p. 15); and incidents in May and June of 2011 when PRC vessels interfered with seismic surveys by Vietnam, and undertaking of such surveys in the EEZ of the Philippines, may indicate that PRC has now has a policy of enforcing its 'sovereign rights and jurisdiction' in all ocean areas within the nine-dashed line. The PRC's harassment of foreign fishing vessels stemming from its existing powers under its maritime legislation has been particularly evident around its disputed insular claims: see, e.g., N.P. Aquino and J. Gujuto, 'Philippines summons China envoy over water cannon use' (25 February 2014, rmathieson3e.bloomberg.net). Some such actions may of course be interpreted as essentially aimed at bolstering territorial claims to disputed islets.

243 See the Philippines Notification and Statement of Claim of 2013, at para. 13: 'In June 2012, China placed the entire maritime area within the "nine-dash line" under the authority of the Province of Hainan, which, in November 2012, promulgated a law that requires foreign vessels to obtain China's permission before entering the "nine-dashed

Conclusion

As seen above, if the Chinese claim within the nine (or now 10)-dashed line is supposed to be claim to *historic waters*, it fails, in my opinion, to make the mark on most of the supposed rules, and indeed sub-rules, said to underlie the doctrine; and any claim to historic fishing rights there is now, as seen, of little or no legal consequence in the contemporary law of the sea.[244] On the other hand, the origins of the maps and PRC statements since are generally consistent with the line indicating at least a (historic) *territorial claim* to the islands enclosed, as indeed most recent commentators have concluded;[245] and if, of course, such territorial claims prove to be valid in international legal terms, conventional *juridical maritime* zones as spelt out in UNCLOS may proceed from the appropriate insular baselines. As a Chinese commentator has pointed out, most Chinese scholars regard the line as a 'island ownership' line; as the 1948 dashed map is itself entitled 'The *Geographical Location Map of the Islands in the South China Sea*'.[246] This method of territorial delineation in maritime areas (particularly involving clusters of islands) accords with the 'international convention of the time': whether the boundary lines were declared bilaterally by the claimants of relevant territory (as in the Alaska/Russia boundary of 1867) or the so-called 'treaty line' of the Philippines in 1946; or unilaterally by the claimant, as in the case of the Solomon Islands 'line' of 1899.[247]

line", and provides for inspection, expulsion and detention of vessels that do not obtain such permission'. This Law was in effect on 1 January 2013.

244 But cf. the conclusion of Gao and Jia (*supra* n. 11, at p. 123) ('[w]ith regard to the maritime space that the [nine-dashed] line surrounds, relevant provisions of UNCLOS *in conjunction with historic rights* provide the foundation' for the Chinese claim (emphasis added)). They controversially add that 'to a lesser extent' 'historic title', is a 'occasionally mentioned but not developed in UNCLOS'. This is true about, as seen 'historic title (with its two mentions) but *quite untrue about 'historic rights' eo nomine which are not mentioned as such in any part of UNCLOS.*

245 Dupuy and Dupuy (*supra* n. 3, at p. 132) comment that the PRC's *territorial* claims are certainly confirmed by the 2009 map, the dashes *indicating sovereignty over land*, from which the PRC's maritime claims would then proceed under UNCLOS; but they note (at p. 130) a 'blurring of distinction' between maritime claims to which 'historic rights' traditionally apply and territorial claims. Jinming and Dexia (*supra* n. 80, at p. 291), also interpret the map as delineating ownership of the islands rather than constituting a maritime boundary. This is also the view of other states party to the SCS dispute, such as the Philippines: see Department of Foreign Affairs (Philippines), 'China's U-shaped line' at p. 3 (the 'most legally valid and reasonable interpretation of the u-shaped line remains that of a claim only to the islands within that line'). This seems also to be the US position: see *Limits in the Seas*, *supra* n. 116, at p. 11 (it is apparent that China 'intends to use its nine-dashed maps to indicate the islands in the [SCS] over which it claims sovereignty', even in its note verbale of 2011).

246 Emphasis added.

247 Jinming, *supra* n. 108, at p. 3.

The recent reference to arbitration by the Philippines of aspects of the SCS dispute could, if the case proceeds to judgment on the merits or to substantive issues, bring an objective analysis of the nine (now 10)-dashed-line claim, even if the claim's *historic* element has not been articulated in its pleadings: as the Philippines has been careful to completely avoid use of the word 'historic' in the case.[248] It will, of course, be interesting to see how the tribunal copes with this aspect of the dispute; and already somewhat strained interpretations have been made of the legal effect of Art. 298 of UNCLOS and the 'historic title' exclusion thereunder.[249] It seems to this writer that as China has at the time of

---

248 N. Basiron, S. Permakl and M. Malek in 'Commentary: Philippines arbitral proceedings against China', *Australian Jnl of Maritime and Ocean Affairs* 5 (2013), 3, at p. 38, point out that the Philippines' notification does not include categories of disputes specifically opted out of by China; and that 'although the 9-dash line map was mentioned, no reference was made to the "historic" nature of China's claims', and (at p. 38), 'the arbitral tribunal will ... have the potential effect of de-legitimising China's 9-dash line claim'. The question arises, though, whether such 'de-legitimation' would be specifically effected by way of the tribunal rejecting the possible historic aspect to the Chinese claim therein: see below n. 230 and accompanying text. The Philippines Memorial (filed before the tribunal at the end of March 2014) has not yet been made public and is, out of respect for the tribunal and the arbitral process, *pro tempore* 'confidential'. For a good discussion of these issues, see A. Calvo, 'Manilla, Beijing and UNCLOS: a test case', *Asian Pacific Jnl* 11, issue 34, No. 1 (26 August 2013), who points out that para. 40 of the Philippines claim expressly states that it does not, *inter alia*, 'involve historic bays or titles within the meaning of the relevant provisions' of UNCLOS.

249 See, e.g., R. Beckman and L. Bernard paper at the Third International Workshop (entitled '[SCS]: cooperation for regional security and development' (Hanoi 2011): in 'Disputed areas in the SCS: prospects for arbitration or advisory opinion'. They argue (at p. 15) that Art. 298 and the Chinese declaration excludes interpretation of the provisions in UNCLOS involving only 'historic bays and titles'; but that Art. 15 (on territorial sea delimitation) 'does not mention "historic rights", only "historic title"' and that 'there are no provisions in UNCLOS on historic *rights*': thus they maintain such historical aspects are *not excluded* by the Chinese declaration (p. 16). However in this writer's opinion this is a very semantic argument in the light of the loose terminology relating to historic maritime claims: see Symmons, *supra* n. 1, at p. 5. See also the perceptive comments of J. Ku (in his *Opinio Juris* blog): 'The first serious defense of China's position on the Philippines' UNCLOS arbitration'.Here he argues that Prof S. Talmon's recent negative view on a challenge to the nine-dash line on the basis of Art. 298 is 'hardly obvious' on the basis of the *historic title exception*; and that such an interpretation would tend to exclude jurisdiction 'even if it undermines all the other principles of UNCLOS': opiniojuris.org/.../the-first-serious-defense-of-chinas-position-onthePhilippines. S. Talmon and B. Jia, in *The South China Sea Arbitration: A Chinese Perspective* (Oxford: Hart Publishing, 2014), at pp. 10 and 48 et seq., especially, ibid., at p. 54, argue, unconvincingly, that as 'historic titles' do not concern 'the application or interpretation' of UNCLOS, they are thus not subject to the compulsory jurisdiction under Arts 286 and 288(1) of UNCLOS'; and that the question of whether the PRC's claims are 'invalid' or 'unlawful' cannot be answered without deciding upon historic titles and rights which are outside the jurisdiction of the tribunal.

writing ignored the arbitral tribunal's deadline of 15 December 2014 to present its pleadings and is not likely now to appear or be legally represented at the tribunal proceedings (an early *note verbale* of 1 August 2013 stating that the PRC 'would not be participating in the proceedings'), the tribunal will seemingly itself, *sua sponte* and as a preliminary issue, have to consider the gist of the Chinese claim to the waters within the nine (now 10)-dashed line as based on the Chinese official 'position paper' submitted to the tribunal in December 2014; and this may involve the tribunal considering whether the possible Chinese *historic* claim is a *bona fide* one in substance rather than meekly accepting the claim as it stands *in limine*;[250] in ascertaining whether this may be a *prima facie* block to jurisdiction on the issue under Art. 298. If the tribunal adopts this course, it may even then, of course, articulate at least some relevant aspects of international law relating to historic maritime claims[251] even if it does not move on to consider historic issues on the merits. In such an instance, there is a chance that the obscure law on historic claims may at last be objectively and properly considered in a way that has not happened in previous ICJ caselaw where 'historic waters and rights' consideration has, as seen, been brief and incidental.

What is interesting, though, in the latter jurisdictional regard is that the Chinese reaction to reject in advance the tribunal's jurisdiction has been, to date, stated in somewhat in guarded terms. For example, more recent statements, as by a Chinese Foreign Ministry spokesman, have referred simply to his Government's declaration under Art. 298 of UNCLOS 'excluding disputes regarding such matters as those related to *maritime delimitation* from the compulsory dispute procedures', so making no direct reference to 'historic title' also being an optional exclusion for such jurisdiction.[252] And this trend has been continued in the latest

250 It seems clear, particularly in the light of the 'good faith' clause in Art. 303 of UNCLOS, that a state invoking an 'historic title' exemption under Art. 298 cannot *opportunistically* put forward an 'historic element' in a dispute as a sort of 'blanket shibboleth' simply in an attempt to avoid any initial arbitral jurisdiction. See Ku, *supra* n. 233, where he says that it is uncertain how the PRC would have pleaded on this issue, though Judge Xiu Hangui has, in a personal capacity, defended the historic claim. It was initially unclear how much weight the tribunal would give China's late position paper (of 7 December 2014) and sent just before the deadline for its pleadings of 15 December) as an indication of its possible arguments against the tribunal's jurisdiction had it participated: but as seen above n. 218, the tribunal has taken note of it as best representing the possible Chinese arguments in the absence of Chinese participation. It is noteworthy that there is no mention is made of *any 'historic title'* exception to jurisdiction in that Chinese paper.

251 For such reasons, Malek's recent prediction (*supra* n. 93, at p. 33) that 'since the PRC has rejected the arbitral proceedings, legal questions such as critical date and fulfilment of essential elements of historic claim [will] remain moot', may not in fact happen.

252 'Hua Chunying's remarks of the Philippines' efforts in pushing for the establishment of a tribunal in relation to the disputes between China and the Philippines in the [SCS]', 26 April 2013, available at http://www.fmprc.gov.cn/eng/xwfw/2510/t1035577.

Chinese position paper sent to the tribunal on 7 December 2014, which again makes no mention, as seen[253] of a possible Chinese invocation of 'historic title'.

References

Barnard, L. 'The Effect of Historic Fishing Rights in Maritime Boundaries Delimitation'. *LOSI* Conference paper, Seoul, Korea (2012).

Basiron, N., S. Permakl and M. Malek. 'Commentary: Philippines Arbitral Proceedings against China'. *Australian Journal of Maritime and Ocean Affairs* 5 (2013).

Beckman, R. 'Recent Developments and Implications towards Peaceful Dispute Resolution'. Presentation at MIMA Conference on the South China Sea, Kuala Lumpur, Malaysia (12–13 December 2011).

Beckman, R. 'South China Sea: How China Could Justify its Claims'. *RSIS Commentaries*, no. 116/2010 (16 September 2010).

Beckman, R. and L. Bernard. 'South China Sea: Cooperation for Regional Security and Development'. Paper at the Third International Workshop, Hanoi (2011).

'China's U-Shaped Line in the South China Sea: Possible Interpretations, Asserting Actions, and Reactions from Outside'. Paper presented at the conference on 'The Practices of the UNCLOS and the Resolution of the South China Sea Dispute', Taipei, Taiwan (3–4 September 2012).

Duong, H. 'South China Sea Disputes: How Can China Reassure Its Neighbours?'. East Asia Forum (13 July 2013).

Dupuy, F. and P.M. Dupuy. 'A Legal Analysis of China's Historic Rights Claim In The South China Sea'. *AJIL* 107 (2013).

'Eight Experts: How Should We Look on the Nine-Dash Line in The South China Sea?'. 31 July 2012. http://chinaelectionsblog.net/?p=20579.

Franckx, E. and M. Benatar. 'Dots and Lines in The South China Sea: Insights from the Law of Map Evidence'. *Asian Jnl of Intl Law* 2 (2012).

Franckx, E. and M. Benatar. 'Dotted Lines in the South China Sea: Fishing for (Legal) Clarity'. In Diplomatic Academy of Vietnam, 'The South China Sea: Towards a Recognition of Peace Security and Co-operation'. T. Thuy, ed. Vietnam: Gioi Publishers, 2011.

Gao, Z. and B. Jia. 'The Nine-Dash Line in the South China Sea: History, Status and Implications'. *AJIL* 107 (2013).

Huy, D. 'China's U-Shaped Line in the South China Sea'. *Asia Sentinel Consulting*, 19 September 2012.

Jinming, L and Dexia, L, 'The Dotted Line on the Chinese Map of the South China Sea'. *ODIL* 34 (2003).

shtml (emphasis added). This trend has been repeated in press conferences since by PRC Foreign Ministry officials.

253 See above n. 250

Jinming, L. 'Behind the Dotted Line in the Chinese Map of the South China Sea'. 17 June 2013. http://blog.chinadaily.com.cn/?1057682.

The Juridical Regime of Historic Waters, Including Historic Bays. Study prepared for the UN Secretariat. UN Doc. A/CN.4/143 (9 March 1962).

Malek, M. 'A Legal Assessment of China's Historic Claims in the South China Sea'. *Australian Jnl of Maritime and Ocean Affairs* 5 (2013).

'New Map Boosts China's Maritime Claims'. http://blog.geogarage.com/2014/.../new-map-boosts-chinas-maritime-claims.htm.

'Philippines Says China's New Map Shows Unreasonable Expansive Claim'. 26 June 2014. http://www.eaglenews.ph/philippines-says-chinas-new-official-map-shows.

Qifang, T. 'On the Dotted Line: Law and History Support China's Claims over the South China Sea'. 7 February 2013. http://www.bjreview,com.cn.

Schofield, C. and I. Townsend-Gault. 'Brokering Cooperation amidst Competing Maritime Claims: Preventative Diplomacy in the Gulf Of Thailand and the [SCS]'. In A. Chircop, T. Dorman and S. Ralston, eds. *The Future Ocean-Building Regime: Essays in Tribute to Douglas M. Johnston*. Leiden: Nijhoff, 2009.

Symmons, C.R. 'Rights and Jurisdiction over Resources and Obligations of Coastal States: Validity of Historic Rights Claims'. Paper presented at the 5th International Workshop on The South China Sea: Co-operation for Regional Security and Development, Hanoi, Vietnam (11–12 November).

Symmons, C.R. *Historic Waters in the Law of the Sea: A Modern Re-Appraisal*. Leiden: Nijhoff, 2008.

Than, B. 'Nine-Dotted Line: A Vague Claim'. http://baobinthnan.com.vn/en/default.aspex?cat_id=6977news_9d.

Thang, N. and N. Thao. 'China's Dotted Line in the South China Sea: The 2011 Exchange of Diplomatic Notes'. *ODIL* 43 (2012).

'The South China Sea: Evolution or Disregard for International Law', H. Duong and T. Pham. *NAPs net Policy Forum*, 25 June 2013. http:/nautilus.org/napsnet/napsnet-policy-forum/the-south-china-sea-evolution-of-or-disregard-for-international-law.

Valencia, Mark. 'The South China Sea: What China Could Say to Clarify Its Claims and Actions'. http:/nautilus.org/napset-policy-forum-the-south-cvhina-sea-what china-could-say.

Valencia, Mark, J. Van Dyke and N. Ludwig. *Sharing the Resources of the South China Sea*. Hawaii: University of Hawaii Press, 1999.

Yongke, J. 'No Question of Re-Demarcation in the South China Sea'. *Ocean Development and Management* (2000).

Zou, Keyuan. 'Historic Rights in the South China Sea'. In the conference proceedings of 'The South China Sea: UNCLOS and State Practice', 24–25 October 2013, Haikou, China, organized by the National Institute for South China Sea Studies.

Zou, Keyuan. *Law of the Sea in East Asia: Issues and Prospects*. NP: London/NY: Routledge, 2005.

Zou, Keyuan. 'The Traditional Maritime Boundary in the South China Sea and Its Legal Consequences for the Resolution of the Dispute over the Spratly Islands'. *IJMCL* 14 (1999).

Chapter 11
Historic Rights in the South China Sea

Keyuan Zou

Introduction

In recent years, international discussion on China's U-shaped line increased, particularly after China sent its *note verbale* to the United Nations in 2009 with the attachment of the U-shaped line map.[1] This chapter attempts to discuss a couple of legal issues surrounding this line and its implications for the future resolution of the islands disputes as well as maritime boundary delimitation in the South China Sea.

The U-Shaped Line

The U-shaped line in the South China Sea is the line with nine segments off the Chinese coast on the South China Sea, as displayed in the Chinese map, and its official Chinese name is 'traditional maritime boundary line' (*chuantonghaijiangxian*). China's claim to the South China Sea is based on the U-shaped line. On 1 December 1947, the Chinese Ministry of Interior renamed the islands in the South China Sea and formally allocated them into the administration of the Chinese Hainan Special Region.[2] Meanwhile, the same ministry prepared a location map of the islands in the South China Sea, which was then first released for internal use.[3] In February 1948, the Atlas of Administrative Areas of the Republic of China was officially published, in which the above map was included. This is the first official map with the line for the South China Sea. It has two general characteristics: the southernmost end of the line was set at 4° north latitude

---

1 See China's *note verbale*, 9 May 2009, accessed 25 August 2012, http://www.un.org/Depts/los/clcs_new/submissions_files/mysvnm33_09/chn_2009re_mys_vnm_e.pdf.

2 See Ministry of Interior, *An Outline of the Geography of the South China Sea Islands*, National Territory Series, 1947, fig 11, 861, as cited in J.K.T. Chao, 'South China Sea: Boundary Problems Relating to the Nansha and Shisha Islands', in *Fishing in Troubled Waters*, edited by R.D. Hill, N.G. Owen and E.V. Roberts (Hong Kong: Centre for Asian Studies, University of Hong Kong, 1991), 88.

3 The map was named as the Location Map of the South China Sea Islands (*naihaizhudaoweizhitu*), see Li Jinming and Li Dexia, 'The Dotted Line on the Chinese Map of the South China Sea: A Note', *Ocean Development and International Law* 34 (2003): 290.

including James Shoal; and the 11-segment line was drawn instead of the previous continuous line. According to the then official explanation, the basis for drawing the line was: '[t]he southernmost limit of the South China Sea territory should be at the James Shoal. This limit was followed by our governmental departments, schools and publishers before the anti-Japanese war, and it was also recorded on file in the Ministry of Interior. Accordingly it should remain unchanged.'[4] It should be noted that the map is an official map, different from those previously drawn by individual cartographers. Since then, maps officially published both in mainland China and Taiwan are the same regarding the line since both have used the official map published in 1948.

As China claims that it 'has indispensable sovereignty over the islands in the South China Sea and the adjacent waters and enjoys sovereign rights and jurisdiction over the relevant waters as well as the seabed and subsoil thereof. China's sovereignty and related rights and jurisdiction in the South China Sea are supported by abundant historical and legal evidence'. China further stated that 'since 1930s, the Chinese Government has given publicity several times the geographical scope of China's Nansha Islands and the names of its components. China's Nansha Islands therefore clearly defined'. It is indicated that the historic aspect is an essential element in China's claim to the South China Sea islands.

The Concept of Historic Rights

There is no established definition of the term 'historic rights' under international law. However, some scholars have attempted to explain it in their own ways. For example, according to Blum, 'the term "historic rights" denotes the possession by a State, over certain land or maritime areas, of rights that would not normally accrue to it under the general rules of international law, such rights having been acquired by that State through a process of historical consolidation'. Blum further explains that 'historic rights are a product of a lengthy process comprising a long series of acts, omissions and patterns of behaviours which, in their entirety, and through their cumulative effect, bring such rights into being and consolidate them into rights valid in international law'. Other scholars use the term 'historic rights' to indicate 'those rights which a state has acquired vis-à-vis one or more other states by effectively exercising those rights, with the acquiescence of the state or states concerned'.

Like the concept of 'historic bays', the concept of historic waters is not definitive in international law either. A scholarly definition was offered by Bouchez: '[h]istoric waters are waters over which the coastal State, contrary to the generally applicable rules of international law, clearly, effectively, continuously, and over a substantial period of time, exercises sovereign rights with the acquiescence of the community

4 See Zhenhua Han, *A Compilation of Historical Materials on China's South China Sea Islands* (Beijing, Oriental Press, 1988) (in Chinese), 181–4.

of States'. In international judiciary, the International Court of Justice (ICJ) gave a definition of 'historic waters' in the *Fisheries Case*: '[b]y "historic waters" are usually meant waters which are treated as internal waters but which would not have that character were it not for the existence of an historic title'. According to the late O'Connell, there are three circumstances which could be considered as historic waters: (1) bays, claimed by States which are greater in extent, or less in configuration, than standard bays; (2) areas of claimed waters linked to a coast by offshore features but which are not enclosed under the standard rules; and (3) areas of claimed seas which would, but for the claim, be high seas because they are not covered by any rules specially concerned with bays or delimitation of coastal waters (*mariaclausa*). Accordingly, the concept of 'historic waters' is usually applicable to bays and gulfs. Once established as historic waters, the waters in question are then regarded as internal waters. There may be exceptions to this rule, i.e., some historic waters claimed by States are not bays or gulfs, but open seas, which therefore could be regarded as internal waters.

The United Nations International Law Commission (ILC) had discussed the concept of historic waters, and in 1962 the UN Secretariat, upon the request of the ILC, prepared the study on the juridical regime of historic waters, including historic bays. The study examined the elements of title to historic waters, the issues of burden of proof, the legal status of waters regarded as historic waters, and the settlement of disputes. However, it did not give a conclusive concept of historic waters and the standard according to which this concept could be applied. Thus the theoretical problem in regard to the concept of historic waters has not yet been resolved. Because of the controversy around this concept, the Third UN Conference on the Law of the Sea (UNCLOS III) dropped the issue for discussion and only left it as some wordings in the 1982 United Nations Convention on the Law of the Sea (LOS Convention). Generally speaking, there should be three conditions to be fulfilled to sustain a historic water claim. They are: (1) the exercise of the authority over the area; (2) the continuity over time of this exercise of authority; and (3) the attitude of foreign States to the claim.

The term 'historic rights' is a general framework which is directly linked to the term 'historic waters', and the term 'historic bays'. However, we have to realize that the term 'historic rights' is not equivalent to 'historic waters' or 'historic bays', though 'historic rights' may carry a broader meaning and may include historic waters and bays. The term 'historic rights' also covers certain special rights without involving a claim of full sovereignty, such as historic fishing rights which a State might have acquired in particular areas of the high seas. It is not clear whether such expansion is still going on with China's inclusion of the term 'historic rights' in its Law on the Exclusive Economic Zone and the Continental Shelf (hereinafter referred to as the Chinese EEZ Law). The second point resulting from our observation is that all these terms above are often used interchangeably in the maritime sector.

The UNCLOS III did not discuss the issue of 'historic rights' or 'historic waters'. However, a variant term of historic bay and/or historic title is mentioned in the LOS Convention relating to bays, delimitation of the territorial sea between States with opposite or adjacent coasts, and limitations and exceptions in the settlement of disputes. Article 10(6) provides that '[t]he foregoing provisions [on bays] do not apply to so-called "historic" bays'. Article 15 does not allow the median line to apply to special circumstances such as 'by reason of historic title' for the delimitation of the territorial seas of the two States. The last provision in the LOS Convention which mentions the historic bays or titles is Article 298 which permits the contracting States to exclude the compulsory procedure provided for in the LOS Convention from applying to the disputes 'involving historic bays or titles'. It is obvious that the LOS Convention deliberately avoids the issue of 'historic rights' or 'historic waters', and leaves it to be governed by customary international law as reaffirmed by its preamble. On the other hand, the Convention bears some implications for the concept of 'historic waters' in that those waters are related to the territorial seas or internal waters since the mentioning in the Convention only appears in the sections of the rules for the territorial sea regime and the settlement of territorial disputes.

State Practice

Nevertheless, in state practice, historic rights or waters are reflected in domestic legislation and bilateral agreements. In September 1976 Sri Lanka enacted a Law to Provide for the Declaration of the Territorial Sea and Other Maritime Zones of Sri Lanka, and All Other Matters Connected Therewith or Incidental Thereto, in which Article 9 expressly stipulates that: '(1) The President may by Proclamation published in the Gazette, declare the limits of the historic waters of Sri Lanka. (2) The Republic of Sri Lanka shall exercise sovereignty, exclusive jurisdiction and control in and over the historic waters, as well as in and over the islands and the continental shelf and the sea-bed and sub-soil thereof within such historic waters'. The Law on the State Boundary of the former Soviet Union, entered into force on 1 March 1983, provides that the waters of bays, inlets, coves, and estuaries, seas and straits, historically belonging to the USSR are relegated to internal waters of the USSR. As for bilateral agreements, an example can be found with the agreement between India and Sri Lanka on the Boundary in Historic Waters between the Two Countries on 26 June 1974, in which the vessels of India and Sri Lanka will enjoy in each other's waters such rights as they have traditionally enjoyed therein.

The most relevant case to the historic rights rather than historic waters and historic bays is Tunisia's historical claims, which have also been assessed in the 1980s by an Italian scholar. In addition to its historic claim to the Gulf of Tunis and the Gulf of Gabès, Tunisia also claimed 'historic rights' beyond its territorial sea, particularly the historic fishing rights. In its reply to Libya's objections against Tunisia's claim, Tunisia stated that 'historic rights' acquired in bygone ages could extend over areas of sea or seabed which could today qualify as internal waters, territorial waters, a fishing zone or the continental shelf. But this view was contested by the following arguments that 'a state cannot claim a vast area of sea as internal waters on the sole basis of "historic rights" previously acquired for fishing purposes, unless it is possible to consider that those "historic rights" were in fact indicative of a right of full sovereignty'. As for Tunisia's historic rights beyond its territorial sea, those rights are essentially concerned with the exploitation of 'sedentary fisheries', such as sponge fisheries. Tunisia claimed exclusive jurisdiction over those so-called 'fixed fisheries' whatever their distance from the coast. The claimed historic fishing rights were not disputable, even the contestant State Libya recognized those rights: '[e]vidence of the general recognition of Tunisian proprietary rights and ancillary rights to protection and control over the sedentary species asserted is not the issue. For the fact is that such rights existed'. On the other hand, it should be stressed that such 'historic rights' did not exclude foreigners from the exploitation of sponge and octopus fisheries. Therefore, it is argued that the fishery zone created by the 1951 Tunisian decree on the sole basis of the 'historic rights' previously acquired is not justified, and the 1951 decree put forward a completely new and different claim since, for the first time, the established fishery zone included all biological resources of the sea.

In the case of the continental shelf between Libya and Tunisia in 1982, the ICJ observed Tunisia's unilateral line at 45°ZV (Zenith Vertical) North-East, starting from RasAjdir, as the eastern limit of its 'exclusive fishery zone' by the 1951 Decree, and found that although no State may unilaterally establish international maritime boundary lines, the line adopted by Tunisia which was 'originally intended only as a limit of an area of surveillance in the context of specific fishery regulations, constitutes a unilateral claim, but was never a line plotted for the purpose of lateral maritime delimitation, either in the seas or in the continental shelf'. The Court found instead that the line perpendicular to the coast was the only lateral boundary opposable to Libya of the area claimed by Tunisia as being subject to 'historic rights'.

Meanwhile, Tunisia stressed the importance of its 'historic rights' with a view to the future delimitation of the exclusive economic zone (EEZ) by arguing that its claim was supported either by the new law of the sea or the historic rights acquired through its immemorial exercise of jurisdiction. Libya questioned the nature and extent of Tunisia's 'historic rights', asserting that they did not amount to sovereignty over the seabed and that they had never been exercised throughout the area claimed by Tunisia. In addition, Libya stressed that these rights could not 'deprive a neighbouring State of a shelf area which, according to the law, appertains to it *de jure* and *ab initio*'. The Court avoided the question whether Tunisia's historic rights were relevant for the purpose of delimiting its continental shelf, but the Court did make some important remarks that 'historic rights' must enjoy respect and be preserved as they had always been by long usage. On the other hand, the Court seemed to have denied any relevance of 'historic rights' to the delimitation of continental shelf as it found that 'basically, the notion of historic rights or waters and that of the continental shelf are governed by distinct legal regimes in customary international law. The first regime is based on acquisition and occupation, while the second is based on the existence of rights "*ipso facto*" and "*ab initio*"'. Thus in the view of the Court, the 'historic rights' would perhaps have been relevant for the purpose of delimiting Tunisia's EEZ, but not for the purpose of delimiting its continental shelf. Nevertheless, as concluded by Gioia, 'Tunisia could not unilaterally claim the whole area over which her "historic rights" extended as part of her exclusive economic zone', but 'Tunisia's "historic rights" could operate as an important factor when negotiating delimitation agreements with the interested states'.

Case of Eritrea–Yemen Arbitration

Another international judicial case relating to historic rights is the Case of Eritrea–Yemen Arbitration in 1998. The two contesting parties – Eritrea and Yemen – requested the specially established Arbitral Tribunal to decide on questions of territorial sovereignty over disputed islands in the Red Sea 'in accordance with principles, rules and practices of international law applicable to the matter, and on the basis, in particular, of *historic titles*' (author's italics). Eritrea based its claim to territorial sovereignty over the disputed 'Red Sea Islands' on a chain of title extending over more than a hundred years, and on international law of 'effective occupation'. Eritrea traced this chain of title through the relevant historical records, beginning with the Italian colonization of the Eritrean mainland in the latter part of the nineteenth century. Yemen based its claim to the disputed islands on 'original, historic or traditional Yemeni title', which could be traced to the *Bilad el-Yemen*, or realm of Yemen, which was said to have existed as early as the sixth century AD. Yemen contended that its incorporation into the Ottoman Empire, from 1538 to circa 1635, and again from 1872 to 1918, did not deprive it of historic title to its territory. Yemen also contended that the Treaty of Lausanne had no effect on Yemeni title, because Yemen was not a party to the Treaty, and because Turkey's renunciation of rights could not prejudice the interests of third parties. Yemen took the view that the effect of Article 16 was not to make the 'Islands' *terra nullius*, but rather, territory 'the title to which was undetermined'. Yemen provided an historical review of alleged Yemeni acts of administration and control to supplement and confirm Yemen's historic title to the 'Islands'. It is clear that both sides presented their arguments based on historic rights in addition to evidence, in particular the Yemeni side. The Tribunal reviewed those arguments and held that 'there can be no doubt that the concept of historic title has special resonance in situations that may exist even in the contemporary world'. 'A different situation exists with regard to uninhabited islands which are not claimed to be falling within the limits of historic waters.'[5] The Tribunal then pointed out that 'in the present case, neither party has formulated any claim to the effect that the disputed islands are located within historic waters'. It further confirmed that:

5 Ibid., para. 123.

> the conditions that prevailed during many centuries with regard to the traditional openness of southern Red Sea marine resources for fishing, its role as means for unrestricted traffic from one side to the other, together with the common use of the islands by the populations of both coasts, are all important elements capable of creating certain "historic rights" which accrued in favour of both parties through a process of historical consideration as a sort of "*servitude internationale*" falling short of territorial sovereignty. Such historic rights provide a sufficient legal basis for maintaining certain aspects of a *res communis* that has existed for centuries for the benefit of populations on both sides of the Red Sea.

Here it seems that the Tribunal recognized the historic rights of both sides. That makes it difficult for the Tribunal to render its decision based on historic title and rights in favour of either party. Finally, despite great efforts made by the Tribunal to investigate both claims to historic titles, the Tribunal held that 'neither Party has been able to persuade the Tribunal that the history of the matter reveals the juridical existence of an historic title, or of historic titles, of such long-established, continuous and definitive lineage to these particular islands, islets and rocks as would be a sufficient basis for the Tribunal's decision'. On the other hand, the Tribunal held that 'Yemen shall ensure that the traditional fishing regime of free access and enjoyment for the fishermen of both Eritrea and Yemen shall be preserved'.

Article 14 of the Chinese EEZ Law

On 26 June 1998, China officially promulgated the Law on the Exclusive Economic Zone and the Continental Shelf in which Article 14 provides that 'the provisions of this Law shall not affect the historic rights enjoyed by the People's Republic of China'. It is generally agreed that this clause is connected to China's claim to the South China Sea within the U-shaped line. However, instead of using the term 'historic waters', China wisely chose a more softened term 'historic rights'. The provision of the exclusive economic zone (EEZ) law on historic rights can be understood in the following three interpretations: (1) it might be interpreted to mean that the sea areas which could not become China's EEZ and/or continental shelf should have the same legal status as EEZ and/or continental shelf; (2) it might be interpreted to mean that the sea areas which embody China's historic rights are beyond the 200 nm limit; and (3) it might be interpreted to mean that the sea areas which embody China's historic rights but within the 200 nm limit can have an alternative management regime different from the EEZ and/or continental shelf regime.

On the other hand, while China continues to assert its historic rights in the South China Sea, it is to be noted that since such 'historic rights' are contained in the law on the EEZ and continental shelf, they may not be treated as equivalent to 'historic waters' generally interpreted in international law. Having said that, it is also noted that in other Chinese legislations wordings such as '*other sea areas within China's jurisdiction*' have been used in addition to internal waters, territorial sea, EEZ and continental shelf. The typical example is the amended Law on Marine Environmental Protection in 1999. Article 2 of that law provides that 'the Law shall apply to internal waters, territorial sea, contiguous zone, exclusive economic zone, continental shelf of the People's Republic of China and *other sea areas under the jurisdiction of the People's Republic of China*' (italics added). The original law, which was promulgated in 1982, contained similar wordings referring to China's potential EEZ and continental shelf. However, after the establishment of the EEZ and continental shelf regime, China still made such stipulation, which clearly refers to sea areas other than EEZ and continental shelf. But it is unknown where such a sea area is exactly located. One assumption is: it might refer to the sea areas within the U-shaped line which China is unable to claim as its territorial sea, EEZ and/or continental shelf.

Historic Fishing Rights

LOS Convention

Some relevant provisions in the LOS Convention include the fishery management in the EEZ and the traditional fishing rights concerning the archipelagic waters.

Article 62 provides that the coastal State shall determine its capacity to harvest the living resources of the exclusive economic zone. Where the coastal State does not have the capacity to harvest the entire allowable catch, it shall, through agreements or other arrangements and pursuant to the terms, conditions, laws and regulations, give other States access to the surplus of the allowable catch, having particular regard to the land-locked and geographically disadvantaged States of the same sub-region or region, especially in relation to the developing States.

Article 51 provides that 'an archipelagic State shall respect existing agreements with other States and shall recognize traditional fishing rights and other legitimate activities of the immediately adjacent neighbouring States in certain areas falling within archipelagic waters. The terms and conditions for the exercise of such rights and activities, including the nature, the extent and the areas to which they apply, shall, at the request of any of the States concerned, be regulated by bilateral agreements between them'.

In addition, Article 77 concerning the continental shelf mentions 'sedentary species' as natural resources on the continental shelf that coastal States have the right to exploit.

It is clear that after the creation of the EEZ regime, the historic fishing rights have been significantly diminished. It is rightly pointed out that:

> in terms of "quality", traditional fishing activities are no longer a right enjoyed by a third state but merely one of the factors to be considered by a coastal state when deciding whether to grant a third state access to its EEZ. The ultimate decision rests with the coastal state. In terms of "quantity", third state may only take what was specified in bilateral agreements or an appropriate quota from the surplus of the TAC of the coastal state.

It is recalled that prior to the UNCLOS III, Kenya put forward a proposal of Draft Articles on the Concept of an Exclusive Economic Zone beyond the Territorial Sea and Article 9 suggests that 'neighbouring developing States shall mutually recognise their existing historic rights. They shall also give reciprocal preferential treatment to one another in the exploitation of the living resources of their respective Economic Zones'. Apparently, the call for the recognition of mutual historic rights was not concurred even by other developing countries including China.

China–Vietnam Fishery Agreement

On 25 December 2000, China and Vietnam officially signed the Agreement on Fishery Cooperation in the Gulf of Tonkin (*Beibu* Gulf in Chinese, and *Bac Bo* Gulf in Vietnamese) together with the conclusion of the Agreement on Maritime Boundary Delimitation in the Gulf of Tonkin between the two countries. The purpose of the Agreement, as it stands, is to maintain and develop the traditional neighbouring and friendly relationship between the two countries, to preserving and to sustainably utilize marine living resources in the Beibu Gulf. The Agreement applies to parts of the exclusive economic zones and parts of the adjacent territorial seas of the two countries (hereinafter referred to as 'Agreed Water Area') in the Beibu Gulf. The two parties have agreed to undertake fishery cooperation in the Agreed Water Area based on the mutual respect for sovereignty, sovereign rights and jurisdiction. The major achievements of the Agreement are the establishment of the Common Fishery Zone and the Joint Fishery Committee of the two parties.

China's historic fishing rights seem not to be reflected fully in the Fishery Agreement. The LOS Convention only mentions 'traditional fishing rights' in relation to the archipelagic waters, but not to the EEZs. Nevertheless, there are existing boundary delimitation agreements signed by other countries which retained the traditional fishing activities from the countries concerned and such traditional fishing operations may continue undisturbed. Probably, the transitional arrangements contained in the Fishery Agreement impliedly reflect the traditional fishing rights, as Article 11 provides that:

> Each Contractual Party shall make transitional arrangements for the existing fishing operations of the other Contractual Party in its exclusive economic zone north of the Common Fishery Zone (measured from 20^0N). The transitional arrangements shall be implemented from the date of the entry into force of this Agreement. The other Contractual Party shall take measures to reduce such

> fishing operations year by year. The transitional arrangements will end within four years from the date of the entry into force of this Agreement. The extent of the water area and management measures for the transitional arrangements shall be made by the Contractual Parties in the form of a supplementary protocol, which shall constitute an integral part of this Agreement. Each Contractual Party, upon the end of the transitional arrangements, shall give priority, under the same conditions, to the other party for fishing operations in its exclusive economic zone.

These arrangements can be seen as a partial realization of the Chinese traditional fishing rights in the gulf. Nevertheless, the Agreement does not mention any traditional fishing rights in any of its clauses expressly. That would imply to the Vietnamese favour that the Chinese claim to any traditional fishing rights in the Gulf of Tonkin has been denied. No such rights have been ever recognized by the Vietnamese side. Furthermore, it should be borne in mind that even the transitional arrangements made under the Agreement may only last four years after the entry into force of the Agreement. When the period of four years expires, the Chinese traditional fishing rights in Vietnam's EEZ may be totally rescinded, despite the provision in the Agreement that both parties should give each other the priority for fishing operations in their EEZs.

Some Observations

A number of judicial cases may support the elaboration of the concept of historic waters. At least one historic claim was accepted in 1951 by the ICJ in the *Norwegian Fisheries Case*. The issue before the Court was whether the Norwegian method of delimiting territorial waters was valid on the basis of historic title, even if the method violated international law. After examining the past Norwegian practice, the Court found that the Norwegian system of delimitation had been applied consistently and uninterruptedly for some 60 years and that this practice had not been opposed by other States and instead tolerated by them. Based on these facts, the Court ruled that the Norwegian system was not contrary to international law, thus upholding the validity of the Norwegian claim to historic title. The same Court also accepted the Gulf of Fonseca as a historic bay and its waters as historic waters in the *Gulf of Fonseca Case* in 1992.

From the above cases, it is obvious that international court/tribunals have recognized the existence of 'historic rights' in the maritime area. But on the other hand, except for the *Fisheries Case*, it seems that the international judiciary took a rather conservative attitude towards the concept of 'historic rights' as illustrated in the *Libya–Tunisia Case* and the *Eritrea–Yemen Case* where 'historic rights' were not counted substantially by the court or the tribunal to make their judicial decisions. While it is hoped that the international judiciary could construe the concept of 'historic rights' and its applicability in judging the cases in question, such a conservative attitude makes the regime of 'historic rights'/'historic waters' still relatively underdeveloped.

The U-shaped line has existed for more than half a century before the adoption of the LOS Convention and even before the adoption of the 1958 Geneva Conventions on the law of the sea. The historic rights deriving from this line cannot be disregarded. Usually the regime of historic rights is favourable for states with a long history but relatively unfavourable for the newly independent states founded after the Second World War. This concern was actually expressed when the issue of historic waters was discussed in the UN International Law Commission in the 1950s. As García-Amador contended, the concept of historic bays only benefited old countries having a long history and that there were many comparative newcomers to the international community – countries in Latin America, the Middle East and the Far East – which could not claim such historic rights. In comparison with claims by other countries bordering the South China Sea, China's claim has the longest history. This fact can at least partially explain why other claimants to the islands in the South China Sea are opposed to China's historic claims based on the U-shaped line.

While it is admitted that the historic fishing rights have been diminished significantly after the establishment of the EEZ regime, it is recognized that some such residual rights are still in existence as discussed above and reflected in state practice. In considering the development of the international law of the sea and the ambiguous definition of the concept of 'historic rights', it is reasonably perceived that the concept of historic rights may contain other rights as crystallized by the LOS Convention.

Conclusion

Finally, I would like to pose a couple of questions. If we ask whether the concept of 'historic rights' is dead, my answer is no. The other question is: can the rights derived from the LOS Convention erase the acquired rights prior to the LOS Convention? My answer is also no. But I would like to listen to others' views and comments.

References

Blum, Yehuda Z., *Historic Titles in International Law*.

Blum, Yehuda Z., 'Historic Rights', in *Encyclopaedia of Public International Law*, Instalment 7, edited by Rudolf Bernhardt (Amsterdam: North-Holland Publishing Co., 1984), 120.

Bouchez, Leo J., *The Regime of Bays in International Law* (Leyden: A.W. Sythoff, 1964).

Chao, J.K.T., 'South China Sea: Boundary Problems Relating to the Nansha and Shisha Islands', in *Fishing in Troubled Waters*, edited by R.D. Hill, N.G. Owen and E.V. Roberts (Hong Kong: Centre for Asian Studies, University of Hong Kong, 1991), 88.

Gioia, Andrea, 'Tunisia's Claims over Adjacent Seas and the Doctrine of "Historic Rights"', *Syracuse Journal of International Law and Commerce* 11 (1984): 328.

Gros-Espiell, Hector, 'Gulf of Fonseca', in *Encyclopaedia of Public International Law*, Instalment 12, edited by Rudolf Bernhardt (Amsterdam: North-Holland, 1990), 110–12.

Kwiatkowska, Barbara, 'The Eritrea/Yemen Arbitration: Landmark Progress in the Acquisition of Territorial Sovereignty and Equitable Maritime Boundary Delimitation', *IBRU Boundary and Security Bulletin* 8, no. 1 (2000): 66–86.

Li, Jinming and Li, Dexia, 'The Dotted Line on the Chinese Map of the South China Sea: A Note', *Ocean Development and International Law* 34 (2003): 290.

O'Connell, D.P., *The International Law of the Sea* (Oxford: Clarendon Press, 1982).

Surya P. Sharma, *Territorial Acquisition, Disputes and International Law* (The Hague: Martinus Nijhoff, 1997)

Song, Yann-huei and Kien-hong Yu, Peter, 'China's "Historic Waters" in the South China Sea: An Analysis from Taiwan, R.O.C.', *The American Asian Review* 12 (1994): 91.

Tseng, Huan-Sheng and Ou, Ching-Hsiewn, 'The Evolution of the Traditional Fishing Rights', *Ocean and Coastal Management* 53 (2010): 277.

United Nations, Office for Ocean Affairs and the Law of the Sea, *The Law of the Sea: Maritime Boundary Agreements (1970–1984)* (New York: United Nations, 1987).

United Nations, Office for Ocean Affairs and the Law of the Sea, *The Law of the Sea: Maritime Boundary Agreements (1985–1991)* (New York: United Nations, 1992).

Zou, Keyuan, 'Implementing Marine Environmental Protection Law in China: Progress, Problems and Prospects', *Marine Policy* 33, no. 3 (1999): 211.

Zou, Keyuan, 'Maritime Boundary Delimitation in the Gulf of Tonkin', *Ocean Development and International Law* 30 (1999): 235–54.

Zou, Keyuan, 'Historic Rights in International Law and in China's Practice', *Ocean Development and International Law* 31 (2001): 162.

Chapter 12
Legal Framework for Joint Development in the South China Sea[1]

Robert Beckman

Introduction

The features in the South China Sea, especially those in the Spratly Islands, have been a source of tension and potential conflict in the region for many years. Some or all the features in the Spratly Islands are claimed by Brunei Darussalam, China, Malaysia, the Philippines, Vietnam and Taiwan.

It is generally assumed that given the number of claimants and the sensitivity of the disputes on sovereignty over the Islands, it will not be possible for the claimants to resolve the disputes through negotiation for the foreseeable future. Further, it is assumed that the claimants will not be willing to agree to refer the sovereignty disputes to an arbitral or judicial tribunal.

Since the 1980s, it has been suggested that the best way to defuse tension in the Spratly Islands is to set aside the sovereignty disputes and jointly develop the resources in and under the waters surrounding the Islands. Deng Xiaoping, the late paramount leader of China, promoted the principle of 'setting aside disputes and pursuing joint development'. This concept was first openly advanced by Deng on 11 May 1979 in relation to China's dispute with Japan over Diaoyu (Senkaku) Islands.[2] He stated that consideration may be given to joint development of the resources adjacent to the Diaoyu Islands without touching upon its territorial sovereignty.[3]

When China entered into diplomatic relations with Southeast Asian countries in the 1970s and 1980s, Deng Xiaoping made the same proposal for resolving disputes over the Nansha (Spratly) Islands, stating:

> The Nansha Islands have been an integral part of China's territory since the ancient times. But disputes have occurred over the islands since the 1970s.

---

1 Note: This chapter is a revised version of a paper presented at the International Workshop on Cooperation & Development in the South China Sea, which was organized by the China Institute of Maritime Affairs in Beijing in August 2011.

2 'Set Aside Dispute and Pursue Joint Development', Statement of Ministry of Foreign Affairs of the People's Republic of China, 17 November 2000, accessed 16 November 2012, http://www.fmprc.gov.cn/eng/ziliao/3602/3604/t18023.htm.

3 Ibid.

> Considering the fact that China has good relations with the countries concerned, we would like to set aside this issue now and explore later a solution acceptable to both sides. We should avoid military conflict over this and should pursue an approach of joint development.[4]

China and the Association of Southeast Asian Nations (ASEAN) have also taken steps that could lead to setting aside the sovereignty and maritime boundary disputes and jointly developing the resources. The 2002 Declaration on the Conduct of Parties in the South China Sea (2002 DOC) was adopted by the Foreign Ministers of ASEAN and the People's Republic of China at the 8th ASEAN Summit in Phnom Penh on 4 November 2002.[5] The 2002 DOC contains provisions on the following: (a) peaceful resolution of the territorial and jurisdictional disputes; (b) self-restraint in the conduct of activities that would complicate or escalate disputes and affect peace and stability; (c) confidence-building measures; and (d) co-operative activities.

In 2011, China and ASEAN agreed on Guidelines for the Implementation of the 2002 DOC.[6] Despite this, little discussion has taken place on setting aside the disputes and jointly developing the resources in the disputed areas.

UNCLOS as a Legal Basis for Joint Development Arrangements

The 1982 United Nations Convention on the Law of the Sea (UNCLOS) establishes a legal framework to govern all uses of the oceans.[7] UNCLOS was adopted in 1982 after nine years of negotiations. It entered into force in November 1994 and has been almost universally accepted. The States making claims to sovereignty over all or some of the islands in the South China Sea – Brunei Darussalam, China, Malaysia, Philippines and Vietnam – are all parties to UNCLOS.[8] Taiwan

4 Ibid.

5 2002 Declaration on the Conduct of Parties in the South China Sea signed at the 8th ASEAN Summit on 4 November 2002 in Phnom Penh, Cambodia, by the Foreign Ministers of ASEAN and the People's Republic of China, ASEAN website, http://www.asean.org/asean/external-relations/china/item/declaration-on-the-conduct-of-parties-in-the-south-china-sea.

6 'Guidelines for the Implementation of the DOC', accessed 16 November 2012, http://biengioilanhtho.gov.vn/eng/TempFiles/Guidelines%20on%20the%20implementation%20of%20the%20DOC.pdf.

7 United Nations Convention on the Law of the Sea, 1833 U.N.T.S. 397, adopted in Montego Bay, Jamaica, on 10 December 1982, entered into force on 16 November 1994. As of 12 November 2012, there are 164 parties, including the European Union.

8 The dates of ratification of the five claimant States are: Brunei Darussalam, 5 November 1996; China, 7 June 1996, Malaysia, 14 October 1996, Philippines, 8 May 1984, and Vietnam, 25 July 1994. UN Treaties Collection, Status of Treaties, accessed 16 November 2012, http://treaties.un.org/.

is not able to ratify UNCLOS because it is not recognized as a State by the United Nations, but it has taken steps to bring its domestic legislation into conformity with UNCLOS.[9]

UNCLOS has no provisions on how to resolve sovereignty disputes over offshore features. However, it does have provisions on maritime boundary delimitation. The UNCLOS provisions on the delimitation of the exclusive economic zone (EEZ) and continental shelf boundaries assume that it will not always be possible to negotiate boundary agreements in overlapping claim areas because of sovereignty disputes or for other historical reasons.

UNCLOS Provisions on Maritime Boundary Delimitation

The UNCLOS provisions on boundary delimitation purport to provide a solution to the fact that it may be extremely difficult for States to reach agreement in areas of overlapping EEZ and continental shelf claims. This solution is found in paragraph 3 of Articles 74 and 83, which provides that if delimitation cannot be effected by agreement:

> [T]he States concerned, in a spirit of understanding and cooperation, shall make every effort to enter into provisional arrangements of a practical nature and, during the transitional period, not to jeopardize or hamper the reaching of the final agreement. Such arrangements shall be without prejudice to the final delimitation.

This provision is designed to 'promote interim regimes and practical measures that could pave the way for provisional utilization of disputed areas pending delimitation' and 'constitutes an implicit acknowledgement of the importance of avoiding the suspension of economic development in a disputed maritime area'.[10]

Obligations Regarding 'Provisional Arrangements of a Practical Nature'

The use of the word 'provisional' implies that the arrangements are interim measures pending the final delimitation of maritime boundaries.[11] It is commonly observed that the use of the term 'arrangements' implies that the arrangement

9 For the action taken by Taiwan to pass legislation claiming maritime zones as provided in UNCLOS, as well as a comparison of the positions of China and Taiwan, see Y.H. Song and Z. Keyuan, 'Maritime Legislation of Mainland China and Taiwan: Developments, Comparison, Implications, and Potential Challenges for the United States', *Ocean Development and International Law* 31 (2000): 310–12.

10 *Guyana v. Suriname*, Award of the Arbitral Tribunal, 17 September 2007, 153, para. 460, accessed 16 November 2012, http://www.pca-cpa.org/showpage.asp?pag_id=1147.

11 R. Lagoni, 'Interim Measures Pending Maritime Delimitation Agreements', *American Journal of International Law* 78 (1984): 356.

can include both informal documents, such as *Notes Verbale*, Exchange of Notes, Agreed Minutes, Memorandum of Understanding, etc.,[12] as well as more formal agreements, such as treaties.[13] With regards to the meaning of 'practical nature', the Article itself does not give much guidance, but has been interpreted to mean that such arrangements 'are to provide practical solutions to actual problems regarding the use of an area and are not to touch upon either the delimitation issue itself or the territorial questions underlying this issue'.[14]

It is clear that there are two aspects to the obligation in Articles 74(3) and 83(3). First, States concerned shall make every effort to enter into provisional arrangements of a practical nature. Second, States, in good faith, shall make every effort not to jeopardize or hamper the reaching of the final delimitation agreement.

The obligation of States to make every effort to enter into provisional arrangements of a practical nature has been succinctly summarized by scholars, based on judicial precedents such as the *North Sea Continental Shelf Cases*:

> The states concerned are obliged "to enter into negotiations with a view to arriving at an agreement" to establish provisional arrangements of a practical nature and … "not merely to go through a formal process of negotiation". The negotiations are to be "meaningful, which will not be the case when either [state] insists upon its own position without contemplating any modification of it". However, the obligation to negotiate does not imply an obligation to reach agreement.[15]

This view was endorsed in the 2007 arbitration between Guyana and Suriname by an Arbitral Tribunal constituted under Annex VII of UNCLOS.[16] While it was acknowledged that the language 'every effort' leaves 'some room for interpretation by the States concerned, or by any dispute settlement body', it imposes on the parties 'a duty to negotiate in good faith'. This requires the parties to take 'a conciliatory approach to negotiations, pursuant to which they would be prepared to make concessions in the pursuit of a provisional arrangement'.[17] Further, the obligation to negotiate in good faith 'is not merely a nonbinding recommendation

---

12 S.P. Kim, *Maritime Delimitation and Interim Arrangements in North East Asia* (The Netherlands: Martinus Nijhoff, 2004): 47. Kim notes that 'some States may prefer MOUs to formal agreements for provisional arrangements because these have some advantages in several aspects: no need to publish them as these are not treaties: no need for elaborate final clauses or the formalities surrounding treaty-making: easy amendment; and no need to be submitted for an approval of the parliament'. See also Lagoni, 'Interim Measures', 358.

13 Kim, *Maritime Delimitation and Interim Arrangements*.

14 Lagoni, 'Interim Measures', 358.

15 Ibid., 356.

16 *Guyana v. Suriname*.

17 Ibid., 153, para. 461.

or encouragement, but a mandatory rule whose breach would represent a violation of international law'.[18]

However, it is clear that States are under no obligation to enter into any provisional arrangement but must only 'make every effort' to negotiate in good faith. Articles 74(3) and 83(3) also leave States with significant discretion as to the type of provisional measures that should be taken.[19]

The obligation to negotiate in good faith appears to include an obligation for States to consult with each other if they intend to carry out unilateral activities in a disputed area and to continue to negotiate even after such unilateral activities take place. In the *Guyana v. Suriname* arbitration, it was found that the parties had breached their obligation to negotiate provisional arrangements of a practical nature pending maritime delimitation of their territorial sea, EEZ and continental shelf boundary. This stemmed from an incident in 2000 where an oil rig and drill ship engaged in seismic testing under a Guyanese concession were ordered to leave the disputed area by two Surinamese vessels. It was found that Guyana had violated its obligation under Article 83(3) as it should have, in a spirit of co-operation, informed Suriname of its exploratory plans, given Suriname official and detailed notice of the planned activities, offered to share the results of the exploration, given Suriname an opportunity to observe the activities, and offered to share all the financial benefits received from the exploratory activities.[20] Similarly, the Tribunal found that when Suriname became aware of Guyana's exploratory efforts in disputed waters, 'instead of attempting to engage it in a dialogue which may have led to a satisfactory solution for both Parties, Suriname resorted to self-help in threatening the oil rig and drill ship in violation of [UNCLOS]'.[21]

The second part of the obligation provides that during this transitional period States are obliged not to jeopardize or hamper the reaching of a final agreement on delimitation. It is said that a court or tribunal's interpretation of this obligation must reflect the delicate balance between preventing unilateral activities that affect the other party's rights in a permanent manner, but at the same time not stifling the parties' ability to pursue economic development in a disputed area during a time-consuming boundary dispute.[22]

International courts and tribunals have found that 'any activity which represents an irreparable prejudice to the final delimitation agreement'[23] is a breach of this obligation and that 'a distinction is therefore to be made between activities of the kind that lead to a permanent physical change, such as exploitation of oil and gas

18 Lagoni, 'Interim Measures', 354.

19 N. Klein, 'Provisional Measures and Provisional Arrangements in Maritime Boundary Disputes', *International Journal of Marine and Coastal Law* 21, no. 4 (2006): 444.

20 *Guyana v. Suriname*, para. 477.

21 Ibid., para. 476.

22 Ibid., para. 470.

23 Lagoni, 'Interim Measures', 366.

reserves, and those that do not, such as seismic exploration'.[24] For example, in the *Guyana v. Suriname* arbitration it was found that allowing exploratory drilling in disputed waters was a breach of the obligation to make every effort not to hamper or jeopardize the reaching of a final agreement, as this could result in a physical change to the marine environment and engender a 'perceived change to the status quo'.[25] This was in contrast to seismic testing, which did not cause a physical change to the marine environment.

Notably, it was also found that Suriname's actions in using the threat of force in getting the Guyana-licensed vessel to leave was not only a breach of its obligation not to jeopardize the final agreement, but also a breach of its obligation not to use force under UNCLOS, the UN Charter and general international law.[26]

Provisional Arrangements are 'Without Prejudice' to the Final Delimitation of Boundaries

The key aspect of provisional arrangements of a practical nature is that they are 'without prejudice' to the final delimitation. The effect of such a feature is that:[27]

- Nothing in the arrangement can be interpreted as a unilateral renunciation of the claim of either party or as mutual recognition of either party's claim.
- The arrangement itself does not create any legal basis for either party to claim title over the area and its resources.
- The States concerned cannot claim any acquired rights from the interim arrangement.
- Final delimitation does not have to take into account either any such preceding arrangement or any activities undertaken pursuant to such arrangement.

Essentially, parties are preserving their claims either to sovereignty over disputed territory or to sovereign rights over the waters surrounding such territory and, at the same time, shelving the sovereignty disputes and the final boundary delimitation.[28]

It is debatable whether it is necessary to have an express 'without prejudice clause' in a provisional arrangement because there is a general 'without prejudice

24 *Guyana v. Suriname*, para. 467.

25 Ibid., para. 480.

26 Ibid., para. 445.

27 As succinctly summarized by Dr Zhiguo Gao in Gao, Z., 'Legal Aspects of Joint Development in International Law', in *Sustainable Development and Preservation of the Oceans: The Challenges of UNCLOS and Agenda 21*, edited by M. Kusuma-Atmadja, T.A. Mensah and B.H. Oxman (Honolulu: Law of the Sea Institute, 1997): 639.

28 H. Fox et al., *Joint Development of Offshore Oil and Gas: A Model Agreement for States with Explanatory Commentary* (Great Britain: British Institute of International and Comparative Law, 1989): 378.

clause' in the final sentence of Articles 74(3) and 83(3). Arguably, 'simply referring to the provisions of Articles 74(3) and 83(3) in an arrangement would be sufficient for preserving the positions of each party on final delimitation, if the parties to the arrangement are also parties to the LOS Convention'.[29] However, it is of course preferable in terms of legal certainty to have an express 'without prejudice clause'. The 'without prejudice' clause in the 1959 Antarctic Treaty is a good example of a 'without prejudice clause':

1. Nothing contained in the present Treaty shall be interpreted as:
   a. a renunciation by any Contracting Party of previously asserted rights of or claims to territorial sovereignty in Antarctica;
   b. a renunciation or diminution by any Contracting Party of any basis of claim to territorial sovereignty in Antarctica which it may have whether as a result of its activities or those of its nationals in Antarctica, or otherwise;
   c. prejudicing the position of any Contracting Party as regards its recognition or non-recognition of any other State's rights of or claim or basis of claim to territorial sovereignty in Antarctica.
2. No acts or activities taking place while the present Treaty is in force shall constitute a basis for asserting, supporting or denying a claim to territorial sovereignty in Antarctica or create any rights of sovereignty in Antarctica. No new claim, or enlargement of an existing claim, to territorial sovereignty in Antarctica shall be asserted while the present Treaty is in force.

The Area to which Provisional Arrangements Apply

Articles 74(3) and 83(3) do not specify the area to which the provisional arrangements apply, although some suggestions and proposals raised during the negotiations of UNCLOS contained references to specific geographical lines or areas.[30] Ranier Lagoni opines that the obligation to negotiate provisional arrangements has a geographical connotation:

> In accordance with the above-mentioned object and purpose of paragraph 3, the obligation applies only to those areas about which the governments hold opposing views. These views must be expressed formally, for example by declarations, or may be implied, for example through protests filed against the acts of other states or foreign nationals, by acts of the national legislator, or by the granting of licenses and concessions.[31]

29 Kim, *Maritime Delimitation and Interim Arrangements*, 53.
30 Lagoni, 'Interim Measures', 356.
31 Ibid.

Types of Provisional Arrangements

As discussed above, Articles 74(3) and 83(3) do not mandate the type of provisional arrangements States can enter into, but leave it to the discretion of the States concerned. State practice shows that provisional arrangements can include a wide variety of arrangements, such as mutually agreed moratoriums on all activities in overlapping areas, joint development or co-operation on fisheries, joint development of hydrocarbon resources, agreements on environmental co-operation, and agreements on allocation of criminal and civil jurisdiction. The next section will explore one type of provisional arrangement, namely, the joint development of hydrocarbon resources.

Provisional Arrangements involving Joint Development in the Spratly Islands

Arguably, the claimant States have an obligation under Articles 74(3) and 83(3) of UNCLOS to make every effort to negotiate, in good faith, provisional arrangements of a practical nature. The claimant States also have an obligation not to undertake unilateral activities which would irreparably damage resources or the interests of other claimants. Such obligations would apply even though negotiations on maritime delimitation have not begun and even though the overlapping claim area has not been defined due to the lack of clarity in both the sovereignty and maritime zone claims of the claimant States.[32]

One type of provisional arrangement that could be agreed upon in the South China Sea is the joint development of hydrocarbon resources and fisheries resources.

Rationale for Joint Development in the South China Sea

There are good reasons why the claimants should make an effort to enter into joint development arrangements in the South China Sea. First, there is unlikely to be a resolution of the sovereignty disputes and maritime delimitation disputes in the immediate or near future.

Second, there are considerable economic incentives for claimants to enter into joint development arrangements. Admittedly, the exact amount of hydrocarbon resources in the South China Sea is unknown and may not be as much as estimated in some accounts. However, the cost of oil is rising and, coupled with shortage in supply, the claimants will want to and may need to exploit every resource possible. The claimants will face considerable difficulties in exploiting any oil in areas that

32 As mentioned above, Lagoni observed that the obligations in Articles 74(3) and 83(3) may arise 'in exceptional situations if no definite claim can be asserted because the principles of delimitation are at issue, or if the delimitation is contingent on the resolution of a dispute over sovereignty of an island'. See Lagoni, 'Interim Measures', 357.

are subject to competing claims, particularly if the exploration and exploitation is done in areas near the disputed features.

Third, joint development arrangements in the South China Sea have the potential to reduce tension and facilitate co-operation between claimants. The disputes relating to the Spratly Islands have been a major irritant, which spills over to other aspects of bilateral and multilateral relations.

Identifying the Area Subject to Joint Development Arrangements

One practical obstacle to any joint development arrangements being negotiated in the South China Sea is that there will have to be agreement on the geographic area or areas that will be subject to joint development and in which claimants will participate in joint development arrangements.

The Philippines and Vietnam have maintained that certain areas of their EEZs are not in dispute because they are close to the coast of their mainland territory or main archipelago and far from any of the disputed islands. Their position is that joint development arrangements must be limited to those maritime areas that are in dispute.

It will be difficult to agree on the areas in dispute and subject to joint development in the Spratly Islands unless agreement can be reached on the status of the geographic features and the maritime zones to which such features are entitled. There is no agreement on which features in the Spratly Islands are 'islands' entitled to maritime zones of their own because they are naturally formed areas of land above water at high tide, as set out in Article 121(1) of UNCLOS. Scholars have estimated that less than one-third of the features in the Spratly Islands are naturally formed areas of land above water at high tide. Furthermore, many of the features, which meet the definition of an island in Article 121(1), are very tiny and might be classified as 'rocks' that cannot sustain human habitation or economic life of their own as provided in Article 121(3) of UNCLOS. If so, such features would not be entitled to an EEZ or continental shelf of their own, but only a 12 nautical mile (nm) territorial sea.

Uncertainty as to the status of the features and the maritime zones they generate could be a serious obstacle to the claimants reaching agreement on the areas in dispute which are subject to joint development. The Philippines maintains that Reed Bank is not an area in dispute because it is a submerged bank, which is part of its continental shelf and is outside the maritime zone that can be measured from any disputed island. Its position seems to be that the disputed features near Reed Bank either do not meet the definition of an island in Article 121 or, if they are islands, they are rocks within Article 121(3) that are not entitled to an EEZ or continental shelf of their own. Therefore, its position is that the Reed Bank area is not an area in dispute and is not to be subject to joint development.

Currently, the only areas that are clearly 'in dispute' in the Spratly Islands are the features that are islands because they are naturally formed areas of land above water at high tide, and the 12 nm territorial sea adjacent to such islands.

One approach to reaching agreement on the area in dispute in the Spratly Islands is to determine the status of all geographic features and the maritime zones to which they are entitled. However, this would be exceedingly difficult to negotiate because the claimants are likely to take positions on the features that favour their national interest. One possible way this could be done is for the claimants to agree to have a neutral third party conduct a study on the status of the various features. However, it would still be difficult to reach agreement because of the ambiguity of the definition of a rock in Article 121(3).

A more fruitful way to reach agreement on the area for joint development arrangements might be for the claimants concerned to enter into serious negotiations to try to reach agreement on the area for joint development. Discussions could begin by focussing on the area where most of the larger islands are located, which is in the northern part of the Kalayaan Island Group (KIG) claimed by the Philippines. All these islands are claimed by China, the Philippines, Vietnam and Taiwan, and all the larger features in this area are occupied by one of those claimants. Therefore, the islands and the 12 nm territorial waters adjacent to them are areas in dispute. In addition, some of these islands are arguably large enough to be entitled to an EEZ of their own, at least in principle. Therefore, the claimants concerned may be able to agree that the maritime zones measured from these disputed islands will overlap with the EEZ claims and extended continental shelf claims of the ASEAN claimants. This area of overlap could be the agreed area in dispute. Vietnam and the Philippines may be amenable to such an approach as it would exclude areas close to their mainland coasts. Such an approach would also be advantageous to China as it could be done without any reference to the nine-dashed line map.

A more cautious approach might be to first attempt to negotiate joint development arrangements in the areas where there are only two claimants. It might be possible for China and the Philippines to agree on a joint development area surrounding Scarborough Shoal. It might also be possible for China and Vietnam to agree on a joint development area in the Gulf of Tonkin, especially since they have been able to negotiate part of the maritime boundary in this area.[33]

33 2000 Agreement between the Vietnam and China on the Delimitation of the Territorial Seas, Exclusive Economic Zones and Continental Shelves of the Two Countries in the Beibu Gulf/Bac Bo Gulf. Article VII provides: 'If any single petroleum or natural gas structure or field, or other mineral deposit of whatever character, extends across the delimitation line defined in Article II of this Agreement, the two Contracting Parties shall, through friendly consultations, reach agreement as to the manner in which the structure, field or deposit will be most effectively exploited as well as on the equitable sharing of the benefits arising from such exploitation'. '2000 Agreement between Vietnam and China', http://biengioilanhtho.gov.vn/eng/TempFiles/Bac%20Bo%20Gulf%20Agreement.pdf.

Recommendations for Moving Forward on Joint Development

On 16–17 June 2011, the Centre for International Law (CIL) at the National University of Singapore organized a Conference on Joint Development and the South China Sea. The Conference brought together international legal experts on joint development, representatives from the oil and gas industry and government officials from the region to examine the law and policy issues relating to the joint development of oil and gas resources in areas of overlapping claims in the South China Sea.

The Report of the Conference makes several recommendations for moving towards joint development in the South China Sea.[34] Although these recommendations are focussed on the Spratly Islands, many of them would be equally applicable to the other areas in dispute in the South China Sea. These recommendations are summarized below.

1. Encourage Claimants to Clarify Claims in Conformity with UNCLOS

At present, there is a significant lack of clarity on the basis, nature and extent of the maritime claims surrounding the Spratly features. It is not clear what maritime zones, if any, are being claimed from the Spratly features by the various claimants. The ASEAN claimants, at least for now, appear to be treating the Spratly features as either 'rocks' entitled only to a 12 nm territorial sea or low-tide elevations that are not entitled to any maritime zone, but they have not expressly stated this.

China's claim from the Spratlys remains ambiguous. While it has recently confirmed that it believes the Spratly Islands are entitled to a territorial sea, EEZ and continental shelf, its nine-dashed line map surrounding the Spratly Islands and covering a large part of the waters of the South China Sea continues to raise suspicions that China is claiming 'historic rights' to explore and exploit the natural resources inside the nine-dashed line.

Clarification of the claims would help the claimants move towards joint development in two ways. First, it would be a step towards clarifying the areas that could be subject to joint development. Until agreement can be reached on which marine spaces in the South China Sea are in dispute and subject to joint development, and which marine areas are not in dispute and will not be subject to joint development, it will be impossible to begin discussions on joint development.

Second, a clarification of the claims would foster an atmosphere of trust and confidence, which is necessary for joint development. Once the nine-dashed line is clarified and the prospect of claims based on historic rights is put to rest, the necessary trust and confidence to pursue joint development will be present.

---

34 'Conference Report for the CIL Conference on Joint Development and the South China Sea', http://cil.nus.edu.sg/wp/wp-content/uploads/2011/06/Report-of-CIL-Conference-on-Joint-Development-and-the-South-China-Sea-2011-04.08.2011.pdf.

2. Increase Knowledge of Features in the Spratly Islands

The number and nature of the features in the Spratlys remain shrouded in mystery. While there are accounts of physical descriptions of some of the features made by geographers and academics, they are not up to date and the accounts are not consistent with each other. The lack of definitive information on the number and nature of the features contributes to the uncertainty and lack of clarity of the claims made by the claimants. It also makes it difficult to identify disputed areas in which joint development can take place. Therefore, there should be further research on the features in the Spratly Islands.

3. Increase Knowledge of Hydrocarbon Resources through Joint Seismic Surveys

While the Spratlys are often referred to as 'oil rich', estimates of hydrocarbon resources differ widely and there is an absence of reliable publicly available data regarding hydrocarbon reserves. Actual knowledge of hydrocarbon resources will enable the claimants to know where the hydrocarbons are located and, hence, assist in identifying areas that could be suitable for joint development.

Joint seismic surveys between some or all the claimants conducted on a 'without prejudice' basis in areas that are clearly in dispute would be a tremendous step towards joint development. The parties to the joint seismic survey should be the claimants that have bona fide claims made in good faith to the area in which the survey will be taking place. It should also involve all claimants that have claims in that area so as to avoid protests and persistent challenges. The agreement for the joint seismic survey should have robust 'without prejudice' clauses to allay concerns of States and their national populations.

4. Implement the 2002 DOC

The 2002 DOC was an important milestone as it set down a series of conflict avoidance mechanisms, such as mutual restraint and co-operative activities designed to build confidence between parties. The co-operative activities that the parties are encouraged to undertake are marine environmental protection, marine scientific research, safety of navigation and communication at sea, search and rescue operations and combatting transnational crime. These are arguably less controversial than joint development of hydrocarbon resources and hence, may be easier to reach agreement on. Small incremental steps such as these will help foster the goodwill and trust necessary for discussions on joint development.

5. Enhance Understanding on Nature and Importance of Joint Development Arrangements

There appears to be a lack of understanding in some countries on the nature of joint development arrangements, particularly that joint development can be done without compromising the sovereignty claims of the claimants. Seminars, workshops and meetings can be organized by think-tanks and research institutes on a Track 2 basis so as to enhance understanding of joint development arrangements. Given the role of the media in fanning the flames of nationalism, some of the sessions should include members of the media.

6. Better Management of Domestic Politics and Nationalistic Rhetoric

The Spratly Islands have become potent symbols of nationalism for the populations of the claimants. Accordingly, the public often perceives its government as weak if it fails to aggressively assert its claims over the Spratlys. This makes it difficult for the claimants to make reasonable compromises in negotiations without being accused of surrendering their sovereignty. This is a major obstacle to any joint development agreement in the South China Sea (and any peaceful settlement of the disputes for that matter).

Accordingly, the governments of the claimants and the media have a significant role to play in managing domestic politics and nationalist rhetoric associated with the Spratlys. First, governments and the media can refrain from stoking national sentiments when incidents occur that are perceived as a threat to national sovereignty. Second, the governments can avoid taking extreme positions that are difficult to back down from. Third, the governments can educate the public on the benefits and importance of joint development and the fact that it does not involve a surrender of sovereignty. Last, the governments should be as transparent as possible or, at the very least, give the appearance of transparency, in any negotiations relating to joint development.

7. Greater Discussion on Appropriate Institutional Framework for Discussion and Negotiations

There is a lack of agreement on the appropriate institutional framework for discussion and negotiations on joint development. There appears to be a lack of agreement between claimants on the forum where such issues should be discussed and on who should be included in the discussions. The confusion on the proper forum is exacerbated by China's insistence that sovereignty disputes and competing claims be discussed bilaterally between individual claimants and by the actions of some ASEAN claimants to organize conferences and workshops that appear to be intended to internationalize the issues. There also seems to be some confusion on the role of ASEAN in the Spratly disputes.

ASEAN can provide a forum for discussion between the claimants without it becoming a dispute between the ASEAN claimants and China. In fact, there is little likelihood that ASEAN will have a common position since the non-claimant members view the issues differently than the claimants. Once the claims of all the claimant States have been clarified, all the claimants should be able to agree that there are areas in the EEZs of the ASEAN claimant States that are not in dispute and are not subject to joint development. While it may be difficult to reach a formal agreement clarifying the areas not in dispute, such a consensus can be achieved by State practice. For example, if the Philippines licenses a company to do a seismic survey in an area of its EEZ and none of the other claimants protest when the survey is done, they will have impliedly agreed that the area in question is solely within the EEZ of the Philippines.

8. Involve Oil Companies in the Discussions

Oil companies (both state-owned and privately owned) have a significant role to play in facilitating joint development in the South China Sea. They are the contractors who will ultimately be carrying out exploration and exploitation and will be providing considerable capital input. They have the potential to exert influence on States to enter into a joint development arrangement in order to ensure political and legal certainty for their investment.

A more indirect way for oil companies to facilitate joint development is through education and dialogue with the claimants on the benefits of joint development and on technical matters related to joint development (such as licensing regimes, petroleum laws, safety of installations, etc.). This would not only enhance understanding on joint development, but would also improve the lines of communication between the claimants and oil companies.

9. Do Research on Joint Development Regimes Suitable for the South China Sea

While examining common provisions in existing joint development arrangements in Asia was useful for setting out the issues and considerations that need to be addressed in any joint development arrangement, it also demonstrated that each situation is unique and that the terms of any joint development agreement will depend on the needs and circumstances of the States at the time. Accordingly, it would greatly move forward joint development if more research was done on joint development regimes that would specifically be suitable for the South China Sea.

If the claimants were to actually see *how* and/or *on what terms* joint development can be done in real terms (as opposed to the abstract way joint development has been discussed to date), it would significantly increase the chances of them coming to an agreement on joint development. While the joint development regime put forward would not bind the claimants in any manner, it would provide an excellent starting point for negotiations.

Conclusions

The sovereignty disputes in the Spratly Islands are intractable and are unlikely to be resolved in the foreseeable future. Another extremely difficult problem is the status of the features in the Spratly Islands and the maritime zones those features can generate. Given these obstacles, it is unlikely that the States concerned will be able to reach agreement on the maritime boundaries in the Spratly Islands.

Nevertheless, the claimant States have obligations under UNCLOS to make every effort to enter into provisional arrangements of a practical nature pending final agreement on maritime boundaries. Furthermore, until the sovereignty and boundary issues are finally resolved, the claimants have an obligation not to take any measures in the areas of overlapping claims that would jeopardize or hamper the reaching of a final agreement on the boundaries. The provisional arrangements of a practical nature include the cooperative measures called for in the 2002 DOC. More importantly, they include the measure called for by the late Deng Xiaoping of 'setting aside disputes and pursuing joint development'.

It is in the interests of all the claimants to begin discussion on provisional arrangements of a practical nature concerning joint development of the resources in the Spratly Islands. Such arrangements would be without prejudice to the sovereignty claims or the final determination of the maritime boundaries. They would be in the common economic interests of the claimants and would further mutual trust and confidence in the region.

One major obstacle to agreement of provisional arrangements concerning joint development in the Spratly Islands is the lack of consensus on the precise geographic areas that would be subject to joint development. This problem is exacerbated by the fact that the claimants have fundamental differences over the appropriate forum for addressing these issues. China argues for bilateral negotiations and the ASEAN claimants argue for negotiations between China and ASEAN.

There may be a 'middle way' of going forward to define the areas in dispute. As stated earlier, the area that seems to be the most obvious candidate for joint development is centred in the KIG group where the largest islands (with the exception of Taiwan-occupied Itu Aba) are claimed and occupied by China, the Philippines and Vietnam. If these three claimants could begin serious discussions on defining the areas in dispute, it would be a major step forward. If the focus of the negotiations was to reach a consensus on the area of overlapping claims surrounding the larger islands, and define it as the area in dispute that is subject to joint development by the three States (and possibly Taiwan), it would go a long way towards finding an amicable solution. An advantage to such an approach is that it would enable the parties to completely avoid discussing the nine-dashed line map or China's right to undertake activities in certain areas in the EEZ of the other two claimants.

Another approach would be to first attempt to negotiate joint development arrangements in the areas where there are only two claimants. It might be possible for China and the Philippines to agree on a joint development area surrounding Scarborough Shoal. It might also be possible for China and Vietnam to agree on a joint development area in the Gulf of Tonkin, especially since they have been able to negotiate part of the maritime boundary in this area.

If the claimant States are able to generate the necessary political will to take the steps required to move towards joint development, it will be a major step in managing potential conflicts in the region.

References

'Conference Report for the CIL Conference on Joint Development and the South China Sea'.

Declaration on the Conduct of Parties in the South China Sea, signed at the 8th ASEAN Summit on 4 November 2002 in Phnom Penh, Cambodia, by the Foreign Ministers of ASEAN and the People's Republic of China, ASEAN website, http://www.asean.org/asean/external-relations/china/item/declaration-on-the-conduct-of-parties-in-the-south-china-sea.

Fox, H., McDade, P., Reid, D.R., et al., *Joint Development of Offshore Oil and Gas: A Model Agreement for States with Explanatory Commentary* (Great Britain: British Institute of International and Comparative Law, 1989).

Gao, Z., 'Legal Aspects of Joint Development in International Law', in *Sustainable Development and Preservation of the Oceans: The Challenges of UNCLOS and Agenda 21*, edited by M. Kusuma-Atmadja, T.A. Mensah and B.H. Oxman (Honolulu: Law of the Sea Institute, 1997): 639.

'Guidelines for the Implementation of the DOC', accessed 16 November 2012, http://biengioilanhtho.gov.vn/eng/TempFiles/Guidelines%20on%20the%20implementation%20of%20the%20DOC.pdf.

Guyana v. Suriname, Award of the Arbitral Tribunal, 17 September 2007, 153, para. 460, accessed 16 November 2012, http://www.pca-cpa.org/showpage.asp?pag_id=1147.

Kim, S.P., *Maritime Delimitation and Interim Arrangements in North East Asia* (The Netherlands: Martinus Nijhoff, 2004).

Klein, N., 'Provisional Measures and Provisional Arrangements in Maritime Boundary Disputes', *International Journal of Marine and Coastal Law* 21, no. 4 (2006): 444.

Lagoni, R., 'Interim Measures Pending Maritime Delimitation Agreements', *American Journal of International Law* 78 (1984): 356.

'Set Aside Dispute and Pursue Joint Development', Statement of Ministry of Foreign Affairs of the People's Republic of China, 17 November 2000, accessed 16 November 2012, http://www.fmprc.gov.cn/eng/ziliao/3602/3604/t18023.htm.

Song, Y.H. and Zou, K., 'Maritime Legislation of Mainland China and Taiwan: Developments, Comparison, Implications, and Potential Challenges for the United States', *Ocean Development and International Law* 31 (2000): 310–12.

United Nations Convention on the Law of the Sea, 1833 U.N.T.S. 397, adopted in Montego Bay, Jamaica, on 10 December 1982, entered into force on 16 November 1994.

Chapter 13
State Practice of UNCLOS in the South China Sea[1]

Nong Hong

State practice is a broad and flexible term. It includes such matters as legislation enacted by national parliaments, instances on the practical enforcement of such legislation by national authorities, decisions of domestic courts, statements made by Government ministers and their legal advisers as to what they believe international law on a particular question to be, diplomatic correspondence between states, protest by states against the acts of other states that are considered to infringe international law, and so on.[2] State practice may also be considered to have a broader sense and includes treaties and collective state actions within international organizations.[3]

State practice in ocean affairs over more than four decades, which was accelerated by the UNCLOS III process, has complicated relations among Southeast Asian states considerably, and between China and the ASEAN states. The semi-enclosed South China Sea (SCS) is now covered by actual claims by littoral states to exclusive economic zones (EEZ) or the Continental Shelf (CS), creating or exacerbating disputes over boundaries and resources. The approaches which the SCS claimants take to jurisdictional and functional issues with which the law of the sea process is concerned – sovereignty, sovereign rights or jurisdiction in the Territorial Sea (TS), EEZ and CS; navigation rights in the TS and EEZ and through international straits; access to fisheries, petroleum exploration and exploitation, and marine research; pollution control; access to deep seabed resources – have implications both within and beyond the region for cooperation or conflict.

This chapter addresses both the legal and political impact of state practice. There are various ways in which state practice could have a legal impact on

---

1 This chapter is revised based on the author's work from Chapter 4 of Nong Hong, *UNCLOS and Ocean Dispute Settlement: Law and Politics in the South China Sea* (Abingdon and New York: Routledge, 2012).

2 See further M. Akehurst, 'Custom as a Source of International Law', *BYIL*, 47 (1974–5): 1–53 at 1–11; M.E. Villiger, *Customary International Law and Treaties*, 2nd edn (The Hague: Kluwer Law International, 1997), 16–28.

3 Robin R. Churchill, 'The Impact of State Practice on the Jurisdictional Framework Contained in the LOS Convention', in Alex G. Oude Elferink (ed.) *Stability and Change in the Law of the Sea: The Role of the LOS Convention* (Leiden: Martinus Nijhoff, 2004), 92.

UNCLOS. First, it could be used as an element in interpreting the Convention. Second, state practice could give rise to a new rule of customary international law modifying or supplementing the Convention. Third, inconsistent state practice may have various possible legal consequences not falling into either of the previous two categories.[4] In this chapter, the attitude towards international law, participation in UNCLOS negotiation, maritime legislation, and dispute settlement practice of relevant states will be considered in turn to elaborate the practice of littoral states of the SCS.

Attitude towards International Law

This section explores the Asian attitude towards international law, in particular that of China and other Southeast Asian states involved in the SCS dispute. It is important to examine how the concept of international law is interpreted in different political cultures, and to what extent international law is considered important in the practice of dispute settlement, if we wish to answer the question of whether UNCLOS plays a positive role in SCS dispute resolution.

China

Modern international law has its origin in Christian civilization. It emerged from the natural law tradition of Western Europe and was confined originally to those states. After the nineteenth century, China gradually accepted the norm of international law[5] and utilized it for protecting its national interests in international relations.[6] However, after the founding of the PRC, its attitude towards traditional international law changed.[7] In accordance with the orthodox Marxist point of view, international law is the instrument of bourgeois nations to perpetuate their favoured position in the world.[8] 'All States attempt to utilize international law to cloak their foreign policy with the mantle of legality.'[9] The PRC is not an exception. Writers in the PRC spoke more frankly on this point than Western scholars.[10] The purpose of international law education in political science and law departments is to train incumbent political-legal cadres and teachers in the way of Marxism-Leninism.[11]

4 Ibid., 93.

5 Byron N. Tzou, *China and International Law: The Boundary Dispute* (New York: Praeger, 1990), 7.

6 Ibid.

7 Ibid.

8 Ibid.

9 Text in White Paper 1, 98–107.

10 See 'China's Note to India of July 10 1958', White Paper 1, 60–62.

11 Peter Cheng, *A Chronology of the People's Republic of China: From October 1 1949* (Totowa: Rowman & Littlefield, 1972), 34.

The PRC's foreign policy has been influenced by a mixture of traditional culture, political reality, nationalism and Marxist-Leninism, among which nationalism has been the most important element.[12] It is the common feeling of the Chinese that their country was reduced to the status of a semi-colony after the middle of the nineteenth century.[13] China was forced to cease and lease territories, to give up maritime customs, salt tax, and other economic and industrial privileges, to grant extraterritorial jurisdiction, and to accept foreign troops in its territory.[14] It is understandable that both the Republic and Communist China's basic foreign policy have been striving for political independence, territorial integrity, and equity with other nations.[15]

To achieve these goals, the PRC urged that the proletarian science of international law based on 'the principles of peace and democracy' should be established to serve its national interests.[16] The PRC believes that international law possesses a strong character of class. Bourgeois international law serves the interests of the bourgeoisie only. Thus, the PRC as a socialist country should develop a new science of international law to serve its own foreign policy, and refuse to accept certain norms of Western international law. The Chinese proposed a new definition of international law. They offered a new theory of territorial changes and put it into practice while concluding the Sino-Burmese Boundary Treaty.[17] They suggested that nations in the process of forming states should be subjects of international law.

Although there are differences among socialist theoreticians, essentially contemporary international law is the law for the historical period of coexistence. It consists of rules and norms created by various means of agreements among the clashing wills of socialist and capitalist states and has 'a general democratic character'.[18] Initially, in the 1950s, Chinese scholars also followed the Soviet definition. The Sino-Soviet split, the decline of the study of international law in China from the late 1950s until the late 1970s, and the absence of scholarly publication in the field from 1965 to 1979 meant that there was uncertainty concerning the position taken by Chinese scholars and that they had nothing to contribute during that period.[19]

The PRC proposed the 'Five Principles of Peaceful Coexistence'[20] as a basic border policy. Of the five principles, the principle of sovereignty ranks first for

12 Tzou, *China and International Law*, 7.

13 Ibid.

14 Ibid.

15 Ibid.

16 Ibid.

17 Ibid., 16.

18 Ibid., 29.

19 Ibid., 30.

20 The Five Principles of Peaceful Coexistence were first put forth by Premier Zhou Enlai of China at the start of negotiations that took place in Beijing from December 1953

China. According to China, sovereignty can be interpreted as independence and includes the internal powers of independence (such as legislation, establishment of national system, etc.) as well as its external powers (such as freedom to deal with international affairs, participation in international conferences and signing treaties).[21] Strict adherence to the principle of inviolability of sovereignty has become a distinctive feature of foreign policy of the PRC and is treated as the basis of international relations and the cornerstone of the whole system of international law.[22] Thus, China's external powers are inherent in its principle of sovereignty; therefore, China does not allow any violation or infringement of its sovereignty and independence, which is justifiable if we look back at the bitter Chinese history when the weak China was bullied by the Western powers in the nineteenth and the early twentieth centuries. Sovereignty guarantees complete independence in political, economic and other areas. When a state is independent, it can exercise jurisdiction over its controlled territory as well as over its citizens. Based on these essential elements of sovereignty, aggression and intervention are illegal in China's view.[23] Chinese scholars are of the opinion that although some forms of intervention were allowed in traditional international law, such as intervention by rights and humanitarian intervention, modern international law has prohibited all forms of intervention.[24] In practice, China strongly opposes any intervention from other countries. This is well illustrated by its stand in opposing any intervention from external players on the SCS dispute. And this is why China insists on its position in the SCS, a part of which it regards as its jurisdictional waters.

Other than the above analysis on China's attitude towards international law, one should never neglect the very strong realist view of International Relations (IR) in China, which has a strong influence on China's security analysts. Realists are the great sceptics about international law. E.H. Carr argued that law within states was a reflection of the 'policy and interests of the dominant group in a given state at a

---

to April 1954 between the Delegation of the Chinese Government and the Delegation of the Indian Government on the relations between the two countries with respect to disputed territory. Later, the Five Principles were formally written into the preface to the 'Agreement Between the People's Republic of China and the Republic of India on Trade and Intercourse Between the Tibet Region of China and India' concluded between the two sides. Since June 1954, the Five Principles were contained in the joint communique issued by Zhou Enlai and Prime Minister Jawaharlal Nehru of India, and have been adopted in many other international documents. As norms of relations between nations, they have become widely recognized and accepted throughout the region.

21 Bai Guimei, 'Basic Rights and Obligations of the State', in Wang Tieya (ed.) *International Law* (Beijing: Law Press, 1995), 107–8 (in Chinese).

22 J.A. Cohen, 'Attitudes toward International Law', in J.A. Cohen (ed.) *Contemporary Chinese Law: Research Problems and Perspectives* (Cambridge, MA: Harvard University Press, 1970), 287.

23 Keyuan Zou, *China-ASEAN Relations and International Law* (Oxford: Chandos Publishing, 2009), 27.

24 Guimei, 'Basic Rights and Obligations of the State', 113.

given period'.[25] Consequently, law could not 'be understood independently of the political foundation on which it rests and of the political interests which it serves'.[26] By implication, law is fundamentally political and the content of international law is determined by dominant states and will not be upheld when it conflicts with their perceived political interests. It is deployed by these states for their ends, against subordinate or weaker entities and in this respect cannot be uncoupled from politics. International law is thus not enforceable independently of the will of powerful states, and cannot be regarded as binding.

And on the historical side, it is necessary to look closely at the very hierarchical thinking of world order and power structure, which have had, and will have influence on Chinese thinking on international law as it is emerging as a global power. With China's involvement as a mediator in many international issues in recent years, international law has become a more and more important tool and concept for Chinese government in dealing with many global problems.

> China faces a dilemma in the study of international law: on the one hand, it realizes that international law is developing with the globalization of the world community and new branches have emerged, such as law relating to human rights and environmental protection. On the other hand, it seems that China is not ready fully to respond to such new developments, particularly in the field of human rights law.[27]

ASEAN

This subsection focuses on two countries of ASEAN – Vietnam and Indonesia – which are two interesting representing countries of this regional organization. Indonesia has been playing a leadership role within ASEAN from ASEAN's formation and its functional operation, while Vietnam is a latecomer after being excluded by other Southeast states due to its invasion of Cambodia. Another reason for selecting these two countries is based on the nature of their claims in the SCS. Indonesia is the only state, among other disputants, that did not occupy any islands or other features of the Spratly Islands. Vietnam, on the other hand, has occupied the majority of the Spratlys features, thus being considered the major ASEAN competitor with China.

Vietnam

Historically, the Vietnamese legal tradition is derived from that of the Chinese and French, to which since the Second Indochina War the Democratic Republic of

---

25 E.H. Carr, *The Twenty Years' Crisis, 1919–1939: An Introduction to the Study of International Relations*, 2nd edn (London: Macmillan, 1946), 176.

26 Ibid., 179.

27 Keyuan Zou, *China's Legal Reform: Towards the Rule of Law* (Leiden and Boston: Martinus Nijhoff, 2006), 248.

Vietnam (DRV)/Socialist Republic of Vietnam (SRV) has added an emphasis on Soviet scholarship. In their approach to the issues addressed here, the Vietnamese use the ideologically based socialist concept of a contemporary international law, which developed as a result of fundament changes wrought by the 1917 Russian Revolution.[28]

The socialist concept of contemporary international law emphasizes state sovereignty, the equality of states and self-determination of peoples, all of which Vietnam particularly insists upon as both a socialist and newly independent developing state. Further, it emphasizes the peaceful settlement of disputes, non-interference in internal affairs, and prohibition of the threat and use of force.[29] Vietnam shares the preference of other socialist and developing states for normative development of international law without compliance mechanism,[30] an approach that is reflected in the SRV's positions on law of the sea issues.

It is not surprising that as the unified country emerged to participate in the international community, the leaders of the SRV would perceive international law as fitting into the ideological framework of the three revolutionary currents.[31] As one Vietnamese analyst put it, contemporary international law was developing in an increasingly positive fashion under the impetus provided by the socialist states and, with the historic worldwide success of the national liberation movement, by the non-aligned states.[32]

In the Vietnamese law journal *Luat Hoc*, UNCLOS III was described as a struggle between aggressive, exploitative capitalist states, in particular the imperialist United States, on one hand, and socialist and developing countries and the 'progressive forces' in the world, on the other. The signing of the Convention was judged a 'big victory', primarily for newly 'independent and socialist countries'.[33]

International law is perceived by the Vietnamese as having political and ideological utility, as having public relations and symbolic value, and as providing a mechanism for the attainment of foreign policy goals.[34] At one level, they have used international law in a pragmatic fashion to further and support

28 Luu Van Loi, 'Le Sud Est asiatique: un point chaud du globe au cours de l'histoire de ces quarante dernieres annees', *Bulletin de droit* (Hanoi), 1 (1985): 21.

29 Tunkin, Grigory, ed. *Contemporary International Law* [Translated from the Russian by G. Ivanov-Mumjiev], pp. 277–87.

30 Antonio Cassese, *International Law in a Divided World* (Oxford: Clarendon Press, 1986), 114–15 and 121.

31 Epsey Cooke Farrell, 'The Socialist Republic of Viet Nam and the Law of the Sea: An Analysis of Viet Namese Behaviour within the Emerging International Oceans Regime', PhD dissertation, 1997, 46.

32 Van Loi, 'Le Sud Est asiatique', 21.

33 Le Quoc Hung, 'Luat Bien Va van De Bao Ve Moi Truong Bien' [The Law of the Sea and the Problem of the Protection of the Marine Environment], *Laut Hoc* (Hanoi), 3 (1979): 38–43 and 51; and Pham Giang, 'Cong Uoc Moic Ve Luat Bien Nam 1982' [The New 1982 Convention on the Law of the Sea], *Luat Hoc*, 1 (1983): 20–31.

34 Farrell, 'The Socialist Republic of Viet Nam', 46.

external policies. At another, the SRV has dealt in moralistic generalities aimed at embarrassing Western capitalist states and at helping to move the world in the desired direction. Because they feel so ambivalent towards the UN, the Vietnamese use it as a forum for their views while continuing to excoriate the organization for not living up to the Charter's principles in general or towards the Indochinese states in particular.[35] In their writing, the Vietnamese have emphasized the broad principles contained in the UN Charter and expressed in certain UN resolutions as well as in the 1975 Helsinki final Act, regardless of whether they have political rather than legal effect, as providing a basis for future relationships and for the settlement of disputes in Southeast Asia.[36] Because they perceive themselves as the victims of so many wars of aggression and as so in need of security, the Vietnamese have envisioned multiple political or legal acts within this framework, even though their significance may be only symbolic. In particular, the Vietnamese have advocated coexistence through bilateral nonaggression pacts or pacts between the Indochinese states and ASEAN. They blamed Chinese sabotage and 'possible mistrust among some parties' for the unwillingness of other Southeast Asian states to sign nonaggression pacts, which embodied mutual respect for independence, sovereignty and territorial integrity, and for non-interference in the internal affairs of the other.[37]

The Vietnamese, however, remain sceptical concerning the utility of international law in controlling aggression. Experience tells them, according to analyst Luu Van Loi, that the role of international law in interstate relations should not be overestimated.[38] In principle, any state, which has accepted the principles and norms of contemporary international law, must follow them. In practice, however, this is not always the case for all states or for any given state in a particular case. This statement would appear to include socialist states. Ultimately, only the struggle of the forces of peace, democracy and progress among the peoples of the countries concerned can guarantee independence, peace and détente. Legal means are supported by the struggle of the people of Southeast Asia, who in turn are supported by progressive forces worldwide.

Because of their insistence upon state sovereignty and lack of experience in international affairs, the Vietnamese both have created some confusion concerning the status of obligations undertaken by the former South Vietnamese government and have been cautious in undertaking substantive international obligations through multilateral conventions and membership in intergovernmental organizations (IGOs). When acceding to the International Maritime Organization's (IMO)

35 See United Nations General Assembly, *Official Records, 32 d session* (1977), vol. 1, 41–3. The Vietnamese attitude towards the UN has been expressed in numerous addresses at the annual opening of the General Assembly, and elsewhere.

36 See Nhu Ngoc, 'Some Essential Notions about Border Law', *Laut Hoc*, 3 (1978), in *JPRS 72542*, 2 January 1979, 11–19; and Van Loi, 'Le Sud Est asiatique', 24–6.

37 Farrel, 'The Socialist Republic of Viet Nam', 49.

38 Van Loi, 'Le Sud Est asiatique', 26–7.

Convention in 1984, the SRV made a declaration that its consideration of activities under the organization would be based on state sovereignty.[39] The SRV's 1980 accession to the Seabed Treaty[40] contained a reservation that no treaty provision should be interpreted as contradicting the rights of coastal states with regard to their continental shelves, including the right to take security measures.[41]

Like its socialist counterpart, China, Vietnam is very conservative on the role of the third party compulsory dispute settlement mechanism under Part XV of UNCLOS, though it has not made a declaration in accordance with Article 298 of UNCLOS to exclude relevant disputes from compulsory procedures.

Indonesia

While international treaties function as a catalyst for legal and administrative development in Indonesia, Indonesian law, or Indonesian legal philosophy, has in one way or another also found its way to international fora and international documents. A number of very basic international principles of government, laid down in the preamble of the 1945 Constitution, are recognized in the Ten Principles (Dasasile) of the 1955 Asian-Africa Conference at Bandung.[42] They must be respected in the course of international cooperation between (at least the Asian-African) states.

While international law has very much influenced Indonesia's political history in the past, and continued influencing Indonesia's law after the Proclamation of Independence in 1945, it seems to have a particular effect on the development of new bureaucratic legislation and administration law, as well as international business law and the development of private international law in principle.[43] One feature of the effect of international law on Indonesian law is the fact that domestic law tends to be superseded by international law, for instance in the case of the Investment Guaranteed Agreement vis-à-vis the Foreign Investment Law (no. 1 of 1967), or the GATT will cause the regulations on export credits to be repealed.[44]

---

39 United Nations Legislative Series (hereinafter UN Leg. Ser.), *Multilateral Treaties Deposited with the Secretary-General, Status as at 31 December 1988* (ST/LEG./SER.E/7), 1989, 539.

40 'Treaty on the Prohibition of the Emplacement of Nuclear Weapons and other Weapons of Mass Destruction on the Seabed and the Ocean Floor and in the Subsoil Thereof'.

41 Stockholm International Peace Institute, *SIPRI Yearbook 1988: World Armaments and Disarmament* (Oxford: Oxford University Press, 1988), 575.

42 Sunaryati Hatono, 'The Interrelation between National Law and International Law in Indonesia', 43, http://books.google.ca/books?id=Er760ECzZiIC&pg=PA35&lpg=PA35&dq=international+law+in+Indonesia&source=bl&ots=Eyxef_NgWx&sig=VTMfkxw1uI4k0fkOZL0ub5lJo7Q&hl=en&ei=CppXSpr0BZC3lAfWlpzjBA&sa=X&oi=book_result&ct=result&resnum=10.

43 Ibid.

44 Ibid.

Although the interaction of national law and international law is still lopsided, it is hoped that in future a more balanced situation may be achieved, when developing countries strengthen their position through the increase of South–South cooperation, and so gain not only self-esteem, but also respect from the 'old' industrialized countries, which will be more ready to accept the transformation of the old colonies from being merely objects of international law to becoming full-fledged subjects of international law.[45]

As other ASEAN states, Indonesia has long adhered to the principle of non-interference and non-intervention as core values of the so-called ASEAN way of dealing with their matters. Some Asian countries accept compulsory jurisdiction of the ICJ, while others do not. However, despite their diverse legal and cultural backgrounds, these countries share identical viewpoints on the dispute settlement mechanisms under UNCLOS.

Participation in UNCLOS Process

All the states in the SCS, except for Cambodia, are party to UNCLOS.

China

China ratified UNCLOS on 15 May 1996, which was considered by the PRC as 'a victory of the long-term struggle of the third world countries for equal maritime right and against the superpowers' maritime hegemony'.[46] The PRC also viewed UNCLOS as part of the establishment of a new international economic order and an important step towards the establishment of the new legal order for the oceans.[47] This helps to explain why the PRC was one of the 119 states that signed UNCLOS the first day the Convention was opened for signature in 1982. However, two major reasons have been given to account for why it took more than 13 years for the PRC to ratify UNCLOS. First, the PRC was not certain about the financial obligations of ratification. Second, the PRC was not entirely satisfied with some of the provisions contained in UNCLOS, in particular, those dealing with innocent passage in the territorial sea (Articles 17–26).[48]

45 Ibid.

46 *People's Daily*, 4 May 1982, as quoted in Zhiguo Gao, 'China and the LOS Convention', *Marine Policy*, 15(3) (1991): 213.

47 See Shen Weiliang and Guangjian Xu, 'The Third UN Conference on the Law of the Sea and the Convention on the Law of the Sea', *Chinese Yearbook of International Law*, 433 (1983) (in Chinese).

48 In addition to those provisions dealing with innocent passage in the territorial sea, reportedly the PRC was not satisfied with the definition of the continental shelf (Article 76), the delimitation of the EEZ and the continental shelf (Articles 74 and 83), and the deep seabed regime (Part XI). See generally Weiliang and Guangjian, 'The Third UN

In the early 1990s, it was also believed that UNCLOS would receive nearly universal acceptance once Part XI was revised in accordance with the developed states' demands. As a result of these developments, the PRC had to consider whether or not to ratify UNCLOS.[49] In 1996, Li Zhaoxing, Vice Minister of Foreign Affairs, presented an explanation before the Standing Committee of the Eighth National People's Congress of the PRC why UNCLOS as a whole was consistent with the PRC position and therefore why it would be beneficial to the PRC if it were ratified. Li listed four principal reasons why the PRC should ratify UNCLOS.[50] First, UNCLOS was conducive to preserving and protecting the PRC maritime rights and interests and to enlarging the PRC's maritime jurisdiction. Second, it was helpful to maintain the substantive status of the PRC as 'a pioneer investor' in deep seabed resource development activities and thus fulfilling the PRC's long-term interests. Third, it would benefit the PRC's participation in those institutions established under UNCLOS[51] and bring the PRC's role in global maritime affairs into full play. Finally, it was useful in shaping a good image for the PRC.[52]

On the other hand, Li also noted four concerns that required consideration.[53] First, there was a discrepancy between the PRC's domestic laws and regulations (namely, the 1958 Declaration,[54] the 1984 Law on Safety of Maritime Transportation,[55] and the 1992 Territorial Sea Law[56] and UNCLOS[57] concerning

---

Conference on the Law of the Sea and the Convention on the Law of the Sea'; see also Yann-Huei Song and Keyuan Zou, 'Maritime Legislation of Mainland China and Taiwan: Developments, Comparison, Implications, and Potential Challenges for the United States', *Ocean Development & International Law*, 31 (2000): 303–45.

49 Song and Zou, 'Maritime Legislation of Mainland China and Taiwan', 308.

50 Ibid.

51 The institutions referred to include the International Seabed Authority, the International Tribunal for the Law of the Sea, and the Commission on the Limits of the Continental Shelf.

52 The PRC official document is on file with the authors.

53 Article 11 of the 1984 Law states that 'foreign vessels for military uses shall not enter into the territorial sea of the People's Republic of China without the permission of the Government of the People's Republic of China'. See also Office of Laws and Regulations, State Oceanic Administration (ed.), *Collection of the Sea Laws and Regulations of the People's Republic of China* (Beijing: Ocean Press, 1991), 283–302.

54 Paragraph 3 of the 1958 Declaration, *supra* note 21, provides that '[n]o foreign vessels for military use and no foreign aircraft may enter China's territorial sea and the air space above it without the permission of the Government of the People's Republic of China'.

55 Article 6 of the 1992 Law provides that '[f]oreign ships for military purposes shall be subject to approval by the Government of the People's Republic of China for entering the territorial sea of the People's Republic of China'.

56 Ibid.

57 Song and Zou, 'Maritime Legislation of Mainland China and Taiwan', 309.

the right of innocent passage for warships[58]). Second, the settlement of maritime boundary problems in the East China Sea between the PRC and Japan could be affected by the provisions in UNCLOS concerning the delimitation of the EEZ and the continental shelf. Third, the SCS issues needed to be taken into account. Although UNCLOS does not apply to the settlement of territorial disputes, its provisions concerning historic waters[59] could be used to strengthen China's rights and interests in the waters adjacent to the Spratly Islands in the SCS. Finally, there were concerns about the dispute settlement processes of UNCLOS. However, Beijing was not required to accept the compulsory procedures provided in UNCLOS for settling disputes involving sovereign rights over the living resources within the EEZ, disputes involving boundary delimitation for the territorial sea, EEZ and continental shelf; disputes involving historic bays; or disputes involving ownership over land or islands. On all these issues, Mr Li recommended that further measures and actions be taken when and after the PRC ratified UNCLOS. On 15 May 1996, the Standing Committee of the Eighth National People's Congress of the People's Republic of China at its 19th session decided to ratify UNCLOS, and at the same time made a declaration.[60]

China has committed itself to develop its domestic laws and regulations on marine affairs in line with UNCLOS and to establish its marine legal system to meet the demands and changed circumstances in the use of oceans.[61] On the other hand, the entry into force of UNCLOS and China's ratification of it also pose a new challenge to be coped with by the Chinese in the resolution of both domestic and international issues regarding the SCS. One Chinese expert on the SCS, for instance, claims that China's ratification of UNCLOS plays a limited role in the

58 Ibid.

59 Article 17 of UNCLOS states that '[s]ubject to this Convention, ships of all States, whether coastal or land-locked, enjoy the right of innocent passage through the territorial sea'.

60 1. In accordance with the provisions of the United Nations Convention on the Law of the Sea, the People's Republic of China shall enjoy sovereign rights and jurisdiction over an exclusive economic zone of 200 nautical miles and the continental shelf; 2. The People's Republic of China will effect, through consultations, the delimitation of maritime jurisdiction boundaries with the states with coasts opposite or adjacent to China respectively on the basis of international law and in accordance with the equitable principle; 3. The People's Republic of China reaffirms its sovereignty over all its archipelagos and islands listed in Article 2 of the Law of the People's Republic of China on the Territorial Sea and the Contiguous Zone which was promulgated on 25 February 1992; 4. The People's Republic of China reaffirms that the provisions of the United Nations Convention on the Law of the Sea concerning innocent passage through the territorial sea shall not prejudice the right of a coastal state to request, in accordance with its laws and regulations, a foreign state to obtain advance approval from or give prior notification to the coastal state for the passage of its warships through the territorial sea of the coastal state.

61 Keyuan Zou, *China's Marine Legal System and the Law of the Sea* (Leiden and Boston: Martinus Nijhoff, 2005), 3.

settlement of the SCS dispute; instead, it is the main and direct source of conflict among the SCS countries.[62]

Amid rising tensions in the seas surrounding China, on 11 May 2009, the Chinese Government submitted to the Commission on the Limits of the Continental Shelf (CLCS) China's Preliminary Information Indicative of the Outer Limits of the Continental Shelf beyond 200 Nautical Miles. The submission deals only with China's claims to the continental shelf in the East China Sea. But the Government reserves the right to submit claims in other areas and challenged the submissions from Vietnam and Malaysia on the continental shelf in the SCS.

Vietnam

At UNCLOS I and II the South Vietnamese generally supported positions congenial to the United States.[63] In addition to security, which was tied to the United States, South Vietnam had a strong interest in the protection of coastal fisheries and a growing interest in the continental shelf and offshore petroleum, as indicated by national legislation and activities. At UNCLOS III, however, as the US military presence ended, South Vietnam cast its lot with the developing countries. This was indicated clearly in the address at the opening of the first substantive session of UNCLOS III in Caracas by Foreign Minister Vuong Van Bac, who stated that 'his country could not forget that it was a developing country and therefore a part of the third world, many of whose ideas it shared'.[64]

The DRV perspective on UNCLOS III was political and ideological and reflected Vietnamese concern with state sovereignty and equality. In substantive terms, its strong interest lay in the maritime boundary issue area. In a subsequently controversial October 1974 interview with a Thai journalist, the editor of *Nhan Dan* stated that at the Caracas UNCLOS session 'big' states wanted to draw big lines and 'small' states small lines for the limits of 'territorial waters'.[65] Limits must be based on equality between large and small states, and 'if the U.S. wants to have 200 miles of territorial water, we also will have that. If she has 20 miles of territorial water, this, too, must be applied to all'.[66] Essentially, what mattered was equal status with the United States and other 'big' states. Apparently, it did not occur to the Vietnamese that it was developing African and Latin American states, regardless of size, which so strongly advocated expansive maritime boundaries.

62 Interview with Dr Shicun Wu, President of the National Institute for the SCS Studies in June 2009.

63 Farrel, 'The Socialist Republic of Viet Nam', 60.

64 UNCLOS III, *Official Records*, 1: 64–5.

65 Farrel, 'The Socialist Republic of Viet Nam', 60.

66 Interview by Thai journalist Phansak Winyarat with *Nhan Dan* editor Hoang Tung in Hanoi carried in the *Nation* (Bangkok), 23 October 1974, and reported in *FBIS-APA*, 23 October 1974, J3.

During this period, the DRV was awaiting both control of the South and departure of the imperialists, as well as the expected conclusion of UNCLOS, before making any claims of its own.[67] At that time, according to *Nhan Dan*'s editor, a conference of Southeast Asian states could be called to settle their maritime boundaries.[68] The desire to settle maritime boundaries and link island disputes with China and Cambodia, in particular, before entering the conference seems quite probable, with the intention of engaging in petroleum exploration providing a strong impetus. Approximately a month after rejecting to UNCLOS III, the DRV had requested maritime boundary negotiation with China in the Gulf of Tonkin because the Vietnamese intended to begin petroleum exploration there.[69] The Vietnamese also had attempted to reach maritime boundary agreements with Democratic Kampuchea up through May 1976. By the time the SRV began to attend UNCLOS, solutions to any boundary or resource disputes with either China or Cambodia appeared increasingly remote. It is also clear that establishing their own legal positions prior to participating in UNCLOS III became essential to the Vietnamese, as the SRV made its declaration on maritime zones immediately before first attending the conference for the 1977 session.[70]

With the fall of the Republic of Vietnam (RVN), most of the legal and technical experience and expertise in law of the sea matters that had developed in South Vietnam became unavailable to the DRV/SRV. There was a small group of French-educated experts in the bureaucracy, however.[71] From articles appearing in *Luat Hov* beginning in 1975, it is evident that the North Vietnamese were following developments at UNCLOS III. These articles dealt with topics under discussion in UNCLOS III, giving historical background, current developments and ideological interpretation on a number of issues. Ideologically, the Vietnamese found it difficult to reconcile the fact that, because the Soviet Union had become a maritime power, it shared a number of interests and positions with the imperialist United States.[72]

Before the 1990s, only one book appeared to have been written on the subject, a 186-page work entitled *Luat Bien* [Law of the Sea], which was written in 1977 by Nguyen Ngoc Minh, who in 1986 was listed as editor of *Luat Hoc* and head of the Institute of Jurisprudence in Hanoi.[73] *Luat Bien* deals with the development of the law of the sea from the 1930 Hague Conference through the fourth session (spring 1976) of UNCLOS III and undoubtedly was written in preparation for

67 The DRV, like other states at the time, expected UNCLOS III to conclude in 1975. See 'Hanoi Reports Conclusion of Caracas Sea Law Conference', Hanoi Radio, in *FBIS-APA*, 30 August 1974, K1.

68 Farrel, 'The Socialist Republic of Viet Nam', 64.

69 Ibid., 86.

70 See the synoptical table in UNCLOS, *Official Records*, 158.

71 'Common Fishing Zone Plan Proposed to S. Vietnam', *The Nation* (Bangkok), in *FBIS-APA*, 3 September 1974, J7.

72 Farrel, 'The Socialist Republic of Viet Nam', 88.

73 Ibid.

Vietnam's entry into the law of the sea process. The book cites numerous French sources and makes frequent reference to Soviet doctrine and practice.[74] In 1990, a 123-page work on the continental shelf was published, which is indicative of the SRV's strong interest in that subject. It is entitled *Them Luc Dia: Nhung Van De Phap Ly quoc Te* [The Continental Shelf: Problems of International Jurisdiction].[75]

As an UNCLOS III participant, the SRV was quick to make political statements.[76] The Vietnamese used the opportunities available to support political positions congenial to the Group of 77 and to the nonaligned movement. They hailed the completed Convention as 'a first step in the establishment of a just and equitable new international economic order',[77] long a tenet of the Group of 77. The SRV has not developed policies concerning nor commented upon all aspects of the law of the sea either in UNCLOS III or elsewhere.[78] Further, statements made publicly in UNCLOS must be treated with some caution as they may be negotiating positions or intended for particular audiences. Nevertheless, it is possible to identify Vietnamese positions in major jurisdictional and functional areas and to give the background to those positions.

Vietnam became the 64th state to ratify UNCLOS, despite the financial burdens of participation. The ratification by the National Assembly on 24 July 1994 indicated that, having weighed the perceived benefits and shortcomings of the Convention, Vietnam believed its law of the sea interests would be better served within the Convention regime shortly to come into force.[79] Ratification also served to further Vietnam's image as a law-abiding state intent upon regional cooperation.

On 7 May 2009, Vietnam submitted to the CLCS information on the limits of the continental shelf beyond 200 nautical miles from the baselines from which the breadth of the territorial sea is measured in respect of the North Area (VNM-N). On 6 May 2009, Vietnam and Malaysia submitted jointly to the CLCS information on the limits of the continental shelf beyond 200 nautical miles from the baselines from which the breadth of the territorial sea is measured in respect of the southern part of the SCS.

---

74 But see the concerns expressed in D. O'Connell, *The Influence of Law on Sea Power* (Manchester: Manchester University Press, 1975), 133.

75 On this point, see Churchill, R. and A. Lowe, *The Law of the Sea* (Manchester: Manchester University Press, 1988), 172. States are allowed to enforce their laws against ships of their own nationality on the high seas. Article 22 of the 1958 Convention on the High Seas and Article 110 of the 1982 CLOS cover ships reasonably believed to be of the same nationality as the inspecting warship, though not flying that flag.

76 R.L. Schreadley (Cdr., U.S. Navy), 'The Naval War in Viet Nam, 1950–1970', *Naval Review* (1971), reprinted in Frank Uhlig, Jr. (ed.), *Viet Nam: The Naval Story* (Annapolis: Naval Institute Press, 1986), 283–5. The Market Time operation was 'the U.S. Navy's first large-scale operational participation in the Viet Namese War' (281).

77 Colonel Duy Duc, 'The Maritime Ho Chi Minh Trail', *Viet Nam Courier*, 6 (1985): 19–20.

78 Farrel, 'The Socialist Republic of Viet Nam', 92.

79 Ibid., 276.

Indonesia

As many other countries, Indonesia considers the Convention as one of the most – if not the most – spectacular achievement of the international community since the singing of the Charter of the United Nations in 1945.[80] For Indonesia, it is also the culmination of its effort during 25 years, to get the principle of the archipelagic state formally accepted as part of the law of the sea by the international community.[81] When Indonesia became independent, the Indonesian territorial waters were regulated by the 'Territorial Zee en Maritieme Kringe Ordonantie 1939' (*Staatsblad* 422).[82] This ordinance established a three-mile territorial sea around each island of the Indonesian archipelago, thereby virtually dividing Indonesia in many parts separated by water, some of which were governed by the regime of the high sea. The provisions on the EEZ and CS in UNCLOS reflect more of Indonesia's national aspirations than previous treaties on the law of the sea. In accordance with the provisions of this Convention, Indonesia, on 12 March 1980, adopted a declaration on the EEZ.

The members of the Group of Archipelagic States during UNCLOS negotiation were Indonesia, Fiji, Mauritius and the Philippines. Generally, their common interest was to ensure that the Convention would recognize the special method of drawing archipelagic straight baselines connecting the outermost points of the outermost islands so as to create a sense of political unity. The territorial sea would be measured seawards from such baselines. Waters landwards from these baselines would be archipelagic waters over which the archipelagic states would exercise sovereignty analogous to internal waters. Specially, their objective was to adopt a common position on passage through archipelagic waters, on claims by neighbouring states for provisions on guaranteed access and communication and on fishing rights.[83]

Under the legitimacy of UNCLOS, as an archipelagic state, Indonesia in 1996 revised the Law No. 4/Prp.1960 with the Law No. 6/1996 on the Indonesian Waters.[84] (The Law No. 4/Prp.1960 announced Indonesian baselines system and how it enclosed the high seas pocket within the Indonesian archipelago. The Law No. 6/1996 was passed on 8 August 1996 in accordance of the law on archipelagic

80 E. Hey and A.W. Koers, *The International Law of the Sea: Issues of Implementation in Indonesia* (Rijswijk: The Netherlands Institute of Transport, 1984), 12.

81 Ibid.

82 Ibid.

83 Myron H. Nordquist (ed.), *United Nations Convention on the Law of the Sea 1982: A Commentary*, vol. I (Dordrecht, Boston and Lancaster: Martinus Nijhoff, 1985), 77–8.

84 See respectively, *Law No.4 Concerning Indonesian Waters 1960* (United Nations The Law of the Sea: Practice of Archipelagic State (New York: United Nations, 1992)); and *Law No. 6 of 1996 concerning the Indonesian Territorial* http://www.gmat.unsw.edu.au/ablos/ABLOS08Folder/Session6-Paper2-Patmasari.pdfWaters (1998) 38 LOSB 32, preamble para. (c) and arts 11–21.

states as contained in Part IV of the UNCLOS.) Indonesia also constructed its new archipelagic baseline, using the new definition of straight archipelagic baseline in UNCLOS, through the GR Number 38/2002 on the Geographical List of Coordinates of the Indonesian Archipelagic Baselines.[85] The law is one of the important instruments to protect Indonesia's territorial integrity. Besides that, it also becomes the basis of the Indonesian sea as a uniting factor of the archipelago. Due to various political developments and some special circumstances, which have occurred and influenced the configuration of Indonesian archipelagic baselines, on 19 May 2008, the Indonesian Government established GR Number 37/2008 that revised the GR Number 38/2002 on Geographical List Coordinates of Indonesia's Archipelagic Baselines.[86]

On 16 June 2008, Indonesia submitted to the CLCS information on the limits of the continental shelf beyond 200 nautical miles from the baselines from which the breadth of the territorial sea is measured relating to the continental shelf of North West of Sumatra Island.

The Philippines

The Philippines has retained its original archipelagic legislation[87] to which accords the waters enclosed by archipelagic baselines that status of internal waters and says nothing about other states' navigational rights therein, although according to a Philippine *note verbale* of 1955[88] there is a right of innocent passage. When ratifying UNCLOS the Philippines made a declaration that the

> Provisions of the Convention on archipelagic passage through sea lanes do not nullify or impair the sovereignty of the Philippines as an archipelagic State over the sea lands and … that the concept of archipelagic waters is similar to the concept of internal waters under the Constitution of the Philippines, and removes straits connecting these waters with the economic zone or high seas from the rights of foreign vessels to transit passage of international navigation.[89]

---

85 Hey and Koers, *The International Law of the Sea*, 12.

86 'The Indonesian Archipelagic Baselines: Technical and Legal Issues and the Changing of Environment', http://www.gmat.unsw.edu.au/ablos/ABLOS08Folder/Session 6-Paper2-Patmasari.pdf.

87 Republic Act No. 3046 of 17 June 1961, as amended by *Republic Act No. 5446 of 18 September 1968* (United Nations, The Law of the Sea: Practice of Archipelagic States, at 75).

88 Philippine *note verbale* of 7 March 1955 to the UN Secretary-General (UN Doc. A/2934 (1955)), reproduced in M.M. Whiteman Digest of International Law (U.S. Department of States, Washington, DC: 1963) vol. IV, 52–3.

89 United Nations, at United Nations, *Multilateral Treaties Deposited with the Secretary-General*, vol. II, 279.

In February 2009, the Philippine Congress passed a bill that spelt out the archipelagic baselines of the Philippines and claimed Huangyan Island (Scarborough Shoal) and Nansha Islands (Spratlys) as 'a regime of islands under the Republic of the Philippines' (known as Republic Act (RA) 9522 or the Philippine Archipelagic Baseline Law). RA 9522 was enacted in time to meet the deadline of UNCLOS for countries and archipelagic states to submit their respective claims to their extended continental shelf, set on 13 May 2009. On 8 April 2009, the Philippines submitted to the CLCS information on the limits of the continental shelf beyond 200 nautical miles from the baselines from which the breadth of the territorial sea is measured in the Benham Rise region.

Practice of Dispute Settlement

This following section will unfold the state practices in terms of dispute settlement in the SCS, in order to present the political culture and context of China and Southeast Asia when addressing international disputes.

China

Ways of peaceful settlement of dispute cover good office, mediation, consultation, negotiation, arbitration, courts, etc. In most cases, China prefers selecting negotiation and/or consultation directly with the other party. This orientation is mostly original from and owing to the Chinese culture and history. China has always advocated bilateral negotiations as the most practical means of dispute settlement between states. In practice, China has resolved several of its bilateral disputes with other countries through negotiation and consultation, such as border disputes and dual nationality, among other issues. So far as judiciary is concerned, China's attitude is very conservative. Thus far, no dispute between China and any other state has been brought to the ICJ or other international tribunals. During the Sino-India border conflict in 1962, China refused India's proposal to submit the dispute to international arbitration by stating that 'Sino-India border dispute is an important matter concerning the sovereignty of the two countries, and the vast size of more than 100,000 square kilometres of territories. It is self-evident that it can only be resolved through direct bilateral negotiations. It is never possible to seek a settlement from any form of international arbitration'.[90] However, after the 1980s, it changed its policy by consenting to arbitration in treaties that it ratified, but confined this only to economic, trade, scientific, transport, environmental and health areas.[91] Some conventions require the contracting states to accept compulsory judicial dispute settlement procedures. For instance, UNCLOS makes

90 Gao,Yanping, 'International Dispute Settlement', in Wang Tieya (ed.) *International Law* (Beijing: Law Press, 1995), pp. 611–612 (in Chinese).

91 Zou, *China-ASEAN Relations and International Law*, 31.

it obligatory for its state parties to select at least one of the compulsory procedures: ICJ, ITLOS, arbitration and special arbitration. Upon ratification of the convention, China did not state which mechanism it had accepted. Therefore, it was deemed to accept the mechanism of arbitration.[92]

Meanwhile, China's perception of the role of international courts in dispute settlement is also passive. In treaties in which it is a party, China has usually made a reservation about the clause of judicial settlement by the ICJ. On 5 September 1972, China declared not to recognize the statement of the former Chinese government on Acceptance of the Compulsory Jurisdiction of the ICJ. In fact, it refused to settle any dispute with other countries through the ICJ.[93] On the other hand, as a UN Security Council member, China has nominated judges of its nationalist to the ICJ as well as to other international courts, such as ITLOS. Since these courts are composed mainly of judges from the West, developing countries, including China, are doubtful about the impartiality and justice the international judiciary can maintain.[94] As for UNCLOS, China declared on 7 September 2006 under Article 298 the exclusion of certain disputes (such as concerning maritime delimitation territorial disputes or military use of the ocean) with other countries from the jurisdiction of international judiciary or arbitration.[95] As one Chinese scholar points out, there is slim hope for China to change its attitude towards third-party forums in the near future with regard to its dispute in the SCS.[96]

Nevertheless, some other international legal scholars in China began to bring to the table the issue of third party compulsory dispute settlement forums. At the 'Symposium on China's Energy Security and the South China Sea', which was held China in December 2004, for example, Yu Jia explained the reasons why China feels reluctant to go to an international court to address its disputes with other countries, especially on claims of sovereignty and maritime jurisdiction. Unlike the assumption from some Western scholars, China' hesitation does not come from the lack of evidence finding in terms of sovereignty claims in the case of its East China Sea and SCS claims. In fact, as the past ITLOS Judge Chan Ho Park pointed out, compared with Vietnam and other SCS countries, China has more historic evidence to show its jurisdiction in the SCS.[97] Yu Jia argued that China's reluctance to accept a third party settlement forum comes from, first of all, the lack of experience in international litigation, and second, the lack of expertise

92 See Article 297(3) of UNCLOS.

93 Yanping, 'International Dispute Settlement', 612.

94 Zou, *China-ASEAN Relations and International Law*, 32.

95 'China's Declaration in Accordance with Article 298 of UNCLOS', 7 September 2006, accessed 6 February 2007, http://www.fmprc.gov.ch/chn/wjb/zzjg/tyfls/wizdtyflgzlzg zhyflydgz/t270754.htm.

96 Interview with Dr Shicun Wu.

97 Interview with Judge Chan HO Park in Shanghai, 2005.

in the international law field with regard to dispute settlement.[98] Apart from the reasons given by Yu Jia, the political culture of China, and many Asian countries – believing that good neighbourly relations will be jeopardized if their difference has to be resolved by a third party involvement – sets the psychological obstacle for pursuing a third party mechanism.

China and the ASEAN countries have been negotiating for years to conclude a code of conduct for the SCS. The DOC is based on a multilateral dimension as well as on a convergence of views on the need to peacefully manage the dispute. With the exception of Vietnam and the Philippines, who feel threatened by China's actions, the problem of sovereignty in the SCS is not regarded as a direct danger to the national security of the individual ASEAN countries. A similar situation of status quo exists on the diplomatic front. China and the ASEAN countries have been negotiating for years to conclude a code of conduct for the SCS. Beijing has preferred a non-binding multilateral code of conduct limited to the Spratlys that would focus on dialogue and the preservation of regional stability rather than on the problem of sovereign jurisdiction.

China has on several occasions used force to consolidate its position in the SCS. In January 1974, China and South Vietnam exchange small-scale fire over the control of the Paracels.[99] A naval confrontation with Vietnam on 14 March 1988 led to recover Chinese 'lost territory', while Vietnam used the term 'seize the territory' to describe this event.[100] Since the Mischief Reef incident, China in its foreign policy has increasingly been acting as a status quo power respecting standard international norms, rather than as a revisionist power seeking to undermine the international order. Shambaugh explains that, both at a bilateral and multilateral level, 'Beijing's diplomacy has been remarkably adept and nuanced, earning praise around the region'.[101] This has been reflected in its actions toward the SCS, as China has not seized disputed features in the Spratlys since the Mischief Reef incident. Even though it expanded its structures on the Reef in November 1998, Beijing's policy towards the SCS has been moderate in recent years in an attempt not to antagonize the ASEAN countries. China's readiness to accommodate the Southeast Asian countries over the SCS can be explained by Beijing's economic priorities as well as by its difficult relations with Japan and its

98 Yu Jia, presentation on the Conference of 'Energy Security and the South China Sea', Haikou, 2004.

99 See Gerald Segal, *Defending China* (Oxford: Oxford University Press, 1985), 197–210.

100 See Shee Poon Kim, 'The March 1988 Skirmish over the Spratly Islands and its Implications for Sino-Viet Namese Relations', in R.D. Hill, N. Owen and E.V. Roberts (eds) *Fishing in Troubled Waters: Proceedings of an Academic Conference on Territorial Claims in the SCS* (Hong Kong: Centre of Asian Studies, University of Hong Kong, 1991), 177–91.

101 David Shambaugh, 'China Engages Asia: Reshaping the Regional Order', *International Security*, 29(3) (Winter 2004/5): 64.

concern over increased US military presence in the region, particularly since the terrorist attacks of 11 September 2001.

On 25 December 2000, China and Vietnam signed an agreement on the delineation of the Tonkin Gulf. After three years of talk, on 29 April 2004, an additional protocol on fishery cooperation in the Tonkin Gulf was signed; two Agreements on delineation of the Tonkin Gulf and an Agreement on fishery cooperation in the Tonkin Gulf entered into effect on 30 June 2004.[102]

In a joint communiqué with Vietnam issued on 8 October 2004, China and Vietnam agreed to strictly follow the SCS Conduct Declaration:[103]

> Both parties agree to strictly follow the consensus reached by the high-level leaders of both governments and the purpose and principles of the Declaration on The Conduct of Parties in The SCS (DOC) signed between China and the member states of ASEAN. The two parties will remain restrained, neither adopting unilateral action which might add to the complexity or expand existing disputes nor resorting to force or threats by force, including not resorting to force against fishing boats. Both sides will take tangible actions to maintain the stability of the SCS.[104]

On 28 August 2007, Chinese Ambassador Liu Zhenmin made a statement on prevention and resolution of conflicts at the Open Debate of the Security Council.[105] He put forward four points on this issue on behalf of the Chinese government:

> Firstly, greater importance should be attached to preventative diplomacy … Secondly, more reform and ingenuity should be encouraged … While dealing with domestic conflicts of a country, it is essential to bring into full play the active role of the government of the country concerned, and the overall objective of the Council in this exercise is to help the national government to establish social stability … Thirdly, coordination and cooperation with regional and sub-regional organizations should be significantly enhanced. It is widely acknowledged that, in recent years, African Union has played an ever more important role in coping with the conflicts in African region on behalf of the international community and made invaluable contributions to maintaining world peace and security … Lastly, more efforts must be made to fully utilize

---

102 Embassy of Vietnam in China website, accessed 29 July 2009, http://www.vnemba.org.cn/en/nr050706234129/.

103 Chen, Qiang, 'Chinese Practice in Public International Law: 2004(II)', *Oxford Journals*, http://chinesejil.oxfordjournals.org/cgi/content/full/4/2/607#SEC4.

104 'China and Viet Nam Issues a Joint Communiqué', www.fmprc.gov.cn/eng/wjdt/2649/t163759.htm.

105 Lijiang Zhu, 'Chinese Practice in Public International Law: 2007(I)', *Oxford Journals*, http://chinesejil.oxfordjournals.org/cgi/reprint/7/2/485.

> the system-wide resources of the United Nations and give full play to the good offices of the Secretary General.

Chinese leaders in many occasions stress the its preferred approach of addressing the SCS dispute. For example, Chinese Premier Wen Jiabao said in Beijing on 3 June 2009 that China and Malaysia should enhance dialogue and cooperation and handle relevant issues in a proper way to jointly safeguard peace and stability on the SCS.[106] China and Vietnam signed an agreement in October 2011 that seeks a peaceful resolution for the dispute. Chinese President Hu Jintao spoke positively about settling the dispute.

Vietnam

Along with other socialist states and a number of other states participating in UNCLOS negotiation, the SRV refused to accept compulsory dispute settlement procedures in delimitation cases. When the Vietnamese co-sponsored NG7/10, they reserved their position on paragraph 2, which called for resort to procedures in Part XV of the Convention if agreement could not be reached within a reasonable period of time.[107] By the spring of 1979 they had 'firmly opposed' any compulsory third party settlement because that would violate 'the principles of the sovereign equality of states'. Any settlement must be 'through agreement of the parties by means of procedures freely chosen by them'. As a compromise, they would consider resort to a conciliation commission whose recommendation would be nonbinding.[108]

Le Kim Chung gave a fuller exposition of the Vietnamese position in a 1980 UN Sixth (Legal) Committee debate on criteria for a general declaration on peaceful settlement of dispute between states. Elaborating on the same points made earlier by Vietnamese UNCLOS delegates and with maritime boundaries obviously in mind, he emphasized that the SRV could not accept compulsory settlement procedures, including ICJ jurisdiction, in disputes involving sovereignty or sovereignty rights. 'In such cases, only the parties themselves would be in a position to appreciate all the sensitive aspects, specific circumstances and particular interest involved; only they would be able to reconcile their positions with a view to reaching an equitable and mutually acceptable solution.'[109] He noted that the UNCLOS proposal on nonbinding conciliation could be a possible solution. Beyond that, only if both parties agreed, could a compulsory procedure be used.

106 *People's Daily Online*, 'China Calls for Dialogue, Cooperation Over South China Sea', 4 June 2009, http://english.peopledaily.com.cn/90001/90776/90883/6671212.html.

107 Farrell, 'The Socialist Republic of Viet Nam', 120.

108 See UNCLOS III, *Official Records*, vol. 11: 13 and 31.

109 United Nations General Assembly, *Official Records*, 35th sess., 1980/1981, vol. 12, Sixth Ctee., 7-8 (Doc.A/C.6/35/sr.43).

Le Kim Chung had already indicated at UNCLOS III ninth session in April 1980 Vietnam's willingness to accept 'in a spirit of compromise' Article 298(1)(a) on dispute settlement procedures.[110] This allows states to declare at any time from signature of the Convention onward that they do not accept any or all of the compulsory dispute settlement procedures, which would entail a binding decision, and which are listed in Part XV, section 2, with regard to disputes concerning delimitation of territorial seas, EEZ, CS, or historic bays or title. While states may make use of nonbinding conciliation procedures if all parties agree, only 'when such a dispute arises subsequent to the entry into force of this Convention and where no agreement within a reasonable period of time is reached in negotiations between the parties' may a state be compelled by the action of the other party to undertake conciliation (under Annex V, section 2). Even then, in practice, the process may end without an agreement.

In the SRV's case, there can be no disputes that all the Vietnamese maritime boundary disputes arose before the Convention will have gone into effect. In any event, under Article 298 no state may be required to submit a dispute to compulsory conciliation if the dispute involves 'the concurrent consideration of any unsettled dispute concerning sovereignty or other rights over continental or insular land territory'. Vietnam's disputes with China, the Philippines, Malaysia and Cambodia all involve such question.

Stretching out along the SCS and having borders with several countries, Vietnam is a country with numerous boundary disputes. In the north, Vietnam has completed maritime delimitation in the Gulf of Tonkin with China. In the south, Vietnam has disputes with Cambodia, Thailand, Malaysia and Indonesia. In the east, there is a conflict over the Paracels and Spratlys.[111] Vietnam holds the position that all disputes should be settled through peaceful means. Concerning this issue, Clause 7 of the 12 May 1977 Declaration of the Socialist Republic of Viet Nam (SRV) on the Territorial Sea, the Contiguous Zone, the EEZ and the Continental Shelf of Viet Nam clearly states: 'The Government of the Socialist Republic of Viet Nam shall, together with the concerned countries through negotiations on the basis of mutual respect of independence and sovereignty, in compliance with international law and practices, resolve the issues relating to the maritime zones and the continental shelf of each side.'[112]

On 29 March 1990, Vietnam and the Philippines exchanged views in Manila about extending bilateral political and economic exchanges, as well as measures

110 UNCLOS III, *Official Records*, vol. 13: 28.

111 Nguyen Hong Thao, 'Viet Nam and the Code of Conduct for the SCS', *Ocean Development & International Law*, 32 (2001): 105–30, at 111.

112 Reprinted in Thao Nguyen Hong, *Le Viet Nam face aux problèmes de l'extension maritime dans la mer de Chine méridionale* (Paris: Septentrion Presses Universitaires, 1997), annex 10, 848–9 and Kriangsak Kittichaisaree, *The Law of the Sea and Maritime Boundary Delimitation in Southeast Asia* (Singapore: Oxford University Press, 1987), annex IV.

for reinforcing security, stability and peace in the region.[113] The Joint Statement on the Fourth Annual Bilateral Consultations between the SRV and the Republic of the Philippines in November 1995 reaffirmed that the two sides 'shall settle all disputes relating to the Spratlys through peaceful negotiations in the spirit of friendship, equality, mutual understanding and respect'.[114] In September 1983, when the troops of Malaysia landed on Swallow Rock, Vietnam and Malaysia agreed to settle their claims over islands, islets and shoals in the SCS through negotiations.[115] Vietnam has supported the 1992 ASEAN Manila Declaration on the SCS. In November 1995, Vietnam signed a document with the Philippines containing eight principles of code of conduct, which incorporates a firm mutual commitment of both states to promoting bilateral and multilateral efforts to find a long-term solution to the various disputes in the SCS.

Yet claimant states have used military means to take control of reefs claimed by other states, and friction over the disputed territories has continued.[116] Tensions have surged between the Philippines and Malaysia, Malaysia and Vietnam, and Vietnam and the Philippines. In March 1999, Malaysia's seizure of Navigator Reef, claimed by the Philippines, strained relations with Manila and was criticized by Vietnam, Brunei and China. In August 2002, Vietnamese troops based on one islet fired warning shots at Philippine military planes. Additionally, some claimants have also used non-military means to protect their interests. In May 2004, Vietnam started re-building a runway on the disputed island of Truong Sa Lon (Big Spratly) with the purpose of sending small groups of Vietnamese tourists to the SCS. China strongly criticized the Vietnamese actions and described them to be in violation of the DOC. In sum, all these initiatives and counter-initiatives have been part of an attempt by the claimant states to secure their presence in the Spratlys.

The Philippines

Compared with its ASEAN counterparts, the Philippines pioneers in leaning for a third party compulsory dispute settlement mechanism. On many occasions, the Philippines has called for the UN to get involved in the settlement of the SCS. Although the United States does not want to get involved in this dispute and does not feel obligated to come to the rescue of the Philippines in its territorial conflict over the Spratlys, there are some indications that US–Philippine security cooperation might be increased. After all, the US security alliance with Manila is among the oldest in the Pacific. And, in 1999, the Visiting Forces Agreement (VFA) between the Philippines and the United States entered into force, making it possible for Washington to resume normal US–Philippine military-to-military

113 *AP du Viet Nam*, 30 March 1990; Nguyen Hong Thao, 'Viet Nam and the Code of Conduct for the SCS', 113.

114 Nguyen Hong Thao, 'Viet Nam and the Code of Conduct for the SCS', 113.

115 BBC, 6 October 1983.

116 http://www.rsis.edu.sg/publications/WorkingPapers/WP87.pdf.

contacts, such as warship visits and joint military exercises. In fact, the two countries held their first large-scale joint exercise since 1993 in February 2000, involving more than 2,500 US military personnel.[117] In the wake of 11 September 2001, the United States and the Philippines have begun to hold joint operations against the Al-Qaeda-linked Abu Sayyaf. In 2011, US Secretary of State Hillary Clinton said the United States would honour its mutual defence pact with Manila and offer the Philippines affordable weapons. Along with this statement, the United States and the Philippines have conducted joint military exercises in the SCS on a regular basis.

Other ASEAN States

Not all the claimants wish to see the United States becoming involved in the resolution of this issue. In contrast to the Philippines' apparent preference for a multilateral and, if necessary, international process of conflict resolution, Malaysia agrees with China that a bilateral solution is the best. Malaysia is also concerned about a PRC announcement of baselines in the SCS and its impact on Malaysia's EEZ and the continental shelf claims.[118] In July 1996, during the PRC–ASEAN dialogue, Malaysia's foreign minister, on behalf of ASEAN, asked the PRC foreign minister to clarify the meaning and implications of the announcement of the baselines for the Paracel Islands.[119]

Indonesia has not been a direct participant in the Spratly Islands sovereignty dispute. However, since 1990 when it organized the unofficial Workshops on Managing Potential Conflicts in the South China Sea (SCS Informal Workshop) attended by the countries of the SCS area, it has played an important role as an 'honest broker'.[120] After the PRC announced its baselines around the Paracel Islands and that the baselines around the Spratly Islands would be set in the future,[121] it has been questioned whether Indonesia can retain its role as 'honest broker' in the Spratly Islands dispute.[122] Should the PRC establish baselines around the Spratly Islands, the PRC could extend its EEZ and the continental shelf to the Natuna Islands area, which is within Indonesia's claimed 200-nautical-mile EEZ. Accordingly, it would be necessary for the two countries to delimit as a maritime boundary an area that is believed to have 'the largest concentration of

117 ASEAN Regional Forum, 2000: 11.

118 Song and Zou, 'Maritime Legislation of Mainland China and Taiwan', 327.

119 *Central Daily News*, 29 May 1996, 2.

120 The 10th Workshop was held in December 1999 in Borgor, Indonesia. Funding has been provided by the Canadian International Development Agency.

121 The 1996 Baseline Declaration. For the Declaration of the Government of the People's Republic of China on the Baselines of the Territorial Sea, 15 May 1996, see *Law of the Sea Bulletin*, no. 32 (1996): 37–40.

122 See Douglas Johnson, 'Drawing into the Fray: Indonesia's Natuna Islands Meet China's Long Gaze South', *Asian Affairs* (1998): 153–61.

gas reserves in the world'.[123] However, there is a belief among Chinese scholars that China does not have any maritime dispute with Indonesia, which is interpreted to have sent a friendly signal to Indonesia authority.

Vietnam, the only claimant to have actually gone to war with China over the Paracels and the Spratlys, has an obvious stake in deterring Chinese military actions, but it has not openly supported US involvement, preferring also to focus on bilateral negotiations and ASEAN's confidence-building processes with China.[124] Meanwhile, China has also tried to play down the significance of its recent territorial assertions, whether through separate bilateral consultations with ASEAN claimants or assurances given to ASEAN as a whole. It has pledged to abide by international law, including UNCLOS, in seeking a resolution to the disputes, and agreed to sign a regional 'Declaration of Conduct' with ASEAN to govern their behaviour in the disputed areas. China has also embarked on defence diplomacy with Southeast Asia, consisting of high-level visits among defence officials, port calls of its ships, exchanges of defence attaches, and cross-invitations to military training courses, among others.

In comparison with China, some ASEAN member states are more willing to resort to the international judiciary for settling their disputes. In 1998, Indonesia and Malaysia jointly brought a dispute of sovereignty over Pulau Ligitan and Pulau Sipadan Island to the ICJ.[125] In 2003, Malaysia and Singapore jointly submitted a dispute concerning sovereignty over Pedra Branca/Pulau Batu Puteh, Middle Rocks and South Ledge to ICM.[126] A request for the prescription of provisional measures on land reclamation activities in and around the straits of Johor was submitted to ITLOS by Malaysia against Singapore in September 2003.[127] Besides, the scenario of resorting infrequently to the international judiciary may change in the future with the realization of the proposed 'ASEAN Court of Justice, comprising designated judges nominated by each member-state'.[128] However, whether a third party forum will be welcomed in settling sovereignty of islands and maritime delimitation in the SCS, still remains an unanswered question. When asked this question, the respondents, including scholars and government officials of foreign affairs or marine affairs from Indonesia, the Philippines, Vietnam, Malaysia and

123 *United Daily News*, 19 May 1995, 2.

124 Aileen San Pablo-Baviera, 'The China Factor in U.S. Alliances in East Asia and the Asia Pacific', *Australian Journal of International Affairs*, 57(2) (July 2004): 339–52.

125 For the judgment, see 'Sovereignty over Pulau Ligitan and Pulau Sipadan (Indonesia/Malaysia)', International Court of Justice, http://www.icj-cij.org/docket/index.php?p1=3&p2=3&k=df&case=102&code=inma&p3=4.

126 For the judgment, see 'Sovereignty over Pedra Branca/Pulau Batu Puteh, Middle Rocks and South Ledge (Malaysia/Singapore)', International Court of Justice, http://www.icj-cij.org/docket/index.php?p1=3&p2=3&k=2b&case=130&code=masi&p3=4.

127 See http://www.itlos.org/start2_en.html.

128 Jusuf Wanandi, 'ASEAN Future Challenges and the Importance of an ASEAN Charter', *Asien: Deutsche Zeitschrift fuer Polik, Wirtschaft und Kulture*, 100 (2006): 87.

Brunei, are reluctant to express their opinions, even though the author encourages them to speak in their personal capability, rather from a government's position.

Although the East Asian countries are not as active as their African and Latin American counterparts in their recourse to legal means for dispute settlement, they frequently and usually use political forms, particularly direct negotiation and consultation, or regional arrangements, as reflected in the agreements reached among the ASEAN members as well as those between the ASEAN/its members and China. Through the operations of ASEAN, the unique 'ASEAN way' has been created, which refers to a loose arrangement including 'informal processes, weak regional institutions, and decisions by consensus'.[129] It contains three core values: (1) consultation – due to various diversities and contradictions between/among the states in Southeast Asia, regional integration must rely on consultation rather than on coercive forces; (2) harmony – ASEAN regards itself as a harmonious entity of states, like an orchestra consisting of its member states, without interfering in their domestic affairs and resort to peaceful dispute settlement; and (3) cooperation – unlike the 'hard way' of law used by the European Union (EU), ASEAN adopts the 'soft way' for cooperation.[130] It is commented that the ASEAN way has played an active role in establishing the regional order, constructing a platform for states from outside the region to be involved in participation and dialogue, maintaining regional stability and balancing the influence of the big powers.[131]

The Philippines versus China Arbitration Case in the SCS

The Philippines set a precedent among the SCS claimant states to resort to the third party compulsory settlement mechanism of UNCLOS. On 22 January 2013 it sent the Notification and Statement to China that it will sue China by establishing an arbitration tribunal according to Annex VII of United Nations Convention on the Law of the Sea (UNCLOS).[132] In response, China, on 31 January, rejected this request. On 30 March 2014, the Philippines submitted its Memorial to the Arbitration Tribunal.[133] The formal institution of the Arbitral Tribunal under Annex 7 of UNCLOS, in August 2013, triggered legal and political debates between

129 Rodolfo C. Severino, 'Framing the ASEAN Charter: An ISEAS Perspective', in Rodolfo C. Severino (ed.), *Framing the ASEAN Charter: An ISEAS Perspective* (Singapore: Institute of Southeast Asian Studies, 2005), 4.

130 Yunlin Zhang, 'The Valuable ASEAN Way', *People's Daily*, 8 August 2007, 3 (in Chinese).

131 Ibid.

132 Department of Foreign Affairs (DFA Philippines), 'DFA: Notification and Statement Claim on West Philippine Sea', Official Gazette, 22 January 2013, http://www.gov.ph/2013/01/22/dfa-notification-and-statement-claim-on-west-philippine-sea-january-22-2013/.

133 'China Reiterates Opposition to Philippines' Arbitration Bid', SinaEnglish, 20 February 2013, http://english.sina.com/china/2013/0220/563275.html.

China and the Philippines, between China and the United States and among the international community.[134] 15 December 2014 was the deadline granted by the Arbitral Tribunal for China to submit its counter-memorial according to its rules of proceedings.[135] The report issued by the US Department of State on 5 December 2014, analysing China's maritime claims in the South China Sea (the U.S. No. 143 report),[136] and the position paper issued by the MFA of China on matters of jurisdiction in the South China Sea on 7 December 2014 (China's position paper),[137] reflect the legal dimension of Beijing and Washington's debate. But while the two papers may not be considered so-called replies or rejoinders, underneath the legal arguments, they do reflect the policy choices of the two countries concerning maritime domains in the South China Sea. In addition to that, the Philippines' response on 8 December, Vietnam's Statement of Interest with the Permanent Court of Arbitration on 11 December, drag both the claimant states and user states to the stage of this seemingly legal fight, but what is in essence a geopolitical competition.

Overwhelming comments and analysis arose one after another following these two papers that were interpreted as 'White Papers' of each government. Relevant governments also responded officially. Philippine foreign ministry spokesman Charles Jose denied Manila was taking its complaint to a UN tribunal as a way to put China under foreign pressure. He predicted that the tribunal may decide the case by 'early 2016'.[138]

Vietnam's statement to the Permanent Court of Arbitration (PCA), submitted on 11 December, made three main claims in opposition to China's stand, recognizing the court's jurisdiction over the case submitted by the Philippines, requesting that the court give 'due regard' to Vietnam's own legal rights and interests in the Spratlys, Paracels, and in its exclusive economic zone and continental shelf while deliberating on the case, and rejecting China's nine-dash line as being 'without legal basis'.[139]

---

134 http://www.pca-cpa.org/showpage.asp?pag_id=1529.

135 Ibid.

136 Limits in the Seas, No. 143 China: 'Maritime Claims in the South China Sea', by Office of Ocean and Polar Affairs Bureau of Oceans and International Environmental and Scientific Affairs, U.S. Department of State, 5 December 2014, http://www.state.gov/documents/organization/234936.pdf (accessed 7 December 2014).

137 Chinese Government's Position Paper on Matter of Jurisdiction in South China Sea Arbitration Initiated by Philippines, http://news.xinhuanet.com/english/china/2014-12/07/c_133837498.htm (accessed 7 December 2014).

138 'Philippines Stands Firm on Sea Dispute with China', at Channel NewsAsia, http://www.channelnewsasia.com/news/asiapacific/philippines-stands-firm/1517968.html, 8 December 2014.

139 'Vietnam Launches Legal Challenge Against China's South China Sea Claims', *The Diplomat*, 11 December 2014, http://thediplomat.com/2014/12/vietnam-launches-legal-challenge-against-chinas-south-china-sea-claims/.

This statement is not a 'statement of claim' as made by the Philippines in January 2013 but a statement of interest in the China–Philippines case before the Arbitral Tribunal. But it has also been interpreted that Vietnam was prepared to take stronger legal action and advised its close friends accordingly. The Philippine quickly voices the support of the Vietnamese intervention.

On 17 December, the Arbitral Tribunal requested further written argument from the Philippines. The Philippines has until 15 March 2015 to file a supplemental written submission addressing the Arbitral Tribunal's Request, and China will have until 16 June 2015 to provide any comments in response to the supplemental written submission of the Philippines. What actions may be taken during this period from China, the Philippines and Vietnam remains a very significant issue for observers of the South China Sea development.

What Next for China and the International Community?

As Mark Valencia pointed out, the 'good' policies and actions by China (ratifying the UNCLOS along with other 164 countries, its agreement with Vietnam at the Gulf of Tonkin, its participation in the anti-piracy efforts in the Gulf of Aden, offering the China-ASEAN Maritime Cooperation Fund) 'have been tarnished by alleged "bad" policies and behavior that have been trumpeted by some media, some of which may be deserved but much is exaggerated or heavily biased'.[140]

What is the choice for China in managing maritime disputes with its neighbours? The 'carrot' is attractive but does not earn reciprocity. Economic contracts and investment agreements do not play down the tensions arising from any small-scale incidents at sea, be it fishery conflicts or others. The 'stick', which is not necessarily appreciated and taken by China, but often interpreted by the media, is certainly not what everyone is delighted to see. Public relations campaign and a smart power, as Valencia suggests, may be what China lacks. But it is far from being sufficient. China shall use the same language as the United States, as the Philippines and Vietnam, and maybe others – 'international law'. China, as it always claims, does not lack historical and legal evidence to support its territorial and maritime claims. The position paper, which provides the detailed explanation on why it believes that the Tribunal does not have jurisdiction, with lots of references to case laws and treaty law, proves this very well. It is a good start and it puts China in the same language context with the international community. China has frequently used the dispute settlement mechanism of the WTO to resolve its economic issues with other WTO members. It helps China convey the right and precise image of the country to the international community that it is a close follower of international norms. To do that, it does not suggest that China should accept any compulsory,

140 Mark Valencia, 'China's Maritime Machinations: The Good, the Bad, and the Ugly', *The Diplomat*, 10 December 2014, http://thediplomat.com/2014/12/chinas-maritime-machinations-the-good-the-bad-and-the-ugly/.

unilateral litigation or arbitration proceedings, which fall into the category of 'exception', provided by Article 298 of UNCLOS, but it gives China a platform to explain why.

Conclusion

This chapter elaborates the state practices of UNCLOS in the SCS, from four aspects respectively, namely attitude to international law, process in UNCLOS negotiation, marine legislation and dispute settlement practice. A conclusion may be drawn from this. No Asian state has ever claimed to reject the whole system of international law; the claims have always been more discrete and have related to specific issues. The Asian states had no part in the creation of much of modern international law, which has been fashioned largely by European states in the past three or four hundred years. In other words, the states of Asia may reject those parts of international law, developed without their participation, which they consider contrary to their interest. Asian states and people are said to be less legalistic, less in favour of codes, and more prone to settlement according to more flexible criteria. This contention, especially in the context of the Asian attitude to compulsory third party settlement of disputes, has, of course, a wider significance; it goes to the very basis of a system ordered by objective rules. Since the Second World War, Asian states, together with African states, which often have similar interests, have in acquired considerable numerical strength in international organizations, especially the General Assembly of the United Nations. They realize that this voting power can be used to press their views in the process of codifying and progressively developing international law. This point is well demonstrated from the analysis on the process of UNCLOS negotiation, in which both China and other disputant states of the SCS have actively participated and pushed the direction, to different extents, towards what their own interests.

All the states involved in the SCS disputes have developed a comparatively comprehensive marine legal system under the framework of UNCLOS, which can be illustrated from the marine legislation by these states. These legislations provide a legal framework to deal with many maritime issues in a domestic context. Nevertheless, in the situation where multiple issues interrelate with each other, such as the SCS, a theoretically sound legal system does not always do a good job in many fields, such as maritime delimitation, overlapping maritime jurisdiction claims, fishing disputes, trans-boundary marine environmental pollution, etc. Hence, a third party compulsory dispute settlement regime needs to play its desired role. The practices of dispute settlement in the SCS were elaborated by unfolding the political culture of relevant states on their attitude to a third party forum. China, Vietnam and Indonesia oppose of international litigation, and on all occasions insist on the merit of negotiation, while the Philippines is more willing to bring an extra party to the stage of SCS, and it did make the first move by initiating the Arbitral proceedings against China in 2013. Nevertheless, as some

Chinese scholars in recent years bring to the table for discussion, China should be encouraged to place more weight on the third party dispute settlement mechanism, given its desired responsibilities in many contemporary global issues and its role in international organizations.

References

Akehurst, M. 'Custom as a Source of International Law', *BYIL*, 47 (1974–5): 1–53.

Carr, E.H. *The Twenty Years' Crisis, 1919–1939: An Introduction to the Study of International Relations*, 2nd edn. London: Macmillan, 1946.

Cassese, Antonio. *International Law in a Divided World.* Oxford: Clarendon Press, 1986.

Cheng, Peter. *A Chronology of the People's Republic of China: From October 1 1949*. Totowa: Rowman & Littlefield, 1972.

'China and Viet Nam Issues a Joint Communiqué'. www.fmprc.gov.cn/eng/wjdt/2649/t163759.htm.

'China Reiterates Opposition to Philippines' Arbitration Bid'. *SinaEnglish*, 20 February 2013. http://english.sina.com/china/2013/0220/563275.html.

'China's Declaration in Accordance with Article 298 of UNCLOS'. 7 September 2006. http://www.fmprc.gov.ch/chn/wjb/zzjg/tyfls/wizdtyflgzlzgzhyflydgz/t270754.htm (accessed 6 February 2007).

Chinese Government's Position Paper on Matter of Jurisdiction in South China Sea Arbitration Initiated by Philippines. http://news.xinhuanet.com/english/china/2014-12/07/c_133837498.htm (accessed 7 December 2014).

Churchill, Robin R. 'The Impact of State Practice on the Jurisdictional Framework Contained in the LOS Convention'. In Alex G. Oude Elferink (ed.) *Stability and Change in the Law of the Sea: The Role of the LOS Convention.* Leiden: Martinus Nijhoff, 2004.

Cohen, J.A. 'Attitudes toward International Law'. In J.A. Cohen (ed.) *Contemporary Chinese Law: Research Problems and Perspectives*. Cambridge, MA: Harvard University Press, 1970.

'Common Fishing Zone Plan Proposed to S. Vietnam'. *The Nations* (Bangkok). In *FBIS-APA*, 3 September 1974, J7.

Department of Foreign Affairs (DFA Philippines). 'DFA: Notification and Statement Claim on West Philippine Sea'. Official Gazette, 22 January 2013. http://www.gov.ph/2013/01/22/dfa-notification-and-statement-claim-on-west-philippine-se a-january-22-2013/.

Duc, Duy. 'The Maritime Ho Chi Minh Trail'. *Viet Nam Courier*, no. 6 (1985), pp. 19–20.

Embassy of Vietnam in China website. http://www.vnemba.org.cn/en/nr050706234129/ (accessed 29 July 2009).

Farrel, Epsey Cooke. 'The Socialist Republic of Viet Nam and the Law of the Sea: An Analysis of Viet Namese Behaviour within the Emerging International Oceans Regime'. PhD dissertation, 1997.
Gao, Yanping. 'International Dispute Settlement'. In Wang Tieya (ed.) *International Law*. Beijing: Law Press, 1995 (in Chinese).
Gao, Zhiguo. 'China and the LOS Convention'. *Marine Policy*, 15(3) (1991): 213.
Giang, Pham. 'Cong Uoc Moic Ve Luat Bien Nam 1982' [The New 1982 Convention on the Law of the Sea]. *Luat Hoc*, 1 (1983), pp. 20–31.
Guimei, Bai. 'Basic Rights and Obligations of the State'. In Wang Tieya (ed.) *International Law*. Beijing: Law Press, 1995.
Hatono, Sunaryati. 'The Interrelation between National Law and International Law in Indonesia'.
Hey, E. and A.W. Koers. *The International Law of the Sea: Issues of Implementation in Indonesia*. Rijswijk: The Netherlands Institute of Transport, 1984.
Hung, Le Quoc. 'Luat Bien Va van De Bao Ve Moi Truong Bien' [The Law of the Sea and the Problem of the Protection of the Marine Environment]. *Laut Hoc* (Hanoi), 3 (1979), pp. 38–43.
Jia, Yu. Presentation on the Conference of 'Energy Security and the South China Sea', Haikou, 2004.
Johnson, Douglas. 'Drawing into the Fray: Indonesia's Natuna Islands Meet China's Long Gaze South'. *Asian Affairs* (1998), pp. 153–61.
Kim, Shee Poon. 'The March 1988 Skirmish over the Spratly Islands and its Implications for Sino-Viet Namese Relations'. In R.D. Hill, N. Owen and E.V. Roberts (eds) *Fishing in Troubled Waters: Proceedings of an Academic Conference on Territorial Claims in the SCS*. Hong Kong: Centre of Asian Studies, University of Hong Kong, 1991.
Kittichaisaree, Kriangsak. *The Law of the Sea and Maritime Boundary Delimitation in Southeast Asia*, annex IV. Singapore: Oxford University Press, 1987.
Limits in the Seas, No. 143. China: 'Maritime Claims in the South China Sea'. Office of Ocean and Polar Affairs Bureau of Oceans and International Environmental and Scientific Affairs, U.S. Department of State, 5 December 2014. http://www.state.gov/documents/organization/234936.pdf (accessed 7 December 2014).
Ngoc, Nhu. 'Some Essential Notions about Border Law'. *Laut Hoc*, 3 (1978). In *JPRS 72542*, 2 January 1979.
Nguyen, Hong Thao. *Le Viet Nam face aux problèmes de l'extension maritime dans la mer de Chine méridionale*, annex 10. Paris: Septentrion Presses Universitaires, 1997.
Nguyen, Hong Thao. 'Viet Nam and the Code of Conduct for the SCS', *Ocean Development & International Law*, 32 (2001): 105–30.
Nordquist, Myron H., ed. *United Nations Convention on the Law of the Sea 1982: A Commentary*, vol. I. Dordrecht, Boston and Lancaster: Martinus Nijhoff, 1985.
O'Connell, D. *The Influence of Law on Sea Power*. Manchester: Manchester University Press, 1975.

People's Daily Online. 'China Calls for Dialogue, Cooperation Over South China Sea', 4 June 2009. http://english.peopledaily.com.cn/90001/90776/90883/6671212.html.

'Philippines Stands Firm on Sea Dispute with China'. Channelnew Asia, 8 December 2014. http://www.channelnewsasia.com/news/asiapacific/philippines-stands-firm/1517968.html.

Qiang, Chen. 'Chinese Practice in Public International Law: 2004 (II)'. Oxford Journals. http://chinesejil.oxfordjournals.org/cgi/content/full/4/2/607#SEC4.

San Pablo-Baviera, Aileen. 'The China Factor in U.S. Alliances in East Asia and the Asia Pacific'. *Australian Journal of International Affairs*, 57(2) (July 2004): 339–52.

Schreadley, R.L. (Cdr., U.S. Navy), 'The Naval War in Viet Nam, 1950–1970'. *Naval Review* (1971). Reprinted in Frank Uhlig, Jr. (ed.) *Viet Nam: The Naval Story*. Annapolis: Naval Institute Press, 1986.

Segal, Gerald. *Defending China*. Oxford: Oxford University Press, 1985.

Severino, Rodolfo C. 'Framing the ASEAN Charter: An ISEAS Perspective'. In Rodolfo C. Severino (ed.) *Framing the ASEAN Charter: An ISEAS Perspective*. Singapore: Institute of Southeast Asian Studies, 2005.

Shambaugh, David. 'China Engages Asia: Reshaping the Regional Order'. *International Security*, 29(3) (Winter 2004/5).

Song, Yann-Huei and Keyuan Zou. 'Maritime Legislation of Mainland China and Taiwan: Developments, Comparison, Implications, and Potential Challenges for the United States'. *Ocean Development & International Law*, 31 (2000): 303–45.

'Sovereignty over Pedra Branca/Pulau Batu Puteh, Middle Rocks and South Ledge (Malaysia/Singapore)'. International Court of Justice. http://www.icj-cij.org/docket/index.php?p1=3&p2=3&k=2b&case=130&code=masi&p3=4.

Stockholm International Peace Institute. *SIPRI Yearbook 1988: World Armaments and Disarmament*. Oxford: Oxford University Press, 1988.

Tzou, Byron N. *China and International Law: The Boundary Disputes*. Praeger Publishers, 1990.

United Nations. *Multilateral Treaties Deposited with the Secretary-General*, vol. II.

United Nations General Assembly. *Official Records, 32 d session* (1977), vol. 1.

United Nations Legislative Series. *Multilateral Treaties Deposited with the Secretary-General, Status as at 31 December 1988* (ST/LEG./SER.E/7).

Valencia, Mark. 'China's Maritime Machinations: The Good, the Bad, and the Ugly'. *The Diplomat*, 10 December 2014. http://thediplomat.com/2014/12/chinas-maritime-machinations-the-good-the-bad-and-the-ugly/.

Van Loi, Luu. 'Le Sud Est asiatique: un point chaud du globe au cours de l'histoire de ces quarante dernieres annees'. *Bulletin de droit* (Hanoi), 1 (1985), p. 21.

'Vietnam Launches Legal Challenge against China's South China Sea Claims'. *The Diplomat*, 11 December 2014. http://thediplomat.com/2014/12/vietnam-launches-legal-challenge-against-chinas-south-china-sea-claims/.

Villiger, M.E. *Customary International Law and Treaties*, 2nd edn. The Hague: Kluwer Law International, 1997.

Wanandi, Jusuf. 'ASEAN Future Challenges and the Importance of an ASEAN Charter'. *Asien: Deutsche Zeitschrift fuer Polik, Wirtschaft und Kulture*, 100 (2006), p. 87.

Weiliang, Shen and Guangjian Xu. 'The Third UN Conference on the Law of the Sea and the Convention on the Law of the Sea'. *Chinese Yearbook of International Law*, 433 (1983) (in Chinese), pp. 433–4.

Zhang, Yunlin. 'The Valuable ASEAN Way'. *People's Daily*, 8 August 2007 (in Chinese).

Zhu, Lijiang. 'Chinese Practice in Public International Law: 2007(I)'. Oxford Journals. http://chinesejil.oxfordjournals.org/cgi/reprint/7/2/485.

Zou, Keyuan. *China-ASEAN Relations and International Law*. Oxford: Chandos Publishing, 2009.

Zou, Keyuan. *China's Legal Reform: Towards the Rule of Law*. Leiden and Boston: Martinus Nijhoff, 2006.

Zou, Keyuan. *China's Marine Legal System and the Law of the Sea*. Leiden and Boston: Martinus Nijhoff, 2005.

Chapter 14

Case Study on the Application of Part XV of UNCLOS to the Annex VII Arbitration Case Concerning the South China Sea Disputes between China and the Philippines

Michael Sheng-ti Gau*

Introduction

On January 22, 2013, the Philippines presented a diplomatic notification to China under Article 287 and Annex VII of the United Nations Convention on the Law of the Sea (UNCLOS). It aimed at initiating arbitral proceedings to challenge China's claims and entitlement to areas of the South China Sea (SCS) and the underlying seabed, which the Philippines requests the Tribunal to declare as its exclusive economic zone (EEZ) and continental shelf.[1] Based on the Philippines' claims and the relief sought under Sections III and V of the 'Notification and Statement of Claim' (the Notification),[2] there are five groups of claims as follows.[3]

---

* This chapter is a condensed and revised version of the paper published in the *Ocean Yearbook*, vol. 28, pp. 81–133 (2014), entitled "The Sino-Philippine Arbitration of the South China Sea Nine-Dash Line Dispute: Applying the Rule on Default of Appearance." The points presented in this chapter only comment on the Philippines' statement and arguments contained in its diplomatic notification released on January 22, 2013. The opinions expressed here do not represent those of any government agencies.

1 See online: http://www.dfa.gov.ph/index.php/newsroom/dfa-releases/7300-statement-by-secretary-of-foreign-affairs-albert-del-rosario-on-the-unclos-arbitral-proceedings-against-china-to-achieve-a-peaceful-and-durable-solution-to-the-dispute-in-the-wps. For the information released by the Permanent Court of Arbitration, serving as Registry of this arbitration, see online: http://www.pca-cpa.org/showpage.asp?pag_id=1529.

2 The Notification and Statement of Claims, issued by Department of Foreign Affairs of Republic of the Philippines in Manila to the Embassy of the People's Republic of China in Manila, serial no. 13-0211, January 22, 2013, available online: http://www.dfa.gov.ph/index.php/downloads/doc_download/523-notification-and-statement-of-claim-on-west-philippine-sea.

3 See paras 31 (Section III: The Philippines' Claims) and 41 (Section V: Relief Sought) of the Notification, ibid.

First, China's rights concerning the SCS maritime areas are those established by UNCLOS only and consist of the territorial sea, the contiguous zone, the EEZ and the continental shelf. China's maritime claims therein based on the "nine-dash line (U-Shaped Line)"[4] contravene UNCLOS and are invalid.[5] *Second*, the Mischief, McKennan, Gaven and Subi Reefs are submerged features not above sea level at high tide, and should not be deemed as islands or rocks according to Article 121 of UNCLOS. None of them are located on China's continental shelf. The Mischief and McKennan Reefs are part of the Philippines' continental shelf. China's occupation of these four maritime features and construction activities thereon are unlawful and should be terminated.[6] *Third*, Scarborough Shoal and the Johnson, Cuarteron and Fiery Cross Reefs should be considered as rocks under Article 121(3), and may only generate state entitlement to the territorial sea. Having unlawfully claimed maritime entitlements beyond 12 nautical miles (NM) *from* these features, China should refrain from preventing Philippine vessels from exploiting the living resources in waters adjacent to the Scarborough Shoal and Johnson Reef, and from undertaking other activities inconsistent with UNCLOS at or in the vicinity of these features.[7] *Fourth*, the Philippines is entitled under UNCLOS to a 12-NM territorial sea, a 200-NM EEZ, and a continental shelf measured from its archipelagic baselines. China has unlawfully claimed and exploited the living and non-living resources in this EEZ and continental shelf, and prevented the Philippines from exploiting the living and non-living resources therein.[8] *Fifth*, China has unlawfully interfered with the Philippines' exercise of its navigational rights and other rights under UNCLOS within and beyond the Philippines' EEZ. China should desist from these unlawful activities.[9]

On February 19, 2013, China officially refused to join the litigation.[10] However, the default rules under Annex VII were applied to proceed in establishing the

4 The term "nine-dash line" is interchangeable with "U-Shaped Line" and "11-dash line." For various names of this line, see K.Y. Zou, "China's U-Shaped Line in the South China Sea Revisited," *Ocean Development and International Law* 43 (2012): 18.

5 See 1st–2nd claims under para. 31 and 1st–3rd reliefs under para. 41 of the Notification, n. 2 above.

6 See 3rd–5th claims under para. 31 and 4th–7th reliefs under para. 41 of the Notification, ibid.

7 See 6th–7th claims under para. 31 and 8th–9th reliefs under para. 41 of the Notification, ibid.

8 See 8th–9th claims under para. 31 and 10th–11th reliefs under para. 41 of the Notification, ibid.

9 See 10th claims under para. 31 and 12th–13th reliefs under para. 41 of the Notification, ibid.

10 See the statement made on February 19, 2013 by the spokesman of the Foreign Ministry of China (English translation): "China's position on the South China Sea issue is clear and consistent. China's sovereignty over the Nansha Islands and their adjacent waters is based on sufficient historical and jurisprudential evidence. Meanwhile, bearing in mind the larger interests of China-Philippines relations and regional peace and stability,

arbitral tribunal. On June 25, 2013, the fifth arbitrator was appointed and the arbitral tribunal was established for this case (the Tribunal). As there is an obvious dispute concerning whether the Tribunal has jurisdiction over the disputes, the Tribunal should follow Article 288(4) of UNCLOS to decide such an issue as a preliminary matter.

As revealed by its official statements, China will neither appear in this litigation nor present written or oral arguments in the court room as the respondent. Such default of appearance makes certain procedural rules applicable. According to Article 9 of Annex VII to UNCLOS, the Tribunal, before making its Award, is obligated to satisfy itself not only that it has jurisdiction over the *dispute*, but also that the *claims* brought by the Philippines are well-founded in fact and law. It is necessary for the Tribunal to look into *all* the claims brought forward by the Philippines and *all* the disputes forged by the claims in the procedural phase. The possible arguments China could make should also be explored during this process.

To assist the Tribunal in making informed and balanced decisions, this chapter addresses the three categories of questions for the Tribunal to answer:

i. whether the inherent conditions for the Annex VII Tribunal to be applicable under Articles 286 and 288 are fulfilled;
ii. whether the Philippines' claims are well-founded in fact and law under Article 9 of Annex VII to UNCLOS; and
iii. whether jurisdictional requirements of the disputes presented by the Philippines are all fulfilled under Article 9 of Annex VII.

To answer these questions, this chapter discusses the rules and then applies them to the Chinese and Philippine situations. To this end, information will be provided to explore the following factual and legal problems concerning whether or not:

i. the disputes formulated by the Philippines are real and contentious;
ii. the disputes brought by the Philippines are identical with the unsettled Sino-Philippine SCS disputes;
iii. the disputes presented by the Philippines are concerning the interpretation or application of UNCLOS; and

China has always been committed to solving disputes through bilateral negotiations and has made unremitting efforts to safeguard stability in the South China Sea and promote regional cooperation. It is also the consensus reached by ASEAN (Association of Southeast Asian Nations) countries and China in the *Declaration on the Conduct of Parties in the South China Sea* (DOC) to resolve disputes through negotiations between directly concerned sovereign states. The Philippines' note and its attached notice not only violate the consensus, but also contain serious errors in fact and law as well as false accusations against China, which we firmly oppose." Available online: http://www.fmprc.gov.cn/eng/xwfw/s2510/2511/t1015317.shtml.

iv. the disputes as correctly re-characterized have been excluded by the 2006 Chinese Declaration in accordance with Article 298.

Finally, based on these examinations and analyses, a conclusion will be drawn and a suggestion will be made to the Tribunal.

The Rules on the Jurisdiction of the Tribunal and Default of Appearance

Article 288: Inherent Conditions for the Tribunal to be Applicable

As the chosen forum, the Tribunal must have jurisdiction over the disputes presented under Article 288(1) of UNCLOS. It reads "[a] tribunal referred to in article 287 shall have jurisdiction over any dispute *concerning the interpretation or application of this Convention* which is submitted to it *in accordance with this Part*" (emphasis added).[11]

Two preconditions must be fulfilled before the Tribunal becomes bound to address the jurisdictional problems. First, the dispute must concern the interpretation or application of UNCLOS. Second, such a dispute must have been submitted to the Tribunal in accordance with Part XV.

At first glance, these conditions are all met. The Philippines is asking the arbitral tribunal to apply UNCLOS to decide the entire dispute, and in particular, to evaluate the legality of: (1) the U-Shaped Line claimed by the PRC; (2) the legal status given by the PRC to eight self-occupied SCS maritime features; (3) the maritime areas surrounding these maritime features claimed by the PRC; and (4) the range of maritime zones claimed by the Philippines measured from its archipelagic baselines. These disputes all concern the interpretation or application of UNCLOS. Besides, as the Philippines specifically states at the beginning of the Notification,

> the Government of the Philippines has the honor to submit the attached Notification *under Article 287 and Annex VII of the 1982 United Nations Convention on the Law of the Sea (UNCLOS)* and the Statement of Claim on which the Notification is based, in order to initiate arbitral proceedings to clearly establish the sovereign rights and jurisdiction of the Philippines over its maritime entitlements in the West Philippine Sea.[12] (Emphasis added)

Therefore, the Philippines will probably argue that it has submitted the disputes to the Tribunal *in accordance with UNCLOS*, and thereby has met the second

11 United Nations Convention on the Law of the Sea, open for signature on December 10, 1982, 1833 United Nations Treaty Series 397, available online: http://www.un.org/Depts/los/convention_agreements/texts/unclos/unclos_e.pdf.

12 Para 1 of the covering letter for the Notification, n. 2 above.

condition under Article 288(1). However, certain situations may prevent the fulfillment of these two conditions.

First, certain disputes presented by the Philippines may not concern the interpretation or application of UNCLOS as required by Article 288(1).

Second, the way the Philippines submitted the disputes to the Tribunal may not conform with Part XV, because: (1) as this chapter will explain, *there is lack of dispute*, as the 'disputes' submitted by the Philippines may be either non-contentious or hypothetical, making one of the inherent requirements for all the provisions of Part XV unfulfilled; (2) the Sino-Philippine SCS disputes that failed to be settled through the means indicated by Section 1 of Part XV (Section 1 Means) *may not be the same as* the disputes presented by the Philippines to the Annex VII Tribunal, thus violating Article 286 first,[13] and consequently breaching Article 288(1).

Assuming these preconditions were fulfilled and Article 288(1) became applicable, the Tribunal would be obligated to satisfy itself that it has jurisdiction over the case. In this respect, China claimed that the 2006 Declaration has the effect of depriving the Tribunal of jurisdiction over this case.[14] The Philippines argued in its Notification that "the Philippines' claims do not fall within China's Declaration of 25 August 2006."[15] Article 288(4) of UNCLOS, as the way out, provides that: "in the event of a dispute as to whether a … tribunal has jurisdiction, the matter shall be settled by decision of that … tribunal."[16]

Article 9 of Annex VII: Default of Appearance

As default of appearance on the part of China will occur, Article 9 of Annex VII applies, which provides:

> If one of the parties to the dispute does not appear before the arbitral tribunal or fails to defend its case, the other party may request the tribunal to continue the proceedings and to make its award. Absence of a party or failure of a party to defend its case shall not constitute a bar to the proceedings. *Before making its award, the arbitral tribunal must satisfy itself not only that it has*

13 Article 286 (Application of procedures under this section) reads: "Subject to section 3, any dispute concerning the interpretation or application of this Convention shall, where no settlement has been reached by recourse to section 1, be submitted at the request of any party to the dispute to the court or tribunal having jurisdiction under this section." See n. 11 above.

14 See remarks made by the spokesperson of the Chinese Ministry of Foreign Affairs on April 26, 2013, available online: http://www.fmprc.gov.cn/eng/xwfw/s2510/2535/t1035577.shtml.

15 Para. 40 of the Notification, n. 2 above.

16 See UNCLOS, n. 11 above.

> *jurisdiction over the dispute but also that the claim is well founded in fact and law.*[17] (Emphasis added)

The drafting history shows that the final decision in choosing the word "claim" (instead of "award") in the last sentence of Article 9 brings the sentence back to the language of Article 53 of the Statute of the International Court of Justice (ICJ).[18] Therefore, the commentary to Article 53[19] can be the guidance when interpreting and comprehending the last sentence of Article 9 of Annex VII.

In the event of default of appearance, the "default" award of the Tribunal will not automatically be in favour of the appearing party. The Tribunal will not necessarily find that it has jurisdiction, that the case is admissible or that the underlying claim is well-founded. Rather, the Tribunal may only decide in favour of that party if such an award is justified both in procedure and in substance.[20]

Given the opposing position of China in the present case, the Tribunal must not decide such preliminary matters lightly due to China's absence and the lack of its legal arguments submitted formally. If applying the analogous ICJ judgments in two Icelandic Fisheries cases, the Tribunal, in examining its own jurisdiction, should consider those objections of China which *might*, in its view, be raised against its jurisdiction.[21]

In the present case, China as a party has raised and could further provide *informal* jurisdictional objections, though neither in the form of preliminary objections nor in the way requested by Part XV of Annex VII or by the Tribunal. If following the ruling of the *Aegean Sea Case*,[22] the Tribunal should nevertheless consider such "informal objections" to be relevant.[23]

---

17 See online: http://www.un.org/depts/los/convention_agreements/texts/unclos/annex7.htm.

18 S. Rosenne and L.B. Sohn, *United Nations Convention on the Law of the Sea 1982: A Commentary, Vol. V* (Virginia: Martinus Nijhoff, 1989), pp. 433–4 and 389–90.

19 The most authoritative guide is by A. Zimmermann, K. Oellers-Frahm, C. Tomuschat and C.J. Tams, eds, *The Statute of the International Court of Justice: A Commentary*, 1st edn (Oxford: Oxford University Press, 2006), pp. 1141–70. To be noted, the Commentary to Article 53 was written by Von Mangoldt and Zimmermann.

20 Ibid., pp. 1159–60.

21 Fisheries Jurisdiction Case (UK v. Iceland) (Jurisdiction) [1973] ICJ Rep 3, 7–8 (para. 12), available online: http://www.icj-cij.org/docket/files/55/5749.pdf. Fisheries Jurisdiction Case (FRG v. Iceland) (Jurisdiction) [1973] ICJ Rep 49, 54 (para. 13), available online: http://www.icj-cij.org/docket/files/56/10713.pdf.

22 Aegean Sea CS Case (Greece v. Turkey) [1978] ICJ Rep 3, 20 (para. 46), available online: http://www.icj-cij.org/docket/files/62/6245.pdf. In this case, Turkey, as the non-appearing party, had in informal written observations invoked a reservation with regard to the General Act for the Pacific Settlement of Disputes and the ICJ took note of it. See Zimmermann et al., n. 19 above, p. 1160.

23 Zimmermann et al., ibid.

The last sentence of Article 9 of Annex VII imposes an obligation upon the Tribunal to investigate whether it has jurisdiction or not. One question arises: To what extent is the Tribunal obliged to search for possible jurisdictional problems and to discuss every *conceivable* objection to the Tribunal's jurisdiction that a creative party like China *may* raise? As this is also a question for the ICJ when applying Article 53 of its Statute, the commentary to the ICJ Statute again provides insightful guidance.[24]

In short, the ICJ's obligation under Article 53(2) is much higher than that for establishing *prima facie* jurisdiction, as required by Article 41 of the ICJ Statute governing provisional measures.[25] It is because Article 53(2) allows for a judgment on jurisdiction and eventually also on the merits of the case, which is final.[26] Applying this differentiation to the UNCLOS regime, the level of investigatory obligation incumbent upon the Tribunal under Article 9 of Annex VII (governing award-making process) would be thus higher than that under Article 290 of UNCLOS (governing provisional measures and *expressly* provide *prima facie* test).[27]

Now, what does it mean by claims being well-founded in fact and law? The ICJ in the *Nicaragua Case* discussed Article 53(2) of the ICJ Statute by saying:

> The use of the term 'satisfy itself' in the English text of the Statute … implies that the Court *must attain the same degree of certainty as in any other case that the claim of the party appearing is sound in law, and so far as the nature of the case permits, that the facts on which it is based are supported by convincing evidence.* For the purpose of deciding whether the claim is well founded in law, the principle *jura novit curia* signifies that the Court is not solely dependent on the argument of the parties before it with respect to the applicable law, so that the absence of one party has less impact … As to the facts of the case, in principle the Court is not bound to confine its consideration to the material formally submitted to it by the parties. Nevertheless, the Court cannot by its own enquiries entirely make up for the absence of one of the Parties; that absence, in a case of this kind involving extensive question of fact, must necessarily limit the extent to which the court is informed of the facts.[28] (Emphasis added)

24 Ibid., 1161.

25 However, the *prima facie* test is not part of the wording of Article 41 of the ICJ Statute, available online: http://legal.un.org/avl/pdf/ha/sicj/icj_statute_e.pdf.

26 Zimmermann, n. 19 above, p. 1161.

27 See Article 290(1), which provides the *prima facie* test, whereas Article 9 of Annex VII does not. See n. 11 above.

28 Case Concerning Military and Paramilitary Activities in and against Nicaragua (Nicaragua v. USA) (Merits) [1986] ICJ Rep 14, 24, 25 (paras 29–30), available online: http://www.icj-cij.org/docket/files/70/6503.pdf.

Additionally, given the principle of *juria novit curia*, issues on the burden of proof do not arise as to whether the claim is well-founded in law.[29] The ICJ held that "It being the duty of the Court itself to ascertain and apply the relevant law in the given circumstances of the case, the burden of establishing or proving rules of international law cannot be imposed upon any of the parties, for the law lies within the judicial knowledge of the Court."[30]

On the other hand, the ICJ does not examine the factual basis of the claim to the same degree of certainty. Besides, the ICJ has so far been reluctant to define a clear general rule as to what standard is to be applied in order to determine whether the claim is well-founded in fact. The ICJ has further held that while "Article 53 … obliges the Court to consider the submissions of the Party which appears, it does not compel the Court to examine their accuracy in all their details; for this might in certain unopposed cases prove impossible in practice." On the other hand, it is "especially incumbent upon the Court to satisfy itself that it is in possession of all the available facts."[31]

The above-mentioned test and jurisprudence of the ICJ in applying Article 53(2) of its Statute are both pertinent to the present case for the Tribunal to apply Article 9 of Annex VII to UNCLOS.

In the following sections, relevant factual information and legal opinions are offered to assist the Tribunal in fulfilling the above-mentioned assignments when examining each of the disputes to ascertain if it has jurisdiction. More fundamentally, whether the Philippines' claims are all well-founded in fact and in law will be studied first, as part of the questions the Tribunal must answer.

In the judgment of *The Mavrommatis Palestine Concessions Case*, the Permanent Court of International Justice has defined a dispute as "a disagreement on a point of law or fact, a conflict of legal views or of interests between two persons."[32] Seen as an elaboration of such a definition, J.G. Merrills said that, "a dispute may be defined as a specific disagreement concerning a matter of fact, law or policy in which a claim or assertion of one party is met with refusal, counter-claim or denial by another."[33] A.V. Lowe and J. Collier also describe the dispute

29 Zimmermann, n. 19 above, p. 1162.

30 Fisheries Jurisdiction Case (UK v. Iceland) (Merits) [1974] ICJ Rep 3, 9 (para. 17), available online: http://www.icj-cij.org/docket/files/55/5977.pdf. Fisheries Jurisdiction Case (FRG v. Iceland) (Merits) [1974] ICJ Rep 175, 181 (para. 18), available online: http://www.icj-cij.org/docket/files/56/6001.pdf.

31 Zimmermann, n. 19 above, pp. 1162–3.

32 The Mavrommatis Palestine Concessions [August 30, 1924] PCIJ Series A, No. 2, 11, available online: http://www.icj-cij.org/pcij/serie_A/A_02/06_Mavrommatis_en_Palestine_Arret.pdf.

33 J.G. Merrills, *International Dispute Settlement*, 4th edn (Cambridge: Cambridge University Press, 2005), p. 1.

as "a specific disagreement relating to a question of rights or interests in which the parties proceed by way of claims, counter-claims, denials and so on."[34]

Clearly, a dispute must be built upon a combination of a claim and counter-claim. In the present case, the examination of the dispute and, more fundamentally, the *existence* of it, should follow the analysis of the claims actually made by the disputing parties, not the other way around.

Are the Philippines' Claims Well-Founded in Fact and Law?

The First Group of Claims Concerning China's U-Shaped Line and SCS Maritime Area

Such claims challenge the legality under UNCLOS of China's maritime claims in the SCS allegedly *based on, within, and encompassed by* the U-Shaped Line. The first claim contends and the first relief requests the Tribunal to declare that:

> China's rights in regard to maritime areas in the SCS, like the rights of the Philippines, are those that are established by UNCLOS, and *consist of* its rights to a Territorial Sea and Contiguous Zone under Part II of the Convention, to an EEZ under Part V, and to a Continental Shelf under Part VI. (Emphasis added)

Based on such a position, the second claim contends and the second relief requests the Tribunal to declare that "China's maritime claims in the SCS based on its so-called 'nine dash line' are contrary to UNCLOS and invalid." Importantly, the wording "based on" as used by the Philippines in this claim is interchangeable with "within"[35] or "encompassed by."[36] The third relief then "requires China to bring its domestic legislation into conformity with its obligations under UNCLOS."[37]

Being by nature counter-claims against Chinese positions, these Philippines' claims seem less than well-founded in fact and law. This is because the object challenged is far from what China actually asserts, for the following three major reasons.

34 J. Collier and A.V. Lowe, *The Settlement of Disputes in International Law: Institutions and Procedures*, 1st edn (Oxford: Oxford University Press, 1999), p. 1.

35 Paras 2 and 11 of the Notification, n. 2 above.

36 Paras 3 and 12 of the Notification, ibid.

37 Underlying such line of claims is the principle of State responsibility for an internationally wrongful act, as codified by the International Law Commission (ILC). The Philippines' second claim and second relief point out the internationally wrongful act of China, while its third relief demonstrates what China needs to do in terms of reparation. The text on the Responsibility of States for Internationally Wrongful Acts was adopted by the ILC at its fifty-third session in 2001, and submitted to the General Assembly of the UN as a part of the ILC's report, which is available online: http://legal.un.org/ilc/texts/instruments/english/draft%20articles/9_6_2001.pdf.

First, by virtue of its 2011 official statement, China's SCS maritime claims are not based on, within, or encompassed by the U-Shaped Line, as challenged by the Philippines. Following the 2009 Chinese Note Verbale (NV)[38] invoked but misunderstood[39] by the Philippines in the Notification, China sent a NV (CML/8/2011) on April 14, 2011 as a response to the Philippine NV (No. 000228) on April 5, 2011.[40] The 2011 Chinese NV asserts that:

> China has indisputable *sovereignty* over the islands in the South China Sea and the *adjacent waters*, and enjoys *sovereign rights and jurisdiction* over the *relevant waters* as well as the seabed and subsoil thereof. China's sovereignty and related rights and jurisdiction in the South China Sea are supported by abundant historical and legal evidence ... Since 1930s, the Chinese Government has given publicity several times the geographical scope of China's Nansha Islands[41] and the names of its components [*sic*]. China's Nansha Islands is [*sic*] therefore clearly defined. In addition, under the relevant provisions of the 1982 United Nations Convention on the Law of the Sea, as well as the Law of the People's Republic of China on the Territorial Sea and the Contiguous Zone (1992) and the Law of the EEZ and the Continental Shelf of the People's Republic of China (1998), *China's Nansha Islands is* [*sic*] *fully entitled to Territorial Sea, EEZ and Continental Shelf.*[42] (Emphasis added)

Obviously, China's maritime claims in the SCS are those regulated by UNCLOS as far as, *inter alia*, Nansha Islands (Spratly Islands Group) are concerned. It is hard to imagine how any dispute can exist between these Chinese positions

38 Dated on May 7, 2009, the two Chinese Notes Verbales (CML/17/2009 and CML/18/2009) were issued to oppose the Malaysia-Vietnam Joint Submission and Vietnam Individual Submission for Outer CS beyond 200 miles in the SCS region. See online: http://www.un.org/Depts/los/clcs_new/submissions_files/mysvnm33_09/chn_2009re_mys_vnm_e.pdf and http://www.un.org/Depts/los/clcs_new/submissions_files/vnm37_09/chn_2009re_vnm_c.pdf.

39 The last three sentences of para. 11 of the Notification read "China first officially depicted the 'nine dash line' in a letter of 7 May 2009 to the United Nations Secretary General. It is reproduced below. According to China, it is sovereign over all of the waters, all of the seabed, and all of the maritime features within this 'nine dash line'." See n. 2 above. The Chinese 2009 NV did not say that China is sovereign over all of the waters, all of the seabed, and all of the maritime features within the U-Shaped Line. Moreover, the 2009 Chinese NV is not the first official statement of China in terms of claiming territorial sovereignty in the SCS.

40 See online: http://www.un.org/Depts/los/clcs_new/submissions_files/mysvnm33_09/phl_re_chn_2011.pdf.

41 Here, the Nansha Islands are the Spratly Islands, as touched upon by the Philippines' claims in the present case.

42 See online: http://www.un.org/Depts/los/clcs_new/submissions_files/mysvnm33_09/chn_2011_re_phl_e.pdf. The document is no. CML/8/2011.

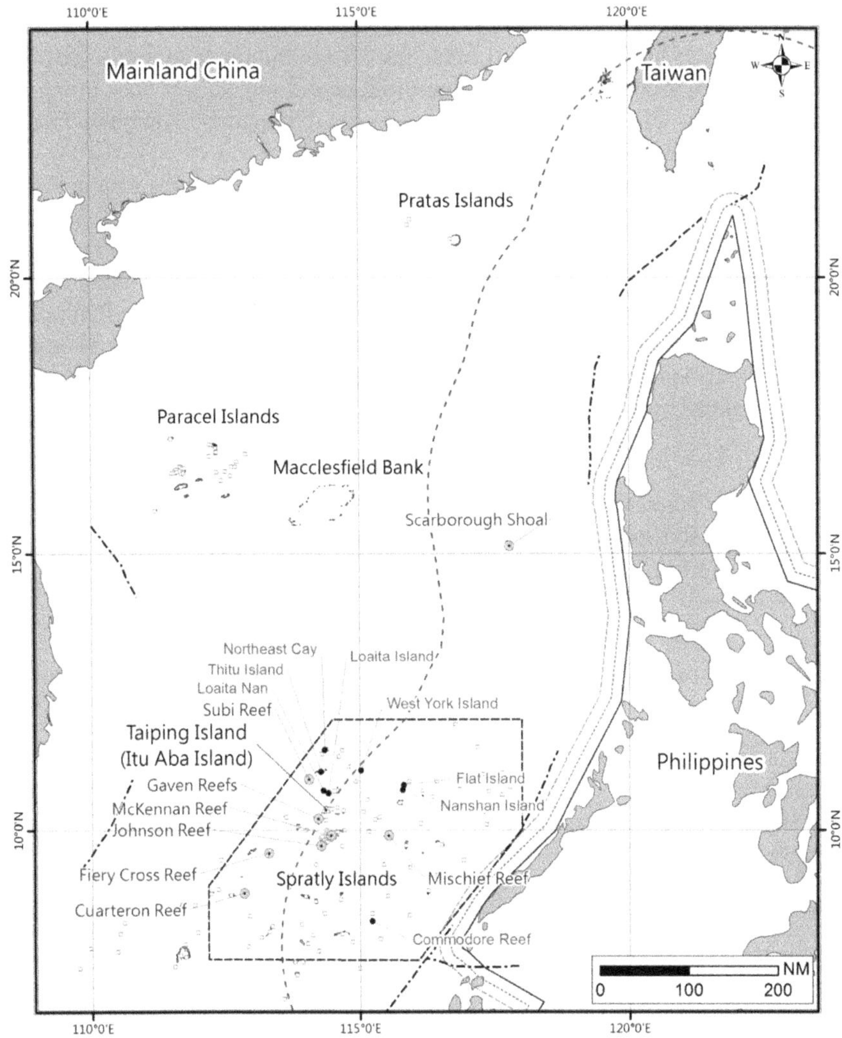

Figure 14.1 Maritime features occupied by China and the Philippines in the Spratly Islands

Source: Prepared for the author by Mr Jui-Hsien Huang.

and the Philippines' first claim and first relief sought. Though having no dispute *concerning UNCLOS as the legal basis* for China to generate maritime zonal claims in the SCS, a sharp Sino-Philippine disagreement exists concerning the total *size* of maritime areas over which China may claim sovereignty, sovereign rights, and jurisdiction there. This underpins the complaints raised by the first group of the Philippines' claims. The anxieties of the Philippines (and other contenders) are based on a perception that the body of SCS waters China claims may be as large as that enclosed by the U-Shaped Line. Such Sino-Philippine maritime disputes probably result from, *inter alia*, a Sino-Philippine disagreement concerning the territorial status of *all* maritime features in the Philippines' Kalayaan Islands Group (KIG) and Scarborough Shoal.[43]

To illustrate Sino-Philippine territorial disputes, eight dots on the map in Figure 14.1 represent the maritime features in the KIG (part of the Spratly Islands) occupied and claimed by the Philippines.[44] These maritime features are also claimed by China as part of its Nansha Islands.[45] On the map there are another seven maritime features occupied by China within the Spratly Islands that are identified by the Philippines in its second and third groups of claims (while Scarborough Shoal as the eighth identified maritime feature is not located in the Spratly Islands). These seven features are also claimed by the Philippines as part of its KIG.

Table 14.1 Names and coordinates of the islands occupied by the Philippines in the Spratly Islands

Chinese name	English name	Philippine name	Coordinates
Beizi Dao 北子島	Northeast Cay.	Parola	11°27'N., 114°22'E
Zhongye Qunjiao 中業島	Thitu Island	Pagasa	11°01'–11°06'N., 114°11'–114°24'E
Nanyue Dao 南鑰島	Loaita Island	Dugao Kota	10°40'N., 114°25'E
Feixin Dao 費信島	Flat Island	Patag Flat	10°49'N., 115°50'E
Mahuan Dao 馬歡島	Nanshan Island	Lawak	10°44'N., 115°48'E
Xiyue Dao 西月島	West York Island	Likas	11°05'N., 115°02'E
Siling Jiao 司令礁	Commodore Reef	Rizal Reef	8°22'–8°24'N., 115°11'–115°17'E
Shuanghuang Shazhou 雙黃沙洲	Double Egg Yolk Shoal	Panata	10°42'–10°43'N., 114°19'–114°20'E

Source: The names of the South China Sea islands are those adopted by the PRC National Committee on Geographical Names and published in the *People's Daily*, April 25, 1983. The list of all names of South China Sea islands may be found online: http://www.unanhai.com/nhzddm.htm. Double Egg Yolk Shoal is also known as Loaita Nan.

43 N.T.A. Hu, "South China Sea: Troubled Waters or a Sea of Opportunity?" *Ocean Development & International Law* 41, no. 3 (2010): 203, 206.

44 R. Beckman, "The UN Convention on the Law of the Sea and the Maritime Disputes in the South China Sea," *American Journal of International Law* 107 (2013): 142, 144; see D. Heinzig, *Disputed Islands in the South China Sea* (Wiesbaden: Harrassowitz Verlag, 1976), p. 36; Zou, n. 4 above, p. 19; J.L. Batongbacal, "The Maritime Territories and Jurisdiction of the Philippines and the United Nations Convention on the Law of the Sea," *Philippine Law Journal* 76 (2001): 123, 140–41.

45 Y.H. Song, "The South China Sea Workshop Process and Taiwan's Participation," *Ocean Development & International Law* 41, no. 3 (2010): 253, 254.

Table 14.1 shows the names (in Chinese, English and Filipino) and coordinates of the eight maritime features currently occupied and claimed by the Philippines,[46] but contested by China. These territorial disputes are not mentioned by the Philippines in its Notification. Due to the overall territorial disputes, the Chinese maritime claims generated by the SCS maritime features are denied by the Philippines (and some other States). Consequently, the maritime dispute over 'the size' occurs. However, the Tribunal is powerless to settle the entire territorial disputes *inseparable from* the disputes on China's maritime zonal claims the Tribunal is now called upon to settle. Hence, the first group of Philippines' claims should not be considered as well-founded in law, because the core legal basis is missing and can neither be provided by the Tribunal nor by the Philippines.

Second, China did attach a map with the U-Shaped Line in its 2009 NV. But China did not say that its SCS maritime claims of "adjacent waters" and/or "relevant waters" are based on, within, or encompassed by the U-Shaped Line. It was said by the 2009 Chinese NV that,

> China has indisputable sovereignty over the islands in the SCS and the adjacent waters, and enjoys sovereign rights and jurisdiction over the relevant waters as well as the seabed and subsoil thereof *(see attached map)*. The above position is consistently held by the Chinese Government, and is widely known by the international community.[47] (Emphasis added)

The second page of the 2009 Chinese NV contains the map, reproduced in Figure 14.2.

What is probably meant by China here is that it has sovereignty over the four groups of islands[48] enclosed by the U-Shaped Line on the map. What was said is "(see attached map)," which indicates four groups of islands over which China claims territorial sovereignty and two kinds of maritime areas ("adjacent waters" and "relevant waters") *attached to* the islands. As observed by a famous Japanese scholar, the U-Shaped Line is not continuous and incapable of enclosing water.[49]

China claims sovereignty over the "adjacent waters" to those islands, due to its sovereignty over the islands and based on the "the land dominates the sea"

46 L.B. Bautista, "The Legal Status of the Philippine Treaty Limits and Territorial Waters Claim in International Law: National and International Legal Perspectives" (2010) University of Wollongong Thesis Collection, 245. Available online: http://ro.uow.edu.au/theses/3081/.

47 See n. 38 above.

48 They are Dongsha Qundao (the Pratas Islands), Xisha Qundao (the Paracel Islands), Zhongsha Qundao (the Macclesfield Bank) and Nansha Qundao (the Spratly Islands). Qundao means archipelago in Chinese.

49 See Masahiro Miyoshi, "China's 'U-Shaped Line' Claim in the South China Sea: Any Validity Under International Law?" *Ocean Development & International Law* 43, no. 1 (2012): 1–17.

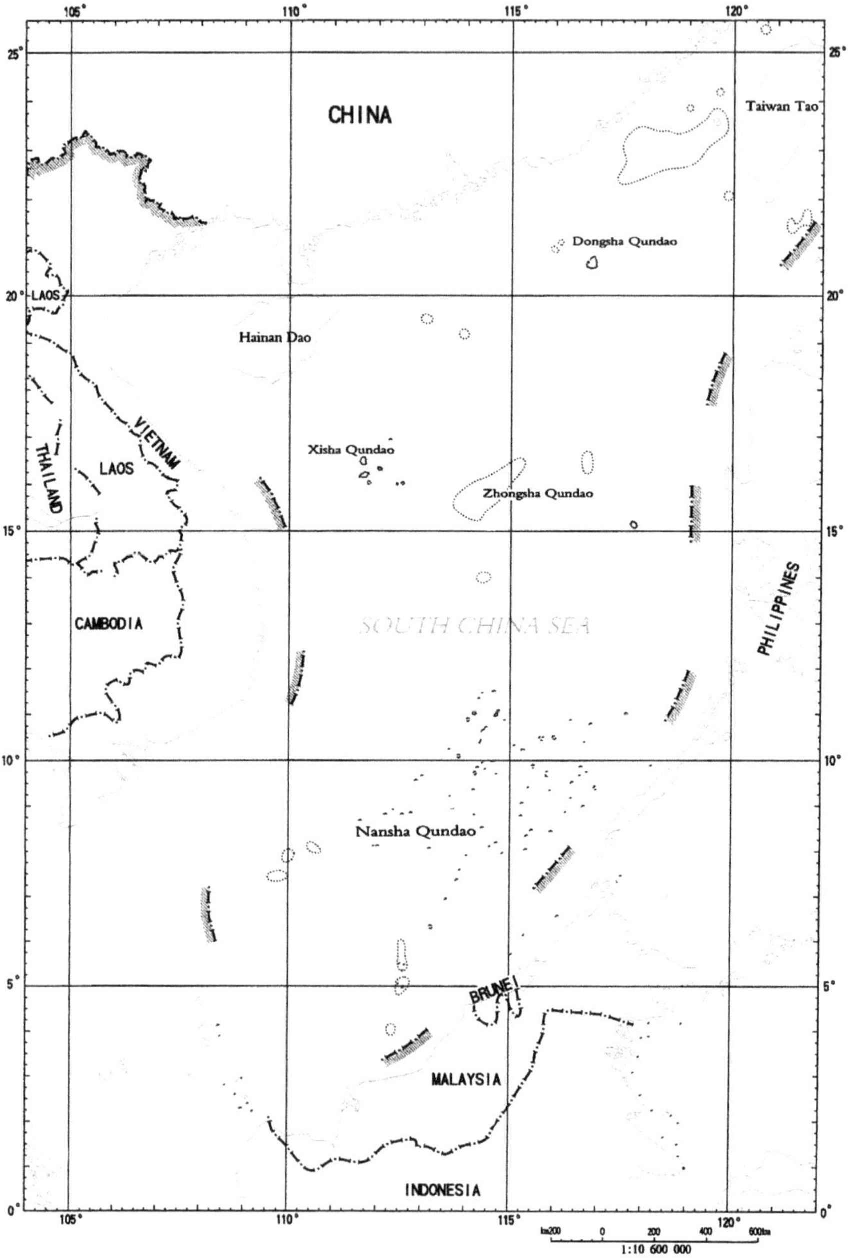

Figure 14.2 Map provided by China in its 2009 NV

Source: Chinese (PRC) Government released in 2009 in its NV delivered to the United Nations.

principle.[50] China does not specify how far its sovereignty goes in the "adjacent water." It probably will not exceed 12 M from the baselines, as it has to follow the 1992 Law of PRC on the Territorial Sea and the Contiguous Zone which complies with UNCLOS.

The next question is about the range of 'relevant waters' that China claims to have sovereign rights and jurisdiction over. This is most controversial as both foreign governments and scholars suspect the boundary for it to be the U-Shaped Line on the map attached to China's two NVs of 2009.[51] If this is true, then China would be acting inconsistently with UNCLOS. However, such a view ignores the background indicated by the word "relevant." In fact China's two NVs in 2009 to the UN were used to protest[52] against (1) the Vietnam/Malaysia Joint Submission[53] and (2) the Vietnamese individual Submission[54] for the limits of their Outer Continental Shelf in SCS. Figure 14.3[55] and Figure 14.4[56] are the illustrations provided by these two submissions respectively. Putting these two zones submitted by Vietnam and Malaysia into Figure 14.2, it becomes evident *why* China raised objections and *what* China objected to in its 2009 NVs. It was because the two submissions overlap with *China's* EEZ and continental shelf generated by the Spratly Islands Group and the Paracel Islands over which China maintains territorial claims. It proves that the phrase 'relevant waters' means *the waters (and the seabed and subsoil thereof) enclosed by these two submissions*, instead of the waters enclosed by the U-Shaped Line. Figure 14.5[57] combines all these factors. Doubtlessly, China's 2009 NVs do not use the U-Shaped Line as the boundary of its maritime claims in SCS.

50 See North Sea Continental Shelf, ICJ Reports 1969, p. 51, para. 96. And see Aegean Sea Continental Shelf, ICJ Reports 1978, p. 36, para. 86. And see Case Concerning Maritime Delimitation and Territorial Questions between Qatar and Bahrain, Merits, ICJ Reports 2001, p. 97, para. 185.

51 Robert C. Beckman and Clive H. Schofield, "Defining EEZ Claims from Islands: A Potential South China Sea Change," *The International Journal of Marine and Coastal Law* 29 (2014): 204–6. Also see n. 2 above, p. 4, para. 11.

52 Para. 5(a) of Annex I to the Rules of Procedure of the CLCS, available online: http://daccess-dds-ny.un.org/doc/UNDOC/GEN/N08/309/23/PDF/N0830923.pdf?OpenElement.

53 Available online: http://www.un.org/depts/los/clcs_new/submissions_files/mysvnm33_09/chn_2009re_mys_vnm_e.pdf.

54 Available online: http://www.un.org/depts/los/clcs_new/submissions_files/vnm37_09/chn_2009re_vnm.pdf.

55 See page 5 of Executive Summary of the Vietnam/Malaysia Joint Submission dated May 6, 2009. Available online: http://www.un.org/depts/los/clcs_new/submissions_files/mysvnm33_09/mys_vnm2009excutivesummary.pdf.

56 See page 5 of Executive Summary of the Vietnam individual Submission dated May 7, 2009. Available online: http://www.un.org/depts/los/clcs_new/submissions_files/vnm37_09/vnm2009n_executivesummary.pdf.

57 Lori Fisler Damrosch and Bernard H. Oxman, "Agora: The South China Sea, Editors' Introduction," *American Journal of International Law* 107 (2013): 96.

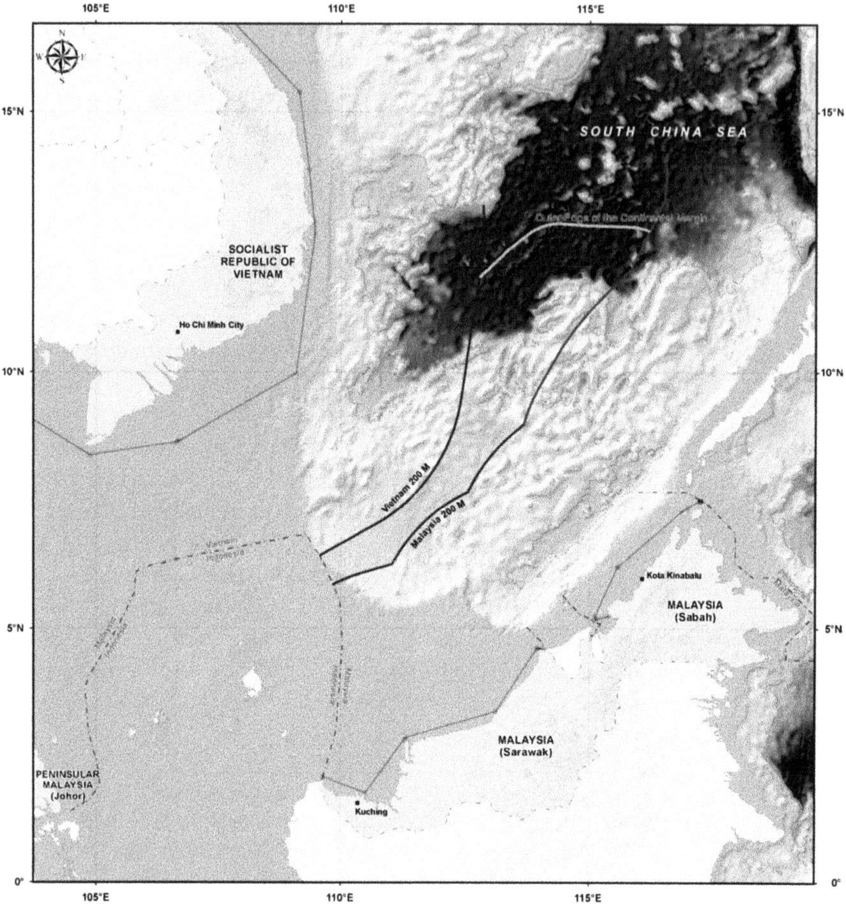

Figure 14.3 Limits of Outer Continental Shelf in SCS submitted by Vietnam/Malaysia jointly in 2009 to the CLCS

Source: Governments of Vietnam/Malaysia in their 2009 Joint Submission of limits of their outer continental shelf to the CLCS.

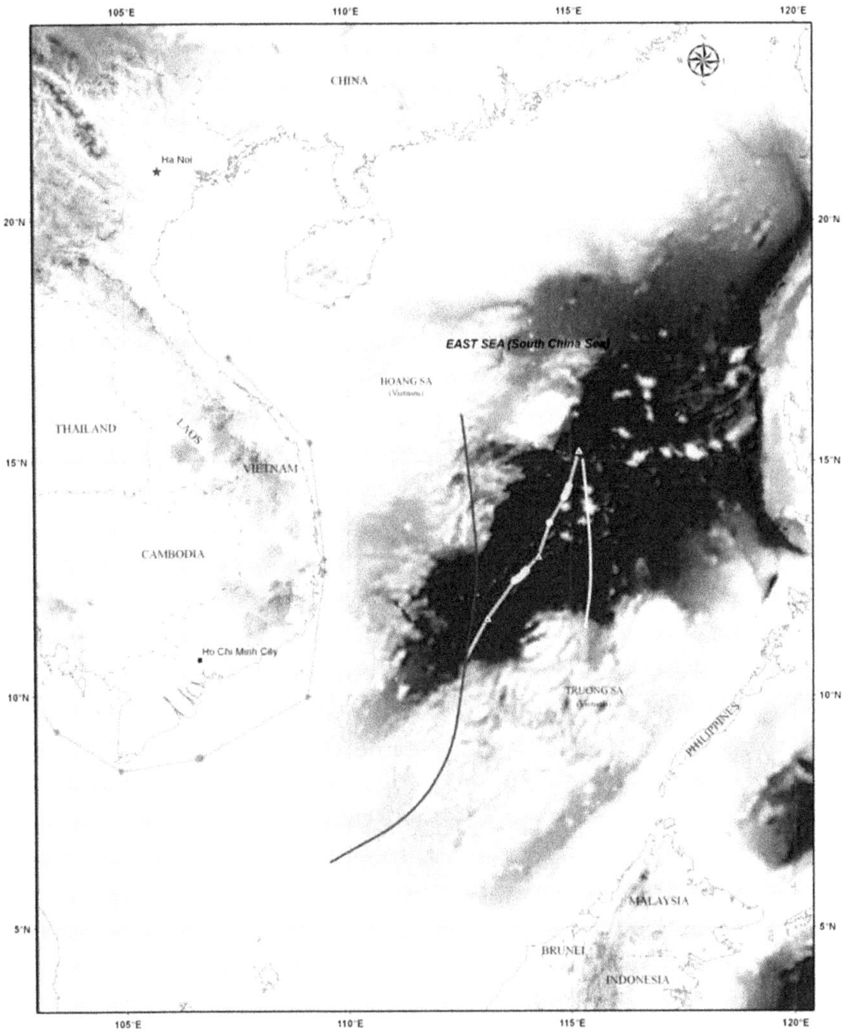

Figure 14.4 Limits of Outer Continental Shelf in SCS submitted by Vietnam in 2009 to the CLCS

Source: Vietnam's Government in its 2009 Submission of limits of its outer continental shelf to the CLCS.

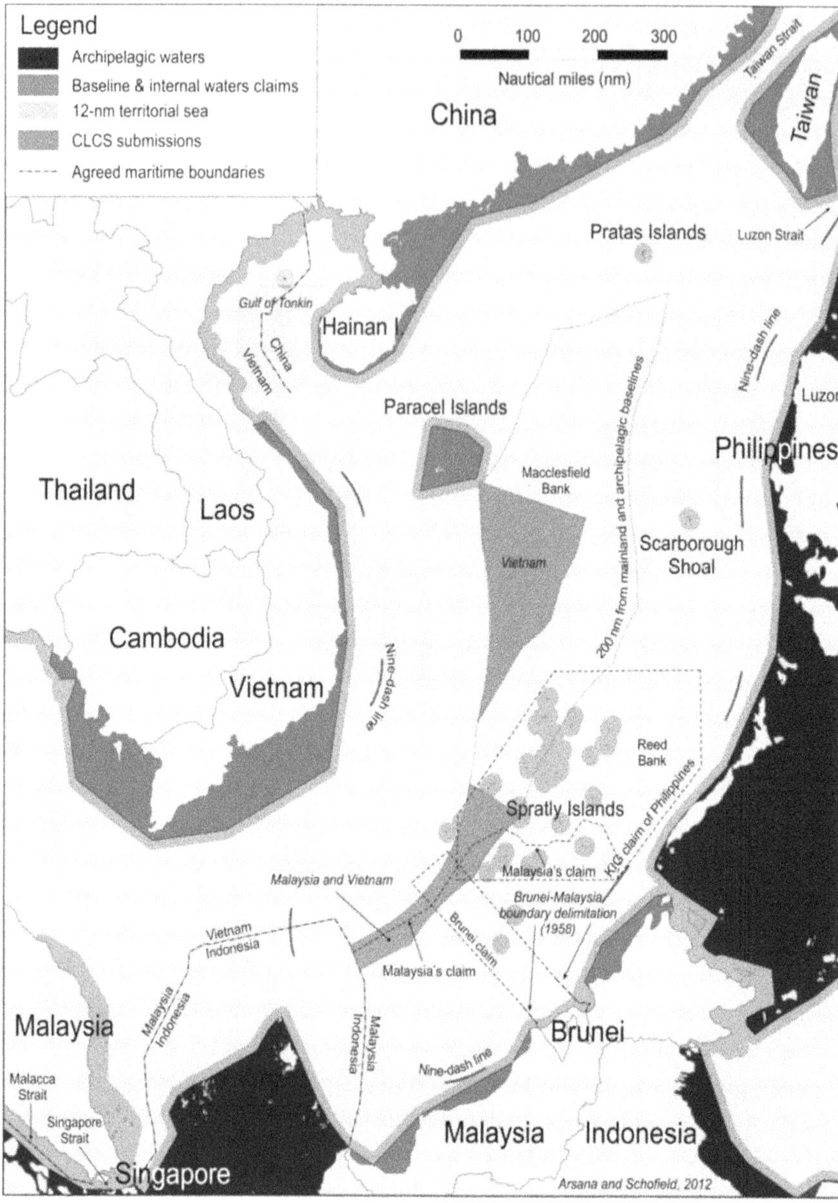

Figure 14.5 Illustration of territorial and maritime claims in the SCS by various governments

Source: 107 American Journal of International Law 95, at 96 (2013).

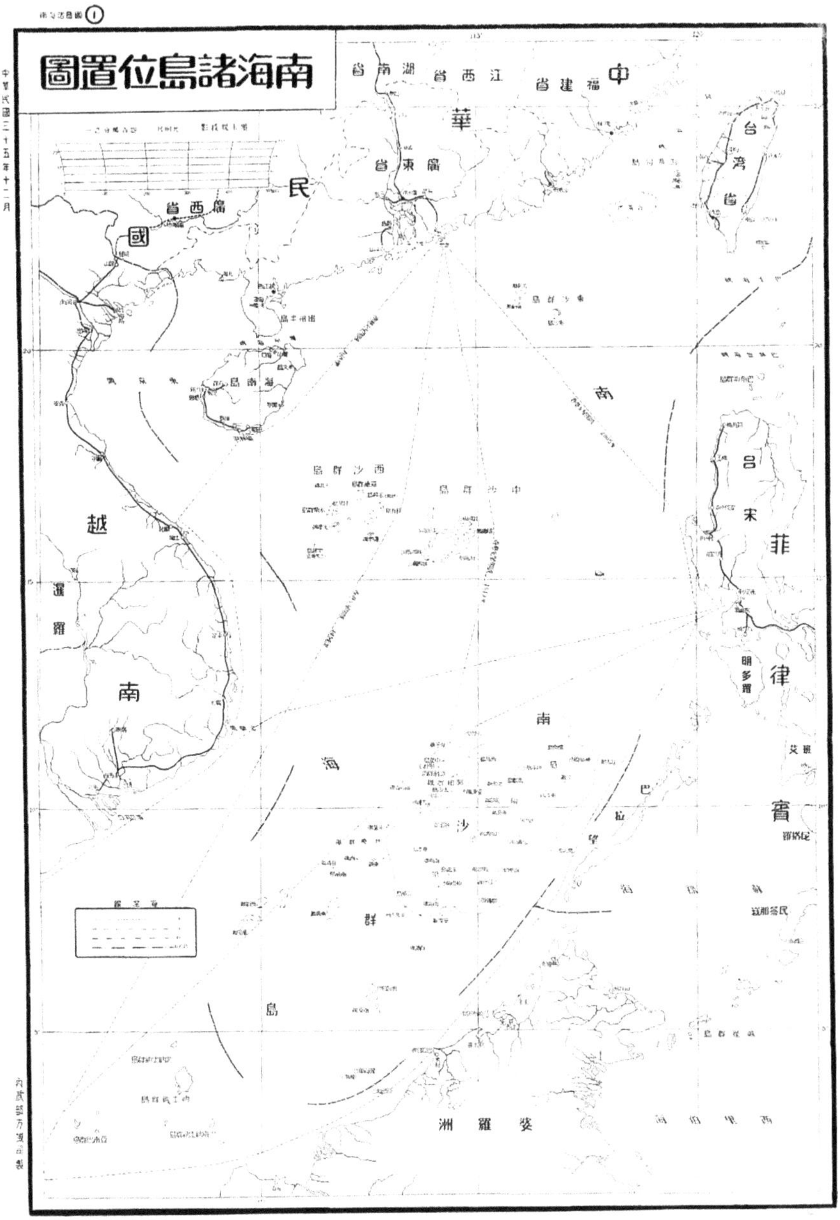

Figure 14.6 The 1948 location map for the South China Sea Islands
Source: Chinese (ROC) Government (published in 1948).

Third, the U-Shaped Line upon its genesis was not meant to be a line enclosing water over which China made maritime zonal claims. The line indicates the 'whereabouts' of the maritime features over which China asserts territorial sovereignty. The original 1948 map showing the U-Shaped Line published by the Republic of China (ROC) Government is entitled "Location Map for the SCS *Islands* (南海諸島位置圖)," shown in Figure 14.6.[58]

Therefore, the U-Shaped Line issue should be considered an issue of China's territorial claims, whose legality can hardly be judged according to the rules of UNCLOS. As the Philippines is applying the inapplicable rule (UNCLOS), the second claim becomes not well-founded in law.

The Philippines may argue that, even if U-Shaped Line was originally meant to be a territorial claim, it has been transformed into a maritime claim. The Philippines may contend that the choice of ambiguous wording ("relevant waters") in the 2009 and 2011 Chinese NVs signifies Chinese historic water claims in the SCS.[59] This possible argument of the Philippines has just been refuted. However, if such a view were accepted by the Tribunal, the legality of the U-Shaped Line to be judged according to UNCLOS would then become an issue concerning historical titles under Article 298(1)(a)(i) of UNCLOS. As has been carved out from the jurisdiction of an Annex VII Tribunal by the 2006 Chinese Declaration, this dispute may not be settled by the present Tribunal.[60]

Summing up, the foregoing three major legal problems make it hard to believe that the first group of Philippine claims is well-founded in fact and law.

The Second Group of Claims Concerning Four Low-Tide Elevations

The second group of Philippine claims tackles the Chinese-occupied Mischief, McKennan, Gaven and Subi Reefs, and the maritime zones surrounding them.

According to the fourth Philippine claim, these four reefs are submerged features not above sea level at high tide that should neither be deemed as islands nor rocks according to Article 121 of UNCLOS. All of them are *not* located in China's continental shelf. The fifth Philippine claim argues that the Mischief

58 This well-known map was produced by the Ministry of the Interior of the ROC Government in December 1946. See the tiny Chinese words at the right hand side of the map. It was kept in the archives of the Presidential Office in Taiwan, serial no. 50082355. This map was published in 1948. See Gao and Jia, "The Nine-Dash Line in the South China Sea: History, Status, and Implications," *American Journal of International Law* 107 (2013): 98, 109.

59 Z.G. Gao and B.B. Jia, ibid., 108. Also see F. Dupuy and P.-M. Dupuy, "A Legal Analysis of China's Historic Rights Claim in the South China Sea," *American Journal of International Law* 107 (2013): 124, 129–30, 135. Also see Beckman, n. 44 above, 155–6; Zou, n. 4 above, p. 18–19, 21–2, 28. Miyoshi, n. 49 above, pp. 3–4. E. Franckx and M. Benatar, "Dots and Lines in the South China Sea: Insights from the Law of Map Evidence," *Asian Journal of International Law* 2 (2012): 89, 93.

60 Zou, n. 4 above, p. 29. Miyoshi, n. 49 above, p. 10.

and McKennan Reefs are part of the Philippines' continental shelf. The fourth and fifth reliefs request the Tribunal to make a declaration that, having violated Philippine sovereign rights, China's occupation of the Mischief and McKennan Reefs, as well as construction activities taken thereon, are unlawful and should be ended. The sixth and seventh reliefs request the Tribunal to declare that China's same conduct with respect to the Gaven and Subi Reefs, which are not part of its continental shelf, are unlawful and shall be terminated, too.[61]

Being components of a Sino-Philippine contention, these Philippine claims and relief sought are supposed to counter China's following possible claims that:

i. the four reefs are located in China's continental shelf, which entitles China to claim and exercise maritime jurisdiction under UNCLOS in the seabed areas surrounding them, or the four reefs should be considered as islands or rocks defined by Article 121 of UNCLOS that may generate for China considerable maritime zones of their own, like the territorial sea, the EEZ or continental shelf; and
ii. the Mischief and McKennan Reefs are not part of the continental shelf of the Philippines.

The Philippines denies all these claims, based on:

i. the application of the rule in the third Philippine claim to these four alleged "low-tide elevations";
ii. that the other four maritime features identified by the third group of claims are rocks capable of generating a 12-NM territorial sea only, and the territorial sea so generated cannot cover the maritime areas surrounding the four reefs under the second group of claims;
iii. even if those four features under the third group of claims were islands, the EEZ and continental shelf generated thereby could not be considered as Chinese, as the Philippines denies Chinese territorial claims over those four "islands"; and
iv. apart from those eight maritime features occupied and claimed by China as indicated by the Notification, China's territorial claims over the *remaining* maritime features located in the Spratly Islands are inadmissible or non-existent in this litigation.

The rule invoked by the third Philippine claim reads:

> Submerged features in the SCS that are not above sea level at high tide, and are not located in a coastal State's territorial sea, are part of the seabed and cannot

---

61 To be noted, the Philippines again is applying rules of State responsibility for internationally wrongful act here. See n. 37 above.

> be acquired by a State, or subjected to its sovereignty, unless they form part of that State's continental shelf under Part VI of the Convention.

Being the third Philippine claim, such a rule is supposed to challenge China's claim or position that opposes this rule, which seems hardly the case. Besides, the following four significant obstacles will probably preclude the second group of the Philippine claims from being deemed well-founded in fact and in law.

First, although the rule is legally sound,[62] the third claim containing the rule is not contesting any claim China has made in fact. Consequently, the third Philippine claim should be considered unfounded in fact.

Second, it seems that the Philippines has not released the whole truth in the Notification. The Chinese territorial claims over SCS maritime features are not limited to those eight identified by the second and third group of Philippine claims (see Figure 14.1 and Table 14.1). For the purpose of this litigation, China claims territorial sovereignty over *all* maritime features in the Spratly Islands (part of which is KIG) and Scarborough Shoal. Quite a few good-sized islands located inside the Spratly Islands may lawfully generate the EEZ and continental shelf on which these four maritime features stand.[63] Being incapable of settling such overall Sino-Philippine territorial disputes and, *a fortiori*, rejecting these Chinese territorial claims, it would be inconceivable for the Tribunal to hold that China's territorial claims over all the foreign-occupied maritime features in the Spratly Islands are groundless, inadmissible or ignorable. Equally unfair would be to deny that Mischief, McKennan, Gaven and Subi Reefs are located on the continental shelf that China may claim in the SCS.

Third, the Philippines fails to indicate Taiwan-occupied Itu Aba (or Taiping) Island in its Notification, as it should. On June 9, 1975, the Philippines and the PRC signed a Joint Communiqué to establish diplomatic relations at the ambassadorial level. It was declared by the Philippines that:

> *The Philippine Government* recognizes the Government of the People's Republic of China as the sole legal government of China, *fully understands and respects the position of the Chinese Government that there is but one China and that Taiwan is an integral part of Chinese territory*, and decides to remove all its official representations from Taiwan within one month from the date of signature of this communiqué.[64] (Emphasis added)

62 Beckman, n. 44 above, pp. 150, 152–3.

63 J.W. McManus, K.T. Shao and S.Y. Lin, "Toward Establishing a Spratly Islands International Marine Peace Park: Ecological Importance and Supportive Collaborative Activities with an Emphasis on the Role of Taiwan," *Ocean Development & International Law* 41, no. 3 (2010): 270, 271.

64 Joint Communiqué of the Government of the People's Republic of China and the Government of the Republic of the Philippines (Peking, June 9, 1975), available online: http://ph.china-embassy.org/eng/zfgx/zzgx/t183265.htm.

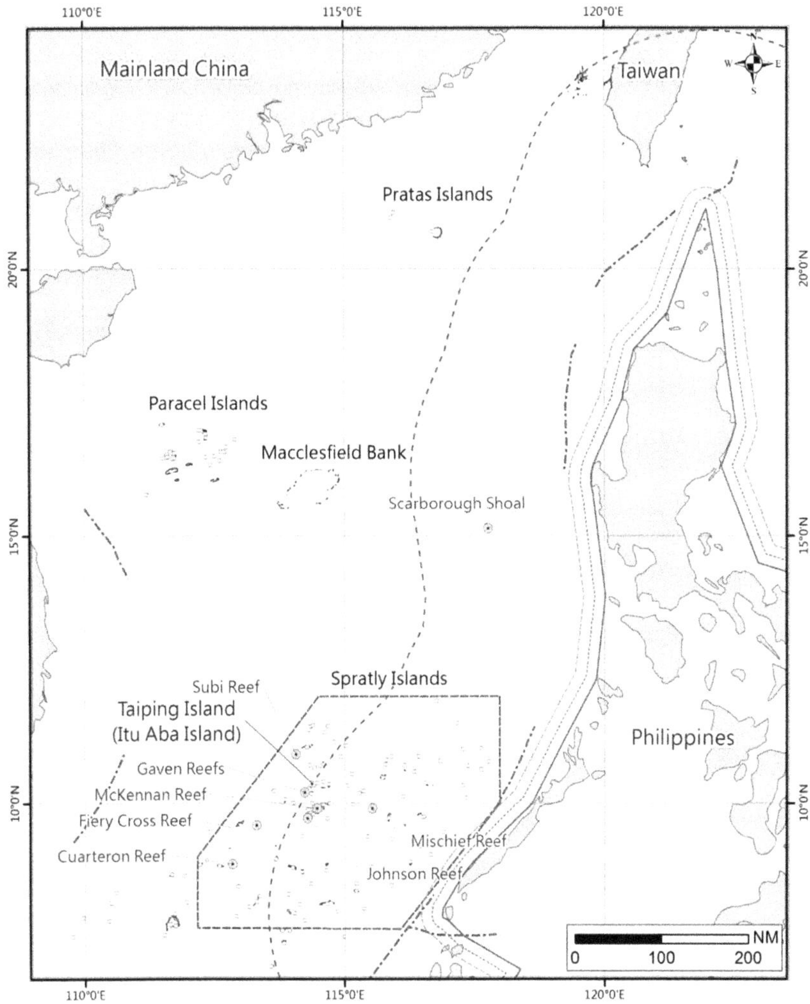

Figure 14.7 Location map of Itu Aba and the Eight Reefs identified by the Philippines

Source: Prepared for the author by Mr Jui-Hsien Huang.

Clearly, the Philippines respects the Chinese territorial claim and, *a fortiori*, may not deny that Taiwan forms part of the State of China. Besides, the Philippines respects the "One China Policy" and, therefore, may not recognize the independence of Taiwan,[65] which has actually not been proclaimed by Taiwan.[66] Hence, the islands claimed and occupied by the ROC in Taiwan, including Itu Aba,[67] should be considered as territories of the State of China opposable to the Philippines under international law. As a proper island, Itu Aba[68] is located at 10°23'N and 114°22'E,[69] less than 200 NM from each of the seven maritime features identified by the Philippines in its second and third group of claims. The map in Figure 14.7 and Table 14.2 show the relative geographical positions and distance between Itu Aba and each of the seven maritime features.

Table 14.2 Distance between Itu Aba and each of the seven reefs in the Spratly Islands

Maritime features	Location	Distance from Itu Aba	Position in Philippine claim
Mischief Reef	9°54'N., 115°32'E	74.7 NM	4th–5th claims
McKennan Reef	9°53'5"N., 114°28'E	29 NM	
Gaven Reef	10°13'N., 114°13'E	12.9 NM	4th claim
Subi Reef	10°55'N., 114°05'E	36.7 NM	
Johnson Reef	9°42'N., 114°22'E	39.7 NM	6th–7th claims
Cuarteron Reef	8°51'N., 112°50'E	128.2 NM	6th claim
Fiery Cross Reef	9°33'N., 112°54'E	78.8 NM	

The eight maritime features identified by the Philippines in the present case are claimed by China and the Philippines. This fact did not prevent the Philippines from mentioning these maritime features in the Notification. Why did the Philippines leave out the name of Itu Aba and the rest of proper islands and

65 Even the United States, the biggest ally of and weapon provider for Taiwan, does not give such a recognition. See "A Strong and Moderate Taiwan," by T.J. Christensen, Deputy Assistant Secretary of State, to Defense Industry Conference held by the U.S.-Taiwan Business Council on September 11, 2007 in Annapolis, Maryland, available online: http://www.us-taiwan.org/reports/2007_sept11_thomas_christensen_speech.pdf.

66 J. Crawford, *The Creation of States in International Law*, 2nd edn (Oxford: Oxford University Press, 2006), pp. 198–221. A.V. Lowe, *International Law* (Oxford: Oxford University Press, 2007), p. 165.

67 Heinzig, n. 44 above, p. 35.

68 Beckman, n. 44 above, p. 144.

69 See online: http://www.anchorageworld.com/content/itu-aba-island.

maritime features unoccupied but claimed by China in the Spratly Islands? Itu Aba is an island fulfilling every condition under Article 121(1) of UNCLOS.[70] The four reefs identified in the second group of claims are all within 200 NM from Itu Aba. Therefore, the second group of claims that these four reefs are not located on China's continental shelf is: (1) unfounded in fact as it omits the vital factor of Itu Aba and other nearby islands claimed by China; and (2) unfounded in law, as such an omission of the Philippines violates the One-China Commitment it has given to the PRC since 1975.

Fourth, the fifth Philippine claim said that Mischief and McKennan Reefs are part of the Philippines' continental shelf under Part VI of the Convention. However, no record shows that China has denied that the Philippines, as another Contracting Party to UNCLOS, may make such a claim from its baseline in accordance with UNCLOS, provided these two reefs are low-tide elevations. Since the fifth Philippine claim is not challenging any Chinese claim that exists, it is difficult to consider this claim well-founded in fact. In conclusion, the second group of the Philippine claims is not well-founded in fact and law.

The Third Group of Claims Concerning the 'Rock' Status of Four Reefs

In the third group of claims, another four reefs are covered, namely, Scarborough Shoal,[71] and the Johnson, Cuarteron and Fiery Cross Reefs. All of them are occupied by China, which claims large maritime zones *from* these reefs, as perceived and challenged by the Philippines.

Here, the sixth Philippine claim and the eighth relief requests the Tribunal to declare that: (1) Scarborough Shoal, and the Johnson, Cuarteron and Fiery Cross Reefs shall qualify as rocks under Article 121(3) of UNCLOS; (2) they are only capable of generating entitlement to a 12-NM territorial sea and nothing else; and (3) China has unlawfully claimed maritime entitlements beyond 12 NM *from* these four maritime features. The seventh claim argues that China has unlawfully prevented Philippine vessels from exploiting the living resources in waters adjacent to Scarborough Shoal and Johnson Reef. Therefore, in the ninth relief the Philippines requests the Tribunal to require China to refrain from: (1) preventing Philippine vessels from exploiting in a sustainable manner the living resources in the waters adjacent to Scarborough Shoal and Johnson Reef; and (2) conducting other activities inconsistent with UNCLOS at or in the vicinity of all the four features.

Once again, to examine whether such Philippine claims are well-founded in fact, we need to see what claims China must have made that are challenged here. According to the Philippines, China must have claimed that: (1) the four maritime features are islands capable of generating maritime zones larger than 12 NM; and

70 R.W. Smith, "Maritime Delimitation in the South China Sea: Potentiality and Challenges," *Ocean Development & International Law* 41, no. 3 (2010): 214, 222.

71 Beckman, n. 44 above, p. 145.

(2) China legally enjoys maritime zones like the EEZ or continental shelf extending *from* these four features. However, such 'Chinese' positions are neither correct nor a complete picture of the situation based on the following three difficulties.

First, no evidence proves that China claims an EEZ or continental shelf in the SCS extending *from* or generated *by* these four maritime features. In terms of the maritime areas where the Spratly Islands are situated, China in fact need not rely on the Johnson, Cuarteron and Fiery Cross Reefs individually to generate the EEZ or continental shelf, regardless whether these three maritime features are considered as rocks or islands under Article 121 by the Tribunal.[72] There are several islands fulfilling every condition of Article 121(1) that China can use to claim the EEZ or continental shelf to cover the water and seabed surrounding Johnson, Cuarteron and Fiery Cross Reefs. The island of Itu Aba is a perfect example.[73] However, these factors are not mentioned by the Philippines in its Notification. Consequently, the third group of the Philippine claims does not seem well-founded in fact. Besides, the sixth Philippine claim is unfounded in law like the fourth claim just discussed, because the omission of Itu Aba by the Philippines is inconsistent with the Philippines' One-China commitment.

Second, concerning the alleged Chinese activities in preventing Philippine vessels from exploiting the living resources in the waters adjacent to or in the vicinity of the four 'rocks,' the Philippines again fails to inform the Tribunal of the real cause. The situations are attributable to a set of compound SCS disputes China has with the Philippines and other States: (1) territorial disputes over all the maritime features in the KIG and Scarborough Shoal, for the purpose of the present litigation; and (2) maritime boundary delimitation disputes for the overlapping maritime zones extending from the disputed maritime features claimed by China, and from the Philippines' archipelagic baselines. Since the third group of the Philippine claims omits these factual situations facing both China and the Philippines, it seems unreasonable to consider such claims as well-founded in fact.

Third, as the overall disputed situations of overlapping maritime areas are not presented to the Tribunal by the Philippines, the Sino-Philippine legal relation as formulated by the Philippines turns into the one between a non-coastal State (China) and a coastal State (the Philippines), instead of a relation between two coastal States. This incorrect characterization of the legal relations between the two disputing parties makes it hard to consider the third group of Philippine claims well-founded in law.

---

72 See China's 2011 NV, n. 42 above.

73 There are more examples, such as Thitu Island (or Zhongye Dao, Pagasa Island). See Smith, n. 70 above, p. 222.

The Fourth Group of Claims Concerning the Philippines' Entitlement to Maritime Zones

In the eighth claim and the tenth relief, the Tribunal is requested to declare that the Philippines is entitled under UNCLOS to a 12-NM territorial sea, a 200-NM EEZ, and a continental shelf measured from its archipelagic baselines. The ninth claim and the eleventh relief requests the Tribunal to declare that China has unlawfully claimed and exploited the living and non-living resources in the Philippine EEZ and continental shelf, and has unlawfully prevented the Philippines from exploiting living and non-living resources therein.

To answer the question as to whether such claims are well-founded in fact or in law, we still need to see which Chinese claims, from the Philippines' perspective, constitute the object contested here. In the eyes of the Philippines, China must have said that: (1) the Philippines is *not* entitled under UNCLOS to a 12-NM territorial sea, a 200-NM EEZ, and a continental shelf measured from its archipelagic baselines; and (2) China has lawfully claimed and exploited the living and non-living resources in the very maritime area not considered as the Philippine EEZ and continental shelf, and lawfully prevented the Philippines from exploiting living and non-living resources therein.

However, due to the following two reasons, these so-called Chinese claims are both factually incorrect and based on a mischaracterization of Sino-Philippine legal relations.

First, it will be hard, if not impossible, to prove that China has denied the Philippines' right to claim a territorial sea, EEZ and continental shelf, as implied by the Philippine claims.[74] Hence, it is hard to consider the eighth Philippine claim, as a component to create a Sino-Philippine contention, well-founded in fact.

Second, as mentioned, the real unsettled SCS disputes China has with the Philippines are maritime delimitation disputes harboring territorial disputes over all the maritime features in the KIG (part of the Spratly Islands) and Scarborough Shoal. This can better explain the confrontations indicated by the ninth claim and the eleventh relief of the Philippines. On the contrary, the Philippines' explanation for the confrontations is less than convincing. As implied by the Philippines, China is not a coastal State in the West Philippine Sea as it may not claim an EEZ or continental shelf. However, the Tribunal is powerless to endorse such a characterization (that China is no coastal State). To do this, a preliminary judicial settlement must have been made by the Tribunal on the Sino-Philippine territorial disputes over all the maritime features in the KIG and Scarborough Shoal *in favor of the Philippines*. The Tribunal simply is not authorized to make such a decision in the Philippines' or China's favor.

74 Beckman, n. 44 above, p. 146.

The Fifth Group of Claims Concerning the Philippines' Right to Navigation

In the fifth group of claims, the tenth claim argues for and the twelfth relief requests the Tribunal to declare that China has unlawfully interfered with the Philippines' exercise of its rights to navigation and other rights under UNCLOS in areas within and beyond the Philippines' EEZ. The thirteenth relief requests the Tribunal to require that China desist from these unlawful activities.

Several legal problems exist that may render these claims unfounded in fact and in law. To begin with, legal errors may exist in the choice of UNCLOS provisions to build up such claims. Judging by the formulation of these claims and reliefs, Articles 58[75] and 78(2)[76] probably serve as the chosen rules. According to these two articles, it is non-coastal States whose rights and high seas freedoms are protected. Meanwhile, the presupposition of the fifth group of claims is that China has violated the Philippines' rights. But, is the Philippines a non-coastal State in the region? Does the Philippines recognize China as a coastal State in the SCS whose EEZ and continental shelf were entered by the Philippines' vessels exercising high seas freedoms? Based on the above-mentioned Philippine claims, both answers should be negative. As a result, the fifth group of Philippine claims is defeated by the third and fourth groups of its own claims.

A legally irreconcilable situation thus arises between the fifth group of Philippine claims on the one hand, and the third and fourth group of its claims on the other hand. It seems impossible to consider the fifth group of Philippine claims well-founded in law since the legal grounds used by the fifth group of claims would be rendered inapplicable in the context of the Philippine claims as a whole, provided Articles 58 and 78(2) are invoked as the legal grounds.

Summary of Legal Problems concerning the Philippine Claims

Having examined all five groups of Philippines' claims contained in its Notification dated on January 22, 2013, it seems unjustified to say that the first to tenth claims are well-founded in fact, and that the second, fourth, sixth, seventh, ninth and tenth claims are well-founded in law. Specifically, the first, third, fifth and eighth Philippine claims assert something China does not oppose. For the second Philippine claim, it denies something that China does not claim. Besides, the second claim is based on UNCLOS, which is inapplicable to judging the legality of the U-Shaped Line. The fourth and sixth Philippine claims are premised on an incomplete factual foundation, for omitting Itu Aba, which should be considered as belonging to the State of China as opposed to the Philippines. Consequently, the fourth and sixth claims are not well-founded in law. The seventh and ninth Philippine claims are based on an incorrect characterization of the factual and legal situations. It qualifies China as a non-coastal State in the maritime areas

75 UNCLOS, n. 11 above.

76 Ibid.

concerned. The tenth claim is probably not well-founded in law, as Articles 58 and 78(2) of UNCLOS, which may serve as legal bases, are inapplicable to govern China's conduct, based on the positions taken by the Philippines in its third and fourth groups of claims.

Is the Requirement of Jurisdiction Over the Disputes Fulfilled?

Identity of the Disputes Submitted and the Real Disputes

Article 286 of UNCLOS, which is the first article of section 2 (entitled 'Compulsory Procedures Entailing Binding Decisions') of Part XV (entitled 'Settlement of Disputes'), dictates that the dispute submitted to the Section 2 Tribunal must be identical to the dispute that has not been settled under Section 1 Means. If the disputes brought by the Philippines to this Tribunal are different from what China and the Philippines have disputed about regarding the SCS according to Articles 279–285 of UNCLOS, the Tribunal would be rendered inapplicable in the first place and should declare the claims presented by the Philippines inadmissible.

Moreover, Article 288(1)[77] requires an Annex VII Tribunal to have jurisdiction over any *dispute* concerning the interpretation or application of UNCLOS "which is submitted to it according to Part XV." When the disputes *as submitted and formulated* by the claimant are considered either hypothetical/unreal or different from the disputes that the claimant and respondent have according to Section 1 Means, the disputes cannot be deemed as submitted to the Tribunal according to Article 286, as part of Part XV. Therefore, the condition ("which is submitted to it according to Part XV") under Article 288(1) is not met, rendering Article 288(1) inapplicable. In such a situation, it will be premature for the Tribunal to be engaged with the obligation to satisfy itself of the needed jurisdiction to proceed to the merits part.

It is time to explore the real Sino-Philippine SCS disputes, which have been there for four decades.[78] Countless statements and counter-statements have been made. It is useful to observe the most recent and *conclusive* exchange of Sino-Philippine positions at the Commission on the Limits of the Continental Shelf (CLCS) since 2009.[79] The position of the PRC is demonstrated by its NV delivered to the United Nations on May 7, 2009, and the map attached thereto[80] to challenge

77 Ibid.

78 Gao and Jia, n. 58 above, p. 105. See Heinzig, n. 44 above, p. 36.

79 N.-D. Thang and N.H. Thao, "China's Nine Dotted Lines in the South China Sea: The 2011 Exchange of Diplomatic Notes Between the Philippines and China," *Ocean Development & International Law* 43, no. 1 (2012): 35, 39–46.

80 Notes Verbales, n. 38 above.

the Malaysia/Vietnam Joint Submission[81] and the Vietnam Submission[82] to the CLCS concerning extended continental shelf in certain SCS areas on May 6 and 7, 2009 respectively. The 2011 NV by the Philippines[83] was delivered to challenge the 2009 Chinese NV. As a response to the 2011 Philippines' statement, the PRC produced its 2011 NV.[84]

Based on such exchange of legal positions the real Sino-Philippine SCS disputes are four-fold: (1) territorial disputes over all the maritime features within Philippines' KIG, which is part of China's Nansha Islands; (2) disputes concerning legal capability of certain reefs or rocks in China's Nansha Islands to generate the territorial sea, the EEZ, and the continental shelf; (3) disputes concerning the legality under UNCLOS of China's historical waters claims within the U-Shaped Line; and (4) disputes concerning maritime boundary delimitation for the overlapping Sino-Philippine maritime claims.[85]

However, what has been presented to the Tribunal by the Philippines' claims stated in the Notification is far from the aggregation of these disputes. First, as discussed already, the first, third, fifth and eighth Philippine claims cannot *create* any dispute. The real Sino-Philippine dispute behind the fifth and eighth claims is a maritime boundary delimitation dispute for the overlapping maritime areas identified by the Philippines. As said by the Philippines, this dispute was not even presented to the Tribunal. The second Philippine claim can hardly create any dispute as to the legality of China's maritime claims in the SCS based on, within, and encompassed by the U-Shaped Line under UNCLOS. No evidence shows that China has made such a "maritime claim." The fourth and sixth Philippine claims are premised on an incomplete factual foundation that excludes the island of Itu Aba and other islands in the Spratly Islands. China would probably argue that those seven maritime features situated in the Spratly Islands are located in China's continental shelf, generated by other *nearby* maritime features qualifying as islands. The Philippines would deny China's sovereignty over these islands. Such territorial disputes are the root issues of the confrontations indicated by these two claims but not presented by the Philippines to the Tribunal, either. The dispute to be created by the seventh Philippine claim concerns the illegality of China's prevention of Philippine vessels from exploiting the living resources in

81 The executive summary of this joint submission is available online: http://www.un.org/Depts/los/clcs_new/submissions_files/mysvnm33_09/mys_vnm2009excutivesummary.pdf.

82 The executive summary of this submission is available online: http://www.un.org/Depts/los/clcs_new/submissions_files/vnm37_09/vnm2009n_executivesummary.pdf.

83 Dated April 5, 2011, and the Document No. is 000228. Available online: http://www.un.org/Depts/los/clcs_new/submissions_files/mysvnm33_09/phl_re_chn_2011.pdf.

84 NV, n. 42 above.

85 Damrosch and Oxman, n. 57 above, p. 95; M.S.T. Gau, "The U-Shaped Line and a Categorization of the Ocean Disputes in the South China Sea," *Ocean Development and International Law* 43 (2012): 57, 62; Beckman, n. 44 above, pp. 143–4, 151–2. Song, n. 45 above, pp. 254–6. Smith, n. 70 above, pp. 214–36, 220.

the waters adjacent to Scarborough Shoal and Johnson Reef. However, the real Sino-Philippine dispute demonstrated by such Philippine complaint is maritime boundary delimitation dispute, not presented to the Tribunal. The basis of such dispute is the Sino-Philippine territorial disputes over all the maritime features in KIG. The territorial dispute and boundary delimitation disputes are inseparable from the dispute to be created by the seventh claim of the Philippines. However, no territorial disputes are presented for settlement. The disputes to be established by the Philippines based on its ninth claim concern: (1) the illegality of China's claims and activities in exploiting the living and non-living resources in the Philippines' EEZ and continental shelf; and (2) the illegality of China's prevention of Philippine people from the same activities in the areas. The real Sino-Philippine disputes behind this concern territorial claims and maritime delimitation which are again not presented to the Tribunal. The tenth claim of the Philippines seems to be an alternative argument based on the Philippines' recognition of China as a coastal State entitled to claim an EEZ in the region. However, what is between China and the Philippines are not the disputes between a coastal State (in this case, China) and a non-coastal State (in this case, the Philippines).

To conclude, what the present Tribunal is requested to resolve is far from the aggregation of those four kinds of real Sino-Philippine disputes. The failure of presenting Sino-Philippine territorial and maritime boundary delimitation disputes as core disputes to the Tribunal by the Philippines would be inconsistent with Articles 286 and 288(1). The Tribunal is facing the disputes that should not have been brought to it *at this time*, as the disputes presented are either unsupported by the facts, non-contentious, unreal and self-contradictory, or different from the existing Sino-Philippine SCS disputes. As Articles 286 and 288(1) are not complied with, the Tribunal should not have been established in the first place. *Being also inapplicable*, the Tribunal as presently constituted should be considered without jurisdiction over the disputes as formulated by the Philippines.

The Re-Characterization of the Disputes

Should the Tribunal consider the disputes presented to be identical with the real but unsettled Sino-Philippine SCS disputes without violating Articles 286 and 288(1), the Tribunal should then examine whether the disputes *presented* have already been removed from the scope of its jurisdiction by the 2006 Chinese Declaration. Prior to this, the Tribunal still needs to properly characterize the nature or the scope of the disputes presented. As put in paragraph 40 of the Philippines' Notification,

> It follows that the Philippines' claims do not fall within China's Declaration of 25 August 2006, because they do not: concern the interpretation or application of Articles 15, 74 and 83 relating to sea boundary delimitation; involve historic bays or titles within the meaning of the relevant provisions of the Convention; concern military activities or law enforcement activities; or concern matters

over which the Security Council is exercising functions assigned to it by the UN Charter.[86]

Clearly, the Philippines said that it does not bring any dispute falling within the category of disputes as indicated by Article 298(1)(a)–(c) and excluded by the 2006 Chinese Declaration. This characterization is still subject to judgment by the Tribunal. It is worth mentioning the Barbados Arbitration in this connection. The tribunal in that case did not accept Barbados' argument that the terms of notification it submitted to institute the arbitration excluded the delimitation of the outer continental shelf.[87] In the present case, it is critical to properly characterize the scope of the Sino-Philippine dispute, as formulated by the Philippines alone. But with what test can this job be done? The test is to see the 'scope of the legal differences between the Parties' as indicated by the record with reasonable clarity, as declared and applied by the 2006 Award of the Barbados Arbitration, in particular, paragraphs 198 and 213 of the Award.[88]

As indicated by the open records of the 2009–2011 Sino-Philippine exchange of Notes Verbales in the UN concerning their compound disputes with more than reasonable, if not crystal, clarity, the real Sino-Philippine SCS disputes are four-fold, as discussed above. As stated previously, the core Sino-Philippine disputes of: (1) territorial sovereignty over all the maritime features in the KIG and Scarborough Shoal; and (2) maritime boundary delimitation cannot be separated from the partial, if not hypothetical, disputes as presented by the Philippines. However, should the Tribunal consider it lawful for such core disputes to be cut off from the disputes presented under Article 286 and 288(1), then the Tribunal must find out *what these disputes presented really are* before deciding if these disputes still fall within the 2006 Chinese Declaration.

Looking at all the 10 claims and the 13 reliefs sought as presented by the Philippines *in its entirety*, the result the Philippines wishes to achieve is clearly the Sino-Philippine maritime boundary delimitation indirectly drawn, which gives the Philippines the entire 200-NM EEZ in the SCS extended from the Philippine archipelagic baselines free from Chinese interference, while China receives no more than four circles of territorial sea surrounding four rocks[89] whose legal status remain disputable. Let us see how the Philippines can do this step-by-step through its claims.

Specifically, the first and second claims, if upheld by the Tribunal, would render the U-Shaped Line unlawful and void. The U-Shaped Line would be useless for

86 Para. 40 of the Notification, n. 2 above.

87 See para. 213 of the Award of the Arbitral Tribunal in the matter of arbitration between Barbados and the Republic of Trinidad and Tobago, available online: http://www.pca-cpa.org/showpage.asp?pag_id=1152.

88 Ibid., paras 198, 213.

89 Beckman, n. 44 above, p. 152. J. Greenfield, *China's Practice in the Law of the Sea* (Oxford: Oxford University Press, 1992), p. 164.

China in negotiations for maritime boundary delimitation with the Philippines, Malaysia and Vietnam. The result of upholding the Philippines' fourth to seventh claims is that the eight maritime features do not assist in generating maritime zones for China in the SCS. The Philippines accepts that Scarborough Shoal and the Johnson, Cuarteron and Fiery Cross Reefs may legally generate no more than 12 NM of territorial sea, *without* recognizing that the four circles of territorial sea belong to China. The Tribunal is unauthorized to determine the territorial disputes. Therefore, it is impossible for China to be granted ownership or sovereignty over these four maritime features as well as their 12-NM territorial sea by the Tribunal. Furthermore, the third to fifth Philippine claims, once upheld, would justify the eviction of Chinese presence from the Mischief, McKennan, Gaven and Subi Reefs.

Therefore, the first six claims mean that in the maritime areas surrounding those eight maritime features, China becomes a non-coastal State, if the Tribunal upholds these claims while neglecting the overall territorial disputes. Following this logic, it is easy to understand the Philippines' goal in making its seventh to tenth claims. As China would be considered a non-coastal State in the relevant maritime areas, all the law enforcement activities by China in preserving its various maritime zonal rights, jurisdiction or even sovereignty in the areas concerned become totally illegal. To conclude, it is fair to consider the disputes *presented* by the Philippines to be *de facto* maritime boundary delimitation disputes by nature.

Disputes Concerning the Interpretation or Application of the Convention

Article 4 (entitled 'functions of arbitral tribunal') of Annex VII to UNCLOS provides: 'An arbitral tribunal constituted under Article 3 of this Annex shall function *in accordance with* this Annex and *the other provisions of this Convention*' (emphasis added). While Annex VII does not regulate the subject matter for settlement by the Tribunal, Part XV of UNCLOS confines the disputes to those concerning the interpretation or application of UNCLOS. Such limitation was required by Articles 279–284, 286–288 and 297 in Sections 1, 2 and 3 of Part XV, respectively. Two points must be made here.

First, the alleged dispute in the first group of claims indicated by the Philippine Notification does not seem to concern the interpretation or application of UNCLOS. As discussed already, the U-Shaped Line from the very beginning has been a demonstration of Chinese territorial claims relating to four groups of maritime features in the SCS, instead of a maritime zonal claim for the body of sea enclosed.[90] The applicable law governing the legality of such claims consists of the rules concerning acquisition of territorial sovereignty. Such body of rules is neither part of UNCLOS concluded in 1982,[91] nor the four Geneva Conventions signed in 1958. Such rules cannot be found in any standard textbook on public

90 Smith, n. 70 above, p. 224.

91 Beckman, n. 44 above, p. 142. Smith, n. 70 above, p. 220.

international law of the sea, either. In short, the rules concerning the acquisition of territorial sovereignty are not part of conventional or customary international law of the sea.

Second, *even assuming* 2009 was the first time for China to make its official *maritime zonal claims* in the SCS by its NV to the UN Secretary-General, what was stated in that communication cannot contribute to the creation of *any* dispute concerning the interpretation or application of UNCLOS. Critically, the 2009 Chinese communication cannot be detached from the context which includes the subsequent clarifying NV of China dated April 5, 2011, in which China *invokes* UNCLOS when making maritime zonal claims in the SCS region. Therefore, it will be unjustified to say that the 2009 Chinese communication that contains the U-Shaped Line constitutes an element to build up a Sino-Philippine maritime 'dispute' concerning the interpretation or application of UNCLOS.

Optional Exceptions to the Applicability of the Present Tribunal: The 2006 Declaration of China

According to China's 'Declaration under Article 298' on August 25, 2006, as discussed above, the PRC has excluded an Annex VII Tribunal as a means to settle, *inter alia*: (1) disputes concerning the interpretation or application of Articles 15, 74 and 83 relating to maritime boundary delimitation; (2) disputes involving historic bays or titles; and (3) disputes necessarily involving the concurrent consideration of any unsettled dispute concerning sovereignty or other rights over continental or insular land territory. To be noted, these disputes are covered by paragraph 1(a)(i) of Article 298.

As just concluded, the disputes presented by the Philippines, after careful re-characterization, amount to *de facto* maritime boundary delimitation disputes to secure the integrity of the Philippines' EEZ in the SCS. It is submitted that such disputes fall within the scope of excluded disputes indicated above. However, if such a re-characterized nature of the disputes is not accepted by the Tribunal, three issues remain hard to be resolved by the Tribunal.

First, the Sino-Philippine disputes as *presented* to the Tribunal basically have different layers. The central disputes are the territorial disputes over all the maritime features in KIG and Scarborough Shoal. The maritime boundary delimitation disputes are the middle layer disputes. The outer layer disputes are made by all the claims brought by the Philippines in its Notification. The core and middle layer disputes are the *real* causes of the confrontations indicated by the Philippines in its claims. In fact, the core and middle layer disputes must first be settled by the Tribunal *in favor of the Philippines*, before the Tribunal can entertain the outer layer disputes formulated by the Philippines. However, both the core and middle layer disputes have been excluded by the 2006 Chinese Declaration. It would be incorrect to say that the Tribunal has jurisdiction to settle the outer layer disputes.

Second, for the first group of Philippine claims, it was submitted above that the dispute over the legality of the U-Shaped Line should not be deemed to concern the interpretation or application of UNCLOS. However, should the Tribunal consider the U-Shaped Line as a maritime claim of China, this dispute should then be regarded to concern historical title. Hence, the Tribunal may not adjudicate such an issue, as it has been excluded by the 2006 Chinese Declaration.

Third, concerning the fifth group of the Philippine claims (the tenth claim and twelfth and thirteenth relief sought of the Philippines) marine scientific research may be considered as the Philippines' high seas freedom that has been interfered by China.[92] The Tribunal also lacks jurisdiction to adjudicate such a case, if raised by the Philippines. The 2006 Chinese Declaration has removed the dispute under Article 298(1)(b) of UNCLOS from the scope of jurisdiction of the Annex VII Tribunal. That provision provides the scope of such dispute as "disputes concerning law enforcement activities in regard to the exercise of sovereign rights or jurisdiction excluded from the jurisdiction of a … tribunal under article 297, paragraph 2."

Which disputes are excluded from the Tribunal's jurisdiction under Article 297(2)? They are the ones arising out of the exercise by the coastal State of a right or discretion in accordance with Article 246.[93] Paragraph 2 of Article 246 provides that "Marine scientific research in the EEZ and on the Continental Shelf shall be conducted with the consent of the coastal State." Paragraph 3 of this article provides that, in normal circumstances, coastal States shall grant their consent for marine scientific research projects by other States in their EEZ or continental shelf "to be carried out in accordance with this Convention exclusively for peaceful purposes and in order to increase scientific knowledge of the marine environment for the benefit of all mankind." Paragraph 5(a)–(c) of this article allows the coastal States to withhold their consent when the project "(a) is of direct significance for the exploration and exploitation of natural resources, whether living or non-living; (b) involves drilling into the Continental Shelf, the use of explosives or the introduction of harmful substances into the marine environment; (c) involves the construction, operation or use of artificial islands, installations and structures referred to in articles 60 and 80."

Therefore, if the situation indicated by the fifth group of Philippine claims is characterized as marine scientific research for the purpose of the exploration and exploitation of natural resources in China's continental shelf as defined by Article 246(5)(a)–(c), China will have the right to withhold its consent and exercise jurisdiction by interfering with the team dispatched or authorized by the Philippines. Under the 2006 Chinese Declaration, the disputes arising out of such a refusal or interference by China will be excluded from the jurisdiction of the present Tribunal.

92 For the Reed Bank incident between China and the Philippines and Chinese official positions, see Beckman, n. 44 above, pp. 157–8.

93 See UNCLOS, Article 297(2)(a)(i), n. 11 above.

Summary of Tribunal's Lack of of Jurisdiction over the Disputes Presented

Based on the above examination, it seems unjustified to conclude that the Tribunal has jurisdiction over the disputes brought by the Philippines for several reasons. First, there is serious doubt as to whether the disputes presented to the Tribunal are both real and identical with what China and the Philippines have disputed about in the SCS. Second, assuming there is identity, the disputes articulated in the first group of the Philippine claims do not concern the interpretation or application of UNCLOS. Third, assuming the legal problems identified in the above two points are all resolved, the Philippines' characterization of the disputes should be reviewed and dismissed by the Tribunal. The disputes presented are *de facto* maritime boundary delimitation disputes involving unsettled territorial disputes over all the maritime features in the KIG (part of the Spratly Islands) claimed by China and opposed by the Philippines. No matter whether the re-characterization of the disputes is accepted by the Tribunal or not, the disputes presented by the Philippines should be deemed as falling within the scope of disputes excluded by the 2006 Chinese Declaration. With no jurisdiction over the disputes, the Tribunal should take no action to entertain the merits part of this litigation in accordance with relevant provisions of Part XV of and Annex VII to UNCLOS.

Conclusion

Since China has declined to participate in the litigation, Article 9 of Annex VII becomes applicable. The Tribunal is accordingly required to satisfy itself, before making its award, not only that it has jurisdiction over the disputes but also that the claims are well-founded in fact and law. Article 10 of Annex VII also obligates the Tribunal to state the reasons on which the award is based. Even before applying Article 9 of Annex VII, major preliminary problems may preclude the fulfillment of some *inherent* conditions for the disputes to be lawfully brought to the Annex VII Tribunal under Articles 286 and 288(1).

First, certain disputes alleged by the Philippines' claims should be considered hypothetical, non-contentious and self-defeating. The first, third, fifth and eighth claims contend something that China does not oppose. The second claim denies something China has not claimed. The tenth claim treats China as a coastal State in the SCS while denies the Philippines this status, which is irreconcilable with the first to ninth claims, treating the Philippines as a coastal State in the SCS while denying China this status. Second, the disputes brought to the Tribunal may not be identical to the disputes that both parties failed to settle through Section 1 Means. The real unsettled disputes are compound, consisting of territorial issues, maritime boundary delimitation issues, the legality of maritime features to generate maritime zones under UNCLOS, and historical titles. The core components of these disputes are not presented by the Philippines to the Tribunal. Third, the dispute to be established by the first and second Philippine claims, namely, the legality of the U-Shaped Line under UNCLOS, as an issue of territorial claim by nature, should not be considered as concerning the interpretation or application of UNCLOS. Fourth, the disputes were not submitted to the Tribunal in accordance with Article 286. Consequently, the condition of Article 288(1) cannot be fulfilled. This renders the Annex VII Tribunal inapplicable to the present case.

Assuming the above preliminary issues are all resolved, major conditions under Article 9 of Annex VII for the Tribunal to give its award may not be fulfilled.

It has been submitted that the first to tenth claims may not be well-founded in fact, while the second, fourth, sixth, seventh, ninth and tenth claims are not well-founded in law. Assuming the claims are all well-founded in fact and law, the disputes presented, after careful re-characterization, turn out to be a *de facto* maritime boundary delimitation disputes excluded by, *inter alia*, the 2006 Chinese Declaration. Assuming such a re-characterization is not accepted by the Tribunal, the disputes presented would have two layers as components. The core layer disputes are territorial disputes, while the middle layer disputes are maritime boundary delimitation disputes. Both components must be all settled *in favor of* the Philippines before the Tribunal can actually resolve the outer layer disputes formulated by the Philippines. The 2006 Chinese Declaration, which expressly excluded the core and middle layer disputes, should be considered as having also excluded the *inseparable consequence* of these *component* disputes, namely, the disputes presented by the Philippines.

To conclude, many serious factual and legal problems exist which serve to preclude the application of Articles 286 and 288(1) of UNCLOS, rendering the Annex VII Tribunal inapplicable right from its establishment. Assuming the Tribunal may function legally, it would then be bound by Article 9 of Annex VII to refrain from giving an award for this case. Therefore, the Tribunal is advised to take no actions in the merits part of the litigation but to declare its lack of jurisdiction over the disputes presented by the Philippines.

References

Aegean Sea CS Case (Greece v. Turkey) [1978] ICJ Rep 3, 20 (para. 46), available online: http://www.icj-cij.org/docket/files/62/6245.pdf.

Batongbacal, J.L., "The Maritime Territories and Jurisdiction of the Philippines and the United Nations Convention on the Law of the Sea," *Philippine Law Journal* 76 (2001): 123, 140–41.

Bautista, L.B., "The Legal Status of the Philippine Treaty Limits and Territorial Waters Claim in International Law: National and International Legal Perspectives" (2010) University of Wollongong Thesis Collection, 245. Available online: http://ro.uow.edu.au/theses/3081/.

Beckman, R., "The UN Convention on the Law of the Sea and the Maritime Disputes in the South China Sea," *American Journal of International Law* 107 (2013): 142, 144.

Beckman, R.C. and Schofield, C.H., "Defining EEZ Claims from Islands: A Potential South China Sea Change," *The International Journal of Marine and Coastal Law* 29 (2014): 204–6.

Collier, J. and Lowe, A.V., *The Settlement of Disputes in International Law: Institutions and Procedures*, 1st edn (Oxford: Oxford University Press, 1999).

Crawford, J., *The Creation of States in International Law*, 2nd edn (Oxford: Oxford University Press, 2006).

Damrosch, Lori and Oxman, Bernard H., "Agora: The South China Sea, Editors' Introduction," *American Journal of International Law* 107 (2013).

Dupuy, F. and Dupuy, P.-M., "A Legal Analysis of China's Historic Rights Claim in the South China Sea," *American Journal of International Law* 107 (2013): 124, 129–30, 135.

Executive Summary of the Vietnam/Malaysia Joint Submission dated on May 6, 2009.

Fisheries Jurisdiction Case (FRG v. Iceland) (Jurisdiction) [1973] ICJ Rep 49, 54 (para. 13), available online: http://www.icj-cij.org/docket/files/56/10713.pdf.

Fisheries Jurisdiction Case (UK v. Iceland) (Jurisdiction) [1973] ICJ Rep 3, 7-8 (para. 12), available online: http://www.icj-cij.org/docket/files/55/5749.pdf.

Franckx, E. and Benatar, M., "Dots and Lines in the South China Sea: Insights from the Law of Map Evidence," *Asian Journal of International Law* 2 (2012): 89, 93.

Gao, Z.G. and Jia, B.B., "The Nine-Dash Line in the South China Sea: History, Status, and Implications," *American Journal of International Law* 107 (2013): 98, 108.

Gau, M.S.T., "The U-Shaped Line and a Categorization of the Ocean Disputes in the South China Sea," *Ocean Development and International Law* 43 (2012): 57, 62.

Greenfield, J., *China's Practice in the Law of the Sea* (Oxford: Oxford University Press, 1992).

Heinzig, D., *Disputed Islands in the South China Sea* (Wiesbaden: Harrassowitz Verlag, 1976).

Hu, N.T.A., "South China Sea: Troubled Waters or a Sea of Opportunity?" *Ocean Development & International Law* 41, no. 3 (2010): 203, 206.

Joint Communiqué of the Government of the People's Republic of China and the Government of the Republic of the Philippines (Peking, June 9, 1975), available online: http://ph.china-embassy.org/eng/zfgx/zzgx/t183265.htm.

Lowe, A.V., *International Law* (Oxford: Oxford University Press, 2007).

McManus, J.W., Shao, K.T. and Lin, S.Y., "Toward Establishing a Spratly Islands International Marine Peace Park: Ecological Importance and Supportive Collaborative Activities with an Emphasis on the Role of Taiwan," *Ocean Development & International Law* 41, no. 3 (2010): 270, 271.

Merrills, J.G., *International Dispute Settlement*, 4th edn (Cambridge: Cambridge University Press, 2005).

Miyoshi, M., "China's 'U-Shaped Line' Claim in the South China Sea: Any Validity Under International Law?" *Ocean Development & International Law* 43, no. 1 (2012): 1–17.

Rosenne, S. and Sohn, L.B., *United Nations Convention on the Law of the Sea 1982: A Commentary, Vol. V* (Virginia: Martinus Nijhoff, 1989).

Smith, R.W., "Maritime Delimitation in the South China Sea: Potentiality and Challenges," *Ocean Development & International Law* 41, no. 3 (2010): 214, 222.

Song, Y.H., "The South China Sea Workshop Process and Taiwan's Participation," *Ocean Development & International Law* 41, no. 3 (2010): 253, 254.

Thang, N.-D. and Thao, N.H., "China's Nine Dotted Lines in the South China Sea: The 2011 Exchange of Diplomatic Notes Between the Philippines and China," *Ocean Development & International Law* 43, no. 1 (2012): 35, 39–46.

The Mavrommatis Palestine Concessions [August 30, 1924] PCIJ Series A, No. 2, 11, available online: http://www.icj-cij.org/pcij/serie_A/A_02/06_Mavrommatis_en_Palestine_Arret.pdf.

The Notification and Statement of Claims, issued by Department of Foreign Affairs of Republic of the Philippines in Manila to the Embassy of the People's Republic of China in Manila, serial no. 13-0211, January 22, 2013, available online: http://www.dfa.gov.ph/index.php/downloads/doc_download/523-notification-and-statement-of-claim-on-west-philippine-sea.

United Nations Convention on the Law of the Sea, open for signature on 10 December 1982, 1833 United Nations Treaty Series 397

Zimmermann, A., Oellers-Frahm, K., Tomuschat, C. and Tams, C.J. (eds), *The Statute of the International Court of Justice: A Commentary*, 1st edn (Oxford: Oxford University Press, 2006).

Zou, K.Y., "China's U-Shaped Line in the South China Sea Revisited," *Ocean Development and International Law* 43 (2012): 18.

Index

For Product Safety Concerns and Information please contact our EU
representative GPSR@taylorandfrancis.com
Taylor & Francis Verlag GmbH, Kaufingerstraße 24, 80331 München, Germany

www.ingramcontent.com/pod-product-compliance
Ingram Content Group UK Ltd.
Pitfield, Milton Keynes, MK11 3LW, UK
UKHW022008180926
475701UK00003B/258

9780367668693